Burt Reynolds
on Screen

Burt Reynolds on Screen

WAYNE BYRNE

Foreword by Nick McLean Sr.
Afterword by C. James Lewis

McFarland & Company, Inc., Publishers
Jefferson, North Carolina

LIBRARY OF CONGRESS CATALOGUING-IN-PUBLICATION DATA

Names: Byrne, Wayne, 1983– author. | McLean, Nick, 1941– writer
of foreword. | Lewis, C. James, 1948– writer of afterword.
Title: Burt Reynolds on screen / Wayne Byrne ;
foreword by Nick McLean Sr. ; afterword by C. James Lewis.
Description: Jefferson, North Carolina : McFarland & Company, Inc.,
Publishers, 2020 | Includes bibliographical references and index.
Identifiers: LCCN 2019049186 | ISBN 9781476674988 (paperback : acid free paper) ∞ |
ISBN 9781476638119 (ebook)
Subjects: LCSH: Reynolds, Burt—Criticism and interpretation.
Classification: LCC PN2287.R447 B97 2020 | DDC 791.4302/8092—dc23
LC record available at https://lccn.loc.gov/2019049186

BRITISH LIBRARY CATALOGUING DATA ARE AVAILABLE

ISBN (print) 978-1-4766-7498-8
ISBN (ebook) 978-1-4766-3811-9

Front cover: Burt Reynolds as Bandit Bo Darville in *Smokey
and the Bandit*, 1977 (Universal Pictures/Photofest)

Printed in the United States of America

McFarland & Company, Inc., Publishers
Box 611, Jefferson, North Carolina 28640
www.mcfarlandpub.com

This book is dedicated
to the memory of Burt Reynolds.

Table of Contents

Acknowledgments

I am very grateful to all of Burt Reynolds' friends, colleagues, co-stars and directors who have contributed to this book. Your participation has been invaluable to the creation of this tribute to the greatest movie star of them all, and so I offer my sincerest thanks to Matt Battaglia, Bill Bennett, Clive Fleury, Bill Forsyth, Bobby Goldsboro, Michael D. O'Shea, Adam Rifkin, Brian K. Roberts and Rachel Ward. Thank you all for your words, photographs and memories.

Very special thanks to Nick McLean Sr. and C. James Lewis for providing me with your wonderful foreword and afterword, respectively. You both welcomed me into your world with open arms. I cherish the friendship.

Much gratitude and appreciation to my commissioning editor, Layla Milholen, and all at McFarland Publishing for their encouragement and support of this book.

A tip of the hat is also due to all the authors, critics and journalists who have contributed to the wealth of written consideration on my subject over the last six decades, I have drawn valuable inspiration and information from your work.

And thank you, Burt Reynolds. God bless you.

Foreword
by Nick McLean Sr.

"I'm going to make you a cinematographer!"—Burt Reynolds

I first met Burt Reynolds after I got a call from the great cinematographer William Fraker asking me to be his camera operator on *Sharky's Machine*. In the late '70s and early '80s, the best job you could get in Hollywood was on a Burt Reynolds movie. The money was great and you knew you weren't going to work a lot of long hours. To get on that crew was like gold. Burt had control of everything, at that time he was the #1 box office star in the world. You had to be really qualified to land the job on a Burt Reynolds film; he only hired the best of the best.

Burt requested a meeting with me before we started shooting because he wanted to discuss a helicopter shot that he envisioned for the opening of the film. The idea was to follow the exterior elevator of the Peach Tree Plaza in downtown Atlanta, Georgia, and move in close as it ascends to the top of the building. Burt and I got off to a great start because we were both ex–football players; Burt played for Florida State and I had been a running back for the USC Trojans. So we bonded over being former athletes and then we got talking about this idea he had and it became apparent to me that it would be an extremely difficult shot because we would have to fly backwards a quarter of a mile, which is pretty impossible. So I convinced Burt to re-arrange it somewhat. I was known in Hollywood for my aerial photography so Burt had a lot of faith and trust in my skills to get something really great.

When it came time to get the shot, it was a tough ride up in the helicopter. We were about 40 floors up and fortunately we had this real incredible helicopter pilot whose name was Ricky Holley. It was quite dangerous trying to get so close to the building, and to our amazement Burt insisted on coming with us. The wind was blowing like crazy, and at one point the rotor blades were only ten feet from the building. We had to get that close because I couldn't use a zoom due to not having enough light for such. I was using a 50mm prime lens which meant having to get pretty close to that building. It took us two or three takes to get it right but we got it, and it is an amazing shot. It ended up appearing 20 minutes into the film rather than being the opening scene as originally planned, but that shot really cemented my relationship with Burt.

I call that whole period "The Limousine and Learjet Days," because those were our only modes of transportation. One time on *Sharky's Machine*, I got a note from Burt that read "Meet me at Atlanta Airport." When I arrived, he had two Learjets there which took about ten of us back to Jupiter, Florida. When we got there, we jumped straight into these limousines that were waiting for us. They then brought us to these condos that Burt had booked for the night, one for each of us. I used to drink this beer called Olde English, and when I opened the refrigerator in the condo I discovered it had been filled with Olde English. That's the kind of small but very personal gesture that Burt would offer you. He knew I liked that beer and had my condo stocked with it. Who does that?! He said, "You guys have a good time tonight and be ready for four o'clock tomorrow. The limo will be picking you up."

So the car came and dropped us off at this place where we were taken up a back staircase and brought into a room where there were drinks and hors d'oeuvres laid out for us. After a while of enjoying the party, Burt said, "Okay, this is what I wanted you guys to see…." He pressed a button and then this wall rose up into the ceiling and all of a sudden we were looking out into Burt's dinner theater and there were about 400 people sitting down in the auditorium. So we finished our party and they started the show. At the time, I didn't know that he owned a theater so I was absolutely blown away by the whole experience.

I owe my career as a cinematographer to Burt Reynolds. I remember exactly when it happened: It was also during this time shooting *Sharky's Machine*; Burt and I were setting up the shots for the scene where Sharky is looking across staking out Dominoe's apartment and we found ourselves alone. We got talking about *Deliverance*, a film that my old friend Vilmos Zsigmond shot. I told him about the time when I was a camera assistant for Zsigmond and he said to me that one day he would make me a camera operator, and on our very next picture he did. So Burt turns around and says, "Oh yeah? Well, Nick, I'm going to make you a cinematographer!" and then he got up and walked out of the room. Nine months later, there was a knock on my door and a guy from Warner Bros. handed me the script for *Stroker Ace*. It turned out Burt wanted me as the director of photography on that film. I could not believe it. Burt was true to his word. But that was Burt. He remembered.

Burt went to bat for me again years later when he wanted me to direct one of the *B.L. Stryker* TV movies, *High Rise*. The executives at Universal, the studio that was producing the series, told him "no!" but Burt simply replied, "Nick McLean will be directing this film." And so I did, I got my first opportunity to direct a picture and in the end the studio loved it. I was set to direct more had the series continued. That was the kind of loyalty that Burt Reynolds showed his friends.

I was glad I could repay Burt back whenever he needed me. In 1986, I got a phone call from the producers of the movie *Heat*. They told me that there was some trouble going on with the production up in Las Vegas and Burt wanted me to come down and help him finish the film. So I went down there and shot second unit and helped get the film wrapped up on time, but mainly I was there to be a friend to him amidst the chaos that was happening on the film. When I was shooting *Friends*, he asked me to go down to Florida to speak at the Burt Reynolds Institute for Theatre Training, which was a blast because it was an opportunity to see Burt again and catch up with a lot of friends down there from the *B.L. Stryker* days.

When Burt asked me to be his director of photography on *Evening Shade*, I initially resisted the idea of working in television. I had no interest, but then I realized I couldn't

Left to right on the set of *Cannonball Run II* **(1984): Dom DeLuise, Jamie Farr, Dean Martin, Reynolds, Sammy Davis Jr. and Nick McLean Sr. (photograph courtesy Nick McLean Collection.)**

turn down this man who had given me so much. Working on *Evening Shade* was a special experience because Burt directed a lot of them. He had a lot of creative control over that show and he allowed me to be equally creative: I could do anything I wanted with the lighting and compositions, which you don't often get to do in television. That show turned out great and it was the start of another significant chapter in our long-lasting professional relationship.

I had known Burt Reynolds for almost 40 years and my lasting impressions are that of a wonderful actor, a talented director, a loyal friend—loyal to the very end—and generous to a fault. "Generous," that is perhaps the best word to summarize Burt Reynolds. He gave everything away, he loved to gift you things and to offer you a taste of the good life. He loved to make people happy and to make you feel part of his family. That generosity extended to his work in nurturing young talent at his acting workshops in Florida, where he helped launch the careers of many fine actors. He used his power and his wealth to give back to people and to his community. He just kept giving.

Burt was a star in the very best sense of the word. Number one: He had the looks and the charisma, and he brought honesty and truth to every role he played. He made it look so easy but it is a hard thing to do, to be so comfortable and confident in front of the camera like he was. Number two: Burt loved the business and he loved film. And just like Burt, Wayne Byrne is a great student of the movies, someone who understands the art of cinema like few others. He is the real deal. I could not imagine a more ideal writer for this book because I know Wayne deeply loves Burt's work and you can trust that he has put together a brilliant piece of work on a true artist and great man. Burt would have loved Wayne's heartfelt tribute to his career.

When I leave my house every day, I hit the button for the electric gate and I say "Thank you, Burt," because I wouldn't be living in this nice house in Malibu if it weren't for him. I owe that man the amazing career that I've had in the film business and the great life I have because of that. Burt Reynolds was a very special individual, he was a gentleman. There will never be anyone like him.

Thank you, Burt.

Reynolds and Nick McLean Sr. setting up a shot on the B.L. Stryker film, *High Rise*, 1990.

As a camera operator, Nick McLean Sr. shot some of the greatest films of the New Hollywood era, including *Marathon Man*, *The Deer Hunter* and *Being There*. He later became a cinematographer beginning with *Stroker Ace* and moving on to major studio pictures such as *Cannonball Run II*, *The Goonies*, *Spaceballs* and *Staying Alive*. His television work began with the sitcom *Evening Shade* before he filmed *B.L. Stryker*, *Cybill* and *Friends*, the latter earning him three Emmy award nominations.

Introduction

"Success is Burt Reynolds' only handicap."—Orson Welles[1]

As a writer, when I make a commitment of work—temporally, emotionally and contractually—to author a book, my passion for the subject cannot be any less than absolute. The filmmakers that I have chosen to write about thus far have meant something very dear to me and my relationship with cinema. Many people have asked, upon learning that I was writing a book on Burt Reynolds, "Why?" For some, it seems, Reynolds was a meretricious figure of Hollywood excess who embraced the opulent lifestyle it afforded, a studio golden boy who made millions for himself, the producers and the executives, who relished the fame and fortune but then lost his hard-earned cultural capital by appearing to enjoy it all a little too much.

For me, though, Burt Reynolds was one of the great American artists: a truly compelling performer and a distinguished filmmaker. And if he enjoyed himself along the way, he damn well deserved to, because he has entertained millions of fans around the world with a long, prolific career in film and television, all the while imparting the sense of triumph and delight that he so clearly felt in sharing his silver screen dreams with us.

After my first book *The Cinema of Tom DiCillo: Include Me Out* was published, I began wondering what subject I would next devote myself to. To write about Tom DiCillo, the filmmaker whose work introduced me to the art of film, was instinctual; it wasn't something I merely wanted to do, it was something I felt I *had* to do. Selecting a follow-up subject didn't take much time at all. There are a few filmmakers and actors whose work I would consider essential to my love and enjoyment of cinema, so the short list was indeed short, and sitting atop that list was Burt Reynolds. Fortunately, my publisher agreed with my sentiments about Reynolds' importance as an American icon and his significance as an artist throughout a half-century of film and television.

It is always difficult relating into the spoken word the absolute passion we feel for a subject, and so my simple and somewhat ineffectual answer to the question "Why Burt Reynolds?" is always, "He's my favorite movie star." But that answer doesn't do justice to the kind of admiration and respect I have for Reynolds' work. So the act of writing this book is an attempt to turn that passion of mine into something tangible and it will perhaps answer that question more profoundly. For me, Reynolds was much more than an actor; he was an artist, an icon, an image, even a brand. Depending on which period of his career you look at, the name "Burt Reynolds" connoted a certain kind of thrilling, gritty tough guy cinema; other times that name stood for hugely entertaining, mass-appeal comedy with rough-hewn Southern charm and amiability, not to mention huge sex appeal. For five years, from 1978 to 1982, Reynolds was America's top box office attraction, according to the Quigley Publications poll of movie exhibitors, a feat which is a testament to the popularity of the star.

Owing to my age, the earliest conscious memory I have of Burt Reynolds is from a 1988 VHS tape of the film *Innerspace* (I'm sure Burt would have told me he has socks older than that film) which featured a Warner Bros. "Coming Attractions" trailer reel which advertised the film *Heat*. Even though I was roughly six years old when I saw this, the name "Burt Reynolds" and his tremendous screen presence felt instantly familiar to me and stuck with me henceforth. Growing up a child of the '80s, it was impossible to escape television rerun screenings of *Smokey and the Bandit*, *The Cannonball Run* and *Deliverance*; those were staples of our television diet, and of course as children of the video store we were well aware of Reynolds' grimacing mid-action pose on the cover of *Malone*, or the poster art of *Stick*. We were consuming Burt Reynolds even if we didn't realize it.

It certainly feels like Reynolds has always been there with us and it is no wonder, as this book will remind us of the epic span of Reynolds' presence throughout the many cultural and industrial shifts in Hollywood's history. He was one of those artists whose career encompasses many of the major progressive movements in American cinema across many decades: He first appeared in the midst of the Golden Age of the 1950s and 1960s, worked solidly through the New Hollywood of the 1970s and the blockbuster era of the 1980s, then embraced the independent boom of the 1990s and kept going right up to until his passing in 2018. He really was—to reference his final theatrical release—the last movie star.

This book is not, nor ever attempts to be, an intimate insight into the private life of Burt Reynolds; that has been previously accomplished by the man himself in his duo of candid memoirs, *My Life: Burt Reynolds* (1994) and *But Enough About Me* (2015). Rather, this book is a work of film criticism and a long-form tribute. It is an opportunity to discuss in-depth many films which haven't been previously covered in critical, historical or aesthetic contexts of any great scope or consideration. Some of the films have indeed been given much page space over the years and been rightly lauded (*Deliverance*), while the financial success and massive popularity of others has been celebrated (*Smokey and the Bandit*). But many of Reynolds' most interesting works have been grossly overlooked or forgotten, such as the series of classy romantic comedies in which he starred for distinguished filmmakers Peter Bogdanovich (*At Long Last Love*, 1975), Michael Ritchie (*Semi-Tough*, 1977), Alan J. Pakula (*Starting Over*, 1979), David Steinberg (*Paternity*, 1981), Norman Jewison (*Best Friends*, 1982) and Blake Edwards (*The Man Who Loved Women*, 1983).

This book analyzes Reynolds' films and television series in chronological order, relating behind-the-scenes production information and discussing their respective places in history, while making subtextual allusions between the man and the characters he played. Throughout his work, Reynolds was an artist cognizant enough about his rare position in life to make humorous reference to himself and his awesome career. While some may see this as an act of self-indulgence or self-consciousness, I see it more as an act of self-deprecation and self-awareness. In how many movies has he played a film industry figure struggling with various treacherous elements of the motion picture business; or how many times has he played a patriarchal figure endeavoring to nurture a bond with a son or daughter, biological or surrogate? Since his days of fame and fortune began, Reynolds made no secret of his desire to have a child, and his 1973 album *Ask Me What I Am* even features a song called "A Room for a Boy Never Used" in which he openly laments the familial void in his life. Reynolds parlayed this and other personally relevant details into his films along the way. For anyone who follows Reynolds' significant career from film to film, there are a multitude of themes that he generously offers the attentive viewer, those which give far greater insight into the man and his internal machinations than a hundred tabloid profiles and lifestyle magazine articles could do.

Now for a note on the inclusion criteria for the films that receive chapter-length coverage. This book is the most comprehensive critical overview available of Burt Reynold's onscreen career. I have attempted to cover every major work he has appeared in as the lead actor or co-star. Some films included feature Reynolds only in a minor role, but made the cut either due to the film having a major director that Reynold collaborated with or his character being of notable value to the narrative. I have excluded films in which Reynolds makes a brief and inconsequential cameo appearance. A listing of these films appears in Appendix 1. Also excluded were films that proved impossible to track down and therefore were unavailable to me at the time of writing.

Speaking to numerous friends and collaborators of Reynolds for this book, one word recurs more than most: generous. Many of them recall with wonder the actor's resolutely giving nature—giving of his time, talent and experience; giving financially, emotionally and morally. After filming on *Starting Over* wrapped in 1978, Reynolds set to work on realizing his dream of opening the Burt Reynolds Dinner Theatre in his hometown of Jupiter, Florida. The project, conceived with the aim of taking the theater out of the traditionally exclusive cultural realm and making it accessible to everybody no matter their social class, brought some of Hollywood's biggest stars to a humble Jupiter playhouse. To name a few of those who graced the South Floridian stage: Martin Sheen, Sally Field, Elliott Gould, Farrah Fawcett, Sarah Jessica Parker, Kirstie Alley, Parker Stevenson, Jim Nabors and Ossie Davis. The theater also afforded Reynolds the opportunity to direct, which he did on the well-received productions *Two for the Seesaw* (1979), *Same Time Next Year* (1980), *One Flew Over the Cuckoo's Nest* (1982), *Mass Appeal* (1983), *Teahouse of the August Moon* (1987) and *I'm Not Rappaport* (1988).

Along with the theater itself, Reynolds utilized his position and experience and created BRITT, the Burt Reynolds Institute for Theatre Training, an apprenticeship acting program which would later function as a post-graduate course. Visiting lecturers and guest speakers have included Dom DeLuise, Charles Nelson Reilly, Ned Beatty, Joshua Logan, Jerry Lewis and others. BRITT alumni who apprenticed under Reynolds' tutelage include Matt Battaglia, John D'Aquino, Mark Fauser, C. James Lewis and Gigi Rice, all of whom went on to prolific careers on-screen and behind-the-scenes on major film and TV projects.

Throughout the making of this book, I asked one particular question of all my interview subjects, in an effort to understand from as many perspectives as possible what made Burt Reynolds the ultimate film star, what was so magnetic about his image and persona, enough that it made him the top-ranking box office star for five years consecutively. I will let Burt Reynolds' own friends and colleagues tell you themselves as you read on. But before that, let us consider film historian Joe Baltake's astute estimation of the actor's appeal:

> Burt Reynolds, in a nutshell, is the movie star who's a pal … but there's something else, something deeper, something sad that makes Reynolds' playfulness and flippancy wrenching…. In his eyes, we see Reynolds' integrity. They're what make him original in a business full of clones. We look at Reynolds

and we see a man who's believed in old movies, the American Dream and loyalty; we look in his eyes and we see how difficult it's been. Today's devoted film aficionados and even our critics can't fully appreciate what Burt Reynolds represents. Yes, he's out of joint. He may be too good for today's movies. His secret with audiences is that he's one of us.[2]

Reynolds' death on September 6, 2018, sharply reminded us that this legend was indeed mortal. Fortunately, his legacy of work renders him immortal to me and millions of other fans. In a 1979 interview, Reynolds reflected upon his career and his place in film history: "The thought of dying doesn't bother me, I've had a fantastic life. Really fantastic. The only regret I'll have if something happened to me tomorrow is that I didn't prove to everybody that I was as good an actor as I think I am."[3]

In the forty years since Burt Reynolds spoke those very words he more than proved to us what an exemplary actor he could be and this book is a tribute to those words and to the words memorialized in Don Williams' elegiac song, *If Hollywood Don't Need You*, which details the singer's yearning to shake Burt's hand and inform him that he has enjoyed all of his movies. Well, Burt, like Mr. Williams, I too have seen all your movies and I would have loved to shake your hand. But it's too late for that now, so this book is an acknowledgment of the love and respect I have for you and your work.

Notes

1. Orson Welles, "Foreword," in *The Films of Burt Reynolds*, Nancy Streebeck (New York: Citadel Press, 1982), p. 9.
2. Joe Baltake, "Afterword," in *The Films of Burt Reynolds*, Nancy Streebeck (New York: Citadel Press, 1982), p. 256.
3. Bernhardt J. Hurwood, *Burt Reynolds* (New York: Quick Fox, 1979) p. 98.

Riverboat
(TV Series, NBC, 1959–1961)

"Colonel, you're not going to use this boat to risk any more lives!"—Ben Frazer

Burt Reynolds' road to *Riverboat* is the stuff of legend; it marked the beginning of one of the most illustrious screen careers of the twentieth century. It is the story of a small-town boy from the wrong side of the tracks who parlays his athletic skill into academic possibilities, only for a devastating physical injury to leave him without recourse. But rather than limiting the young man's opportunities, he would in convalescence discover another talent which would be nurtured and refined with the support of a respected professor. The rest is history.

The boy was Burton Leon Reynolds Jr., the second child born to Harriette Fernette and Burton Milo Reynolds on February 11, 1936, in Lansing, Michigan. The couple's first child, Nancy Ann, was born on January 21, 1930. To his family and friends, Burton Leon would often be referred to as Buddy or Buddy Lee, but the rest of the world would come to know him as Burt Reynolds. The Reynolds youngster would endure a childhood at war with himself and with his father, a strict disciplinarian. Burton Reynolds Sr., also known as Big Burt, was raised on an Indian reservation in North Carolina and later moved across several states, including Michigan, where he met and fell in love with the Italian Harriette. After a few years living in Michigan and now with two children to support, the couple moved south to Florida, settling down in the tough working-class town of Riviera Beach in Palm Beach County, where Burt Sr. became the chief of police.

With his father's restrictions and penchant for punishment, along with having to fortify himself with a streetwise attitude to evade the taunting of his Riviera Beach peers, young Burt developed a taste for rebellion and recklessness. If he was ever safe from venting his fury and enduring the repercussions of such lashing out, it was in the bosom of the movies. "I would spend entire weekends at the movies starting at 12:45 in the afternoon," Reynolds said. "I'd see three movies a day and get out by 11 at night. Movies were an incredibly important part of my life."[1]

At Central Junior High, Reynolds discovered that he excelled in athletics, meaning he was no longer a target of teasing but a hero within the school halls. Finding his calling on the football field not only made him a popular student, it also opened doors he thought would remain closed forever. Higher education was never a consideration for Reynolds, as it wasn't for many working class youths with limited funds and even less opportunities. But with skill to burn, the star athlete was courted by many colleges with the offer of football scholarships. In 1954, Burt accepted and enrolled at Florida State University, where he played at halfback and won several prestigious college football awards, ultimately attracting the attention of the big leagues. A professional contract with the Baltimore Colts beckoned. However, depending on how you look at it, fate dealt him either the best or the worst hand imaginable. One dark night during his sophomore year, Reynolds put pedal to the metal and ended up coming upon a truck parked in the middle of the road. Blinded by the truck's headlights, Reynolds, on instinct, dove for cover as the car ploughed into the immovable vehicle. Injured, the teen's cries for help were ignored as the truck owners fled the scene. Reynolds survived with broken bones and underwent an operation to remove his spleen. What did not survive was his sporting career.

Throughout his recovery, Reynolds was overcome with the sense of anger and resentment of anyone whose dream—a lifeline to a brighter future—is cut short. With an insurance settlement in hand, Reynolds set out for New York City, settling in Greenwich Village to lose himself in the bohemian lifestyle of actors, artists and alcoholics. Still bruised, literally and figuratively, from the crash, he wandered from one dead-end job to another, ending up back home with the hope of returning to the gridiron. Once again at Florida State University, he enrolled in an English Literature class. Fate intervened and brought him together with Prof. Watson Duncan III. The distinguished academic recognized talent in the despondent youngster and suggested that he try out for a school production of Sutton Vane's *Outward Bound*. Only afterwards did Prof. Duncan tell Reynolds that he had successfully auditioned for the play's lead role. For his acclaimed work as the character of Tom Prior, Reynolds earned a scholarship to the Hyde Park Playhouse, and once more left Florida State University and his family behind. Burt settled back into New York City and became part of the struggling actor fraternity, touring in summer stock companies and working menial jobs to pay the bills. Broadway soon beckoned and he landed the role of Mannon in a production of *Mister Roberts* starring Charlton Heston.

Screen tests for major studios and stunt work on TV shows such as *Omnibus* and *Robert Montgomery Presents* followed this high-profile stint on the legitimate stage, but it was an introduction to noted theatrical agent Maynard Morris of Music Corporation of America (MCA) that proved most fortuitous.

Later, at the insistence of some successful co-stars seeing talent in their eager stuntman, Reynolds went westward. Arriving in Hollywood, he gave a memorable audition in front of Hollywood power players Lew Wasserman, head of MCA, and agent Jay Cantor. Reynolds expected the worst but soon learned that his audition earned him the offer of a seven-year contract with MCA-Universal, which led to his first speaking role on a 1959 episode of the TV series *M Squad*, on which he became friendly with the show's star, Lee Marvin. Next came small parts in other shows, such as that of a murderous bootlegger killing his way to the top of the criminal underworld in the Prohibition drama *The Lawless Years* and a vicious highwayman in *Pony Express*. "I worked in every lousy syndicated show," Reynolds says, "the kind of shows that they shoot with a Kodak and a flashlight. They were depressing years but that's where I finally learned to act."[2] After such appearances, Wasserman sent Reynolds to try out for the co-starring role in a new TV series called *Riverboat*. The actor duly did what the president of the studio told him to do, because "[i]f Lew Wasserman says it's going to rain, everybody puts up an umbrella."[3]

Reynolds was cast and the show, which was produced under MCA's television subsidiary Revue Productions, was broadcast on NBC from 1959 to 1961. A potential rival to the likes of *Maverick*, *Wagon Train* and *Rawhide*, *Riverboat* was a weekly black-and-white western adventure set aboard the *Enterprise* as it navigates the Mississippi, Missouri and Ohio rivers. Darren McGavin played the lead role of the captain and owner of the ship, Grey Holden, who won the vessel in a poker game. Reynolds' character Ben Frazer is the ship's tough co-pilot.

Despite being second-billed, Reynolds doesn't feature in many episodes, relegated to sparse moments in the bridge, pulling on the horn and looking slightly embarrassed about the whole situation. But occasional episodes do give Ben Frazer the opportunity to step forward as the hero, as seen in "Witness No Evil," "A Night at Trapper's Landing," "The Faithless" and "The Boy from Pittsburgh," solid Frazer episodes that offer Reynolds a lot more drama and action than previously afforded to him. Holden's job in these entries was limited to appearing at the end of the episode to look comically bemused at all that has happened in his absence.

"A Night at Trapper's Landing" is of interest to Reynolds historians as it features the first of several screen collaborations between the actor and Ricardo Montalban. Montalban plays Lt. Andre Devereaux, a bon vivant Frenchman serving in the U.S. Army. He commandeers the *Enterprise* in order to maneuver upriver to Trapper's Landing to quash a reported Indian uprising. Ben isn't too happy with the army taking over his boat and the two men butt heads until they learn to respect each other. Montalban plays the decadent bourgeois ladies' man with relish and we see here for the first time the great chemistry between Reynolds and Montalban that served them well in future joint endeavors such as *Dan August*, *Cannonball Run II* and *B.L. Stryker*.

Reynolds' *Riverboat* tenure lasted its first 26 episodes and then he was relieved of duty, having become increasingly disillusioned amidst the acrimony between him and McGavin. The onscreen relationship between Holden and Frazer masked serious tensions between the two actors and much of that anguish arose from McGavin denigrating his younger co-star's methods and abilities as an actor, throwing tantrums when it came time for close-ups of Frazer to the point that the shots were sabotaged and unusable.[4] "Revue [Productions] must have a whole auditorium packed with my close-ups. None of them ever got on the air,"[5] Reynolds joked. With a brief explanation of Frazer leaving for

Darren McGavin and Reynolds on the set of *Riverboat* in 1959.

New Orleans, Reynolds was no longer part of the *Riverboat* crew and was initially replaced by Noah Beery Jr. as Bill Blake before Bart Patton, introduced in the episode "The Salvage Pirates," took over as Terry Blake.

Television's loss would be Cinema's gain as Reynolds was relieved of duty from *The Enterprise*, though his time on *Riverboat* wasn't entirely in vain; it was on this show that he would meet fellow actors with whom he would collaborate again, such as John Hoyt (*About Roger Mowbray*, Episode 3, Season 1), Eddie Albert (*The Unwilling*, Episode 5, Season 1), R.G. Armstrong (*A Night at Trapper's Landing*, Episode 9, Season 1), Mercedes McCambridge (*Jessie Quinn*, Episode 10, Season 1), and Doug McClure (*The Face of Courage*, Episode 15, Season 1). Burt Reynolds and Darren McGavin, however, would never work together again.

Notes

1. Sylvia Safran Resnick, *Burt Reynolds* (London: W.H. Allen, 1983), p. 17.
2. *Ibid.*, p. 40.
3. *Ibid.*, p. 41.
4. Everett Aaker, *Television Western Players, 1960–1975: A Biographical Dictionary* (Jefferson, NC: McFarland, 2017), p. 286.
5. Bernhardt J. Hurwood, *Burt Reynolds* (New York: Quick Fox, 1979), p. 26.

Angel Baby

(1961)

"Jenny, what do you want to learn to talk for, huh? Things are just fine the way they are."—Hoke Adams

Burt Reynolds made his first impression upon the cinema-going public in the steamy Southern melodrama *Angel Baby*. Far from the benevolent Southern gentleman of future films, here Burt plays Hoke Adams as a slimy, unsavory delinquent who lusts after the beautiful mute, Jenny Angel (Salome Jens). Ashamed of her daughter rolling around in the grass with bad boy Hoke, Jenny's mother demands a moral and spiritual cleansing of Jenny and takes her to a touring preacher's tent where a fervent young faith healer named Paul Strand (George Hamilton) inspires the girl to say the word "God." Having restored Jenny's communicative powers and believing it to be a genuine miracle, Paul takes the girl into his ministry and on to the rural back roads of the South where she lectures the susceptible public on the healing powers of believing, an act no doubt helped with her illustrating passages of the Bible by dressing in the alluring wardrobe of Babylonian temptresses. The outfits become her as they bedazzle the male gaze of the audience.

In a marriage of convenience more than amore, Paul is wed to a pious middle-aged woman named Sarah (Mercedes McCambridge). Their union is platonic and more familial in nature, informed by a disturbing mother-son dynamic which grows unsettlingly incestuous as Sarah becomes increasingly jealous of Paul and Jenny's blossoming attraction. Jenny eventually breaks away from the Strands and launches a successful solo tour which

Hoke Adams (Reynolds) and beautiful mute Jenny Angel (Salome Jens) in *Angel Baby* (1961).

attracts the attention of unscrupulous businessman Sam Wilcox (Roger Clark), who wishes to cash in on her popular revivalism. Milking the gullibility of those looking for something, anything, to believe in, Wilcox deceptively plants faux invalids for Jenny to miraculously "heal" on stage. Upon learning of Wilcox's scamming ways and being labeled a fraud, Jenny retreats from her faith.

Angel Baby is less a religious satire and more a damning critique of the abuse of power. The theme of illicit sexual deviances that runs below the film's surface not only provides a suitably seamy soap opera context but also a worthy subtextual consideration of the prurient objectives that motivate the manipulation of the morally weak. Sarah's sanctimony and hypocritical judgment of those who she perceives to sin hides what she truly craves and has been grooming for years: the young flesh of Paul Strand. In Sarah's fear of losing Paul, she condemns Jenny as "a slut," to which the besotted Paul lashes out and physically assaults his older keeper. But Paul's passionate outburst only serves to ignite the secret desire that Sarah has been holding onto since becoming Paul's surrogate mother years ago. She tells Paul, "For eight years I guarded you. You were a boy when God commanded me to take you from the choir to do his holy work, and since that day I've fought to keep you pure" (though maintaining his pubescent purity was not for God's benefit, but her own). If Sarah walks in God's shadow, then the youthful virility of Paul offers her a bit of forbidden fruit. Sexually stimulated as she eyes Paul in his shirtless and agitated state, Sarah suggests that he "exorcise this devil … cut away this sin … pluck out the evil cravings of the flesh." But these are merely sanctimonious platitudes to guilt Paul into fulfilling her erotic desires. "You must cleanse yourself … through me!" commands Sarah as she disrobes and offers her bosom for his delectation; he refuses.

Director Paul Wendkos expertly crafts this scene in fierce hypnotic style, with Sarah conversely switching from raving, zealous apostle to slithering, seductive temptress. As Sarah sidles up behind Paul on the bed, nibbling at his bare back, the soundtrack illustrates her heightened arousal with a sensual, spellbinding choral musical piece. Hamilton recalls shooting the scene, considering McCambridge's steely demeanor and remembering her as "one tough broad … made fun of the Southern gent in me when I couldn't bring myself to give her the violent whack the script called for. 'Don't pull punches with me,' she taunted. So I really let her have it."[1]

It is testament to the veracity of their performances that the scene packs a powerful punch. Wendkos is one of those underrated filmmakers who made plenty of pictures and directed prolifically for television but never rose above the ranks of journeyman. He was courted by Columbia early in his career to direct for its CBS television division (*Playhouse 60*, *Route 66*, *Tightrope*) and ended up helming several of the popular surf movies featuring the eponymous beach bunny: *Gidget* (1959), *Gidget Goes Hawaiian* (1961) and *Gidget Goes to Rome* (1963). Later in his career, Wendkos made distinctive thrillers (*The Mephisto Waltz* [1971]), franchise sequels (*Guns of the Magnificent Seven* [1969]) and the occasional NBC Monday Night Movie, including the Raquel Welch melodrama *Right to Die* (1987). All of them displayed an assured formal style that is evident in *Angel Baby*.

Filmed before, though released after, the similarly themed but higher profile, multi–Oscar-winning hit *Elmer Gantry* (Richard Brooks, 1960), *Angel Baby* may have come across to many as riding the coattails of the Burt Lancaster film. Mercedes McCambridge supported what she considered one of her favorite roles and stood up for the film. "If *Angel Baby* had a tenth of the money that was spent advertising *Elmer Gantry*," the actress lamented, "it would have been recognized for what it is, a much better picture. I told Burt Lancaster that."[2] It would certainly take a person of formidable personality to harness the required chutzpah and temerity to tell Lancaster as much.

It is a curious experience to watch *Angel Baby* in the context of a Burt Reynolds picture. With his slick ducktail haircut and smarmy grimace, there isn't much room for the actor to maneuver; there is no opportunity for him to showcase any of the engaging personality of the beloved movie star to come. What is on display is a good-looking, athletic character actor, capable of turning on the menace upon requirement. *Angel Baby* also has the unfortunate distinction of being the first of two consecutive 1961 films (followed by *Armored Command*) that feature Reynolds as a sexually aggressive sleaze, hardly an image the budding actor would wish to embrace for too long, though perhaps no harm considering the culture of cinematic outsiders and outlaws that were synonymous with a new breed of rising star, such as Marlon Brando, James Dean and Clint Eastwood. Reynolds' rendering of the slimy Hoke is the right amount of rebellious antidote to Hamilton's angelic Strand.

Following a quick run of supporting appearances in slick MGM productions including *Home from the Hill* (Vincente Minnelli, 1960), *All the Fine Young Cannibals* (Michael Anderson, 1960) and *Where the Boys Are* (Henry Levin, 1960), George Hamilton stepped up to leading man status for what he hoped would be "better, more serious" films. As it turned out, Reynolds and Hamilton both attended Palm Beach High School, though graduating several years apart, with Hamilton referring to Reynolds as "the golden boy of my high school." Reynolds recalled with affection Hamilton's desire to emulate David Niven's poise and refinement in an era when most young actors yearned for Brando intensity. He also described the absurd fight sequence between Jenny's love rivals, Paul and Hoke:

> The toughest part of *Angel Baby* was doing a fight scene with George. At that time he was a contender for the title of the World's Most Uncoordinated Human Being. Yet he had to beat me up, something

that was almost impossible for him to fake. In the dumbest fight scene ever, he sort of lifted me, and I leaped into the bushes, hoping it would look as if I'd been thrown. But it looked as if he'd lifted me and I jumped.[3]

Reynolds and Hamilton played adversaries again 12 years later in *The Man Who Loved Cat Dancing*, by which time both men had graduated from supporting actors to Hollywood leading men and were far more coordinated in their combative endeavors.

Notes

1. George Hamilton and William Stadiem, *Don't Mind If I Do* (New York: Simon & Schuster, 2008), p. 148.
2. Ray Hagan and Laura Wagner, *Killer Tomatoes: Fifteen Tough Film Dames* (Jefferson, NC: McFarland, 2004), p. 143.
3. Burt Reynolds, *My Life: Burt Reynolds* (Great Britain: Hodder & Stoughton, 1994), p. 94.

Armored Command
(1961)

"I'm saving this for a special occasion, and you ain't it!"—Skee

Armored Command is set during Operation Nordwind, the German offensive (December 1944 to January 1945) in the Vosges-Alsace region of France, ordered by Hitler to distract Allied forces from mounting significant defense against German forces during the Battle of the Bulge. As the conflict rages, an infantry platoon of the American 7th Army finds a wounded Alsatian woman left for dead on the front lines. Alexandra Bastegar (Tina Louise) is a redhead whose luscious looks and vulnerability capture the romantic interests of several squad members, including the honorable Mike (Earl Holliman) and the sleazy Skee (Reynolds).

Little do the Americans realize that Bastegar is actually a Nazi operative posing as a victim of the Wehrmacht; she was willingly wounded by her German comrades in order to gain the trust of the American squad members. Her mission is to provide reconnaissance to her Nazi masters via a contact in the village, relaying the strategies and hardware inventory of the Americans. Once Bastegar is entrenched, she sells herself as a valuable asset to the squad by displaying her fluency in several languages and proficiency in local dialects. A conflict of ego rages amongst the men of the 7th as they vie for her attention,

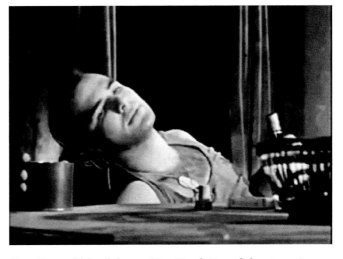

Skee (Reynolds) celebrates New Year's Eve while at war in *Armored Command* (1961).

while their tough commander Col. Devlin (Howard Keel) is actually trying to fight an actual war.

As *Armored Command* is predominantly confined to the single setting of the unit's outpost, the claustrophobic tension simmering between various soldiers underscores the taut, melodramatic love triangle between Mike, Skee and Bastegar, affording these characters some fine moments of power play. Dropping a seductive femme fatale such as Bastegar into the middle of such a macho hotbed—where tension is rife, emotions fragile, and the bellies and libidos of the men are starving—serves the script well with its brewing suspense.

Bastegar uses the two men's distrust of each other to her advantage, insinuating that Skee sexually assaulted her, thus raising Mike's ire. Tina Louise is effectively the centerpiece of the film and, rather than the war itself, it is she who is the cause of antagonism amongst the chief players. The female spy, an unusual concept in war pictures of the period, gives the film a novelty value as well as instilling the story with the required sexual tension and psychological malaise that drives her soldier suitors insane with lust and envy. A low-budget film of this type cannot rely on special effects and elaborately staged action set pieces, but can get by very well with some sizzling sexual chemistry and the right actors to harbor those intense attractions. With Reynolds and Holliman in each other's crosshairs and Louise commanding the attention of their hearts and loins, the film provides the right battleground for these three personalities to go to war. Reynolds manages to out-sleaze his rendering of *Angel Baby*'s Hoke Adams in a role that requires him to charm and repel in equal measure. At first it seems as though Skee's bad boy persona actually intrigues bad girl Bastegar before we realize she is using him to manipulate the affections of the sincere Mike.

Shot in December 1960 in Germany, *Armored Command* is one of the lesser-celebrated films of Byron Haskin, who was a cinematographer in the silent picture era. He's better known for directing Paramount's *The War of the Worlds* (1953) and the cult picture *Robinson Crusoe on Mars* (1968). Haskin does a fine job with the plot's espionage elements, though as a war picture *Armored Command* is quite a staid entry of the genre, with very little of the slick battlefield action that punctuated more spectacular films of the era. However, the grim battle sequence in the final 20 minutes of the picture is brutal—one striking image of a dead soldier's hand being stomped into the muddy ground is a sad and grisly one. The sequence, an invasion of the village by the Panzer Division and subsequent exchange of fire with the Allies, does feel shoehorned into the final act to satisfy the generic conventions of the war picture but is largely disruptive to the tense dramatic flow of the narrative that precedes it. Also, the editing of the battle is undermined by the inclusion of some obvious low-grade stock footage.

The reason for such economy is perhaps due to *Armored Command* being the product of B-movie specialists Allied Artists (an offshoot of Monogram Pictures). In the tradition of privileging story and character over sophisticated production values and finely honed aesthetics, the picture might suffer from appearing less extravagant than its major studio counterparts, but succeeds with its tense scenario and with the realistic, immediate style of shooting from Oscar-winning cinematographer Ernest Haller (*Jezebel*, 1938; *Gone with the Wind*, 1939; *Mildred Pierce*, 1945).

Gunsmoke
(TV Series, CBS, 1955–1975)

"Why should I change? I made my choice when they murdered my pa."—Quint
Asper

America's top-rated show from 1955 to 1961, *Gunsmoke* was a major television event
and huge hit, ultimately becoming the longest-running Western series ever aired. In considering the history of the West as portrayed on screen, the series is as definitive a Western
text as any.

The series takes place in Dodge City, Kansas, in the late 1890s. Marshal Matt Dillon
(James Arness) oversees law and order in the small town which boasts the Long Branch
Saloon, run by Miss Kitty Russell (Amanda Blake), and is home to Doc Adams (Milburn
Stone) and the good-hearted Deputy Chester Goode (Dennis Weaver). Each of these characters brings their own unique personality and sensibility to life in Dodge City. A half-
breed Indian, Quint Asper (Burt Reynolds), ends up in town after a failed quest to exact
vengeance for his fallen father. After saving a white man from certain death at the hands
of the Comanches, Asper is embraced by Marshal Dillon and the community. He trades
the axe of retribution for the hammer of trade by becoming the town's blacksmith, thus
marking the controversial arrival of a minority outsider into Dodge City.

Despite the generic framework of the television western that *Gunsmoke* adheres to, it
managed to far outsize the formal confines of the format with its grand and important
themes. Dodge City at the turn of the century is the setting for small personal dramas that
represent big ideas in American culture, society and politics. This frontier town presents
the virtuous, idealized version of what small town America can be at its best, with law and
order triumphing in tandem with the moral decency of a harmonious community made
up of indigenous and migrant people. When unscrupulous outsiders threaten the Dodge
City way of life, Dillon dispenses a fair and equitable form of justice to rid his town of such
malignancy. Many episodes start with a family or other decent folk being the victims of
highway robbery or massacred by bandits or Indians; those who survive will be harbored
by the town and welcomed into the community while Dillon and other supporting characters become involved in the quest for justice. Grand ideas are explored in *Gunsmoke*,
such as racial-ethnic prejudice, the pursuit of happiness, and the ethical concerns of law
and order, just as each episode hits the generic registers of the western genre with basic
good-vs.-evil narratives which are punctuated with the adventure elements of horseback
pursuits and shootouts. They are occasionally tempered with moments of romance and
levity. The show successfully achieved all of this within its limited television time slot.

While Reynolds waited for his budding film career to take off in earnest, being cast
as a regular character in this beloved series gave him an opportunity to graduate beyond
one-off bit parts in the likes of *Naked City* and *Route 66*. Shows such as these generally cast
Reynolds as a greasy-coiffed delinquent bad boy, which gave viewers much cause to compare
him to Marlon Brando, the actor whom Reynolds perceptively parodied in a Twilight Zone
episode, "The Bard."

As a character of brooding volatility and a representation of racial prejudice, Quint Asper would require a completely sober performance from the actor stepping into the role; this went against Reynolds' naturally gregarious personality. When he screen-tested for the role of Asper, Reynolds was told, "You're too fat in the face for an Indian,"[1] but he gave back as much as he got: "If you want an Indian, go to Oklahoma. I'm an actor."[2] He was hired and Quint Asper became popular with the show's fans, whose letters mentioned Quint in the same breath as Matt Dillon, Doc Adams and Miss Kitty, suggesting the character needed more screen time than he was currently afforded. This posed something of a predicament for producer Norman Macdonnell as the main *Gunsmoke* players were already well-established, with little room for Quint to take up any further space in the narratives. Macdonnell said of Reynolds:

> I have the feeling that if he ever got the bit in his teeth, he'd run away with it. He's not afraid of man, beast or God. He's really made an effort to fit in with us. It's not easy for a newcomer to break into a cast that been working together like a family all these years…. I think he's a good actor. Innately, he's a leading man, which creates something of a problem for us. We can't use him as such.[3]

Gunsmoke star James Arness recalled, "You could tell very quickly that Burt was a guy with a great presence,"[4] and Reynolds duly made that presence felt in his season eight debut episode "Quint Asper Comes Home," when Quint is memorably introduced after tragedy befalls the peaceful Asper homestead. Two wandering peasant prospectors happen across the Asper family land and demand gold from Quint's father (Bill Zuckert) while insulting

his Indian mother, Topsanah (Angela Clarke). The Asper patriarch is killed for punching one of the offenders, but within seconds the young Quint responds with swift and brutal efficiency, killing the two men with extreme prejudice.

With this act of violence, Quint has tasted the blood of the white man and soon develops a fierce thirst, joining the Comanche tribe to go on the warpath to hunt and kill Caucasians. When it becomes evident that Quint can't kill in cold blood, he is scolded by the tribe's chief and humiliated into menial manual labor. Quint releases a white prisoner and escapes alongside him. Dillon tracks down a wounded Quint and brings him to safety, but some of the townsfolk don't take too kindly to Dillon taking in the injured Indian. When Doc Adams asks, "Matt, did it occur to you that this Indian is somewhat lighter than any Indian you

Publicity shot of Reynolds as the *Gunsmoke* TV series' Quint Asper.

ever saw?" Dillon agrees and wonders what the vociferous rabble in the saloon will have to say about an Indian prisoner being sheltered in their close-knit community.

"Quint Asper Comes Home" is typical of the show's sense of compassion and empathy, depicting blind hatred and prejudice as symptoms of further devastation to come, as well as acknowledging that lawless retribution is not something to be tolerated. In the brief outburst of violence that results in the death of Quint's father, we can sympathize with Quint's quick leap into action, but beyond that moment of justified retribution his further bloodlust masks a malignant sense of hatred and a misguided moral compass. The hospitality of Dodge City residents guide Quint towards a more civilized way of life, something which is threatened throughout the character's run on the show. The Season Eight entry "Quint's Indian" affords the eponymous character a central role after he is framed for stealing horses by a couple of lowlifes. The temptation for Quint to exact revenge on the white man is never far from the surface as his is an easily tapped rage which goes all the way back to the death of his father. Just as Dillon thought he had tamed the hot-tempered Asper with the civility of Dodge City, the fury flares up once again: "I'll be wearing a gun tonight, Matt. I'm gonna kill me some white men!"

The financial security of a recurring role, during which he was making $1500 per week, wasn't enough for Reynolds; he was eager to spread his wings beyond hammering an anvil in perpetuity. Despite some episodes revolving around his character, little is developed and Quint Asper is soon relegated to pounding horseshoes in his workshed once again. Reynolds spoke to executives about expanding his character, but the pleas fell on deaf ears. The actor, feeling disgruntled, was on the verge of quitting Hollywood for a regular job in Florida. Appealing to the powerful Dick Clayton of Famous Artists Agency, Reynolds pleaded, "You're the only person who can make it happen. Get me a feature film, anywhere in the world, at any price. If not, I'm going to call it quits and return to Florida—coach football, build barns, paint boats. I swear to you, Dick, this is my last crack at it."[5]

And so Reynolds got out of Dodge, though not without a fondness for the experience and a love for those with whom he became close. "For many years (45 to be exact), I have been asked 'What were the best for you growing up as an actor?' Without hesitation, I have always said, 'The 2½ years I was on *Gunsmoke*.' They were for me 'the best of times'…."

Reynolds said, four decades removed from his departure, "I left *Gunsmoke* only because it was time for me to move on, but I left with everyone's blessings and best wishes … but when I think of those episodes of *Gunsmoke* on that wonderful old stage—sitting and telling stories in front of the Long Branch Saloon with Matt, Kitty, Doc and Festus—well, it just never gets any better than that."[6]

Notes

1. Dianna Whitley, *Burt Reynolds: Portrait of a Superstar* (New York: Grossett & Dunlap, 1979), p. 40.
2. *Ibid.*, p. 41.
3. Sylvia Safran Resnick, *Burt Reynolds* (London: W.H. Allen, 1983), p. 43.
4. "James Arness on working with Burt Reynolds," YouTube, uploaded by FoundationINTERVIEWS, Published May 21, 2010, https://www.youtube.com/watch?v=yJqbQm0j5gY.
5. Nancy Streebeck, *The Films of Burt Reynolds* (NJ, New York: Citadel Press), p. 19.
6. Burt Reynolds, "Foreword," in *James Arness: An Autobiography*, James Arness with James E. Wise Jr. (Jefferson, NC: McFarland, 2001), p. x.

Operation C.I.A.
(1965)

"What is it about me that makes women want to undress me?"—Mark Andrews

This is the picture Burt Reynolds called his worst film ever: "If it played on a plane, people would be killed trying to jump out."[1]

He portrays Mark Andrews, a Central Intelligence Agency man dispatched to Saigon after a colleague is killed in a bomb attack on a crowded street there. Andrews enters the Southern Vietnam city in the guise of an agriculture professor attending an academic conference ("You don't look the professor type," says one skeptic) while trying to intercept information that could uncover a plot to assassinate the U.S. ambassador. Despite his cover, the communist aggressors are already on Andrews' trail. Andrews discovers a completely unstable environment, with political assassinations and guerrilla street attacks devastating the city and its people.

Despite the gravity of the Vietnamese conflict which provides the picture's backdrop, *Operation C.I.A.* indulges in some clichéd tomfoolery, throwing in a jaded, gin-swigging Cockney newspaperman, Withers (Cyril Collick), for cheap laughs; a coquettish French spy, Denise (Danielle Aubry), for titillation; and a maniacal communist agent, Prof. Yen (Vic Diaz), for absurdity. Yen is a villain worthy of any James Bond picture and, apropos to Ian Fleming's said superspy, it is no wonder that Reynolds was later offered a chance to play Bond, considering Reynolds' turn as Mark Andrews is essentially a screen test for

Mark Andrews' (Reynolds) cover is blown in Saigon by Professor Yen (Vic Diaz) in *Operation C.I.A.* (1961).

future Bond vacancies. The variety of chase sequences and fight scenes allow the actor to display his athletic capabilities and to showcase his considerable charm.

After Reynolds exited *Gunsmoke* in search of film work—*any* film work—he was seduced by Peer J. Oppenheimer, executive producer of the celebrity interview show *Here's Hollywood*, with an offer to star in a picture he had co-written with screenwriter-producer Bill S. Ballinger (*The Dinah Shore Show*), *Last Message from Saigon*. It would be a quickie, later renamed *Operation C.I.A.*, made on location in the political volcano of the script's eponymous city. To Reynolds, *Operation C.I.A.* sounded like just the ticket he needed to flee the confines of television, but would just lead to a deeply unpleasant experience for the actor. With filming in proximity of the raging conflicts of the Vietnam War, the production was entangled in a messy security imbroglio as state officials ordered non-military personnel to evacuate the area; cast and crew had to be moved to the less-volatile environs of Bangkok and Laos. Despite the move, the production wasn't without its close calls, such as the accidental use of live ammunition during a gunfight sequence, or shooting a scene with a cobra that was actively venomous. After filming in filthy, polluted waters, Reynolds was struck down with the deadly parasitic disease Schistosomiasis upon arriving back in the United States.

This modestly priced action picture ($70,000) takes full advantage of its location shooting, lending the production a crucial sense of authenticity missing from many espionage pictures filmed on Hollywood soundstages. Such location work provides *Operation C.I.A.* with moments of exotic travelogue scenery as well as taking us into some less-salubrious locales during Andrews' quest for information.

Despite these qualities, the procedural aspect of the plot does tend to drag, with endless scenes of Andrews following up on information, from hotel, to bar, to massage parlor, to alleyway, and back again. Individual scenes are memorable and effective, especially the one in which Andrews humors a couple of street urchins selling flowers only for the moment to turn devastating. As Andrews relinquishes his ten dollars in exchange for the flowers, a grenade is thrown from a passing car. But it is flung too far to injure Andrews, the explosive detonating right under the children. It's a fleeting scene of rare harrow, the tone of the picture returning too quickly to that of jaunty espionage romp for the audience and Andrews to be truly affected by the shocking carnage of child-killing. No time is given to grieve, the plot swiftly moves on to its next piece of exposition.

Director Christian Nyby had worked on some of the best Hollywood studio pictures of the 1940s as an editor, cutting three of Howard Hawks' finest, *To Have and Have Not* (1944), *The Big Sleep* (1946), and *Red River* (1948). As a director, he made minor impact with the influential *The Thing from Another World* (1951) before becoming a hugely prolific television helmer. Between TV jobs, Nyby knocked out the cheap exotic adventure picture *Hell on Devil's Island* (1957) and the Rory Calhoun western *Young Fury* (1965). Few elements of Nyby's direction here suggest the quality of the pictures he worked on before or after. It's merely a merely serviceable translation of Oppenheimer's boilerplate script.

Notes

1. Burt Reynolds, *My Life: Burt Reynolds* (Great Britain: Hodder & Stoughton, 1994), p. 107.

Navajo Joe
(1966)

"There's one way to get rid of your problem ... kill him!"—Navajo Joe

After massacring an Indian village, vile half-breed outlaw Mervyn "Vee" Duncan (Aldo Sambrell) and his band of scalphunters are stalked by a laconic lone rider, Navajo Joe (Burt Reynolds), who demands blood for their killing of his tribe. There's another motive behind Joe's insatiable desire for retribution: His wife was previously murdered and scalped by Duncan. Arriving in the town of Peyote, Duncan and his brother Jeffrey learn about a bounty placed upon their heads—$1000 for Mervyn, $200 for Jeffrey, dead or alive—which naturally displeases the villains and so they proceed to destroy the town. The Peyote sheriff once paid the Duncan gang for returning with the scalps of outlaws and miscreants, a dollar per skin—"a personal hobby," Duncan evilly remarks—but because he has taken to torturing and killing the women and children of peaceful tribes, the law no longer pays up.

Three saloon girls hiding from the gang overhear Duncan scheming with Dr. Lynne (Pierre Cressoy), who is plotting with Duncan to stick up a train carrying a $500,000 state grant. The girls make a break for it on horseback but are chased down by Duncan's goons. Joe appears like an avenging angel, sitting astride his horse in the barren landscape awaiting his moment of vengeance. Joe saves the girls from certain doom but it turns out Joe is an unwitting hero and says as much when he's profusely thanked for saving the girls: "I didn't kill him for you!" Despite his heroism, Joe is met with racism by some of the townsfolk, such as when he suggests assuming an official title of lawman. "But you can't ... an Indian sheriff? The only ones elected in this country are Americans!" scoffs the presiding sheriff, who then admits that his own heritage is actually Scottish before Joe replies, "My father was born here, in America, and his father before him, and his father before him, and his father before him. Now which of us is American?"

Meet Navajo Joe (Reynolds). *Navajo Joe* (1966).

Eschewing the cynicism, irony and dark humor which informed many of the spaghetti westerns of the period, Sergio Corbucci's *Navajo Joe* is a sober, somber and violent film of vengeance; close in tone to stark pictures like *The Hills Run Red* (Carlo Lizzani, 1966) and *Death Rides a Horse* (Guilio Petroni, 1967). While other westerns often utilized the revenge scenario within the context of greater political themes, *Navajo Joe* is more concerned with intimate psychological themes. Duncan's hatred of Indians, we learn, comes from his abusive childhood; he blames the punishment dished out by his disciplinarian preacher father and Indian mother for his own predilection for death and destruction. Duncan tells a priest,

> Nobody ever had mercy on me. When I was a boy, they beat me, even called me *bastard*. I didn't cry and I couldn't fight back. So then I began my revenge to get back at them. I brought out my hatred for the Indians, like my mother, and to kill white people like my father.... I got a bad break when someone killed him and beat me to the punch.

This speech, given in the final act, explains why Duncan reacts so fiercely to his own brother referring to him as a half-breed: "Be careful, brother, I won't ever let anyone call me a bastard!" However, such lofty themes often take a back seat to the macabre and intense action onscreen, which could place the film into the realm of Exploitation Cinema, a somewhat gilded throne from which the likes of Corbucci's *Django* (1966) has enjoyed cult appreciation over the years. As with any good vigilante picture, if we are to cheer the act of vengeance, then the narrative must make us believe that the villains are beyond redemption. Here, the wanton acts of violence visited upon innocents by Duncan and his men is administered with gleeful abandon, marking a clear divide between good and evil that leaves no room for moral ambiguity. Duncan is a monster and Joe is the reluctant savior of the fearful people. As a hero motivated by revenge, Joe is as ruthless as those he smites. "There's one way to get rid of our problem," says Joe coldly and calmly, "kill him!" As a genre piece, *Navajo Joe* works exquisitely as part of the revenge western canon.

It was only a matter of time before Burt Reynolds would make the leap from television dustbowl to the big screen frontier, and in his first cinematic western he teamed

Navajo Joe (Reynolds) isn't one for hanging around. *Navajo Joe* (1966).

with superior director Corbucci (*Django*; *The Great Silence*, 1968; *The Mercenary*, 1968) to produce one of the best spaghetti westerns of the '60s. Reynolds plays Joe as taciturn and enigmatic, with his very first appearance on screen as that of a spectral figure, sitting atop his horse on a mountaintop, eluding the aggressors that he is hunting and taunting.

In the tradition of Roy Rogers and Gene Autry, Reynolds saw the value of a good equine co-star. The production's wranglers introduced Reynolds to an old stunt horse named Destaphanado: plain white and with no tail or mane to speak of. Reynolds suggested dressing the tired and mangy animal to look like a finely coated pinto to use for filming the Spanish scenes. It turned out that the shabby old steed was an excellent stunt horse which enabled Reynolds to engage in some complicated physical work with ease and confidence. In a noble parting gesture, Reynolds granted his fee to Destaphando's keeper to maintain the horse for the rest of its life.

With the considerable commercial clout of producer Dino De Laurentiis, *Navajo Joe* has the aesthetic sheen of a film with a more considerable budget than many of its genre stablemates. But designs on mainstream success didn't stop Corbucci from indulging in the surplus of carnage such a narrative afforded him, with rough imagery to rival that of *Django* and any *giallo* horror picture of the '60s and '70s. The film's neat pacing can be in some part attributed to Corbucci's editorial prowess where he responded to Reynolds' insistence on more story and character, particularly more focus on the romantic subplot, by standing in opposition to such a request. In fact, rather than pleasing his star, the director decided to improve upon the American style of western "by removing all the boring stuff ... the love scenes and all the talk, talk, talk."[1]

It is to the film's advantage that Corbucci took a more direct approach to the "Azione," as *Navajo Joe* works best in the mode of the simple revenge thriller. Other times, the action was dictated by more administrative concerns than aesthetic, as Reynolds needed to be freed from his contract in order to begin work on the television series *Hawk*. With Reynolds being ABC-TV's first choice for the lead role in their imminent cop series, he was required to return to the States immediately as filming of the show was due to begin. But Corbucci was working under the increased pressure of De Laurentiis' demands for further script rewrites, so in order to release Reynolds on time for his big TV break back home, Corbucci and the actor concocted a plan in which they could cover all bases for the remaining schedule. The director filmed coverage of Reynolds engaging in and reacting to various action scenarios that were yet to be staged; this allowed the director to release his star, shoot the remainder of the scenes with the rest of the cast at a later date, and then edit the footage accordingly. After six weeks filming in Italy (exteriors at Tor Caldara and interiors at Dino De Laurentiis Cinematografica Studios) and a further month on location in Spain, Reynolds was finally free to return to New York to begin the next chapter of his career with *Hawk*.

Notes

1. Howard Hughes, *Once Upon a Time in the Italian West: The Filmgoers' Guide to Spaghetti Westerns* (London/New York: I.B. Tauris, 2009 reprint), p. 86.

Hawk

(TV Series, ABC, 1966)

"Who sent you to me to complain about phone calls?! Why don't you take your complaints to the police department? Or have your phone number changed? Or better still, why don't you move back to Ohio, where you came from?"
—Detective Hawk

Trading the Wild West frontier for an urban jungle, Burt Reynolds had his first TV series lead on ABC's *Hawk*, a gritty police procedural centered on the cases of Detective Lt. John Hawk. Working for the New York City district attorney's office, the eponymous detective and his African-American partner Dan Carter (Wayne Grice) investigate murder, extortion, arson and organized crime, as well as departmental bureaucracy and discrimination.

The series got off to an auspicious start with the terrific pilot episode "Do Not Mutilate or Spindle" (September 8, 1966). This tantalizing pilot sees Detective Hawk on the trail of Houston Worth (Gene Hackman), a religious zealot terrorizing New Yorkers with phone calls of him quoting Scripture and announcing "I, the Sword of Jehovah, will destroy thee!" With the body count rising, Hawk must find the killer before he reaches his next victim. Hackman brilliantly inhabits Houston Worth as a walking portent of doom, prone to lethal

fits of rage as he stalks his prey. Worth is triggered by proponents of progress and modernity; even the championing of technology is perceived by Worth as worshipping a false idol and worthy of murder.

Hackman, like Reynolds, was a graduate of the acting trenches of 1950s episodic television and appeared on several of the same shows, including *Naked City* and *Route 66*. "Do Not Mutilate or Spindle" was directed by acclaimed theater director and film actor Sam Wanamaker, who directed the additional episodes "Game with a Dead End" and "How Close Can You Get?" Here, Wanamaker executes the proceedings in a stylishly cinematic aesthetic, markedly different for the television police procedural genre of the period. The innovative and immediate vérité style of *Hawk* anticipated future cop shows that would inhabit the shady back streets and dark alleyways of a metropolitan city and shoot on location in a faux realist manner.

By the time Reynolds was offered

Reynolds and Wayne Grice, the stars of *Hawk* (1966–67).

Hawk, he had tired of capitalizing on his supposed Native American heritage to play Indians, having previously parlayed his ethnic looks into limiting depictions of such in *Navajo Joe*, *Gunsmoke* and "Now Join the Human Race," a 1965 episode of Chuck Connors' TV series *Branded*. But something about Hawk was different. His Iroquois heritage is not a selling point; it is evoked sparingly for set decoration in which native cultural props are strategically placed to give Hawk some sense of identity; though on occasion it does mark him as an exotic creature to some of the local ladies. In the pilot, one woman remarks, "I should have known you the moment I saw you, you even walk like an Indian!" while another character asks, "Are you really an Indian? Now I know why you are so strong and silent." With such an insistent line of questioning, Hawk is given a moment to explain his background and indulge us in some character exposition. When asked where he comes from, Hawk gestures across the city and says, "Over there!" "Brooklyn?!" his inquisitor gasps. Hawk explains that many of his people came to New York City as laborers decades earlier to work in the city's booming construction industry; his father was an ironworker who died during construction of the Triborough Bridge.

"The idea of a TV Indian who didn't talk gibberish or get plastered greatly appealed to me," Reynolds said. "Thanks to producer Renée Valente, I didn't have to run around in moccasins and feathers. In the pilot film, they wanted me to hide knives up my sleeves, but I refused to go along with that."[1] Valente, one of Reynolds' strongest champions at this stage in his career, was not withholding when it came to promoting his multiple attributes. Valente said,

> Burt Reynolds was special. Then, as now, he had charm, vulnerability, strength, gentility, humor, compassion and animal sex. It's a rare combination. Add a pinch of insecurity, a dash of antagonism, and a cup of 'down home,' and you have complexities that add to the versatility of the man. And if you believe, as I do, that the eyes are the mirror of our soul, look into his.[2]

With such support from the show's producer, who was also a major casting agent, it wasn't long before Reynolds got the seal of approval from ABC president Tom Moore, who after screen-testing the young actor found just the right amount of tension and anger for the character of Hawk. Reynolds commented upon the period as "one of the happiest years of my life in this business. For the first time, I didn't feel like a chess pawn. I helped direct, cast and write scripts. And I fought the establishment at every turn."[3]

Long before the likes of *Hill Street Blues*, *Homicide: Life on the Street* and *NYPD Blue* appeared to inject life into television with their gritty realism and handheld camerawork, *Hawk* was there paving the way for them. Shot on 16mm on the streets of New York City, it was as realistic a police procedural as you could get for a mid–60s TV cop show. Adding to the authenticity is Reynolds' own stuntwork, which supplemented the sense of immediacy and danger that the show strived for.

Unfortunately, the show may have been a bit too ahead of its time: Critical plaudits and a petition containing thousands of names was not enough to keep it on the air. *Hawk* was cancelled four months into its debut run. However, the lackluster ratings didn't stop its star from ascending, as the series gave Reynolds the opportunity to simultaneously display his chops as a tough guy hero and dashing leading man. "You try to get across to the actor that whether the series is successful or not, it can make him," Valente said. "I use as an example: Burt Reynolds. The series that I produced in New York: *Hawk*, one season. That's all. But it sure as hell made Burt Reynolds."[4]

Notes

1. Nancy Streebeck, *The Films of Burt Reynolds* (N.J., New York: Citadel Press), p. 22.
2. *Ibid.*, p. 23.
3. Sylvia Safran Resnick, *Burt Reynolds* (London: W.H. Allen, 1983), p. 61.
4. Gordon Hunt, *How to Audition: A Casting Director's Guide for Actors* (Illinois: The Dramatic Publishing Company, 1977), p. 272.

Fade In

(1968)

"All them Hollywood people is on something!"—James Hampton

In this low-key romantic melodrama set in Moab, Utah, Reynolds plays a rancher named Rob who loans his land to movie producers in town to shoot a western for Paramount Pictures. When Rob offers his services as a driver, his first order of business is to collect arriving crew members, among them assistant film editor Jean (Barbara Loden). She is immediately attracted to Rob's homespun rugged charm, and he to her sophisticated bohemia. Jean has adopted California as her home, having come from "a small town nobody ever heard of" in North Carolina; she is arty and intellectual where Rob is a practical working class laborer, and so an unfortunate cultural and social chasm emerges and threatens their relationship.

When Rob takes Jean out, they encounter boorish, jealous and aggressive local folks who consider Rob to be entertaining notions of grandeur as he walks around with his Hollywood honey. While the romance develops, the locals are in awe of the commercial juggernaut that has rolled into their humble town. "Is John Wayne going to be in this picture?" a man asks a well-groomed West Coast executive. "All them Hollywood people is on something!" James Hampton's character says while Rob wonders, "Is that why they wear them sunglasses?" Meanwhile, Jean teaches Rob the mechanical and aesthetic processes of film editing, demonstrating the "Kuleshov Effect," one of the founding principles of film assembly. Meanwhile, Rob introduces Jean to the quiet life of Moab, taking in a game of bowling, a spot of pinball, a little jiving and some rodeo riding. The closer they become, the more the rural blue collar-vs.-urbane sophistication divide becomes evident, at least to us if not to them. Jean refers to having seen Russian films; one suspects that Rob has never even heard of Andrei Tarkovsky or Sergei Eisenstein, much less seen one of their films. Another more significant obstacle is the revelation of Jean's significant other, Bill, who interrupts their post-coitus intimacy one morning. This is the beginning of the end of their ill-fated dalliance.

Reynolds displays a rarely celebrated though distinct ability for the dramatic and the romantic in this early lead role. Unfortunately, nobody saw it. *Fade In* is essentially a lost film, and the first to feature the now-infamous DGA (Directors Guild of America) pseudonym "Alan Smithee."[1] The film's actual helmer was Jud Taylor, a prolific actor-director who performed in episodes of *The Fugitive*, *12 O'Clock High* and *Dr. Kildare*, among many others, while his directorial credits includes episodes of *Star Trek*, *A Man Called Shenandoah* and *The Man from U.N.C.L.E.* Taylor took his name off the picture after Paramount re-cut his initial assembly and used their version for preview screenings; it is this cut of the picture which subsequently surfaced on television in the early 1980s and which exists today in various rarefied forms.

The production being filmed throughout *Fade In* is in fact another genuine Paramount film that was being shot simultaneously, Silvio Narizzano's *Blue*. Narizzano's film was originally to star Robert Redford but script changes led to his withdrawal (and a subsequent lawsuit between actor and studio), and so British actor Terence Stamp stepped into the vacant lead. Stamp and co-star Ricardo Montalban can be glimpsed in some of the real production footage of *Blue* that appears throughout *Fade In*. Filming the making of one studio title while crafting a separate narrative around that footage and then releasing the two simultaneously was the result of a novel idea by the film's producer, Judd Bernard, who sold the pitch to Paramount head Charles Bluhdorn and hotshot producer Robert Evans. For its West Coast exhibition, *Fade In* would play on a double-bill with *Blue*, with the latter as the main feature and the former as added value. But *Blue* suffered from unconvincing performances and a stiff script, which didn't help the reception of the unwanted celluloid stepchild that followed it around. Former Paramount executive Peter Bart was present for the disastrous test screenings at which the film and the Reynolds-Loden romance in particular was poorly received. "Months later, several of us gathered at the old Palace Theater in Westwood," Bart remembered, "packed with filmgoers who had just paid to see another film and were now getting a 'bonus.' By the time *Fade In* had been running for 30 minutes, half the theater was empty. By the close, only 10 or 15 filmgoers had remained."[2]

Paramount duly aborted an idea they had to promote *Fade In* as an arthouse release after another calamitous sneak preview in Manhattan where audience members are reported to have laughed inappropriately during moments of sincere romantic dialogue. *Fade In* managed to be that rare beast: an unpretentious art film concerning regular, unexceptional people just going about their business. There is no particular intellectual insight offered, it is merely a snapshot of a moment in time for these two characters of opposite social class and culture. Neither the characters nor milieu may have been hip and urbane enough for an intellectual East Coast arthouse crowd, yet it may also suffer from being too aesthetically unconventional and avant-garde for a Middle-American audience craving a more streamlined narrative. Unloved in the hands of a major studio that saw no commercial value in it as a theatrical enterprise, *Fade In* was bought by CBS-TV, where it fared little better than on the big screen. And so the film has suffered an unfortunate fate having never been afforded an official theatrical or home video release by Paramount, fading into obscurity since its sparse television appearances throughout the 1970s and in the early 1980s. It has been intermittently available in various DVD editions from independent distributors under the title *Iron Cowboy*, but the print is washed out and the sound at times inaudible. But we can be thankful it is at least somewhat viewable as despite the authorial compromises made in assembling this final cut, *Fade In* is a unique and likable picture.

Exquisitely framed by cinematographer William A. Fraker (who collaborated with Reynolds on several future projects), there are deftly intertextual elements here which one could speculate influenced Dennis Hopper's 1971 masterpiece *The Last Movie*, such as shared plot elements including the immediate context of an ill-fated romance, culture clash, capitalist invasion upon a self-sufficient environment, and rural dwellers beguiled by visiting Hollywood glamour. Let us also consider the film's avant-garde aesthetics, including the back-to-front structure (opening with the dénouement); the cinéma vérité documentation of a film production; the surrealist fantasy sequences; and an iconoclastic deconstruction of classical narrative trajectory. All of these elements mark *Fade In* as an intriguing precursor to some of the more well-known films of the New Hollywood which took a self-reflexive look at their own art form, including the aforementioned Hopper film, plus *Easy Rider* (Dennis Hopper, 1969), *Medium Cool* (Haskell Wexler, 1969), *Alice's Restaurant* (Arthur Penn, 1969), *Alex in Wonderland* (Paul Mazursky, 1970) and *Hi, Mom!* (Brian De Palma, 1970).

Another element that distinguishes the film from the rest of the pack is the sumptuous score by Ken Lauber. While it was hip for films at this time to use contemporary folk, pop and rock songs as a soundtrack replacement for traditional orchestration, *Fade In* uses a rich, romantic trumpet-led original score that also functions as Rob and Jean's romantic theme tune. Lauber contributed music to films such as Jack Nicholson's *Goin' South* (1968) and Peter Fonda's *Wanda Nevada* (1969) and he worked with some of music's preeminent names: Bob Dylan, Johnny Cash, Richie Havens, John Lennon, Willie Nelson and Doc Watson.

Fade In has an easygoing late-60s vibe, and carries a genuinely romanticist heart which is devoid of the countercultural cynicism that would inform other works of the New Hollywood. As a piece of Burt Reynolds history, the film is an excellent insight into the quieter, more refined style of performance and emotional resonance that the actor would harness in his later pictures *Starting Over* and *The Man Who Loved Women*. For Reynolds, *Fade In* was a quiet respite into more romantic territory, even if the actor, along with critics and audiences, failed to find any sign of chemistry between the on-screen coupling. Barbara Loden, who would follow *Fade In* by directing and starring in the brilliant feminist drama *Wanda*, was a graduate of the famed Actor's Studio and wife of lauded auteur filmmaker Elia Kazan. She was as fine an actress as any to portray the intelligent urban straight woman to Reynolds' jocular bumpkin, though perhaps their real personalities, which perhaps reflected their on-screen personas a little too closely, didn't gel. According to Reynolds, the lack of emotional charge between him and his co-star was evident for all to see. "Barbara Loden was on a different frequency…I couldn't tune in, couldn't find the key to turn her on," the actor said. "I kept waiting for her to let loose and blow me right out of the tub, but it never happened on film."[3]

Notes

1. Jerry Roberts, *Encyclopaedia of Television Film Directors* (Maryland: Scarecrow Press, 1971), p. 586.
2. Peter Bart, *Infamous Players: A Tale of Movies, The Mob (and Sex)* (New York: Weinstein Books, 2011), p. 174.
3. Nancy Streebeck, *The Films of Burt Reynolds* (New York: Citadel Press, 1982), p. 25.

100 Rifles

(1969)

"I know all about them big town, big belly, billy club–swinging policemen from St. Louis."—Yacqui Joe

Half-breed bandit Yaqui Joe (Burt Reynolds) steals $6000 from a Phoenix bank to fund the arming of the Yaqui tribe in the face of oppression from the Mexican government.

He soon finds himself tracked by an eager Arizona policeman, Lyedecker (Jim Brown). If Lyedecker retrieves the money, he will receive a bounty and permanent employment as a law enforcer. He and Joe unexpectedly join forces along with Sarita (Raquel Welch), a strikingly beautiful revolutionary who witnesses the brutal hanging of her father by Mexican soldiers. Thrown together by circumstance but committed in the name of personal and political justice, the trio joins the cause against the corrupt Mexican Gen. Verdugo (Fernando Lamas) and his repressive regime.

100 Rifles is an entertaining if pedestrian semi–spaghetti western. Tom Gries was a prolific director of episodic television in the 1960s, helming the likes of *The Westerner*, *The Rifleman*, *The Man from U.N.C.L.E.*, *Mission: Impossible* and *Batman*. His film output was marked with straightforward action pictures of varying critical repute, including some decent thrillers with Charles Bronson (*Breakheart Pass* and *Breakout*, both 1975). However, Gries is best remembered for the 1967 Charlton Heston western *Will Penny*, for which the director received much-deserved plaudits.

That film enjoys a good reputation, while *100 Rifles* is less revered. One of the picture's faults is its absence of any distinguishable filmmaking authority; as a journeyman director, Gries didn't bother with much in the way of recurring themes and ideas. His form was to stick with conservative aesthetic values. Gries worked with the distinctively stylish Sam Peckinpah on TV's *The Westerner*, but none of Peckinpah's sense of poetry for the Old West or visual prowess rubbed off on him. There is action aplenty in *100 Rifles*, but that doesn't matter much when the film remains static even as dozens of people are being blown up or mown down.

As well as being shot on location in spaghetti western country (Almeria, Spain), the picture contains similar themes to the Italian productions of the period, such as Sergio Solima's *The Big Gundown* (1966) and Damiano Damiani's *A Bullet for the General* (1967), in which the political tales of insurgency are framed around the reluctant alliance of a Mexican and a North American who is embroiled in revolutionary acts. The narrative wasn't unusual for the left-field spaghettis, but not the typical scenario for a major Hollywood western. Traditionalist western conventions are further subverted, with three American stars of various ethnic backgrounds leading the film: Jim Brown, African-American; Raquel Welch, Hispanic American; Burt Reynolds, White American. *100 Rifles* was released into a Hollywood and an America in transition, affording it a political edge that could be embraced by a countercultural audience of liberal attitude. Only one year prior George Romero's *Night of the Living Dead*, either deliberately or by chance, made a bold socio-political statement in having a colored actor, Duane Jones, playing the lead hero, prefiguring Jim Brown's central casting here. Indeed, 1969 saw a seismic shift in the American film industry, with the likes of Dennis Hopper's *Easy Rider*, John Schlesinger's *Midnight*

Jim Brown and Raquel Welch get steamy in *100 Rifles* (1967).

Cowboy, Paul Mazursky's *Bob & Carol & Ted & Alice* and Sydney Pollack's *They Shoot Horses, Don't They?* all leaving a searing influence in a new generation of filmmaking; not to mention the western genre experiencing a huge shift in form with Sam Peckinpah's *The Wild Bunch* and George Roy Hill's *Butch Cassidy and the Sundance Kid*.

Audiences were confronted with a new approach to previously censored material, and *100 Rifles*, for all its old-fashioned style, wisely catered to the *à la mode* taste for sensationalist depictions of sex and violence. In perhaps the steamiest display of raw sexuality in a western picture since Jane Russell's iconic appearance in Howard Hughes' *The Outlaw* (1943), Gries utilizes Welch's considerable physical assets to their fullest potential when Sarita teases a trainload of soldiers in an effort to divert their attention enough for Lyedecker and Joe to launch a surprise attack. As well as the tantalizing display of flesh, Welch also engages in an interracial screen kiss and subsequent love scene with Brown, then somewhat revolutionary for Hollywood filmmaking. "That's probably the most memorable thing about the picture,"[1] Reynolds said. "Both of these people were animals, supercharged sexual creatures ... whose mere presence generated major heat before the first frame was even shot."[2] Sure enough, the sexual chemistry and politically charged lust between Brown and Welch energizes the picture.

It is a rare film in which Reynolds isn't the object of female affections. Mike Freeman noted the cultural implications of the interracial pairing:

> Welch and Brown remain one of the more significant turning points in cinematic history because a black man was having sex with America's white carnal queen. Welch, with her full breasts and flowing hair, and Brown, muscled and manly, did the voracious sex scene, complete with Brown sticking his tongue in Welch's ear, on the first day of shooting the film.[3]

Welch's train-stopping moment under the water tower aside, Reynolds steals the picture, skating through it with an ironic, self-conscious sense of humor which belies the somber thematic context of war and oppression. In contrast to his sober turn in the grim but brilliant *Navajo Joe*, Reynolds' farcical demeanor here anticipates his comical turn in *Sam Whiskey*.

Despite the decent chemistry onscreen, tensions often ran high during the making of the film. After Welch and Brown had several run-ins, Reynolds had his own embarrassing moment of miscalculation. He recalled:

> For the first time in the picture, Raquel and I found ourselves alone. I had no idea if she was attracted to me ... she told me recently that she knew I was going to be hot and was very attracted to me. Anyway, as we sat by ourselves on my horse, no one else around us, she said, "Let me ask you a question." "Sure, go ahead," I said. "Why haven't you made a pass at me?" Without the slightest pause, I replied, "Because I'm positive that I'd pull up your dress, pull down your panties, and find an 8x10 glossy of your cunt." What an asshole I was. She had every right to never speak to me again.[4]

Despite the acrimony, the two stars headlined another picture three years later, the crime comedy *Fuzz* (1972); however, this occurred only under the somewhat absurd stipulation that they would not have to be in the company of each other on the set on any given day, despite their characters sharing several scenes. Such antipathy didn't stop Reynolds from gallantly attending court in 1986 to provide character witness testimony for Welch over her firing from the 1982 screen adaptation of John Steinbeck's *Cannery Row*. Welch filed suit against the film's producer Michael Phillips, director David S. Ward and MGM executive David Begelman after she was relieved of duties after only one week of filming for allegedly acting "unprofessional."[5] "Raquel's a lot of things, but she isn't unprofessional," Reynolds recalled. "When we worked together, she was always on time and always knew her lines. When I heard she was suing the studio, I called her agent and said I wanted to testify for her … [S]he won the case and got $10 million. She thanked me for my help, but we still don't send Christmas cards."[6]

Reynolds later directed Welch in a 1993 episode of his CBS sitcom *Evening Shade*, an experience on which he reflected, "After that week, I realized I could've fallen in love with her. She has a good heart, which she hides under beautiful boobs and a tough exterior."[7]

Notes

1. Burt Reynolds, *But Enough About Me* (London: Penguin, 2015), p. 242.
2. Burt Reynolds, *My Life: Burt Reynolds* (Great Britain: Hodder & Staughton, 1994), p. 131.
3. Mike Freeman, *Jim Brown: The Fierce Life of an American Hero* (New York: Harper Entertainment, 2006), p.5.
4. Reynolds, p. 136.
5. Deborah Caulfield, "Welch Licks Wounds of Battle," Los Angeles Times, June 28, 1986, http://articles.latimes.com/1986–06-28/entertainment/ca-25727_1_cannery-row.
6. Reynolds, p. 242.
7. Reynolds, p.137.

Sam Whiskey

(1969)

"Sam Whiskey. He was an orphan child born in a snowstorm crossing the Great Plains. Sam's cradle rocked mostly in the back of Joe Callaghan's saloon, first sounds he heard were the rattlin' of dice and some throwin' chips on a poker table … seemed to influence the boy."—Narrator

Sam Whiskey is a legendary frontiersman, a man of few scruples but much personality; he is well-known for his taste in fighting, gambling and women. When not cavorting with Abilene ladies who wear pink pantaloons, he worked with the U.S. government against the Confederate Army, but that didn't end too well. In response to Gen. Sherman's famous declaration "War is Hell," Sam responded, "Worse than that, the pay is bad!"

After a stint working for the railroad, Sam roamed the Wild West looking for opportunities. Enter the beautiful widow Laura Breckenridge (Angie Dickinson). She seduces Sam into her bed and into retrieving $250,000 in gold buried in a sunken riverboat. Laura's husband had stolen the gold from the Denver Mint and substituted lead fakes. As the Mint's inventory is set to produce new coins, Laura fears her husband's crime will be detected and so she must replace the fakes with the genuine gold to save her family's good name. Laura launches an exhaustive campaign to convince the reluctant Sam to cooperate, eventually offering remuneration of $20,000 for his trouble. Helping Sam is blacksmith Jedidiah Hooker (Ossie Davis) and inventor O.W. Brandy (Clint Walker), but returning the gold to the mint is no easy task, as aside from the logistical difficulties of breaking into a fortress with such a consignment of gold, there is also the issue of greedy outlaw Fat Henry (Rick Davis), who fancies the loot for himself.

Sam Whiskey is a rambunctious affair from the very first scene, in which the picture posits itself as a cartoon western with the droll mythologizing of its opening narration. Soon this gives way to an attempted and ultimately aborted barroom brawl between the buffoonish Sam and the indomitable Jedidiah. You see, Sam is a tongue-in-cheek inversion of the traditional cowboy hero, just as the plot is an inversion of the traditional western narrative. Rather than stealing gold, the loot is being returned—a reverse robbery, if you will. Sam is more comfortable slinging dice than a gun, is garrulous rather than taciturn, is easily manipulated by a woman, and is clumsy in a ruckus. Sam's inflated ego allowed Reynolds to fill the role with his considerable personality and makes the character a likable kind of rapscallion, ideal material for Reynolds to utilize his jocular personality and to promote his action hero credentials. However, the film's biggest asset is the tangible chemistry between the four leads. Angie Dickinson is terrific as the promiscuous seductress, playing the role with enough cunning cuteness as to hypnotize any man. Clint Walker uses his considerable size to endearing effect, playing a simple but lovable oaf of great strength and greater heart, while Davis brings some credible gravitas to his role as an honest, hard-working laborer.

Director Arnold Laven comes well-armed with a history in television westerns, having created *The Rifleman* and co-produced *The Big Valley* as part of the Levy-Gardner-Laven Productions portfolio. Laven knew how to keep things amiable and efficient, at least in the setup of the picture; the second half of *Sam Whiskey* occasionally threatens to grind to a halt, usually when the goofing-around must cease to allow for the execution of the backwards heist. Given the logistical nightmare that Sam, Jed and O.W. go through in the third act, it's no wonder the film itself becomes something of a chore as we watch them struggle through the complexities of their ordeal.

But even when the narrative becomes leaden, there is always director of photography Robert Moreno's flair to keep us interested. Moreno (who subsequently shot Reynolds' *Skullduggery*) tempers the blander elements of the narrative with some interesting visual aesthetics, utilizing long-take tracking shots and nicely composed framing; on more than one occasion, he makes interesting use of the zoom lens. Writer W.W. Norton's witty script was first in a series of collaborations with Reynolds and Dickinson, respectively. Norton worked on the script for Reynolds' excellent western *The Man Who Loved Cat Dancing* before penning the two Gator McClusky pictures, *White Lightning* and *Gator*, thus creating one of Reynolds' truly iconic characters. Norton also provided the script for Roger Corman's *Big Bad Mama* (1974), which stars Dickinson as the eponymous bootlegging matriarch, who returned to the screen in 1987's *Big Bad Mama II*.

Impasse

(1969)

"I can't be prejudiced against a man because he might make me rich."—Pat Morrison

Pat Morrison (Burt Reynolds), who runs a dubious marine salvage company out of the Manila port town of Zamboanga, learns that $3 million worth of gold is hidden on the island of Corregidor. Morrison sets about reassembling the original crack team of World War II U.S. Army soldiers who concealed it under the noses of the Philippine military in the first place, luring them one by one back to Southeast Asia with the promise of attaining riches and well as fulfilling various personal goals. One of the men enlisted to help Morrison is Trev Jones (Clarke Gordon), an ailing war veteran who is estranged from his successful athlete daughter Bobby (Anne Francis). Morrison and Bobby develop a romantic relationship as the men set about their business of gold retrieval.

Impasse is a return to the kind of generic wartime caper milieu that allowed Reynolds to develop his big-screen persona early in his career with the likes of *Armored Command* and *Operation C.I.A.* After the actor took an inspired detour into romantic melodrama territory with *Fade In* only to see it sink in corporate indifference, it may have become clear to him that his box office cachet lay in the action adventure genre and so he took the offer of this United Artists picture.

While not as badly mishandled as *Fade In*, nor as hazardous to the actor's health as *Operation C.I.A.*, *Impasse* too came and went unceremoniously, largely forgotten and little seen. It was directed by Richard Benedict, the erstwhile actor who appeared in the likes of Edward Dmytryk's *Crossfire*, Billy Wilder's *Ace on the Hole* and Lewis Milestone's *Ocean's 11*. Benedict wastes little time in getting down to action: Within the first 15 minutes, several plot strands and multiple characters are introduced with great economy. Benedict crafts an entertaining B-movie caper which takes full advantage of the suitably gritty and sweaty surroundings and successfully plays into the boys-own exotic adventure tradition of *Dark of the Sun* (Jack Cardiff, 1968) and anticipates the higher-profile *Kelly's Heroes* (Brian G. Hutton, 1970). *Impasse* may lack the more considerable production values of those two pictures but it does get by on some cheap thrills, sleaze tourism and decent action set pieces.

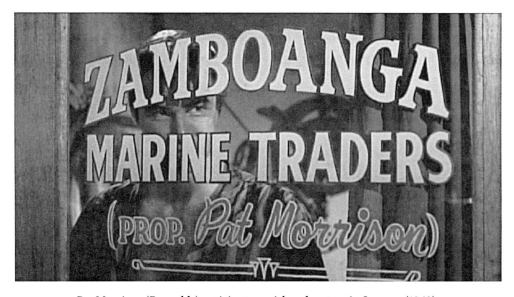

Pat Morrison (Reynolds) anticipates a risky adventure in *Impasse* (1969).

Reynolds gets to showcase his physical ability for this kind of material. His talent for stunts is used to particularly great effect during the picture's foot chase sequence, of which his character Morrison later remarked, "I got an interesting tour of Manila!" The thrilling scene begins with Morrison taking on multiple men in a cage scrap at a cockfighting arena before he begins making its way through the crowded streets, dive bars, cemeteries and rooftops of Zamboanga.

Impasse was released at the height of the counterculture era, and there is a distinct air of cynicism towards the prevalent hippie culture throughout. Several disparaging remarks are made towards the youth movement, not least the horrendous rendering of a hippie in the character of Penny (Joanne Dalsass), a delusional stalker and devoted flower child who seems to be present to merely annoy tennis champion Bobby. There is a strange, barely risqué sexual chemistry between Bobby and Penny that the film doesn't explore beyond a bawdy routine that belongs in a sex farce which has to be seen to be believed. The celebrity-fan relationship between the two sometimes veers into twisted mother-daughter dramatics, with the older Bobby admonishing Penny for her wild, wayward life, and further reprimanding her for not wanting to bathe. Penny, channeling some kind of awful hippie wisdom, says bathing isn't her bag as it's "not macrobiotic"; subsequently the pair tussle on the bed, with the already mostly nude Bobby tearing Penny's clothes off and leaving the younger woman stripped to bra and panties.

Some amusingly ribald though out-of-touch sexual innuendo (even for 1969) is deployed, such as when Bobby asks the macho Morrison if he is gay. Reynolds reaches into his arsenal of flamboyant material for a sarcastically raised-eyebrow retort: "Yeah, but I think you can fix me." And it would be remiss not to mention the greatest single shot of the picture: As Morrison races through a sleazy Zamboanga club, the camera is positioned on the bustling dance floor, brazenly placed between the widespread legs of a female reveler as we view Morrison. If the script lacks verbal wit, then the cinematographer more than makes up for it in his cheeky compositions.

Morrison (Reynolds) in dangerous pursuit in *Impasse* (1969).

Impasse may be somewhat inconsequential in the larger scheme of things but it did have some notable personal results for Reynolds, who met and briefly fell in love with his co-star Miko Mayama, who plays Morrison's erstwhile love interest, Mariko.

Shark

(1969)

"The last time I heard the word 'gunrunner' was in a movie!"—Caine

Caine (Burt Reynolds) is a rough but charming American gunrunner whose illicit cargo is uncovered by border crossing authorities. He flees at high speed but his truck's brakes give out and he makes a daring leap from the truck before it veers off a cliff. Making his way to a Sudanese port town on the Red Sea, Caine becomes a source of interest for Inspector Barok (Enrique Lucero), who isn't well liked and does his best to deport the smuggler. American scientist Dan Mallare (Barry Sullivan) and his lovely mistress Anna (Silvia Pinal) request Caine's help in a supposed study at sea; he accepts the job despite the danger. Dan and Anna are in fact treasure hunters with their eyes on the gold in a sunken boat and it is their greedy pursuit of riches that killed Mallare's previous assistant, a local boy—"a handsome young Arab, built like an Adonis … killed by a shark under suspicious circumstances." He and Anna see Caine as similarly disposable. Caine, looking to get rich quick, doesn't anticipate the level of dishonesty and manipulation of those he is helping.

The screenplay for the picture was written by director Sam Fuller and John Kingsbridge, based on the 1955 Victor Manning novel *His Bones Are Coral*. It's no wonder Fuller retitled the property *Shark*, as every character is out for each other's blood and are snapping eagerly to tear one another apart. The closest thing to a genuine relationship is when Caine befriends a local cigar-chomping child thief who hangs around the bazaars pilfering what he can, including Caine's watch. After catching the little scoundrel, Caine shows him some tough love, teaching him the ways of a good thief and bestowing upon him the suitable title of "Runt."

The cut of *Shark* that exists today is not Fuller's original version, having been compromised by the producers who reassembled the film without its author's consent or presence. "I asked them to take my name off the damn thing, because I didn't like the cut I saw. I thought it was terrible," said the director. "It may be the world's worst picture, or it may turn out to be a surprise to me. I don't know."[1] The unfortunate legacy of *Shark* is that of being despised and disowned by its director, unloved by its star, and generally comprised of perfunctory performances, as if all concerned knew it would languish in B-movie obscurity in perpetuity. The film is also littered with incongruous leaping; actors leap where leaping is neither necessary nor functional.

Though *Shark* simply shouldn't work, there is more going on here than it is usually given credit for, with the film featuring plenty of Fuller's auteurist aesthetics, regardless of how little of the director's initial narrative remains intact. With its complex web of deceit, seedy milieu, shady characters, morally ambiguous anti-hero, alluring femme fatale and multiple double-crosses, *Shark* swims in the dark waters of the film noir genre. Eschewing any form of modesty, Anna's refusal to share the loot with her criminal compatriots proves her own downfall. Icy blonde and coolly detached, Anna is a classic femme fatale, harboring the crucial elements of the character tropes with her ravishing looks and devious demeanor, as cunning as any of her cinematic foremothers. The unfolding layers of deception that reveal the true dark hearts of the protagonists is fresh and unexpected, even if in retrospect it makes perfect sense for the femme fatale to be pulling the strings of her male puppets. The uncompromising Fuller of yore retains his hard-edged, cynical view of humanity—what are the sharks but symbols of the predatory nature and greed of man? If anything, we are worse than sharks, more cunning and deceitful. Instead of making our presence felt at the first sniff of blood, we connive and slowly tear each other apart at the potential for wealth.

Fuller steers away from over-stylizing his picture; it is not a travelogue, the setting is sweaty and grimy rather than fantastic and exotic. A beachside romp between Caine and Anna feels uneasy rather than sexy in the dirt and humidity. Further aesthetic value can be found in Fuller's extensive use of intimate and claustrophobically encasing close-ups, which are not designed to heighten the glamour of the film's good-looking stars as there is little elegant about odious perspiration. Rather Fuller's camera is intrusive and drawing us closer to the ugliness of the vulgar, amoral characters. Out of the shadows that typically veil the misdeeds of a film noir narrative, here Fuller intensifies the vibrant foreign colors and searing sense of heat, all of which adds to the feelings of displacement and distrust. He recalled,

> When I made *Shark*, I had what I felt was a brainstorm: doing a story about four amoral characters. I thought it would be interesting to show not only a double-cross on a double-cross, but when we think we know who the heavy is, we find out that the real heavy behind it all is the girl. She's the lowest. She does have a chance to get out of it alive, if she levels with the lead. But she doesn't…[2]

Shark is complimented with a great jazz score, full of backstreet dive bar saxophone and lounge act xylophone, musical motifs that at times feel inappropriate given the geographical setting. But thematically they underscore the seedy, streetwise film noir elements at play. There are intermittent flourishes of Fuller's skewed genius here as in the well-edited pre-credit sequence in which a skin diver navigates the wreck of a ship in a subjective first-person perspective which is intercut with shots of an approaching shark; the diver is devoured in a bloody underwater ballet between man and monster. In a darkly satirical moment, Fuller cuts from the vicious attack to the victim's mother being satisfactorily reimbursed by Anna for the loss of her son, taking the money and flipping through the paper in businesslike fashion. This is classic Fuller, and moments like this make *Shark* a worthy addition to the auteur's canon, despite the truncation of his initial vision by unscrupulous, philistine producers.

Adding to the film's ignominy, tragedy struck the picture when stuntman Alfonso Raymond, doubling for Reynolds, was attacked by a tiger shark while filming an underwater sequence. At this stage in his career, Reynolds had never used a stunt double, but under orders from his director and producers the actor relented and Raymond was drafted to perform the scene. Barry Sullivan's stunt double Jose Marco was similarly attacked by another shark and later died from his injuries. Shamelessly, the producers of *Shark* cashed in by exploiting the real-life tragedies by promoting the film with insensitive taglines such as "A Realistic Film Became Too Real."

Reynolds recalled,

> I loved Sam Fuller, and he was a good director, but he wasn't as good as he thought he was. And just before we started the scene, instead of saying "Action," he would shoot off a gun. Half the people would jump five feet in the air. You could be doing a love scene, and he'd say, okay, everybody ready, and then *bam*, and the girl you were holding would jump about three feet in the air. I mean, it was not the way to start a scene like that. But that was Sam, you know.[3]

Notes

1. Tom Ryan, "Sam Fuller: Survivor," in *Samuel Fuller: Interviews*, ed. Gerald Perry (Mississippi, 2012), p. 37.

2. *Ibid.*

3. Mike Fleming Jr., "Encore: Burt Reynolds Has Tales to Tell: Passing on 'Cuckoo's Nest,' 007, 'Die Hard,' Bonding with Eastwood, McQueen, Newman & Carson but Not Brando." *Deadline*, September 6, 2018, https://deadline.com/2018/09/burt-reynolds-book-clint-eastwood-johnny-carson-die-hard-1201670957/.

Skullduggery

(1970)

"They're not property, they're people!"—Douglas Temple

Airplane mechanics Douglas Temple (Burt Reynolds) and Otto Kreps (Roger C. Carmel) con their way onto an anthropological expedition to the New Guinea jungle interior under the guise of science exploration, but they are really there to mine for valuable phosphors. The expedition is led by the attractive Dr. Sybil Graeme (Susan Clark), whose long-limbed Amazonian features piqued Temple's interest in the first place ("What a waste of woman that is!"). Also in tow is Father "Pop" Dillingham (Chips Rafferty). Together they are endeavoring to unearth the "missing link" between ape and man, and as such the group stumbles across a race of friendly furry creatures with human-like personalities: Tropis. Temple falls for Sybil, and while acquiescing to his eager charm she makes it clear that her interest in him is purely physical. Though their culture clash renders any potential for a relationship ultimately void, there is an electrifying sexual chemistry between the raffish Temple and the sophisticated, slightly haughty Sybil. On a queasier romantic quest is Kreps, who drunkenly spends a night of intimacy with a female Tropi, Topazia (Pat Suzuki), resulting in a controversial conception; the resulting pregnancy engenders a chain of events that will bring the Tropi to national attention. The baby is stillborn, but Temple takes the blame for its death so that he can be tried. This means that representatives of legal, medical and moral authority must battle out in court the question of whether the Tropis are legitimately human or simply animal. If Temple is found guilty of murder, that would mean the Tropi are to be considered human, and such a controversial ruling would lead to much consternation between the scientific and religious communities.

Skullduggery is an exotic science fiction adventure based on the 1952 novel *Les animaux denatures*, written by French author Jean Bruller under his pseudonym, Vercors. Book editor-turned-movie producer Saul David put the project together for the fledgling ABC Pictures, earmarking the adaptation to be the television network's first theatrical release. But after David experienced some bureaucratic difficulties with top ABC executives, *Skullduggery* was sold off to Universal. Locations had already been scouted in the then-hostile land of New Guinea, but once Universal took over the property it was decided

Douglas Temple (Reynolds) and Dr. Sybil Graeme (Susan Clark) explore each other before analyzing the Tropi in *Skullduggery* (1970).

that the production would be filmed in the less-volatile, and less-expensive, Jamaica.

Writer Nelson Gidding (collaborator with Robert Wise on his films *Odds Against Tomorrow*, 1959; *The Haunting*, 1963; *The Andromeda Strain*, 1971) seems preoccupied with depicting the Tropis as an allegorical species for a number of greater socio-political ideas, far more concerned with the exploitation of indigenous people of Third World countries than he is with the scientific investigations of human behavior. As a new species with basic human capabilities, the Tropis are ripe for exploitation by western industrialists and ideologues. Father Dillingham attempts to baptize them; Temple has them mining for phospurs; and a Dutch capitalist, Vancruysen (Paul Hubschmid), has plans to put them to work on the assembly lines of his textile factories. "Sensational, sir," Vancruysen's sycophantic colleague Bruce Spofford (Edward Fox) triumphantly declares. "In your spinning mills alone, the Tropis will sweep the Japanese right out of the market!" Vancruysen seduces Sybil with talk of winning the Nobel Prize for her studies of the Tropi, though he charmingly admits, "I've had to practice a little deception, darling," when revealing that all he really wants to is to breed the Tropi and create the cheapest labor force in the world: "You have uncovered a vast source of cheap labor, to reduce the sum of human toil."

Even though the picture was fostered by major studio Universal after being orphaned by ABC, the production did not go smoothly and went through several directors, the first being Richard Wilson, a former member of Orson Welles' Mercury Theatre repertory company. Wilson worked on the Mercury's 1930s theatrical productions *Julius Caesar* and *Heartbreak House*, the controversial CBS radio adaptation of *The War of the Worlds* (1938) and Welles' cinematic masterpieces *Citizen Kane* (1941), *The Magnificent Ambersons* (1942) and *The Lady from Shanghai* (1948). He later directed Rod Steiger in the biographical gangster picture *Al Capone* (1959), Ernest Borgnine in the crime drama *Pay or Die* (1960) and Yul Brynner in the western *Invitation to a Gunfighter* (1964).

Despite these fine credits, Wilson's work on *Skullduggery* proved unsatisfactory to Saul

David. David dismissed Wilson's work after seeing the first day's rushes and on short notice replaced him with journeyman filmmaker Gordon Douglas. Gidding, an acquaintance of the newly appointed director, jokes that Gordon was "a very casual director and he has done a lot of pictures, none of them good."[1] Douglas began his career as a child actor and later gag writer in the Old Hollywood world of Our Gang, Laurel and Hardy and various other Hal Roach enterprises. Douglas' prolific output as a director from the 1930s to the 1970s includes several excellent pictures, including the western *The Great Missouri Raid* (1951), the creature feature *Them!* (1954), the Doris Day-Frank Sinatra romantic musical *Young at Heart* (1955), the Sinatra neo-noir duo *Tony Rome* (1967) and *Lady in Cement* (1968) and *In the Heat of the Night* sequel *They Call Me Mr. Tibbs!* (1970).

The Jamaican locations, filling in for Papua New Guinea, are exotic enough without resorting to a glossy travelogue aesthetic, retaining a suitably humid and grubby atmosphere, the uncharted jungle terrain full of potential danger and mystery. Evidently Douglas brought with him the economy of a seasoned studio professional and submitted his assembly of the film on time, though with little love for the material. Universal may have been happy with the footage, but keeping his producer and the executives in the Black Tower happy may have come at the expense of the script, from which the director would discard pages with impunity. Gidding was unforgiving:

> The script was pretty good.... Susan Clark was very good-looking, and had some ability. Not a great actress, but certainly a good actress. Burt Reynolds was excellent in it, he had just the kind of cynical manliness that we wanted in the part.... It's my worst picture, in a way, but in some ways it's the noblest, the way it started off. It was a good book, a good play, and a good script, but you can't tear whole pages out of it and change things around for comfort and convenience.... I was appalled when I first saw it. There were pages, whole pages missing, and there was not much done about the transitions.[2]

With such gaps in the timeline of the plot being leapt over without notice, character motivations appear to change on a whim. Temple suddenly develops a humanitarian conscience with regard to Vancruysen's plan to breed and employ the Tropi; earlier in the film, he seemed quite content to exploit the creatures for their physical strength and endurance when mining for phosphurs.

Skullduggery's sharp turns in tone, interminable pace and elliptical structure mark it as an unusual and at times unintelligible picture. The first half is brutally laborious as director Douglas takes a leisurely approach to marvel at the Tropis and their increasingly human mannerisms, as well as to gaze upon Reynolds and Clark as they perform their own mating dance. Only in the third act does the film come alive with actual drama, but it feels too late to save the floundering narrative, as the time invested in wading through the first hour makes one weary and jaded by the time that we get to the courtroom theatrics.

Most egregious of all, *Skullduggery* is a film unsure of its own generic genetic code. At times it appears to be a light-hearted science fiction romp, then a jungle adventure, and often an exotic romance. As the picture struggles to find its tone and generic identity, it is never afforded an opportunity to reach the gravitas of a work of genuine scientific curiosity.

Notes

1. Tom Weaver, *I Was a Monster Movie Maker: Conversations with 22 SF and Horror Filmmakers* (Jefferson, NC: McFarland, 2001), p. 69.
2. *Ibid.*, p. 72.

Hunters Are for Killing

(Made-for-Television, 1970)

"They don't hand out any diplomas where I've been."—L.G. Floran

L.G. Floran (Burt Reynolds) is just released from prison, having spent six years behind bars for a crime he didn't commit. A known bad boy with an eye for the ladies (particularly the police chief's daughter), L.G. was convicted for manslaughter after he was implicated as the cause of a fatal drunk-driving accident following an alcohol-fuelled party. Tragically, one of the victims was his brother, Tommy. L.G. returns to his home town in Northern California looking to reclaim his life and to claim his inheritance of a big house and the attendant sixty acres of vineyard left to him by his deceased mother. But L.G. is met with fierce resistance and hostility from the townsfolk, and in particular from his elderly step-father, Keller (Melvyn Douglas). Keller believes L.G. deliberately killed Tommy out of jealousy and duly attempts to deny him any financial gain. However, the cunning L.G. and his mother had devised a plan to deceive Keller into thinking that the inheritance would go to a New England charitable organization, not realizing that the person behind the organisation is his estranged stepson, who now stands to gain the property upon his imminent thirtieth birthday. This leads to the two men engaging in a fierce battle of wits and will.

L.G. finds he is also unwelcome elsewhere, such as when he enters a greasy spoon café looking for a bowl of chili, only to be faced with a discriminating proprietor who exclaims "I don't serve ex-cons and murderers!" While trying to move on peacefully he is harassed by the cops for defending himself against two violent thieves who attempt to mug him. He is barely free from prison and has two charges against him. Meanwhile, not everyone is averse to L.G.'s presence in town, particularly his old flame Barbara (Suzanne Pleshette) who is torn between her feelings for her old lover and her new life; things are further complicated when she is warned off by her menacing police chief father, Wade Hamilton (Martin Balsam), who harbours a long-standing hatred of his daughter's former beau. L.G. is also the object of affection of young Holly Fornell (Jill Banner), which sets the gossip mill in motion, though he is wise enough not to get involved with the nubile seventeen-year old temptress.

Hunters Are for Killing shares narrative and thematic similarities to the ABC television movie of the same year, *Run Simon Run*, in which Reynolds also plays an ex-convict making his way back into civilized society only to be greeted with hostility and a cold welcome home. But whereas the ABC film incorporates racially- and socially-charged ideas to fuel its progressive and conscientious narrative, *Hunters Are for Killing* is more concerned with immediate thrills and assumes the essential elements of the film noir tales of the 1940s. Reynolds is suitably stoic here as the cynical protagonist, a troubled man searching for redemption and revisiting the ghosts of his past, only to find antagonism at every turn, all the while battling the allure of the femme fatale.

Hunters Are for Killing received it debut screening on CBS on March 12, 1970, but despite being destined for the small screen the film has abundant cinematic class. Cinematographer Jerry Finnerman's lively camerawork belies the film's humble television origins and beautifully captures the Santa Rosa locations, with the intense heat and searing sunshine of the glorious wine country conversely masking the dark heart of the film's themes of familial deception and betrayal. It is no surprise Finnerman would find more high profile work shooting two theatrical features in the same year, both for director Gordon Douglas, including the western *Barquero* and an *In the Heat of the Night* sequel, *They Call Me Mr. Tibbs!* Perhaps most notably, Finnerman would bring his deft cinematic flair to the eighties television series, *Moonlighting*, and one can see precursors to that show's distinct aesthetic here, particularly in the heavily diffused and highly romantic scenes in the cemetery in the first act. The film also boasts a terrifically bombastic Jerry Fielding score, which gives life to the romances, car chases, and fisticuffs aplenty. The composer imaginatively fuses early-seventies funk grooves with lush string sections and nimble jazz arrangements. It is also worth watching just to observe the verbal sparring and tense dynamic between Reynolds and Old Hollywood heavyweight, Melvyn Douglas. To witness the formidable duo sharing the screen is a treat in itself.

Run Simon Run
(Made-for-Television, 1970)

"I thought I came here to meet some new friends. I'm not an entertainer … [I]f you want to get some Indians to dance, I'm sure you can get some, but not me."—Simon Zuniga

Simon Zuniga (Burt Reynolds) is a Tohono O'odham native (referred to in the film with the Anglicized name of "Papago Indians") released from prison after serving a long sentence for a crime he didn't commit. That crime was the killing of his younger brother, committed by a supposed friend of the family: the dastardly Henry Burroughs (James Best). In a drunken stupor on the night in question, Simon was framed for the murder, and now he is released into a different world, one of fierce acrimony and prejudice, and into the care of a beautiful social worker, Carrol Rennard (Inger Stevens). While Simon was locked up,

Inger Stevens (left) plays the compassionate Carrol Rennard, while Reynolds (right) plays wrongfully imprisoned Simon Zuniga in *Run Simon Run* (1970).

some locals and corrupt authorities colluded to set up a fictional account of Burroughs' death so that Simon wouldn't leave prison seeking retribution.

Escaping the vacuity of her erstwhile bourgeois life and guilty of her inherited privilege as part of an old money oil family, Carrol admits to her own selfish reasons for her social work, which is not entirely altruistic: "It makes me feel superior. It's not very nice but it's true…. I have other reasons: my friends and family, they're affluent and bright and sophisticated … and jaded. I just had to get away to somewhere where life is simple and true, like it is here." While Carrol has noble intentions to help show the natives a better way of life and to take advantage of all they can from society, she still flinches at the casual violence exhibited in their local saloons. When Carrol finds herself falling for her charge, she is disturbed to learn that Simon plans on revenge when he finds out the truth of his framing. But rather than leave him to risk his life and freedom to track down Burroughs alone, she utilizes her wealth to fund Simon's quest, paying up to eight private investigators to locate Burroughs. When word is received that Burroughs is laying low in Arizona under an assumed name, Simon is warned off his vigilante ways by deceitful Sheriff Tacksberry (Royal Dano), who is complicit in the cover-up and is privy to Burroughs' new identity and the location in which he is being protected in anonymity. But neither the sheriff nor the social worker can stop Simon from exacting his vengeance.

Run Simon Run is less a revenge thriller and more a hard-edged romantic drama. In their burgeoning relationship, it is Carrol who leads the seduction. ("I know I'm a paleface and that's terrible, but aside from that, what do you think of me?" she asks Simon by a cozy fireside chat.) Like the love between Reynolds and Loden in *Fade In*, the contrast of their backgrounds is tearing at the heart of the coupling and there are moments of biting social satire to underscore the class tensions. Simon is visibly uncomfortable at a society party at which Carrol takes the opportunity to "show him off." The discreet charm of the bourgeoisie is cast aside as socialites fawn over Simon like a cultural museum exhibit and ask the daftest of questions, such as "Is it true that there's a higher rate of alcoholism and TB among the Indians than any other ethnic group?" Two otherwise respectable ladies further humiliate themselves and Simon when they ask if he would like to partake in a dance, only for one of them to declare, "I think Marilyn maybe meant some kind of Indian war dance, I mean, I'd really like to see that!" Duly, the party gathers around the novelty guest expecting "to learn how to do a real war dance," but Simon schools the supercilious assembly on the sacred beliefs behind his ancient traditions and reiterates the relation of those rituals to the poverty endured by his people.

Just as *Fade In* languishes in limbo, *Run Simon Run* remains another obscure object of desire for Reynolds fans. The film premiered on December 1, 1970, as an ABC Movie of the Week and was financed by TV mogul Aaron Spelling's then-fledgling Aaron Spelling Productions. The films produced for the network under the Movie of the Week banner were often works of respectable pedigree, featuring established stars and veteran character actors such as James Caan (*Brian's Song*, 1971), Walter Brennan and Pat O' Brien (*The Over-the-Hill Gang*, 1969), Dennis Weaver (*Duel*, 1971), Leonard Nimoy (*Assault on the Wayne*, 1971), Richard Burton and Elizabeth Taylor (*Divorce His, Divorce Hers*, 1973) and Lee Remick (*No One Could Save Her*, 1973). As good a film as *Run Simon Run* remains, if it is remembered at all these days it is for holding the unfortunate distinction of being the wonderful Inger Stevens' final role before her premature death from barbiturate overdose on April 30, 1970.

Dan August

(TV Series, ABC, 1970–1971)

"You're gonna foul up again, Junior, and when you do I'm gonna be all over you!"—Dan August

Police Lt. Dan August (Burt Reynolds) works the homicide division in his hometown of San Luisa, California. He and his partner, Sgt. Charles Wilentz (Norman Fell), investigate various murder mysteries and conspiracies throughout the show's 17 episodes, bringing them into contact with the seedier elements of their jurisdiction's high and low society, including politicians, drug dealers, hippies, models, clergymen, trade unionists, industrialists and athletes. As a law enforcer in his own small community, August must sometimes arrest and investigate friends, neighbors and sweethearts.

In the exciting pilot episode "Murder by Proxy," Anne Francis guest stars as Nina Porter, a beautiful lush whose husband is implicated in the murder of a hotshot auto racer. Porter's drunken, aggressive flirting with August leads to some memorable dialogue: When checking her foot size against a shoe that was found at the crime scene, August finds the item far too small for her considerable height—"You've got big feet," August says, coyly ignoring her more notable features. "I've also got sexy legs, you stupid, dumb cop!" Porter exclaims. Previously Reynolds' co-star in the caper film *Impasse*, Francis is one of many of the show's actors who would appear again with Reynolds throughout his career, including James Best, Mike Henry, Ricardo Montalban and Jan-Michael Vincent.

Dan August producer Quinn Martin was a renowned figure in the television industry, having accrued huge success with a string of popular shows (*The Fugitive*, *12 O'Clock High*, *The F.B.I.*) when he began developing a new show called *Dan August* about a hardboiled cop working a small West Coast town. As Martin envisioned a tough and sexy affair, humorless and sober, he initially courted Christopher George (*The Immortal*), but the stubborn actor declined Quinn's insistent offers and instead suggested a friend who would be ideal for the part: Burt Reynolds. At the time, Reynolds was working steadily in film but had tired of being typecast as Native Americans. He told his agent Dick Clayton, "The only Indian I haven't played is Pocahontas…. Dammit, get me a project and let me shine!"[1] But the actor refused to wait for his handlers to find the right script, so he went straight to the source. In a moment of serendipity, Reynolds told Martin about his wanting to find a decent role in a quality series, just as Martin was considering Reynolds upon George's referral. Martin offered the series to the eager star, but Reynolds initially recoiled at the thoughts of another police procedural, having experienced the devastating failure of *Hawk*. "No, I've had it with cop parts," Reynolds said, only for the producer to sweeten the deal even further: "He made a ridiculous offer and I said, 'Gee, I always wanted to play a cop,' and I sold out."[2] That ridiculous offer was $26,000 per week (topping highest television earner Michael Landon's $25,000 per week for *Bonanza*) as well as script approval, the option to perform all of his character's stunts, and a clause allowing him to direct the second unit shots. Despite some reservations about his leading man putting himself in harm's way to execute the required stunts, Quinn agreed and his Dan August was found. With such a lucrative deal

The cast of *Dan August* (clockwise from bottom left): Norman Fell, Richard Anderson, Ena Hartman, Ned Romero, Reynolds.

and the steady employment of 26 guaranteed episodes, *Dan August* finally offered Reynolds the kind of leverage that he was looking for in the industry.

Richard Anderson, who plays Chief George Untermeyer, reminisced fondly on the positive relationship between the star and the producer: "[Burt] was a lot of fun to work with. He was a very good-hearted fellow.... Quinn gave Burt his own office, and his own assistant. Burt and Quinn always seemed to be in communication on how to make things better.... Burt told me he was spending a lot of time with Quinn, that the two of them were talking about the future of the show."[3]

Unfortunately, *Dan August* didn't have much of a future. Reynolds took to the chat show circuit to promote it, but the effect of that endeavor saw Burt Reynolds the man being sold more effectively than Dan August the character. Presenters and audiences gravitated to Reynolds' endearing self-deprecation, which stood somewhat in contrast to the brooding personality of the show's eponymous policeman. Just as *Hawk* had fallen victim to the axe, *Dan August* too failed to be renewed for a second season. The show proved to be an expensive one to maintain (with a budget of $300,000 per episode) and as it went up against *Hawaii Five-O* and *McCloud,* the ratings stagnated, and the network pulled the plug. The show initially aired on ABC from 1970 to 1971. There were primetime reruns on CBS in 1973 and again in 1975 to capitalize on Reynolds' film success and cultural ubiquity.

Rather than sulk about the early demise of *Dan August* and take it as another defeat, Reynolds continued his charm offensive with highly entertaining appearances on *The Tonight Show with Johnny Carson, The Merv Griffin Show* and *Dinah's Place.*

While successfully seducing the American viewing public, the actor began to look through the piles of scripts coming his way from the major Hollywood studios and one potentially lucrative offer on the table was for a James Bond film. Bond producer "Cubby" Broccoli imagined Reynolds as an ideal candidate to take over as the iconic spy from Sean Connery as the star of *Diamonds Are Forever.* It wasn't to be, Connery would be enticed back one more time before the role would be assumed by future Reynolds co-star and pal, Roger Moore. Not that it mattered too much to Reynolds, as the film that he would star in next was to prove a monumental turning point in his career.

Notes

1. Bernhardt J. Hurwood, *Burt Reynolds* (New York: Quick Fox, 1979), p. 35.
2. *Ibid.*
3. Jonathan Etter, *Quinn Martin, Producer: A Behind-the-Scenes History of QM Productions and its Founder* (Jefferson, NC: McFarland, 2003), p. 110.

Deliverance

(1972)

"You don't beat this river...."—Lewis Medlock

The Cahulawassee River Valley, in the backwoods of Georgia, is soon to be flooded for the construction of a dam to accommodate a new lake. Before that happens, a group of middle-class city slickers from Atlanta journey there to experience unbridled, elusive nature in its unspoiled brilliance. Lewis Medlock (Burt Reynolds), Ed Gantry (Jon Voight), Bobby Trippe (Ned Beatty) and Drew Ballinger (Ronny Cox) travel the rapids in pairs. Ed and Bobby encounter trouble when their canoe becomes stranded, forcing them take refuge on the riverbank. Here they stumble upon a duo of dangerous mountain men; what happens next is an act of violence and humiliation upon Ed and Bobby, the latter stripped of clothes and dignity, sodomized and instructed to "squeal like a pig." Ed is tied up in anticipation of his own degradation. Lewis and Drew come to their rescue, with Lewis fatally shooting an arrow through the back of Bobby's abuser; his accomplice flees into the hills. With their trip turning into a living nightmare, the four men face a treacherous voyage home through the uncompromising wilderness.

Lewis Medlock (Reynolds) displays his skill with a bow and arrow in *Deliverance* (1972).

As the men's friendship and courage is tested throughout their traumatic experience, director John Boorman offers a contemplation of male relationship dynamics and traditional masculinity, recalling similar themes in the work of Sam Peckinpah, though minus that maverick filmmaker's predilection for fetishizing and aestheticizing any ensuing chaos. "The idea of masculinity and virility is changing around us," Reynolds said. "The guy I played in *Deliverance* was real macho…. He'd think you were a homosexual if you didn't have a gun rack in your house."[1]

By day, the wealthy and resourceful Lewis is in real estate; his demeanor is stern and cynical, intrepid and vigorous. He is the natural leader of this group which interestingly has its own distinct social structure and unspoken order. Lewis is gifted the physique of an athlete, enviable good looks and a confident swagger that makes him a heroic figure amongst his friends. Ed, an advertising man, is perhaps adept at boardroom politics but far out of his element here; he relies upon the irrepressible Lewis for guidance outside of his conservative lifestyle to the point of adoration. Lewis even appears as a guardian angel, materializing out of nowhere to save Ed's life in his moment of need. But Ed eventually finds that Lewis is not infallible, that his idealized version of a strong, self-sufficient man can be crippled by the same human vulnerabilities as the rest of us. The power dynamic shifts as the diffident Ed finds his will in an effort to preserve himself after Lewis is incapacitated by a leg wound. If Ed looked up to Lewis in hero worship as the kind of masculine beast he could never be, ironically it is he rather than Lewis who must become the mythological conqueror of the volatile duo: Nature and Man.

A burly, perpetually good-humored fellow, Bobby works in insurance and has the benign bluster of an obnoxious salesman; he is not made for the outdoors. Drew, compassionate though meek, represents a holdover of recent 1960s brotherly love. He is a pacifist countercultural figure and quiet suburban family man. Ed refers to the moral decency of Drew when he eulogizes his friend as "the best of us." Throughout the picture, each man's morality and resolve is tested as they face their greatest fears: Lewis, definitive physical specimen, is reduced to an immovable wreck; quiet Ed must step up and embrace survivalist instincts, even resorting to violence; the jocular Bobby's merry demeanor is sullied into solemnity after his sexual assault, an allegorical act echoing Lewis' earlier speculative obser-

Ed (Jon Voight) and Bobby (Ned Beatty) try to help Lewis (Reynolds) in *Deliverance* (1972).

vation that "they're going to rape this whole country"; the civil and conscientious Drew faces the moral dilemma of unlawfully burying their attacker, thus betraying his erstwhile infallible sense of decency and democracy. For these four American males, nature will be everything unsettling to a complacent middle class: ungovernable and disruptive, turbulent and anarchic.

Having already made one of the greatest American films of the 1960s with the neo-noir *Point Blank* (1967), distinguished British filmmaker John Boorman astounded again when he made *Deliverance* one of the truly great American films of the 1970s. He delivered a striking, contentious picture that doesn't offer any easy answers. Are the content suburbanites punished for their privilege, for daring to play primitive? The unfortunate fate of four well-to-do bourgeoisies observing a culture of poverty and depravity backfires even on the most fragile and empathetic of them, Drew, who succumbs first to the unfolding horror.

Deliverance plays upon the prevailing sense of paranoia and guilt that was a major part of 1970s U.S. cinema. As a deeply unsettling, eerie rural drama, the picture is overwhelmingly pessimistic, which is not a criticism but a fact. Even the scene in which Ed and Bobby share a meal with hospitable locals is tinged with melancholy, seeing Ed break down with guilt, shame and remorse. In this heartbreaking moment, the two men are being offered the gifts of nourishment, kindness and warmth from the kind of deeply rural Southern people whose world he has entered through an act of violence. The final images of the dead man's hand rising from the water are unsettling and nightmarish, inescapable in their ability to linger upon Ed's anxious conscience, just as they challenge our own sense of cinematic closure. Most invasively, these images haunt Ed from the comfort of his own bed, what should be the safest place in his world.

James Dickey's 1970 novel celebrated the very American theme of survival against the hostile forces of nature and impending technologies. ("Machines are going to fail, and the system is going to fail ... then survival," Lewis ponders aloud). But Boorman perceived the themes conversely: "For me, the idea that this beautiful river was going to be dammed and destroyed was a fantastic kind of symbol about man's attempt to conquer nature."[2] The director expertly parlayed his protagonists' guilelessness into a feeling of impending dread the deeper into the rural landscape they roam, amplifying the anxiety of Ed, Bobby and

Drew's inexperience and naivety; when Ed is "with Lewis," it is because Lewis is the only one who seems to have absolute assuredness, even if it is the morally and legally wrong sense of the situation. But when Lewis is struck down, wounded and immobile, the men's vulnerability is heightened, their fortitude compromised.

As Lewis, the atypical macho man who craves the adrenaline rush that the adventure of this tragic trip offers, Reynolds is the nominal action hero of the picture, yet Boorman cast the actor not for his tough guy chops but for his distinctive and poised presence when working an even tougher gig: hosting *The Tonight Show*. Having appeared as a guest so memorably many times over the years, Reynolds eventually landed himself in the hot seat filling in for Johnny Carson. Boorman must have seen some elements of Lewis in Reynolds' cocksure, almost vainglorious appearances on the show. Carson even once hilariously ribbed Reynolds on the basis that the more successful the actor became, the more his walk from behind the curtain to the couch became slower and more swaggering, the actor relishing and savoring the uproarious reception of the studio audience. Reynolds often commented on the brilliance of his director: "Without a doubt, John Boorman was the best…. He just had a great deal of faith in me. He thought I could do things that nobody else did, and he was a wonderful man to work for."[3] In the career trajectory of Burt Reynolds, *Deliverance* lent massive credibility to the actor, allowing him to graduate from modestly successful B-picture actor to stratospheric A-list leading man. It showcased to Hollywood and to audiences a figure of commanding screen presence and old-fashioned movie star magnetism.

Deliverance has taken its place in the pantheon of great American cinema, a picture that works exquisitely on several standards of genre: action adventure, revenge thriller, ecological horror and psychological drama. Years of pop-culture parody and everyday citation of its depiction of backwoods rural dwellers, the famous "Dueling Banjos" theme tune, and infamous rape sequence have kept the picture in the public consciousness. But such cultural omnipresence has not diminished its power to shock, repulse and entertain in equal measure. Rather, it has allowed *Deliverance* to be continually appreciated and rightly revered as part of the lexicon of American film history.

Notes

1. Dianna Whitley, *Burt Reynolds: Portrait of a Superstar* (New York: Grossett & Dunlap, 1979), p. 55.
2. John Boorman, "Deliverance: The Beginning," DVD Supplement, *Deliverance*, Warner Bros., 2007.
3. Mike Fleming Jr., "Encore: Burt Reynolds Has Tales to Tell: Passing on 'Cuckoo's Nest,' 007, 'Die Hard,' Bonding with Eastwood, McQueen, Newman & Carson but Not Brando." *Deadline*, September 6, 2018, https://deadline.com/2018/09/burt-reynolds-book-clint-eastwood-johnny-carson-die-hard-1201670957/.

Fuzz

(1972)

"What do you mean, we're inept?"—Detective Bert Kling

Meet the detectives of Boston's 87th Precinct: Steve Carella (Burt Reynolds), Bert Kling (Tom Skerritt), Meyer Meyer (Jack Weston) and Eileen McHenry (Raquel Welch). These four flatfoots are beleaguered by a heavy caseload, but of particular concern are the demands of an enigmatic criminal mastermind, known as The Deaf Man (Yul Brynner), who is extorting $5000 from various politicians and state planners. A drop-off of cash goes awry, the city's parks commissioner is killed and the Deaf Man will kill more senior level civil servants if his demands are not met. In a disturbing subplot, two teenagers prowl the Boston back streets for derelicts that they can douse in lighter fluid and set ablaze. Carella goes undercover posing as a homeless drunk, hoping to provide bait for the suspects. When the tender age of those committing the horrendous acts becomes apparent, he is paralyzed by shock and almost ends up another victim.

Fuzz was one of the first films to afford Reynolds the opportunity to develop the wiseass tough guy persona that would serve him well throughout the '70s and '80s: lethal, efficient and thoroughly charming. Playing straight man to Reynolds' rogue is Tom Skerritt, a rare bird of professionalism in the 87th Precinct nest of bumbling cops. Though Reynolds is the star, it's Skerritt who gets to roll around in a sleeping bag with Raquel Welch, rather than her erstwhile *100 Rifles* co-star, despite his recent ascension to sex symbol status.

Following the acrimony on the set of *100 Rifles*, there was tension between the two stars. Welch reportedly only signed on to act in the film if she was guaranteed that she didn't have to do any scenes with Reynolds. Producers agreed to Welch's request, though there are several scenes in the film in which detectives Carella and McHenry appear together; fortunately for the feuding stars, some well-placed stand-ins and good editing make it appear as though Reynolds and Welch did the scenes together. "We never exchanged one word," Reynolds says. "After I did my close-up, I got in my car and drove off the lot."[1] Welch's character had nothing of dramatic note to do; her presence as a hardboiled detective is merely a cockamamie excuse for male jaws to drop and eyes to pop in appreciation of her physical attributes. The actress is perfectly fine in the role, playing it with the required

Detectives Carella (Reynolds) and Meyer (Jack Weston) go undercover in *Fuzz* (1972).

Yul Brynner plays the sinister Deaf Man in *Fuzz* (1972).

chic and tempering the spirited comedic performances of her jovial co-stars with an air of sobriety. The chemistry of the actors is the core attraction here and much of the camaraderie is wisely kept within the close-proximity confines of the squad room. Further comic relief is provided by the two painters whose laziness is often proudly defended with a declaration of their status as permanent and pensioned city workers from the office of "Public Works: Maintenance and Repair."

Fuzz was based on Ed McBain's 1968 novel, which was part of the writer's *87th Precinct* police procedural series, with the main difference between film and source material being the move in location from New York to Boston. McBain wrote the screen adaptation under the pseudonym of Evan Hunter, lending this lightweight and inconsequential picture some authorial credibility. With its megalomaniacal villain and amusing, anarchic spirit, *Fuzz* would work as a reasonably tame crime comedy for all the family if it weren't for the serious nature of the juvenile arson subplot. As such, the picture displays an uneven tone throughout. It's unclear whether it wants to be a gritty urban crime thriller or a frothy bumbling cop romp; it ends up being a little bit of both. There are some attempts at pathos, such as the scenes with Carella's deaf wife, but this symbolic and jejune gesture of having Carella's love interest afflicted with the same disability as his antagonist is a contrivance too far. It is difficult to take seriously such trite attempts at sentimentality in a picture where the heroes are depicted as so comically inept and ineffective, as well as the absurd rendering of Brynner's cartoonish villain with his ludicrous schemes. Fortunately, such failed attempts at emotional sincerity don't linger too long as *Fuzz* ultimately achieves its goal of providing some frivolous fun in promoting Reynolds' beloved late-night television persona to the big screen.

Note

1. Burt Reynolds, *My Life: Burt Reynolds* (Great Britain: Hodder & Stoughton, 1994), p. 136.

Everything You Always Wanted to Know About Sex (*But Were Afraid to Ask)*

(1972)

"All systems on the alert; we're going to try to ball her there in the car!"—Switchboard Operator

Based on the #1 bestselling 1969 sex manual by physician David Reuben, *Everything You Always Wanted to Know About Sex* (*But Were Afraid to Ask)* is one of Woody Allen's most brilliant works from that lauded period colloquially referred to as "The Early Funny Ones." The picture is a satiric collection of short stories with titles such as "What is Sodomy?" "What Are Sex Perverts?" and "What Happens During Ejaculation?"

Burt Reynolds appears in the latter alongside Allen, Tony Randall and Robert Walden and this segment parodies Reuben's explanation of how the body works when building up to and experiencing a sexual encounter. Reynolds and Randall are operators working the Brain Room control center, commanding various other body parts to function according to the progress of their male owner's romantic date and to ultimately form an erection. The man in whose body the segment is set is on an intimate dinner engagement with a beautiful college student (Erin Fleming) but his sexual interest in the woman begins to wane as she pretentiously pontificates on the cultural significance of Norman Mailer, favorably comparing him to Proust and Flaubert, raising doubts of a sexual conquest amongst the body's operators and engineers. However, the Libido is safe in the knowledge that coitus will be reached when the woman declares "I'm a graduate of New York University!"; Tony Randall

Reynolds tries to stimulate the libido of a man on a date with an NYU student in *Everything You Always Wanted to Know About Sex* (*But Were Afraid to Ask)* (1972).

triumphantly assures his men, "We're gonna make it!" Allen, as one of the sperm para-troopers, naturally endures an existential crisis when it comes time to ejaculate: "You hear these strange stories like there's this pill these women take, or like sometimes the guys will slam their heads up against a wall of hard rubber, or..." he says, looking fretful. "What if it's a homosexual encounter?" After all, he took an oath upon entering Sperm Training School to "fertilize an ovum or die trying."

Despite Reynolds' minimal role, the fact that Allen cast him acknowledges the actor's comedic value, at a time when Reynolds was perhaps the second most beloved person to appear on *The Tonight Show with Johnny Carson* ... the first being Johnny Carson. Reynolds' role as the Switchboard Operator is limited to intermittent shots of him delivering hilari-ously deadpan dialogue such as "Scratch the left leg!" and "Brain Room to Sexual Organs: proceed with erection!" Reynolds utters such commands with the right amount of sober absurdity as he fields directions to and from colleagues in the Stomach and Brain rooms. Allen, one of America's great parodists—when he is in the mood—was in top comedic form here. Yes, *The Purple Rose of Cairo* (1985), *Hannah and Her Sisters* (1986) and *Another Woman* (1988) are better films, but will the writer-director ever top the scene here in which the operators find a rogue priest tampering with the machinery in the Cerebral Cortex after having chained the Conscience to a chair, only then to be dragged away screaming "Blasphemy!" at this sexual encounter of the unwed? I think not.

Ask Me What I Am:
An Interview with Bobby Goldsboro

In 1973, Burt Reynolds was basking in the success afforded him by *Deliverance* and his increased popularity on the chat show circuit. He could do whatever he wanted; he dominated the dual worlds of Film and Television wherein he commanded absolute devo-tion in his vast following. He had yet to direct a film, a goal he achieved in 1976 with *Gator*, but in the meantime he decided to use his stature to become a singer-songwriter and to release a record on a major label.

The LP *Ask Me What I Am* was unleashed on November 5, 1973, by Mercury Records. As he did on his film work, Reynolds surrounded himself with the best in the business, including Nashville's finest session musicians and members of Memphis' legendary Amer-ican Sound Studio house band. Those whose fine playing is featured on the album are gui-tarists Johnny Christopher (who also played for Petula Clark, Kris Kristofferson, Herbie Mann) and Reggie Young (who also played for Elvis Presley, Dusty Springfield, Neil Dia-mond), bassists Joe Allen (who also played for Doc Watson, Don Williams, Waylon Jen-nings) and Mike Leech (who also played for John Prine, Bobby Womack, the Box Tops), drummer Larrie London (who also played for Jerry Reed, Dolly Parton, the Temptations) and many other world-class musicians.

Ask Me What I Am invites the listener into an intimate dialogue with Reynolds, in which the actor addresses parts of his life that he was rarely able to speak about on TV chat shows and in newspaper articles. If the name of the album sounds somewhat enigmatic, Reynolds clarifies his intentions on the title track when he pleads not to be asked what he is going to be, but what he is, and not where he is going, but where he has been. The album is musically outstanding, and lyrically Reynolds draws evocative images of a life that on the surface has it all: riches, the adoration of millions—but one whose heart yearns for the less superficial things. One particular cut proves the deepest of them all: On "A Room for a Boy Never Used," Reynolds laments his childless lifestyle and actively asks God to consider him worthy of fatherhood.

Production of the album was overseen by singer-songwriter Bobby Goldsboro and country music mogul Buddy Killen. With no prior experience behind the microphone, but with performance in his blood and derring-do to spare, Reynolds was convinced by friend Goldsboro to record the album. Goldsboro has worked with his share of legendary artists; after spending several years playing

Cover art for the 1973 album *Ask Me What I Am* (photograph courtesy Album Artwork, Mercury/Phonogram).

with a local Alabama act, The Webs, he got high-profile work when in 1961 he became guitarist for Roy Orbison, with whom he would play for over three years. During that time, he toured England with The Beatles. In 1964, as a solo artist, Goldsboro opened for the Rolling Stones on their first tour of the United States; that same year, he scored the first of many Top 40 hits with "See the Funny Little Clown." In 1968, he scored his biggest hit to date with the classic ballad "Honey." Written by singer Bobby Russell and produced by songwriter Bob Montgomery, "Honey" became a phenomenal success, spending five weeks at the top spot on the Billboard Hot 100 chart and selling over five million copies. From 1973 to 1975, the artist parlayed his talents into a television career with his own variety series, *The Bobby Goldsboro Show*. Around this time, he engaged in several professional collaborations with his friend and fellow Floridian Reynolds, the first of which was *Ask Me What I Am*. Goldsboro recalls his special friendship and working relationship with Burt Reynolds…

Wayne: *What are your earliest recollections of meeting Burt Reynolds?*

Bobby: Burt and I met on Mike Douglas' television show in 1970. We were both from Florida and had a lot in common. We became instant friends. One day we were talking and Burt said, "I always wanted to make an album." I said, "Why don't you come to Nashville and let's do it?" He said, "Really?" and I said, "Why not? We'll pick some songs, I'll set it up and we'll do it!" Buddy Killen, who owned Tree International Publishing, was a friend of mine and I knew he had produced an album for Jack Palance, so I called him and said, "How would you like to co-produce a record for Burt Reynolds?" He said, "Sure!" I said, "All you have to do is pay for it!" He said, "Let's do it!" He contacted the head of Mercury Records, Charlie Fach, who agreed to release the record. So, Buddy and I picked a couple of dozen songs and drove down to north Georgia where Burt was filming *Deliverance*. We stayed for a few days and went over the songs until we narrowed it down to the ones on the album. When Burt finished filming, he came to Nashville and we started recording.

What were your first impressions of Burt as a singer?

Burt wasn't a bad singer but he tended to try to sound like Dean Martin. He was extremely nervous in the studio, so much so that we ended up cutting all the music tracks and then letting the musicians leave. Even then, he'd jump in too early or miss a beat here and there. I finally went into the booth with him and I'd count and point when it was time to come in. Eventually, he relaxed and did a great job. As many times as Burt had recorded lines for movies, this was the first time he was *singing*. Once Burt got comfortable with the recording environment, he relaxed and everything ran pretty smoothly.

Given Burt's success at the time, I would imagine there were a lot of musicians and songwriters offering songs for him to record. Was this the case? And what factors did you consider in choosing the final tracks that would make the cut?

Since Buddy was paying for this project, he obviously wanted Tree Publishing songs on the album. He had some really good writers on his staff and they all wanted a song on Burt's album. We tried to pick songs that Burt felt comfortable with and we brought in a group of musicians who all made him feel at home. It is a who's who of Nashville session guys on that album.

There are some very personal and confessional songs on the album, such as "Childhood 1949," "Til I Get It Right" and "A Room for a Boy Never Used." Was this autobiographical theme a conceptual idea of the album from the beginning?

It was Burt's idea to do songs that were autobiographical. He particularly liked "A Room for a Boy Never Used" and my song, "Childhood, 1949," which he had heard me sing on *The Mike Douglas Show*. We had grown up in the same era and that song reminded him of his childhood. Burt did a few spoken word tracks on the album as well, and I would have liked for him to do more of those, but he wanted to sing.

Did you spend much time with Burt in advance of the recording sessions in terms of songwriting, arrangements, sound, etc.?

I was playing the Fairmont Hotel in San Francisco and Burt flew up to go over the songs. We worked for a couple of days there. Then he came in early to Nashville and we rehearsed some more. We pretty much used the same arrangements that had been on the demos so Burt was comfortable with them.

Burt was one of the biggest stars in the world at the point when you made Ask Me What I Am. *Was there much commercial pressure from the record label to produce any hits from the album or did you, Buddy and Burt have complete autonomy over the sound, style and songwriting on the album?*

Obviously, Burt was so popular at the time that we all knew the album would get a lot of attention. However, we all knew that it wasn't something that would start a new career for Burt. He would later joke, "I did everything backwards! I cut an album, *then* I took singing lessons," which he did for *The Best Little Whorehouse in Texas.* Charlie Fach came to the sessions but left the content of the album entirely to Burt, Buddy and me. The album was just a fun project for Burt and me. Buddy was the money man who also brought in his songwriters and his studio savvy. Buddy published and produced a lot of hits over the years. This album also brought Buddy and me closer and we remained close friends until his death in 2006.

The engineer Ernie Winfrey worked on this record, and he had previously worked on albums by you, Doug Kershaw and Gary Scruggs, among others. What was it about his engineering skill that works so great on an album like Ask Me What I Am?

Ernie was a great "technical" guy but he also had a great ear. He would catch a lot of things we would miss, such as an out-of-tune guitar string, a noise from the drum booth, etc. Ernie worked on so many hit records over the years that he was invaluable to the album.

You and Burt collaborated several times after this album. What was it about working with him that has brought you back repeatedly?

After knowing Burt for so long, I knew what he wanted when he'd say things like, "We need some ice-cream music here…" and "It needs to get *big* here…," so we were comfortable working with each other. Plus, we constantly laughed! We actually enjoyed working together and coming up with ideas.

Your wonderful ballad "For a Little While" closes Burt's film Gator, *and I'm wondering how you came to write that song for the film.*

I was performing in Las Vegas when Burt called one night and said, "I'm doing this movie called *Gator* and we need a love song. I'm walking away from the girl, saying goodbye and even though we were together for just a little while, I'll never forget her!" Well, he had pretty much told me what the song was about so I sat down between shows and wrote "For a Little While." I cut the demo next day with my pianist and sent it to Burt. He *loved* it! After Las Vegas, I flew down to Georgia where they were filming and stayed a couple of days. Later that week, I flew to Hawaii to play in Mac Davis' golf tournament and the day I flew back to L.A., Burt had a car pick me up at the airport and drive me straight to the recording studio. The orchestra was waiting and we recorded "For a Little While."

In the early 1990s, you and Burt collaborated on the hit TV show Evening Shade. *What do you recall of writing and composing that famous theme song?*

I was home one day and Burt called and said, "Did you watch the People's Choice Awards last night?" I said, "No, because I wasn't nominated for anything!" He said *Evening Shade* won several awards and they played a different song every time they went to the stage to accept the award. He said, "We don't have a theme song that anyone knows. Can you write one?" I said I'd give it a try. I knew that *Evening Shade* was this laid-back little southern town, just like I had grown up in, so I wrote the song, made a demo and sent it to Burt. My wife Dianne and I flew to L.A. a few days later and Burt had me come to the CBS studios. The producers of *Evening Shade*, Harry Thomason and Linda Bloodworth-Thomason, were there and asked me if I'd become music director of *Evening Shade* and sing my new theme song. I talked it over with my wife and we decided to move to L.A. for a couple of years. Dianne and Loni Anderson became the best of friends while Burt and I formed a company and we did several projects together over the years. My *Evening Shade* theme song was voted "Best Television Theme" and it won a BMI award. That song would have never happened without my friendship with Burt.

Considering all of the work you've done with Burt, what are your most treasured memories or favorite moments?

Burt was known to call out of the blue and say something like, "I'm doing a tribute to Carol Burnett on CBS day after tomorrow. Can you write a song and sing it to her on the show?" Naturally, I'm thinking, "He wants me to compose a song, lyrics and melody, arrange and produce it and to sing it *live* on TV the day after tomorrow?" and I said "Sure!" So I did it. Burt would do this a lot with many people, and it brought out the best in them. I don't think he ever asked me to do something he didn't think I could do.

Having known and worked with Burt intermittently throughout his long and prolific career, from the early days of his success right up through the height of his fame, I presume you would have a unique personal insight into how Burt worked on his craft and his art. What in your opinion made Burt Reynolds such a distinguished artist and such a tremendous star?

I think that no matter if he was in a drama or a comedy Burt always had that good ol' boy twinkle in his eye. Everybody loved him because he didn't take himself too seriously. He was the kind of guy that women wanted to date and guys wanted as a friend. He was my best friend for a long time. I was with him through the highs and the lows and I'm a better person for it. Burt loved being a movie star but he also loved life. Dianne and I will miss him.

Shamus

(1973)

"I see the cops are still using the same high-powered scientific methods of gathering information that have made them famous: If in doubt, ask the Family."—Shamus McCoy

Shamus opens like few other PG-rated films: An intimate couple is violently interrupted when a masked gang breaks into their bedroom brandishing flame throwers and set the couple on fire. As the carnage rages in the luxury boudoir, the gang steals a safe containing a fortune in diamonds.

Burt Reynolds evokes the spirit of Humphrey Bogart as New York private detective Shamus McCoy, a man with more than a few quirks of his own. He runs his business not out of an office but out of his dingy loft apartment, where he sleeps on a pool table; he is terrified of dogs but loves cats. McCoy, sleeping off a hangover, is awoken by a phone call requesting his presence at the mansion of eccentric diamond dealer E.J. Hume (Ron

Weyand). Hume is set on recovering the stolen diamonds and engages McCoy to retrieve them. The detective wonders why a millionaire would hire such a low-rent P.I. as he; Hume admits McCoy was not his first choice, but his fifty-third: "You could use the cash, and I like to work with people who need my money. It gives me a trump card."

McCoy gets information from his usual dodgy barroom and billiard hall sources and the trail leads to an ex-jock named Felix Montaigne (Alex Wilson) and his stunning sister Alexis (Dyan Cannon). The deeper McCoy digs, the more violently he is warned off. McCoy meets with a respected Mafia godfather who, over wine and pasta, hints at a complicated and treacherous web of intrigue involving illicit military arms dealing.

Reynolds' breezy banter and self-deprecating demeanor tempers the grittier elements of the picture, such as when stoolie Springy (Larry Block) arrives at McCoy's place only to find the detective lying in a full bath entirely clothed; McCoy says, "I'm taking a bath." "Taking a bath with your clothes on?" asks Springy. "Saves on laundry bills," McCoy sarcastically replies. This is the kind of deadpan humor that permeates the picture. *Shamus* uses much of the same kind of low-key satire of Robert Altman's *The Long Goodbye*, crafted with a wink and a nod to the film noir genre and the cynical private detectives of the 1940s, peppered with references to the definitive noir gumshoe, Philip Marlowe. The scene in which McCoy visits a book store looking for information only to end up seducing the female clerk (who is glamorous underneath her glasses and conservative attire) is straight out of *The Big Sleep*.

Shot in the New York City area, the production excellently utilizes plenty of grim, haunting locations for McCoy to follow his leads. Victor J. Kemper's photography serves the sordid milieu exquisitely. Unlike the previous year's *Fuzz*, which struggles to balance its blithe spirit with the dark and troubling plot, here director Buzz Kulik rarely allows the levity that Reynolds brings to the picture to overshadow the gravity of the proceedings, keeping *Shamus* sober and grounded in a seedy New York underbelly populated with unsa-

Cinematographer Victor J. Kemper's brilliantly skewed composition of Shamus McCoy in *Shamus* (1973).

vory characters. Unlike Bogart and his P.I. peers of the forties, McCoy is unable to skate through on steely cynicism alone. Far from invincible, he endures several back alley beat-downs where his smart aleck wit cannot save him.

The Man Who Loved Cat Dancing
(1973)

"One of these days, boy, that mouth of yours is going to get you killed."—Jay Grobart

Taciturn ex-con Jay Grobart (Reynolds) and his fellow reprobates Billy (Bo Hopkins), Dawes (Jack Warden) and Charlie (Jay Varela) pull off a daring train heist. In their efforts to evade the law, they abduct a beautiful bystander, Catherine (Sarah Miles). Tensions are fraught amongst the outlaw gang as the immoral and racist brutes Billy and Dawes clash with the principled, essentially decent Grobart and Charlie. Grobart's conscientious character is set up early on when he chides Dawes for opening fire and killing people during the robbery, "I told you I didn't want anybody killed back there!" Grobart scolds. "Yeah, well, I forgot," Dawes smugly replies. Billy also teases Grobart about his son having Indian blood, a jibe Grobart doesn't take too kindly, striking Billy and issuing a stark warning. Grobart's common law wife was a Native American woman named Cat Dancing; he was jailed for killing in a moment of rage her and the man who raped her. As the title declares, Grobart did indeed love Cat Dancing; he had sacrificed his way of life to be with her, having been ostracized from his community for marrying a Native American girl. Their son is now living on a Shoshone reserve with his uncle and Grobart hopes to reclaim him.

Catherine is similarly on the run, although in her case it isn't the law that she is trying to evade, but rather her refined but overbearing bourgeoisie husband, Willard Crocker (George Hamilton). Willard joins a posse headed up by Harvey Lapchance (Lee J. Cobb),

Reynolds as outlaw Jay Grobart in *The Man Who Loved Cat Dancing* (1973).

the Wells Fargo man assigned to retrieve the stolen money. In his pursuit of Catherine, Willard is less motivated by love of her than as he is for his bloodlust for those who insulted him by stealing his prized possession. Catherine finds herself attracted to the moody but sensitive Grobart, and their romance blossoms. The criminal gang falls apart as personal tensions plague their flight from the law.

The Man Who Loved Cat Dancing sees Reynolds returning to the western genre but this particular foray into cowboy country is miles from the playful antics of *Sam Whiskey* and the more routine action film registers of *100 Rifles*. It's a more somber and reflective melodrama, a bleak vision of the American West which follows the similarly sober genre entries *A Man Called Horse* (Elliot Silverstein, 1970), *Jeremiah Johnson* (Sydney Pollack, 1972), *McCabe & Mrs. Miller* (Robert Altman, 1971), *Ulzana's Raid* (Robert Aldrich, 1972), *The Hired Hand* (Peter Fonda, 1971), *Valdez is Coming* (Edwin Sherin, 1971) and *Soldier Blue* (Ralph Nelson, 1970). Competition in its year of release came in the form of two masterful pictures from genre veterans: Sam Peckinpah's *Pat Garrett and Billy the Kid* and Clint Eastwood's *High Plains Drifter*. In the company of such high-caliber pictures, *Cat Dancing* more than holds its own; it's as stark a meditation on the ruthlessness of frontier life as any other western of the decade.

In a male-dominated genre such as the Western, *Cat Dancing* is a picture of rare feminist alignment. Despite the male at the center of the film, it is Catherine with whom we most recognize and rely upon for emotional cues. She endures several rape attempts and repeatedly endures lascivious behavior. When a band of Indians attacks the group, Dawes offers her to them as a sexual sacrifice in return for sparing his life and money. Grobart responds with action, though Catherine has a forgiving heart and asks that the Indians not to be hurt in retaliation. Grobart instantly betrays her and resorts to retributive justice. Further empathy is depicted after Catherine suffers several instances of sexual abuse at the hands of Billy Bowen yet she still comforts him on his deathbed; then after being raped by Dawes, she cannot bring herself to wound or kill him in defense, something taken care of with no hesitation by Grobart. Unlike the deliberately heightened sexuality of Raquel Welch in *100 Rifles* and Angie Dickinson in *Sam Whiskey*, Catherine is presented as more than a mere object of desire. She is brutalized for her sexuality rather than aestheticized. Both Welch and Dickinson playfully and knowingly used their seductive qualities to lure men for pleasurable or strategic advantage and those films dutifully linger upon their sexually stimulating attributes, but at no point here does director Richard C. Sarafian ogle Miles with his camera; her brief moments of nudity are tastefully shot and never gazed upon to satisfy the prurient interests of the audience. Perhaps owing to the picture's leisurely pace, there is no immediate effort to set up a contrived romance between Grobart and Crocker; both characters are too busy escaping some form of psychological torment. and Sarafian allows the romance to find the pair in its own time, when both have let their guard down just enough to recognize that they are similarly lost, tortured souls seeking connection.

The film's femme-western initiative is no accident. The screenplay was written by Eleanor Perry, based on a 1972 novel by Marilyn Durham. Perry's dramatic pedigree was solid, having written a number of psycho-sexual romantic melodramas directed by her husband Frank Perry: *Ladybug Ladybug* (1963), *The Swimmer* (1968), *Last Summer* (1969) and *Diary of a Mad Housewife* (1970). It's easy to see why *Cat Dancing* appealed to Perry: the strong, independent female refusing domesticity and struggling for sexual and social liberation while enduring objectification by a parade of brutish and boorish men. Catherine flees her abusive husband despite his riches, instigating a romance with Grobart and even deciding to bear his child, thus thumbing her nose at her bourgeois life in earnest.

The decisive action that provides the forward momentum of the narrative is almost entirely dictated upon Catherine's will, essentially making her the hero of the piece. For Perry, the production was a professional debacle; her version of the script seemingly wasn't enough to appease co-producer Martin Poll, who shut Perry out of her creative side of the bargain. Perry soon discovered that her work was being undermined and rewritten by another screenwriter. She said,

> I'm about halfway through the screenplay. So I decide to take a break. I walk down the hall a few offices from me, and I see this guy pounding away at his typewriter. "What are you working on?" I ask him, casually. "I'm writing *The Man Who Loved Cat Dancing*," he says. Of course, I nearly blow my cork and head into the producer's office demanding an explanation. He tells me the other guy is merely writing a back-up script in case mine doesn't work! What a hell of a rotten trick to do to the writer.[1]

One could speculate that said screenwriter was William W. Norton, who performed uncredited writing duties on the picture (and also worked on the Reynolds pictures *Sam Whiskey*, *White Lightning* and *Gator*).

In this slow-burning picture, Reynolds delivers a terrific performance which is allowed time to breathe and unfurl with grace and sensitivity, even exceeding his more celebrated role in *Deliverance* in terms of nuance and range. Grobart is not a traditional hero and it was brave of the actor to accept it just as he was becoming America's favorite movie star. Grobart is a flawed man haunted by demons past and present, his ennui compounded by a sense of displacement at having lost his family as well as losing the respect and honor he previously enjoyed as a soldier. He is an inherently good man blind to racial and social divisions yet lured to violence on a whim in response to acts of aggression against the "Cats" in his life: Dancing and Catherine. Reynolds consummately dramatizes the conflict at the heart of his character and it would be quite a while before the actor again disappeared into a role so completely. The iconic characters he portrayed in succeeding films are almost impossible to consider as mutually exclusive from Reynolds' own larger-than-life persona.

Note

1. William Froug, *How I Escaped from Gilligan's Island: And Other Misadventures of a Hollywood Writer-Producer* (Wisconsin: The University of Wisconsin Press, 2005), p. 154.

White Lightning

(1973)

"My name's Gator McClusky. You know why I'm here, don't you?"—Gator McClusky

White Lightning opens with a shocking title sequence: Two teenage boys, bound and gagged, are led to their death in a desolate Arkansas lake by a pair of law enforcement offi-

A pair of counterculture teenagers are led to a swampy death by corrupt law enforcers in *White Lightning* **(1973).**

cers, including the menacing sheriff of Bogan County, J.C. Connors (Ned Beatty). One of the boys was Donny McClusky, the brother of Bobby "Gator" McClusky, imprisoned for running moonshine and non-payment of liquor taxes. Donny's "crime" was belonging to a group of hippie friends, countercultural college kids whose civil rights protesting made too much noise for the conservative Sheriff Connors' liking. Gator only has one year left on his sentence, but with his blood boiling in anticipation of revenge for his brother's slaying he uses his knowledge of illicit dealings between local moonrunners and the sheriff to strike a deal with federal authorities so that he will be granted temporary release to go undercover to expose the shady operation. Some locals laugh at the idea of McClusky going after Connors, he who "owns Bogan County."

Upon McClusky's return to his home town, we learn he is something of a stud, with comely young ladies fawning over him. McClusky loves the attention but he is fixed on revenge and the film wastes little time in getting down to business. A quick stop at the McClusky family home gives us an insight into the quiet rural farm life the elder McCluskys lead, the scene also serving to tell us how Donny's lifestyle led to his death. We also learn that Mr. and Mrs. McClusky aren't too happy with Gator "taking down names of liquor people" for the federal government to prosecute; their son's quest for vengeance is both dangerous and, to their way of life, immoral.

Gator is introduced to Dude Watson (Matt Clark), a stock car racer and small-time criminal on probation, and the two are joined by local moonrunner Roy Boone (Bo Hopkins) and his woman Lou (Jennifer Billingsley). Lou isn't terribly bright and she proves a source of tension between McClusky and Boone. The quartet infiltrates the illegal whiskey business in order to ensnare the corrupt officials who wield power within Bogan County's civic corridors. However, penal justice is not what Gator has in mind for Connors. Throughout the picture we learn more of Connors' corruption, such as his misappropriation of county funds, for which he is under investigation. The chief instigator of this review is U.S.

Senator Benjamin Fairfield, a former friend and football teammate of Connors' whose work took him to the high offices of Capitol Hill while Connors remained in Bogan County to become the town's sheriff, a title previously held by Fairfield's father. Connors believes he is carrying on the tradition of law enforcement that Sheriff Fairfield believed in, and perceives Senator Fairfield as betraying the old way of life and law of Bogan County. This subplot supports the notion that there is a duel between Old South and New South ideals.

Indignant at this perceived slight against the traditions of Bogan County, Connors even gives a speech that suggests a certain nobility to his shameful endeavors:

> What's it the business of any income tax federal revenuer, anyway, if Pot Willoughby and any other old moonshiner wants to come into this office to put down his paper sack full of money, like he's been doin' for years, and I take that money and I spread it around among 25 men in my department who do not make enough off the taxpayer to buy their wives a washer, a drier and all them things every American family is supposed to have?

Connors promises that Bogan County will continue just like Sheriff Fairfield ran it, no matter what Senator Fairfield and his Washington cronies have planned.

White Lightning is one of the key films in Burt Reynolds' career. As Gator McClusky, he introduced the personality that would endear him to millions of fans: tough yet caring, macho but sensitive. For better or worse, Gator McClusky established his definitive screen persona. If Reynolds would become something of a Southern folk icon with the mammoth success and popularity of *Smokey and the Bandit*, there's a distinct possibility that these seeds of approbation for the cinematic scofflaw as working class hero could well have been sown in *White Lightning*.

McClusky is initially just another rebellious good ol' boy doing time for running 'shine, but just as the Bandit is a benign individual, McClusky too ultimately errs on the side of the law. Like Tom Laughlin's *Billy Jack* (1971), *White Lightning* presents itself as a definitive piece of macho action cinema, a rough vigilante thriller augmented with fisticuffs and

Gator McClusky (Reynolds) arouses the suspicions of Big Bear (R.G. Armstrong) in *White Lightning* (1973).

vehicular stunts to appease adventure junkies, yet the subtext suggests that progressive politics are what drives its aggressive hero to take a moral stance and act accordingly. Conversely, and like Laughlin's character, McClusky uses violence as a means of eradicating bigotry and hatred in a small town mired in such, a town that sees the counterculture and its attendant rebelliousness as a threat to Old South morals. McClusky is torn between the opposing sensibilities of the South; he accepts a life of petty criminality in the guise of tradition (transporting whiskey) yet is sympathetic to the emerging countercultural values of the youth, those which threaten his hometown heritage. Meanwhile, the representative of law and of older conservative values, Sheriff Connors, is depicted unequivocally as a corrupt racist.

But the lines of good and bad in regard to these opposing philosophies are blurred; McClusky at one stage seems to harbor the same attitudes that fuel Connors and his ilk. When a van passes McClusky on the street with a slogan that reads "Legalize Marijuana," he takes offense to "them long-haired hippie freaks; pot-smoking bastards," fearing such liberal acceptance of drugs will undermine the illicit moonshine business and thus upset town traditions and incomes. The act of producing and transporting illegal liquor is seen as less a criminal endeavor and more a way of life; the influx of drugs, burgeoning politicization, and rallying of the youth threatens the black market economy that has supported the Bogan County community for generations.

Similarly, when McClusky learns what happened the night of Donny's death (a booze-fueled anti-war college demonstration turned nasty after Sheriff Connors and his deputy broke it up and traded insults with Donny and his friend), he shifts the blame onto the countercultural movement before accepting that the kids were merely exercising their right to protest. "What the hell's he got to protest about in Bogan County?" McClusky asks rhetorically, "You protest up north, in New York and places like that." Even something as seemingly innocent as a group of college kids staging a sit-in with a six-pack is viewed with suspicions of subversion, something progressive and potentially threatening to traditions and the old ways of Bogan County.

The Gator McClusky of *White Lightning* is very much rooted in the down and dirty life of the anti-hero, but by the time of its 1976 sequel *Gator*, McClusky was a benign malefactor along the lines of future Reynolds protagonists The Bandit, J.J. McLure, W.W. Bright and Walker Ellis. *Gator* crafts an environment of wild stunts, grotesque cartoon villains, heightened violence of little consequence, and a smoothening of McClusky's rougher edges; the sequel displays his nurturing side in looking after his young daughter and elderly father, as well as cultivating a romance with a cosmopolitan lady. The recurring motifs of these Reynolds characters, that which could be attributable to their popularity with audiences, is their the ability to flout the law to an almost comic degree while also putting paid to the more malevolent villains of the pieces (be they booze smugglers, road rivals or rogue lawmen). These characters are able to claim the valor of the moralistic, noble hero while also enjoying the spoils of the anti-hero: engaging in reckless behavior with impunity, enjoying the company of beautiful women, and reveling in being a folk hero. There is no suffering, repression or guilt to be paid for the social disregard that these Reynolds avatars enjoy; they roam the cinematic landscape unscathed and indifferent to the consequences of their endeavors.

While the comedic element would be introduced to a greater degree in following pictures, *White Lightning* takes a more sober approach to the material and its themes. The opening execution of Donny McClusky and his friend commences the film on an unnerving note of menace and dread which are sustained throughout. Much of the credit for this can be attributed to Ned Beatty, who is sterling as the intimidating Sheriff Connors, exuding the kind of brooding intensity that is in exact opposition to the cheerful innocence, later corrupted, that he brought to Bobby Trippe in *Deliverance*. As Connors, Beatty makes you believe the fear instilled in someone like Dude Watson when he says, "When them tax boys put me on a stand in front of a jury, I'm gonna lie…. Five years in a federal pen is no picnic, but J.C. Connors can put me under."

The release of *White Lightning* was a seminal moment in the history of the Southern "hick" flick, embodying the best ramshackle qualities of the fast and the furious B-movies and the skillful aesthetic execution of a well-produced studio picture. However, it is less the out-and-out action extravaganza that its reputation may suggest (a quality more attributable to its sequel). Director Joseph Sargent brings a menacingly quiet and atmospheric quality to the piece that tempers the moments of action.

The "moonshine movie" genre gathered steam in the years following the success of *White Lightning*, though it wasn't a new phenomenon. Robert Mitchum starred in perhaps the first mainstream treatment of the subject, *Thunder Road*, which was released as far back as 1958 and became a cult classic in the interim. Moonshiners were featured as either the protagonists or antagonists of many hard-edged crime thrillers and sleazy exploitation pictures of the 1970s, including *Walking Tall* (Phil Karlson, 1973), *Hot Summer in Barefoot County* (Will Zens, 1974), *Moonrunners* (Gy Waldron, 1975), *Moonshine County Express* (Gus Trikonis, 1977) and *Bad Georgia Road* (John C. Broderick, 1977). While it is not technically a moonshine movie, *Smokey and the Bandit* (1978) could also be considered part of this canon, given its plot concerning the illegal running of Coors beer across state lines. Reynolds notes that the formula for his success in these kinds of pictures is a simple blend of comedy and action:

> Compare *White Lightning* to *Thunder Road*, which was a classic moonshine movie. Robert Mitchum never told any jokes, but in my picture, I was joking almost all of the time. I think it sells tickets and gets your point across…. You've got to like the people in the picture for it to be successful, for it to be a major picture.[1]

Note

1. Bernhardt J. Hurwood, *Burt Reynolds* (New York: Quick Fox, 1979), pp. 84, 85.

The Longest Yard

(1974)

"Shaving points off a game … man, that's un–American."—Caretaker

Former football player Paul Crewe (Burt Reynolds) whiles away his days barely servicing his bored Sugar Mama, Melissa (Anitra Ford), after a point-shaving scandal cost him his illustrious career. Crewe turns nasty after Melissa humiliates him one too many times, physically assaulting her and stealing her Citroen SM. He parks it in a river following a high-speed chase with the cops. Crewe is tracked down to a bar and, after a brawl with officers, he is arrested and sentenced to 18 months at Citrus State Prison. The institution's tyrannical Warden Rudolph Hazen (Eddie Albert) manages a semi-pro football team made up of his prison guards and tries to solicit Crewe's help in coaching the team in anticipation of an upcoming championship game, offering him a pardon in return for his participation. In fear of the sadistic guard and current team coach, Captain Wilhelm Knauer (Ed Lauter), Crewe refuses Hazen's request and is put on swamp reclamation duties. Crewe eventually agrees to arrange for an exhibition game and puts together what he calls his "Mean Machine," a team comprised of the prison's most feared inmates, including himself as quarterback. The cons are more than happy to use this opportunity as a means of attacking the guards on the opposing team. The game becomes a battle not just of scoring points, but of scoring retribution for past grievances within the prison walls, with certain cons becoming players merely to inflict pain and suffering upon various guards. Hazen creates a dilemma for Crewe when he orders the already disgraced star to throw the game so that the guards can triumph, threatening to rescind Crewe's parole if he fails to comply.

To many, *The Longest Yard* is the quintessential Burt Reynolds film; the picture was the ideal property for the actor to leap into superstardom post–*Deliverance*. This was evident from the film's first preview screenings, from which Loews Theatres president Bernard Myerson reported to Paramount head Frank Yablans, "In all my years of attending previews, I have never seen such an overwhelming response from an audience as I did from *The Longest Yard*. They cheered, they stomped, they whistled, they applauded wildly."[1]

It's not hard to understand why audiences embraced Reynolds with this picture, as the actor harnesses all of the comic playfulness of his television appearances into the macho milieu of a sports picture, utilizing his two greatest talents: acting and athleticism. Reynolds recalls director Robert Aldrich's preconceived notion of the actor: "When I met Aldrich, he said, 'I hear you're tough, I hear you're a good guy and the crew loves you, I hear you like to do your own stunts because you think you're some macho putz ... but you play ball, that's important to me.'"[2]

And with that, Aldrich set about creating as authentic a sporting environment as possible, drafting in professionals, semi-pros, actors and stunt doubles to play the game. The director utilized Reynolds' own gridiron experience and placed him amongst them. Ray Nitschke, the tough linebacker for the Green Bay Packers, appears as the aggressive Bogdanski. Mike Henry, linebacker for the Pittsburgh Steelers and the Los Angeles Rams, plays Rasmussen; he went on to co-star in the *Smokey and the Bandit* trilogy. Other football luminaries appearing include Joe Kapp (as Walking Boss), Ernie

Reynolds established one of his most iconic characters, Paul "Wrecking" Crewe, in *The Longest Yard* (1974).

Wheelwright (as Spooner), Ray Ogden (as Schmidt) and Sonny Sixkiller (as Indian). According to Reynolds,

> We worked hard to make the game real. Nitschke might have worked a little too hard. He hit me a couple of shots that made me feel like I'd exploded. I tried not to let anybody know how much they hurt. We had some semi-pros from Savannah in the film who were out to knock my head off, but I was pretty well protected.... A strange thing started happening. I'd look at the faces in the huddle, and this wasn't a movie any more. It wasn't even a game, it was a battle.[3]

In an attempt to keep his star from becoming a target of unruly footballers, Aldrich staged the game in such a way that the defensive team never knew how the offensive were scripted to play. "Under these circumstances," Aldrich recalls, "I thought it would be reasonably safe that Burt would not get hurt and could do much of his 'stuff,' thereby enriching the film."[4]

While the realistic sporting elements are essential to the appeal and longevity of the picture, what makes *The Longest Yard* a unique experience is Aldrich's idiosyncratic storytelling style which is peppered with moments of eccentricity and unusual character performances. For examples of such, look no further than the warden's elaborately coiffed secretary Miss Tott (Bernadette Peters) with her spectacular honeycomb hairdo; she is a lustful lady "as far from Tallahassee as the prisoners"; the bodybuilding Rotka (Tony Cacciotti), who exercises in front of Crewe every chance he gets in an absurdist show of strength; and the weaseling Unger (Charles Tyne) with his catchphrase "How do you like them apples, superstar?" These quirky personalities with their strange line readings and peculiar behavior instill an otherwise hard-edged film with an oddball sense of humor; most of it works while certain other ideas don't. Perhaps the only scene that feels shoehorned in and entirely misjudged is the silent slapstick of the swamp fight between Crewe and Rotka, in which the pair comically dump shovels of mud into each other's boots and pants before wrestling in the mire. The scene is scored as if it were a Laurel and Hardy skit, building in physical and musical momen-

The Mean Machine reigns supreme: Reynolds in *The Longest Yard* (1974).

tum until it turns into an all-out brawl in the brown. In and of itself, the scene is well-timed and quite funny, but in the midst of the jailhouse grit, the intense instances of violence, and bone-crunching sporting mayhem, the farcical routine feels off-tone. The picture excels *not* with this kind of physical comedy, but with its thrilling action set pieces, such as the opening chase sequence choreographed and directed by stuntman Hal Needham, as well as the brutal on-field action which takes over the entire final third of the picture.

Aldrich, one of the Old Hollywood studio filmmakers who left an indelible artistic impression with his body of work, continued his fascination with certain key themes in *The Longest Yard*. Paul Crewe is another of Aldrich's misanthropic men of redemption and men of subversion. In his fall from grace and now wallowing in faded glory and the humiliation of being the kept man of a rich socialite, Crewe steers quite literally off the course of mainstream life and onto a dark path of imprisonment to ultimately regain a sense of self-esteem. We first meet Crewe as selfish and self-pitying, perhaps even savage, as we see in his physical brutality with women. Like another of Aldrich's alpha males in crisis, Mike Hammer from *Kiss Me Deadly* (1955), Crewe's is a life of fast cars, hard liquor and loose women, vacuous and self-destructive in the extreme. Aldrich's males are often men out of time, looking to the past for reassurance that there was once something better and more meaningful in their lives. In *Hustle*, Aldrich's second collaboration with Reynolds, the lead character seeks solace in nostalgia and the art of yesteryear, old movies and music. The entire plot of convicts (as heroes) vs. prison guards (as villains) plays nicely into Aldrich's recurring theme of nonconformist anti-authoritarianism, a theme which affords the director's subversive protagonists a platform to confront moral and physical oppression in an act of personal valor and absolution. Just as Lee Marvin's rebellious Major Reisman in *The Dirty Dozen* turns a gang of unlikely prisoners into a functioning unit, so too does Crewe shape a team of society's castaways into a formidable sporting unit to prevail over their oppressive captors, even just for one afternoon. By flouting Hazen's blackmail attempts and winning the game, Crewe may well endure hard time for the remainder of his sentence at Citrus State Prison, but he regained the important self-esteem that will carry him through the remainder of his time there and back into life on the outside. Crucially, Crewe doesn't do it alone; he is not an infallible hero capable of turning the game or his own life around by himself; it takes the friendship of Caretaker and the skill and wisdom of rugged old pro Nate Scarborough (Michael Conrad) for Crewe to reach the end of the road to redemption. "You've only got two things left they can't sweat out of you or beat out of you," Scarborough says. "Your balls."

Aldrich may have made more outwardly "important" films (the anti-war picture *Attack!* [1956], the Depression-era *Emperor of the North* [1973] as well as his discourses on mental illness, *Autumn Leaves* [1956] and *What Ever Happened to Baby Jane?* [1962]), but *The Longest Yard* takes the director's themes, ideas and auteur resolve and distils them into a mainstream product that is as rich as any in his filmography.

Notes

1. Nancy Streebeck, *The Films of Burt Reynolds* (New York: Citadel Press, 1982), p. 50.
2. Hurwood, Bernhardt J., *Burt Reynolds* (New York, Quick Fox, 1979), p. 80.
3. Burt Reynolds, "Doing Time on The Longest Yard," DVD Supplement, *The Longest Yard*, Paramount Home Entertainment, 2005.
4. Streebeck, p. 50.

At Long Last Love

(1975)

"You remind me of someone I'm really quite fond of … me!"—Michael Oliver Pritchard III

At Long Last Love (20th Century–Fox) is director Peter Bogdanovich's painstakingly crafted love letter to the screwball musical pictures and sophisticated society comedies of the 1930s.

The story, such as it is, contemplates the nature of monogamy as two idle bourgeois New York couples and two of their ne'er-do-well friends become entangled in each other's love lives. Burt Reynolds plays spoiled heir Michael Oliver Pritchard III, a bored playboy who errantly and quite literally runs into Broadway star Kitty O'Kelly (Madeline Kahn) while dangerously drinking and dangling from the side of his moving chauffeured vehicle. Meanwhile, broke heiress Brooke Carter (Cybill Shepherd) meets suave Italian punter Johnny Spanish (Duilio Del Prete) at the racetrack. As if the romantic complications of the four leads aren't enough amore for one film, Brooke's associate Elizabeth (Eileen Brennan) and Michael's driver Rodney (John Hillerman) become embroiled in a steamy and no less contentious liaison.

Bogdanovich was inspired to write the film after being gifted a book of Cole Porter lyrics. The director, acting as an almost Svengali figure, was an instrumental force behind his wife Shepherd's 1974 album *Cybill Does It … to Cole Porter*. Conductor-arranger Artie Butler had previously worked with Bogdanovich on the music for his excellent homage to the screwball comedy *What's Up, Doc?* (1972) and the two reteamed here for a run-through of selections from the Cole songbook. In an unusual move for a contemporary musical film, the actors resorted to a complicated technique from the early days of film sound: The actors sang live to an off-camera keyboard rendition of the respective song, which was broadcast to them via a specially made earpiece which Bogdanovich had Fox commission for $25,000. Shepherd recalls the unorthodox method:

> In movie musicals, actors usually record the vocals in a studio long before the film is shot and then lip-sync to those tracks when filming so the sound of their voices is perfected with millions of dollars of studio enhancement. Audiences are accustomed to hearing this kind of technical quality, which can't be duplicated in live performance. But Peter was more interested in spontaneity than perfection. Inspired by the 1930s Lubitsch musicals, when it was impossible to voice and orchestra separately, he loved the subtle changes in tempo afforded by musicians following the actors. He asked the sound department at Fox to invent a process by which he could record the actors' voices live while we heard a pianist on the set through tiny receivers in our ears, the antennae wired through our hair.[1]

The six ensemble players offer their considerable charm and beauty while Laszlo Kovacs' extraordinary cinematography triumphs over almost every other aspect of the picture, framing the kitsch monochromatic art deco production design in stunning compositions. All of this makes it easier to digest the most egregious element of the film: the incessant songs. With so many tunes rolled out and so little time for narrative or character development, the picture becomes weighed down in its own self-indulgence. Kahn is given a solo performance which is the only true show-stopper, "Find Me a Primitive Man," from Kitty O'Kelly's provocative Broadway show. Careful study of Reynolds choreography during

Cinematographer Laszlo Kovacs' stunning framing of Peter Bogdanovich's decadent characters: left to right, Duilio Del Prete, Cybill Shepherd, Madeline Kahn and Reynolds in *At Long Last Love* (1975).

the musical numbers sees the actor daring to step out of his comfort zone to deliver on his requirements with enough grace, dignity and humor as to avoid any potential foolishness that would render the performance as laughable. Reynolds is a suitable substitute for the genteel soft-shoe men of Old Hollywood such as Fred Astaire and Gene Kelly; the virtuosity of the dancing is highlighted by Kovacs' full-length head-to-toe framing, a filming method that allows the audience to marvel at the intricate footwork on display. This was often done in the films of Astaire and Kelly to privilege the performers and their skill.

Bogdanovich emerged from what was seen as an expensive 1974 vanity project, *Daisy Miller*, with his reputation sullied by the film's poor financial performance and having broken his winning streak after the consecutive success of *The Last Picture Show* (1971), *What's Up, Doc?* (1972), and *Paper Moon* (1973). While *Daisy Miller* received positive notices in some quarters of the press, *At Long Last Love* was universally loathed, shot down with the kind of vehemence normally reserved for the truly reviled. By the time it appeared, reviewers were ready to tear down Bogdanovich for having broken the ranks of the film critic. Judith Crist of *TV Guide* personally warned Bogdanovich of his impending slaughter when she told him the knives were out for him. Was it merely objective criticism or was it the jealousy of former peers? Was it that Bogdanovich dared to make a blatantly Old Hollywood production in the midst of the New Hollywood movement? One would argue that although *At Long Last Love* is heavily indebted to the Golden Age of Hollywood, it remains a piece of work so definitive of its own time and milieu—the artistically indulgent mid-seventies—that it refuses to tie things up as neatly as Fred and Ginger would have done 40 years prior.

Regardless of the aesthetic brilliance and sheer star wattage illuminating the screen, *At Long Last Love* limped towards a $1.5 million box office tally, not even clawing back a third of its $6 million production cost. This, coupled with the scathing reviews, meant the film was prematurely pulled by Fox. According to Boganovich,

> The picture was all right in production and I thought it was gonna be pretty good. What happened was that afterward we got rushed. We had one disastrous preview in San Jose and I recut it, and we had another preview in Denver and it was 100 percent better. And then we screwed it up.... I went back and paid Fox $70,000 to let me recut it again myself.... The picture came out with the worst kind of reviews and general reaction, and unfortunately when that kind of thing happens, it's almost impossible for anyone to be objective. The only way that picture will work is one hundred years from now after everybody's dead, and somebody uncovers it and says, "Hmmm. This is kind of interesting."[2]

Bogdanovich is still around to observe the critical reconsideration of *At Long Last Love*, something that's owed to the accidental discovery of an unauthorized cut which resembled Bogdanovich's original, pre-release assembly. Bogdanovich learned that this version of *At Long Last Love* had been uploaded to YouTube before finding out it was also available for streaming on Netflix. Baffled, he endeavored to find out how this cut was made available.

> I screwed up the picture in the theatrical version because I was badgered.... I made another version for television and for years people would come up to me and say, "Why did that movie get such bad reviews, I saw it on television, it's good!" and I'd say, "Well, it's not the version that was released." I didn't know that what they were referring to wasn't that version that I had cut, but rather this one that had been cut by the 20th Century–Fox editorial department. A guy there named Jim Blakeley ... was a big Cole Porter fan and loved musicals ... he looked at it when we first made it and said, "This is a good picture" and we slowly ruined the picture and he said, "To hell with this!" and he put it back. So from about 1978 or 1979, that version that he did that I didn't see until about a month or two ago was playing all over the place and I didn't know it. People have been saying, "It's a good movie!" [*At Long Last Love*] was loathed, a movie that Cybill Shepherd and I really loved, and then it was so destroyed and mutilated and so hated that we said we don't ever want to talk about it. And now it's like having a child that's been mutilated come back to you whole, it's great! When I look at it now, I say "How did we do this picture?!"[3]

Seen today in Bogdanovich's ultimate, final cut presentation, *At Long Last Love* is indeed a delightfully evocative and lavish piece of old-fashioned entertainment. The director crafted an idyllically decadent world without consequence, a playground of wine, women and song, where the most frightful thing one could imagine encroaching upon such a charmed existence is an uncouth hangover, or, God forbid, boredom. The characters here are mere delivery devices for lines which lead into songs, and that is exactly what this entire enterprise is all about. There is no room for pathos, drama or any kind of subtext at all, and that is perhaps its greatest flaw. A film of this commercial magnitude cannot coast by merely on nostalgia and sex appeal, but taken from the perspective of a loving tribute to the essential elements of the classic musicals, it does feel as though Bogdanovich deliberately wanted to dispense with such trivialities as plot and character; he knows that all we really want to see in a picture like this are song-and-dance numbers and so he duly indulges us. Shepherd said:

> Today many people actually love *At Long Last Love* but when it came out, it was almost universally ravaged. Considering that this frothy cinematic cocktail was released in 1975, just as the country was reeling from a post–Watergate malaise combined with a serious recession, the timing could not have been worse. Though defending it in public, Peter and I privately referred to *At Love Last Love* as our debacle. There was tremendous pressure from the studio to get the movie out in a hurry, and Peter felt he was talked into some bad editing choices, which he would spend $60,000 of his own money to cor-

rect. The film was one of the last to be shown before Radio City Music Hall closed its doors for years, prompting Orson Welles to chastise us, "You shut down the fucking Rockettes!" The film community was thrilled; they'd been waiting for us to fail.[4]

Reynolds said that *At Long Last Love* was "not as bad a film as it was reviewed. I mean, nothing could be that bad." He continued:

> What was reviewed was Cybill Shepherd and Peter Bogdanovich's relationship. You see, Peter Bogdanovich has done something that all critics will never forgive him for doing. That is, stop being a critic, go make a film, and have that film *The Last Picture Show* become enormously successful. Well, what he did then was go on talk shows and be rather arrogant and talk about how bad critics are. That was the final straw. So they were waiting with their hatchets and knives and whatever. And along came Peter, who finally gave them something they could kill him with. Unfortunately, there I was, between Cybill's broad shoulders and Peter's ego. And I got buried with them.[5]

Notes

1. Cybill Shepherd with Aimee Lee Ball, *Cybill Disobedience: My Autobiography* (Great Britain: Ebury Press, 2000), p. 140.

2. J. Thomas Harris, "Peter Bogdanovich Interview," in *Peter Bogdanovich: Interviews*, ed. Peter Tonguette (Mississippi: University of Mississippi Press, 2015) [n.p.].

3. "Peter Bogdanovich Interview—The Seventh Art," uploaded by The Seventh Art, May 13, 2012, https://www.youtube.com/watch?v=MLOhLTB4QoU.

4. Shepherd and Lee Ball, p. 142.

5. Nancy Streebeck, *The Films of Burt Reynolds* (NJ, New Tork: Citadel Press, 1982), p. 175.

W.W. and the Dixie Dancekings

(1975)

"The best thing they got going for them is you, cutie-pie—a combination of horse manure and sincerity...."—Rosie, of Rosie's Nashville Corral

"Once upon a time, in the carefree days of 1957, a legendary hero roamed the southern United States in search of romance and adventure...."

So begins *W.W. and the Dixie Dancekings*, one of the funniest and most delightful films of the Burt Reynolds *oeuvre*. W.W. Bright (Reynolds), a gas station stick-up artist, bumps into a touring country band that unwittingly harbors him while he evades the law. After being spotted by Trooper Carson (played by stuntman Hal Needham), Bright crashes a dancehall performance by the band and cons his way into their hearts. Posing as a music promoter, Bright wards off the suspicious trooper while telling the band he would like to help out by taking them from the dingy stages of amateur open mic bars to the hallowed music halls of Nashville. Dixie (Conny Van Dyke) is smitten with Bright while Wayne (Jerry Reed) is suspicious of the charming huckster.

Bright is a disgruntled former employee of SOS (Southland Oil System), the gas company whose branches he now targets. A most polite gentleman thief who wields nothing more dangerous than a water pistol, Bright compensates the elderly workers that he sticks up with a portion of his takings, knowing the men slog and toil for a mere $40 per week while the company makes $1 million in profits per day. Bright's one request of his captives is that they give the police a false description of him. As they accompany Bright while he robs various gas stations on their way to Nashville, the Dixie Dancekings are now considered accomplices. Because of Bright's conspicuous Oldsmobile Rocket 88 car, Deacon John Wesley Gore (Art Carney) is soon in hot pursuit. Gore is an evangelical former lawman hired by SOS to track Bright down.

Popular songwriter Country Bull (Ned Beatty), a lecherous and egotistical man, offers to write the Dixie Dancekings a hit for $1000. In order to come up with the cash, Bright convinces the band members to rob a bank, the Golden Goose Savings and Loan, which happens to be owned by SOS ("The first drive-in bank in the South!"). Escaping after the heist, Bright decides to leave the band for their own safety, but upon hearing a new song written by Wayne he forgets about Bull and the need for further cash and decides to stay with the band for a concert at the Grand Ole Opry. This proves dangerous as Gore has set a trap to catch his man there. But the devout deacon hits upon a moral and ethical snafu as he hauls Bright to the jailhouse. The clock strikes 12 midnight, ushering in the Sabbath, and Deacon Gore intones, "The book says 'break the Sabbath and lose thy soul,' Exodus 20: Verse 10." And being a man of God, he sets Bright free.

Much of the film's humor is derived from a sense of anti-authoritarian anarchy, as the law, big business and religious fanaticism all provide targets for satire. While these institutions are ripe for comedy and castigation, the picture's scofflaws are presented as a band of naive innocents who are untouchable by danger. They exist on Road Runner–like immunity which, along with the use of comical optical effects (wipes, text zooms), gives the picture a cartoonish edge. Whenever anything as threatening or as real as violence, sex or even bad language appear (Bright chastises Dixie for swearing when she says "dammit"), the picture reverts to its comical tone and playfully skirts around any serious questions that arise.

In perhaps one of the picture's narrative flaws, we are never quite sure if Dixie and Wayne are or were an item; it would certainly explain Wayne's early skepticism about Bright's motives and also Dixie's resistance to Bright's attempts to seduce her. Conversely, when Bright threatens to leave his new surrogate family so he can take sole responsibility for his criminal actions, Dixie offers herself to him ("Can we do it in the backseat?"), only for him to refuse the casual carnal encounter when he overhears the band rehearsing a potential hit song. Sex, like using real firearms and even cussing, would render impure the innocence of our heroes, and therefore when presented with an opportunity to seize upon a sexual encounter with Dixie, Bright instantly dismisses it in favor of getting the band to the Grand Ole Opry with their new song. Even though vengeance and profit motivate Bright and the band, respectively, they outgrow these desires the closer they get to Nashville, whereas the supposed paragons of morality and abstinence, Deacon Gore and his paymaster, SOS chairman Elton Bird, are shown to be gross exaggerations of greed, excess and decadence. What ultimately motivates the gang's growing dependence on each other is a sense of family and unity, as we see them blissfully enjoying chicken wings in a dingy room, or enjoying a campfire sing-along of "I Got the Dirty Car Blues" with Uncle Furry.

Having bowed out of the starring role in 20th Century–Fox's *Zardoz* due to illness (Sean Connery took over), Reynolds was still committed to make a picture for the studio and declared his interest in making *Dixie Dancekings*. Shooting began in late 1974 on location in and around Nashville; it was yet another "perfect fit" vehicle for Reynolds, playing a quick-witted con man with an eye for the ladies and a taste for the good life, a likable character which would further establish his attractive screen persona. Reynolds, a fan of country music, was surrounded by some of the Nashville music scene's leading stars, with whom good times were shared off-set drinking and playing music. The film was a moderate hit and served to introduce Jerry Reed to the Burt Reynolds stock company.

Production was far from a smooth affair. Director John G. Avildsen came to the picture with a great degree of respect from the film community, having made the well-received *Joe* (1970) and *Save the Tiger* (1973), with the latter boasting an Oscar-winning performance from Jack Lemmon. Avildsen was an emerging auteur who went on to massive commercial success directing *Rocky* (1976), *The Karate Kid* (1984) and various sequels to both. But while his work with Sylvester Stallone and Ralph Macchio was conducive to continued critical and financial success, *Dixie Dancekings* proved to be his first and last collaborative effort with Reynolds. Reynolds found Avildsen to be "a picky, arrogant little man, with an entourage of pot-smoking film school eggheads."[1] Avildsen had his own words to say about the discord between them: "That proved to be one of the most unhappy experiences of my career. At a certain point I did not have the knack of getting what I wanted and make him happy."[2] Avildsen was meticulous in preparation, storyboarding to excess, rehearsing to perfection, thus leaving little room for Reynolds' preference for spontaneity on the set. For Reynolds' personality to transcend the restrictions of the script, he needed a director willing to let him play around; it is the difference between "a Burt Reynolds picture" and "a picture with Burt Reynolds." Further antagonism ensued, coming to a head with a jaw-dropping moment of misunderstanding. Avildsen—East Coast and urbane— wasn't familiar with Mel Tillis and his repertoire (which includes "Good Woman Blues" and "Coca-Cola Cowboy") nor his speech impediment. While filming a gas station holdup scene, Tillis stuttered his lines, as expected by those who knew him, but with the film's director not having done an ounce of homework he let rip at Tillis for the gaffe. Reynolds recalled the event:

> "Hold it! Hold it!" Avildsen yelled, interrupting the scene. "Cut the stuttering. It doesn't work…" I stepped out of the car and asked the esteemed little director if I could have a word with him around back…. Once we got behind the filling station, I grabbed Avildsen, literally grabbed him, and hoisted him off the ground.[3]

And with that, Avildsen received a crash course in Mel Tillis via Burt Reynolds. What made the incident even more surreal for the cast and crew, who were watching aghast: When work resumed on the scene, Tillis read his lines perfectly, without a trace of his stutter, having found time for some quick liquid courage during the Reynolds-Avildsen conference. In retrospect, Reynolds said, "I did not mean it to be a combative relationship, because I liked him…. I thought (and quite honestly it was reverse prejudice on my part) this is him not being from the South and not having a sense of what these people are about, that he will have a problem connecting with them."[4] Avildsen said, "The thing that the film taught me was that I could do something that I had no passion for, that my mechanics were such that I could make it work."[5] And though that is as unfortunate a claim to authorship of a text as one could imagine, in fairness to Avildsen the picture does indeed work, remaining thoroughly enjoyable and with no obvious suggestions of on-set discord.

In its own idiosyncratic manner, *W.W. and the Dixie Dancekings* is one of Reynolds' most sensitive works and it features one of his most likable performances.

Notes

1. Burt Reynolds, *My Life: Burt Reynolds* (Great Britain: Hodder & Stoughton, 1994), pp. 189, 190.
2. Larry Powell and Tom Garrett, *The Films of John G. Avildsen:* Rocky, The Karate Kid *and Other Underdogs* (Jefferson, NC: McFarland, 2014), p. 59.
3. Reynolds, p. 190.
4. *Ibid.*
5. Powell and Garrett, p. 64.

Lucky Lady

(1975)

"We're snacking on the booze, not the broad!"—Walker Ellis

When bootlegging club owner Harry Dobbs is killed, his wife Claire (Liza Minnelli) decides to engage a pair of rogue rum-runners, Walker Ellis (Burt Reynolds) and Kibby Womack (Gene Hackman), in a joint business venture. The trio's plan is to assume a big portion of Southern California's bootlegging profits. That doesn't sit well with the East Coast heavies who figure on muscling in on the West Coast smuggling routes. The mob sends an armed envoy in the form of McTeague (John Hillenburg) to deliver a message to the plucky amateurs. Meanwhile, Coast Guard Capt. Moseley (Geoffrey Lewis) also seeks to put the trio out of business with extreme prejudice. While the bootlegging

Walker Ellis (Reynolds) discovers the true meaning of "sea legs" (those of Liza Minnelli) in *Lucky Lady* (1975).

exploits of the three characters provide the essential narrative trajectory of the plot, all of this is background for the love triangle that blossoms amongst them. Walker has been in love with Claire all along and even tries to seduce her literally as soon as Harry is put the ground. Kibby's presence complicates matters and confuses Claire's feelings.

Written by husband-and-wife team Willard Hyuck and Gloria Katz, who had struck gold with *American Graffiti*, the expensive *Lucky Lady* came with a hefty price tag from the very beginning, with 20th Century–Fox paying $450,000 to Hyuck, Katz and producer Michael Gruskoff. It started out as a serious, dramatic picture but turned into something altogether more cartoonish, and fortunately so, as its most enjoyable scenes are played for laughs. The sea battle between the intrepid bootleggers and their antagonists is brilliantly executed, mainly thanks to Reynolds' gift for physical comedy, which he uses to great advantage throughout the picture. In an effort to thwart their enemy, Reynolds, Hackman and Minnelli light Molotov cocktails to be lobbed at the opposing vessel. Reynolds is charged with pitching the bottles but he invariably drops, misses and plain fumbles his throws. It's a scene of fine slapstick that could have been performed in cinema's silent days.

Steven Spielberg had expressed interest in directing the film while having difficulties getting *Jaws* into production. But having been offered the director's chair by Fox, Spielberg came up against a bureaucratic blockade with Universal preempting him from working for another studio at the time.[1] With Spielberg tied to *Jaws*, Stanley Donen entered the fray. Donen, the doyen of the 1950s movie musical, was a man who knew how to create a film of high energy and marvelous production values, but while there is a taste of such evident here, there is a significant lack of energy in the narrative's forward momentum. Part of the problem seems to be that Minnelli is giving everything she has to instill the film with the kind of zippy attitude that Jane Russell or Doris Day once provided, but her vivacious demeanor feels lost in the company of the more aloof Hackman and a Reynolds working overtime to temper the personality extremes of both his co-stars.

In a kind of PG-rated *ménage-à-trois* between Walker, Kibby and Claire, we are expected to be seduced by their disregard for convention and zest for each other. But neither core relationship works particularly well, not Walker and Kibby, not Walker and Claire, not Kibby and Claire. There is not enough backstory to the characters to render them anything beyond vessels of dialogue. Reynolds and Minnelli share a wonderful natural chemistry, one seen to even greater effect in the 1987 thriller *Rent-a-Cop*; they are both performers of immense personality. But *Lucky Lady* doesn't afford them enough of a platform for their characters to develop their own romance. Despite a script in which the story's sympathies were allegedly aligned with Minnelli's Claire, the resulting film feels calculatedly structured to give none of its three major stars any particular time or preference over the other. It is genuinely a movie of three major leads. However, the result is that no character is afforded much time to evolve.

Lucky Lady is a picture of high aesthetic value and supreme craftsmanship, with no expense spared with regard to set design and art direction. George Lucas, a friend of Katz and Hyuck, visited the location in order to gain insight into the mechanics of a major studio operation in preparation for his own Fox film, *Star Wars*. Lucas, inspired by the filmmaking skill on display, went on to hire many of those working on *Lucky Lady*, including production designer John Barry and set decorator Roger Christian. He also sought the services of cinematographer Geoffrey Unsworth, whose use of diffusion particularly attracted him.[2] However, by the time *Star Wars* was ready to roll, Unsworth was committed to working on Richard Donner's *Superman* and thus unavailable to shoot Lucas' iconic space opera.

One of the most notable and perhaps most egregious elements of *Lucky Lady* is Unsworth's photography. Unsworth, the Oscar-winning cinematographer of *A Night to Remember* (Roy Ward Baker, 1958) and *2001: A Space Odyssey* (Stanley Kubrick, 1968), is rightly considered to have been one of the best in his field, but his aesthetic choices on *Lucky Lady* are questionable as despite being graced with the superb production design of John Barry and costuming by Lilly Fenichel, the cinematographer bafflingly decided to obscure almost every scene with a heavily opaque fog filter. So murky is the diffusion that some scenes are literally unwatchable. Unsworth has used such filtering techniques to brilliant and stylish effect in pictures such as *Cromwell* (1970), *Cabaret* (1972) and *Superman* (1978), but here it is purely distracting.

Lucky Lady faced an arduous production and ultimately cost $13 million, shooting on location in Guayman, Mexico, where the seas were unforgiving during filming. Fox was assured that the production would benefit from the Gulf of California seaport's regularly calm weather. Ultimately several boats, some carrying expensive camera equipment, were lost to sea. Further problems, this time more of a bureaucratic nature, ensued in post-production as elements of the original script were compromised. The downbeat ending that Hyuck and Katz had written and which was filmed (Walker and Kibby meeting a violent, watery demise) was re-shot with Reynolds and Hackman surviving. Stanley Donen had final cut privilege and, with the support of the studio, decided that the ending needed to be altered to please audiences looking for a more cheerful dénouement. Reynolds and Hackman returned, free of charge, while Minnelli was absent due to filming *A Matter of Time* for her father, Vincente Minneli. In the aforementioned original ending, Walker and Kibby are gunned down on the beach by a squadron of authorities, with the grim final image of Claire cradling the two fallen men on the harsh seafront at night.[3] Donen recalled,

When I first read the script, the ending touched me, but it also disturbed me, and I was not sure it would work. It left me with a feeling of dissatisfaction that I couldn't quite put my finger on…. You see, the whole picture—with the exception of one battle scene in the middle—had become much funnier. And when it was cut and I saw it all put together, I said to myself, the ending is not integral to the movie. The film seemed to shift tone just to make people cry, to achieve a new sensation, not because it was inevitable in terms of the characters, but because I couldn't find a more adroit way of ending on a comic note. It was as if a play by George Bernard Shaw had an ending written by Clifford Odets.[4]

The re-editing of *Lucky Lady* would prove a classic example of the box-ticking test card focus group mentality that would become standard practice at major studios. Despite the test scores for the original ending coming back strong at 80 percent in favor, the 20 percent negative had to be addressed. Alan Ladd Jr., head of Fox production, remarked, "We are aiming this film at a very broad audience. When you are making an all-family entertainment, you do not want to alienate any segment of the audience that would find the film 'too violent or too unhappy.' I think people in the Midwest prefer a happy ending. I know kids prefer a happy ending."[5]

Katz recalled, "If the movie had a different emphasis, the original ending might have worked better…. Actually, when we saw the direction the film was taking, we added more comic dialogue…. As it stands now, Stanley was right to change the ending."[6]

Hyuck and Katz went on to great success with their associations with George Lucas and Steven Spielberg. Pictures such as *Star Wars* and *Indiana Jones and the Temple of Doom* were part of a commercial movement in Hollywood in the late '70s and early '80s that rang the death knell of the more daring New Hollywood movement. The subversive aesthetic of the New Hollywood infiltrated the corporate Hollywood system and ushered in a kind of bold cultural and artistic revolution in American filmmaking, personal films with fiercely independent resolve but released with studio clout. It was the perfect antidote to the kind of picture that *Lucky Lady* represented: bloated, expensive and irrelevant. Hyuck and Katz were part of Francis Ford Coppola's independent studio American Zoetrope, a radical, countercultural United Artists for the 1970s, but the company became synonymous with bloated excess thanks to the epic scale of self-indulgence that plagued *THX 1138* (George Lucas, 1971), *Apocalypse Now* (Coppola, 1979), *One from the Heart* (Coppola, 1982) and *The Cotton Club* (Coppola, 1984). Today the company is run under the aegis of Coppola's children, Roman and Sofia, and operates as a more modest production company focusing on high-profile independent films. In the annals of Hollywood movie flops, there are plenty of bad films with awful production values and horrendous performances, but there are many well-made (read: expensive) pictures which just failed to strike a chord for whatever reason—think of the aforementioned *At Long Last Love*, or a genuine masterpiece like *Heaven's Gate* (Michael Cimino, 1980). And while both of those pictures bombed upon first release, they enjoyed a second life in the form of director-approved versions and have gained belated critical respectability. *Lucky Lady*, however, hasn't received such critical revision since first emerging in 1975.

Notes

1. Joseph McBride, *Steven Spielberg: A Biography*, Second Edition (Mississippi: University of Mississippi, 2010), p. 240.

2. J.W. Rinzler, *The Making of Star Wars: The Definitive Story Behind the Original Film* (Ballantine Books, New York, 2005), [n.p.].

3. "Lucky Lady 1975 Alternate Ending," YouTube, uploaded by robatsea2009, April 28, 2017, https://www.youtube.com/watch?v=5_tOdtThq0c.

4. Stephen Farber, "Why Couldn't This 'Lady' Have an Unhappy Ending?," *New York Times*, December 4, 1975, https://www.nytimes.com/1975/12/14/archives/why-couldnt-this-lady-have-an-unhappy-ending-why-no-unhappy-ending.html.

5. *Ibid.*

6. *Ibid.*

Hustle

(1975)

"He's just one of those middle-class Americans that believe you get 40,000 miles on a new set of tires."—Phil Gaines

Following their phenomenal success with *The Longest Yard*, Reynolds and director Robert Aldrich reunited for this underrated detective mystery.

Aldrich wastes no time setting the sinister tone in the opening scene: A busload of school kids enjoying a field trip to the beach discovers the washed-up body of young Gloria Hollinger. LAPD detective Phil Gaines (Reynolds) and his partner Louis Belgrave (Paul Winfield) quickly rule the girl's death a suicide by deliberate overdose of barbiturates, yet some aspects of the case remain unsettling, such as the unusual abundance of semen present in her system. The duo trace Gloria to seedy strip joints, sleazy stag films and a highly organized prostitution ring which counts influential Pasadena attorney Leo Sellers (Eddie Albert) among its clientele. Gloria's distraught father, Marty Hollinger (Ben Johnson), refuses to accept the ruling of his daughter's death as a suicide, to the point of accusing Gaines and Belgrave of corruption and a cover-up. Despite the protestations of the detectives, Marty starts his own investigation and uncovers his daughter's nefarious activities and those who supported her lifestyle, from the lowly porn players up to high-powered Sellers. The attorney's involvement puts Gaines in a predicament: His glamorous prostitute girlfriend Nicole Britton (Catherine Deneuve) runs in the same circles as Gloria; as such, Sellers is one of Nicole's loyal clients and he has used his power and influence to help with Nicole's immigration legalities. Gaines could jeopardize such cozy arrangements if he pursues the Hollinger case as a murder inquiry, rather than the convenient write-off of suicide. Gaines also knows that despite Sellers' involvement in labor racketeering and organized crime, he did not kill Gloria. But convincing Marty otherwise is its own dilemma.

By 1975, audiences were enjoying a revival of that great genre staple of Old Hollywood: film noir. Labeled neo-noir to distinguish their contemporary production and settings (a post–Vietnam, post–Watergate, post-counterculture American milieu), these films pay tribute and adhere faithfully to the tropes and traditions of the expressionistic classic texts. "I'm a student of the '30s … don't make fun of my heroes!" Gaines tells Belgrave, referring to Humphrey Bogart and John Garfield. Robert Altman's *The Long Goodbye* (1973) and Roman Polanksi's *Chinatown* (1974) are two oft-cited examples of the neo-noir genre at its

Detective Phil Gaines (Reynolds) and his lover Nicole (Catherine Deneuve) plan to leave Los Angeles for Europe in *Hustle* **(1975).**

best; other notables include *The Late Show* (Robert Benton, 1977), *Hickey & Boggs* (Robert Culp, 1972), *Klute* (Alan J. Pakula, 1971), *Night Moves* (Arthur Penn, 1975) and *Hardcore* (Paul Schrader, 1979).

Hustle works exquisitely on the surface as a procedural police thriller, but it is the complex secondary narrative and its themes that make the film part of the film noir canon. As in many film noir texts, decent citizens, often ex-policemen and war veterans, endure a corrupt society in which they feel temporally and morally out of place. Marty is haunted by his experiences as a Korean War veteran and is disillusioned with the abuse and erosion of a way of life that he fought valiantly for. With his daughter gone and his marriage sullied, the middle-class dream—the American Dream itself—is no longer worth a damn to Marty. His wife Paula (Eileen Brennan), a bitter and emotionally barren lush, admits that she cheated on Marty while he was recovering in a VA hospital years ago; this transgression also resulted in her relationship with Gloria becoming strained, as it was the youngster who discovered that her mother taken a lover into the marital bed. Aldrich creates a city of foul moral poverty. Whether in the decaying back rooms of downtown smut clubs or the neat, wallpapered living rooms of the suburban middle class, perversion, deviance and debauchery are all at home, and home is not where the heart is. The Hollinger house may boast tasteful decor and a fully loaded minibar, but the ghosts of indiscretions past and nightmares present create a hostile environment where even the family's minister is denounced and his unsolicited sanctimony rebuked. "Gloria's death was by divine order," the holy man declares. "Horseshit!" Hollinger replies.

Gaines' domestic life is also precariously balanced. His life with live-in lover Nicole is marked with uncertainty and anxiety as he is privy to her call-girl activities such as working a phone sex line from their lounge, an act which undermines the intimacy they share in the house. *Hustle* depicts depravity as a disease that has infected all walks of society, not just in the Sunset Strip dens of iniquity. The more Marty and Gaines bear witness to the

Marty Hollinger (Ben Johnson) demands information from his murdered daughter's associates, including porn actress Peggy Summers (Catherine Bach), in *Hustle* (1975).

kind of low-rent porn work Gloria was reduced to peddling to support her alternative lifestyle, the more their own moral compass become uncertain.

Like Marty, Phil is a man of many demons: cynical, swift to resort to violence and subterfuge if need be, albeit in the name of protecting innocents. After gunning down a psychopath holding women hostage in a textile factory, Gaines runs to the body and vengefully, if unnecessarily, empties the rest of his ammo into the corpse. And when Marty murders Sellers in a fit of rage, Gaines manipulates the crime scene to make it look like Sellers fired shots at the detectives and Gaines returned fire in self-defense. Though Gaines admits that Sellers has "killed other people, but he didn't do this one," he instinctively saves the life of Marty Hollinger by assuming responsibility for the attorney's death, perhaps tempering the ethical quandary of his actions by reason of meting out justice for the killings that Sellers has, up to this point, been committing with impunity. While some people could consider Gaines' response to violence to be questionable and unlawful in overlooking due process, the greater contexts of these incidents indicates the detective's genuine concern for law and order and the protection of citizens. In the case of the factory scene, Gaines sees bodies of innocent women workers piled up on the floor; aware of the man's proclivity for indiscriminate killing, he knows the remaining hostage is in imminent danger unless desperate measures are taken. That Gaines unloads an entire clip into the perpetrator's lifeless body introduces questions of gratuitous violence. "You know the guy is a psychopath," Aldrich says, addressing questions of the justification, "so that takes away any question of whether it's right or not to kill that man because not to kill him means that an innocent woman is going to get killed…. The hue and cry would be extraordinary if you labeled that he was alive and then Burt killed him. So it's left that you can draw your own conclusions."[1]

With Reynolds' rising popularity and bankability, a picture as grim as *Hustle* was a gamble for the actor and Paramount. The star had yearned for this kind of substantial material as he was being pursued to star in less-challenging projects, but wasn't quite prepared for the fact that starring in an uncompromising picture could jeopardize his commercial status. He said,

> Popularity and money make for a dangerous combination. You think everyone loves you. Everyone doesn't love you. If I'd had any guidance at all, my people would've taken me to Canada, shut me in a frigging room, and kept me there until some really serious filmmakers called and asked them to let me out…. Some thought I was a joke. Realizing that scripts weren't coming to me, I decided to make things happen myself. I found the script for what became *Hustle* and took it to Bob Aldrich, as serious a filmmaker as I knew.[2]

But with Aldrich calling the shots, the picture complied with the pessimistic mood in cinema, society and culture of the times. And, not uncommon for the flawed protagonists of erstwhile film noir, our hero Phil Gaines is killed in the final scene. Gaines' demise in a random liquor store holdup may seem a somewhat flippant denouement considering it is entirely unrelated to the narrative preceding it, but it does make perfect sense in the context of the fatalist world of film noir. Gaines measures his value by his ability to serve and protect, it's his job and it's what he's good at. In this moment he could walk away and meet Nicole at the airport and live happily ever after in Rome, but to allow the thief (a memorable Robert Englund) to walk after assaulting a frail old woman and taking from the cash register, Gaines' sense of value and esteem would diminish. A short burst of violence ensues; Gaines is shot in the melee and the thief flees. It is not a blaze of glory, rather a tragic and pitiful demise. Gaines survives in the original script, but Aldrich had some morally sound ideas for the finale which underscored Gaines' inner conflict, the battle between his heart and his job, and just as though it seemed he and Nicole would realize their dream of seeing Rome, the audience and Gaines are denied the pleasure of such happiness. Gaines isn't a have-a-go-hero; it is his moral and professional duty to resolve this particular moment of conflict, even at the highest price. "The audience should realize he's making up his mind whether to get involved or not get involved," Aldrich says, "knowing what getting involved would mean. And that he thinks: 'Fuck it, I've lived a particular way, and it's my job to not let people get really hurt.'"[3]

Reynolds ultimately regretted the decision to end the picture on this bleak note, recalling some advice a great man once gave him: "*Hustle* got good reviews but lost money, because my character dies at the end. It wasn't in the script, Bob changed it at the last minute, and I couldn't talk him out of it. It was my fault because I'd ignored Duke Wayne's advice: 'Never play a rapist and never die in a movie,' he said. 'People don't like to see their leading men die.'"[4]

Even though *Hustle* performed only moderately, it did nothing to harm Reynolds' rise to the top of the box office. The commercial prospects of the picture might have been limited, but viewed today *Hustle* reveals itself as one of Reynolds' best and boldest pieces of work. With Aldrich's recurring cinematographer Joseph Biroc crafting the *mise-en-scéne*, this collaboration further establishes their unique cinematic style, crafting a rich and highly stylized picture in which the evocative camerawork recalls the high-contrast lighting and distinct compositions of the first wave of film noir.

Notes

1. Edwin T. Arnold and Eugene L. Miller, "Aldrich Interview: Pierre Sauvage 1976," in *Robert Aldrich: interviews* (Mississippi: University Press of Mississippi, 2004), p. 96.
2. Burt Reynolds, *My Life: Burt Reynolds* (Great Britain: Hodder & Stoughton, 1994), p. 199.
3. Arnold and Miller, p. 96.
4. Reynolds, p. 199.

Silent Movie

(1975)

"Hi there, Burt. How would you like to be in a silent movie?"—Funn, Bell and Eggs

After directing one of the most beloved comedies of the 1970s, *Young Frankenstein*, Mel Brooks followed up with one of his funniest though perhaps most forgotten films in *Silent Movie*, a loving ode to Old Hollywood and a satire of the industry's absurdities. Brooks utilized the format and style of early film comedies by Mack Sennett, Harold Lloyd, Charlie Chaplin and Buster Keaton to poke fun at both traditional and topical Tinseltown endeavors.

It's not hard to find Burt's house in Hollywood in *Silent Movie* (1975).

Brooks stars as once-lauded film director Mel Funn, who is no longer in the good graces of Big Picture Studios thanks to his current condition as an alcoholic. Along with associates Dom Bell (Dom DeLuise) and Marty Eggs (Marty Feldman), Funn attempts to convince the studios to fund a novel idea: to produce the first silent film in four decades. The studio chief, simply named Chief (Sid Caesar), is fearful of such a risky, anachronistic project, but his curiosity is piqued when Funn declares that he will cast major stars, a move which could save the studio from being overtaken by The Engulf and Devour Corporation (a reference to the 1966 Gulf + Western corporate takeover of Paramount). Funn, Bell and Eggs set out to seduce a parade of stars to be in their picture, including Burt Reynolds, James Caan, Liza Minnelli, Anne Bancroft, Marcel Marceau, and Paul Newman.

Reynolds proves fine fodder for some of the film's funniest moments. In a poke at the actor's lavish Hollywood lifestyle, Funn, Bell and Eggs don't have too hard a time locating Reynolds' mansion thanks to a wholly conspicuous banner heralding the owner of the residence hanging over a massive portrait of said proprietor. *Silent Movie* was another opportunity for the actor to indulge a recurring theme of his career: movies about moviemaking. Here he delivers a self-mocking portrait of an egotistical superstar actor, drawing upon his gregarious personality that audiences knew and loved from his prolific television appearances.

Pausing to mug exaggeratedly into a mirror every time he passes his reflection, Reynolds literally winks at the audience at every opportunity. Not all of the celebrities appear at ease in playing and mocking themselves as much as Reynold does. James Caan is stiff and joyless; whereas Reynolds allows Brooks to get laughs by satirizing elements of his public persona that were already familiar to many, Caan's is too serious a demeanor to take any joy from the parade of parody thrown his way. Paul Newman comes and goes without much comic effect. Anne Bancroft is afforded more time than most, given a full song-and-dance number and an especially hilarious frog-eyed Marty Feldman impersonation. Liza Minnelli is as game and as spirited as her erstwhile *Lucky Lady* co-star.

As a Brooks picture, plot takes a back seat to the series of celebrity cameos and sketches. It is an often muted affair, quite literally, and many stretches not only go without dialogue but without music as well. Regardless, the film is a winner for anybody with a love of the silent era. But if pre-sound comic films test your patience, *Silent Movie* may only serve to support your opinion.

Gator

(1976)

"You know, I think that's what I missed the most in the morning, your bitchin' and moanin.'"—Gator McClusky

It was perhaps inevitable that when his popularity and bankability afforded him such power, Reynolds would try his hand at directing, and that is what he did in 1976 when he made *Gator*, the electrifying sequel to *White Lightning*.

It opens with New York federal agent Irving Greenfield (Jack Weston), being drafted to clean up Dunston, Georgia, a town rife with corruption thanks to the heavy hand of feared racketeer Bama McCall (Jerry Reed). McCall has his fingers in all kinds of illicit pies, from extortion and protection to prostitution. The governor of Georgia figures one way of getting to McCall is through his old ally, Gator McClusky (Reynolds). If they can nail McClusky on an illegal whiskey charge, they can try to coerce him into gathering a tax evasion sheet on McCall.

McClusky is living in the Okefenokee Swamp with his father and daughter. The family

Reporter Aggie Maybank (Lauren Hutton) investigates her subject, Gator McClusky (Reynolds), up close and personal in *Gator* (1976).

is deracinated from their idyllic rural life when an entire squadron of boats and helicopters ensnare them. After a near–20 minute action set piece involving wild nautical and aeronautical stunts, McClusky is captured. Under threat of jail, as well as fearing the attendant consequences for his father and daughter, McClusky gives in to the demands of the feds and is released onto the mean streets of Dunston, where he can immerse himself in the sleazy underworld that is McCall's kingdom. McClusky becomes a collector for McCall's extortionate affairs, bearing witness to the hardship and oppression caused for his former pal's gain. What brings the compassionate McClusky over the edge is when he is introduced to a brothel in which the sex workers, none older than 16, are all strung out on drugs, working to feed their habit; McCall happens to run the monopoly on all elements of criminality in town, so he benefits entirely from this cycle of abuse. Ambitious TV reporter Aggie Maybank (Lauren Hutton) provides the romantic subplot of the film, her bond with McClusky deepening as she aids the lovable scofflaw to bring down McCall and his evil empire.

Unlike the lean and mean *White Lightning*, everything about *Gator* is wired up for maximum effect. There is a clue in the opening credits as to just how entertainingly excessive the picture will get when we see that the second unit was directed by Hal Needham. Here, the celebrated stuntman cut his teeth calling the shots on some superbly executed and expertly staged pieces of action cinema, from the opening helicopter-boat chase to the final seaside fisticuffs between Gator and McCall.

In this sequel, Reynolds brings a sense of irreverence to the character of Gator McClusky where prior he had been suitably brooding and intense. To identify the diverging tones of both films, one just need look at their respective opening sequences. The former picture opens with a bleak, almost morbid sense of dread with the killing of two college kids by a senior member of local law enforcement. Immediately we are distrustful of the town's supposed good guys; if they are willing to murder a couple of kids in such a callous manner, who can we trust? With the latter picture, the police are seen to be nowhere near as malevolent as J.C. Connors and his deputies; in fact, Greenfield and the cops who assist him in his raid are somewhat bumbling and ineffective. Sure, they have McClusky cornered on a bureaucratic level, as they did in the first picture, but in the physical realm he is in the tradition of the lone cowboy, an untouchable angel of vengeance in blue flare jeans. It is interesting to note that in both films, McClusky's actions are initially seen as a betrayal of hometown ethics: He is a stool pigeon for the federal government. But Gator actually manipulates this position for his own homegrown sense of justice for those left without legal recourse. In *White Lightning* he inadvertently becomes an unwitting champion for the oppressed countercultural college kids, a group to which his felled brother belonged. In *Gator*, he is a savior of another oppressed society of youth, the exploited, drug-addicted juvenile sex workers.

Gator is a protective, patriarchal figure, simultaneously upholding a sense of morality and justice while flouting his own felonies in the face of the law that is using him for their own needs. Aside from the contrasting tones, another narrative oddity serves to distance the two films, if one wishes to be bothered by such a trivial aspect, but it remains nonetheless, and that is the character background of the McClusky family. In *White Lightning*, McLusky's parents are farmers; in the sequel, his father is a swamp rat moonshiner. McClusky also has a nine-year-old daughter here, a character unmentioned in the first pic-

This composite shot of Gator McClusky (Reynolds) and a young prostitute (Stephanie Burchfield) is an example of William Fraker's stunning cinematography in *Gator* (1976).

ture. In a brief moment of exposition, McClusky explains that Suzie's mother got tired of waiting around while he wasted away in prison. Suzie's presence in merely a tool for the picture's revenge motif, so McClusky's revolt against a tainted justice system can be motivated on familial grounds. In this case, McClusky's anger is inspired by the abuse and corruption of young, innocent girls not far in age from Suzie.

Despite its crowd-pleasing resolve, *Gator* still contains some fine moments of drama and pathos, though these normally anticipate the more outrageous scenes of carnage and mayhem. The film's secret weapon is Jerry Reed. In only his second screen performance, following his debut in *W.W. and the Dixie Dancekings*, Reed manages the considerable feat of being truly menacing and disarmingly charming, commanding the screen with ease. With swagger and style to boot, Reed is a villain made likable because his sidekicks are truly bizarre and reprehensible. There's the Amazonian sidekick brute known as Bones, because he tells people to call him that. I doubt that's the name his mother gave him, but if Bones tells you call him Bones, then you call him Bones. And then there's Burton Gilliam's unsavory lech Smiley, who takes a shine to McClusky's good looks.

More than anything, *Gator* is a stunning looking production. While it may have been released with the sole intention to please the masses looking for another blast of that profitable homespun Reynolds charm, the production itself is top class. Shot by lauded cinematographer William Fraker (*Bullitt*, *Rosemary's Baby*, *Paint Your Wagon*), the picture is filled with his distinct visual flair and keen eye for intricate, tasteful composition, often using a notable style in which his shots contain many frames within frames and utilize mirrors to add greater richness and depth to his compositions. The use of color and props in the brothel scene is a master class in *mise-en-scéne*. Edward Rosson's cinematography in *White Lightning* took on a darker, grimmer, perhaps more natural aesthetic, underscoring the searing, unpleasantly humid aura of the corrupt small Southern town; Fraker's photography here is self-consciously stylish and embellished, using his frame and compositional choices to help tell this story of decadence, degeneracy and depravity with notable use of saturated color which heightens the melodrama and cartoonish adventure of this extremely rewarding sequel.

Nickelodeon

(1976)

"Why, you're not from the Patents Company, you don't look dangerous enough."—H.H. Cobb

Nickelodeon is set in 1914, on the cusp of huge advancements in the art of cinema and filmmaking as a business. The bread and butter of the industry is the quickly cranked-out short movie, the kind of picture that could be edited by the simple declaration of "take the first sequence, put it where the second one is, take the third sequence and put it where the first one was!" This is the kind of editorial method used by director and aspiring mogul H.H. Cobb (Brian Keith) of the small-time operation Kinegraph. Leo Harrigan (Ryan O'Neal) is a New Jersey lawyer who ends up in the movie business by accident, having vowed to crusade against the heavy-handed tactics of the Patents Company, who have been muscling out the small studios. Leo becomes a Kinegraph writer after suggesting an interesting plotline, and later becomes a director when he visits a location shoot only to find the real director has gone on a bender with the payroll cash.

Just as Harrigan ends up in pictures by chance, a naive young rodeo rider from Sopchoppy, Florida, Buck Greenway (Reynolds), steps off a train and gets caught up in the affairs of show business when he is scouted by the Clansman Company, who hire him on the spot as a stunt rider for a show where he is ordered to don the white hood and burning cross of a Klansman. Buck is later hired as an enforcer for the Patents Company after he inadvertently helps them bring down a clandestine German film studio operating out of a bagel shop. When Buck is sent west to disrupt a Kinegraph picture being shot by Leo, he is caught in the act and attempts to flee on horseback, only to be spotted by Leo as a potential stuntman and

Leo Harrigan (Ryan O'Neal) and Buck Greenway (Reynolds) discover that making movies can be tough work in *Nickelodeon* (1976).

future star. Buck soon joins Leo and his ragtag crew that includes cinematographer Frank Frank (John Ritter), ingénue Kathleen Cooke (Jane Hitchcock), precocious pre-teen driver and aspiring writer Alice Forsythe (Tatum O'Neal) and other members of their peripatetic film family. Buck becomes as reluctant an actor as Leo does a director, but together they find their calling in life through the movies and endure some Hollywood hardship along the way.

It is hard not to warm to this picaresque comedy, with its clear love of the historical context around which the director Peter Bogdanovich frames his narrative. Bogdanovich neatly uses the tricks of silent cinema in loving recreation, such as the "iris out" shot, and when he has honky-tonk piano scoring fine slapstick comedy that pays tribute to the early film comics. If there were two people qualified enough to make a passionately drawn picture of Old Hollywood, Bogdanovich and Reynolds were eminently suitable. With Bogdanovich, a former film critic and Hollywood historian directing, and Reynolds, with his appreciation of La La Land's grand glory days and love of the silver screen stars of the era, *Nickelodeon* is a film lover's movie made by film lovers. The first two-thirds of the picture are a joyous affair, as it revels in the moviemaking process and physical gags that Bogdanovich renders with great attention to timing and detail. Only when it attempts to become sober and dramatic in the third act by addressing the love triangle between Leo, Buck and Kathleen does the narrative become staid, mired in melodrama that has little place in an otherwise frivolous film. However, just as H.H. Cobb would demand of one of his own pictures, Bogdanovich concludes his story with drama, pathos and humor, as the tired and cynical Kinegraph crew happens upon a production being shot on a soundstage. "They're shooting a picture!" says Leo in hushed reverence of the process so beloved by him and Bogdanovich.

Bogdanovich intended *Nickelodeon* as a tribute to his friend, the great Old Hollywood filmmaker Allan Dwan (*Robin Hood*, 1922; *Heidi*, 1937; *Sands of Iwo Jima*, 1949), who served as a consultant to Bogdanovich throughout. The script is comprised of various tales told to the director by the likes of John Ford, Raoul Walsh and Dwan,[1] and is full of colorful insights into the personalities and early practices of the embryonic film industry. D.W. Griffith, Harrigan is told, never yelled "Cut!" but rather intoned "Cease!" The presence of Griffith, the Father of Cinema, looms large over the whole picture, as *Nickelodeon* documents the seismic shift in the film industry incurred with the premiere of Griffith's 1915 masterpiece, *The Birth of a Nation*, referenced here by its original title taken from the source novel, *The Clansman*. "Did you see what I saw tonight? This thing is going to change the business," says Cobb. "The greatest motion picture of all time was just unfurled!" Having just experienced *The Birth of a Nation*, a game-changer of epic proportions, Cobb & Co. envision a cinema of relevance, not merely a machine for producing "dollars and cents," an art form capable of stirring the soul and empowering the audience through meaning and symbolism, now that its potential has been realized in the form of Griffith's marvel, a picture which makes the case more than any other text for Cinema to be considered the Seventh Art. Emerging from the foyer not a businessman, but a filmmaker, Cobb delivers an idealistic speech which nicely distills the essence of Cinema:

> What are you all standing around here for? This is the beginning of the world! Think of it: all of those people going to see the pictures, a lot of them can't even talk American, and then they don't have to because pictures are a language that everybody understands, it's like music for the eyes. And if you're good, if you're really good, then maybe what you're doing is giving them little tiny pieces of time that they never forget.

To illustrate the sheer power and epic scale of Griffith's film, Bogdanovich shows us scenes from the massive battle sequence where the film's Confederate protagonist Ben Cameron leads a heroic charge against Union forces at the Siege of Petersburg. Bogdanovich also reveals the logistical scale of the monumental theatrical event as it is presented with live sound effects and an orchestra to score the picture from behind the screen. It's no wonder that Cobb and the gang think they've witnessed the greatest of all films: Regardless of its controversial reputation, *The Birth of a Nation* is a spectacle unlike any other, and taken in context of its debut 1915 appearance, one that rightly shook the world of cinema. For those active in the industry, Griffith's picture heralded a seismic shift in the art of film.

Nickelodeon began its difficult pre-production period before the release of Bogdanovich's first major critical and box office misfire, *At Long Last Love*, when the director was still riding high on success and fueled by considerable ego. He was preparing his own project set in the silent days of filmmaking when was offered the chance to direct a script by W.D. Richter called *Stardust Parade* which was to be made with Academy Award–winning producer Irwin Winkler. But the director did not like the script and performed a radical overhaul of the material and in particular imagined realizing his revised script as a black-and-white picture in an effort to give it the authentic feel of an Old Hollywood production. Columbia refused to see any commercial prospects for a black-and-white picture in the mid–1970s commercial milieu and this, coupled with the expensive cast lined up to star, led to the nervous studio cancelling the project. This left an opening for British Lion Films to step in to help bring the film to fruition with a completion fund. British Lion had been a successful production and distribution company since the silent days and boasted a distinguished catalogue of British films such as *The Third Man* (Carol Reed, 1949), *The Entertainer* (Tony Richardson, 1960) and *Don't Look Now* (Nicolas Roeg, 1973). But in 1976, the company was bought out by music industry giant EMI with the view to creating ties between the British film market and the Hollywood studios. British Lion's new mandate of making more commercially viable and easily marketable star pictures in cooperation with Hollywood studios meant a decreased financial risk for wary executives, and as such *Nickelodeon* would once again be a "go" picture at Columbia.[2]

Notes

1. Frederic Lombardi, *Allan Dwan and the Rise and Decline of the Hollywood Studios* (Jefferson, NC: McFarland, 2013), p. 232.

2. Paul Moody, *EMI Films and the Limits of British Cinema* (United Kingdom: Palgrave Macmillan, 2018), p.145.

Smokey and the Bandit

(1977)

"Sumbitch!"—Sheriff Buford T. Justice

Bo Darville, known to the world as "the Bandit," is a renowned trucker and rodeo star. He takes an $80,000 wager to transport a consignment of Coors beer from Texas to Atlanta within 48 hours by the comically mismatched father-son duo, Big Enos (Pat McCormick) and Little Enos Burdette (Paul Williams). Bandit enlists his friend Cledus "The Snowman" Snow (Jerry Reed) to drive the beer truck while he diverts the attention of the law in his blocker car, the iconic black Pontiac Trans Am. After picking up the cargo in Texarkana, all goes smoothly until the Bandit is waved down by a beautiful, diminutive runaway bride in distress. Carrie (Sally Field), or Frog—"because you're always hoppin' around"—is fleein' a hitchin' to Junior Justice (Mike Henry), the dim-witted policeman son of the legend that is Sheriff Buford T. Justice (Jackie Gleason), Texas lawman of high esteem and even higher blood pressure. Justice takes gross offense at Frog ditching his son and pursues the Bandit in vengeance. Disregarding jurisdiction boundaries and basic social graces, nothing will come between Justice and his man, not even the reverence of a funeral cortege—"If they'd-a cremated the sumbitch," Justice declares, "I could be kicking that Mr. Bandit's ass around the moon by now."

No doubt about it, *Smokey and the Bandit* is the definitive Reynolds film. To many, Reynolds and the Bandit are inextricably linked in the context of film history and on a pop-cultural level. The picture is essentially an anarchic road picture that Road Runner and Wile E. Coyote would be proud of, consisting of one long chase sequence featuring a procession of eccentric characters who file past as the plot is punctuated with wild vehicular stunts. The picture's success depends on your goodwill to the kind of irreverent, politically incorrect humor that the script trades on and it would take a particularly curmudgeonly soul to not enjoy this damn fine entertainment. And if box office tallies are any indication, many people were most receptive to *Smokey and the Bandit*, making it the second most successful film of 1977 right behind George Lucas' science fiction behemoth *Star Wars*. If a spectacular space opera with pan-generational appeal to Baby Boomers and their kids, supported by a billion-dollar marketing enterprise, seemed the order of the day, then how did a relatively modest cartoon chase picture about cops and bootleggers become such a profitable cash cow?

With no pretense for inclusion in the elite club of the esoteric auteurist New Hollywood movement, *Smokey and the Bandit* served a populist celebration of working-class country traditionalism, and a major part of such appeal can be attributed to the inclusion of genuine blue collar Southern heroes such as Jerry Reed, as legendary a country music figure as Reynolds was becoming the definitive country movie star. Reed was already a familiar face in the Reynolds canon thanks to his significant roles in *W.W. and the Dixie Dancekings* and *Gator*; and here the actor turns in a fine comedic performance as the Snowman. Reed also significantly contributed to the picture's cultural prevalence with his jaunty theme song "East

Reynolds introduces the legendary Bo Danville aka the Bandit in *Smokey and the Bandit* (1977).

Bound and Down," co-written with country music guitarist Dick Feller. The song became a huge radio hit, adding to the commercial and promotional juggernaut of the picture and spending four months at the #2 spot on the Billboard country singles charts.

Reynolds had been building a massive following in the wake of *Deliverance*, but *White Lightning* and *The Longest Yard* in particular marked the actor as a folk hero of Southern cinema. "There were a lot of things about the South that I was embarrassed about," Reynolds admits, "but there were also things about the South that were wonder-

The Bandit (Reynolds) and Frog (Sally Field) share a tender moment in *Smokey and the Bandit* (1977).

ful. I had hoped to make something out of that in a way that nobody had seen."[1] It is also perhaps a good thing that Reynolds didn't listen to his industry handlers who were urging him to take roles of a more serious caliber and to avoid making *Smokey and the Bandit*. "My friends got down on their knees with tears in their eyes and begged me not to do it," the actor recalls, "A year later, those same people said, 'I'm sure glad I convinced you to make that picture.'"[2]

Much credit for the picture's vigorous energy is due to director Hal Needham's skill as an action-oriented filmmaker with a particular interest in kinetic camerawork. Needham was a man idolized by Reynolds as a pioneer and innovator from his years as the most daring stuntman in the film and TV industries. He doubled for Reynolds as far back as the *Riverboat* and *Gunsmoke* days as well as performing gags on many classic westerns, including some of John Wayne's late-career pictures. Sports journalist Brock Yates considered Needham "perhaps the bravest man I ever met … thought by many to be one of the greatest stuntmen of them all."[3] Needham also happened to be living on Reynolds' property, his pool house to be exact, when he wrote a script influenced by the partial prohibition of Coors beer in the early '70s. Due to its lack of preservatives, Coors required sustained refrigeration and therefore could not withstand prolonged haulage; so sale of the beverage was restricted to markets west of the Mississippi River. The brand enjoyed a mystique that placed it as an attractive and much sought-after product, with such popularity and acclaim meaning it was ripe for bootlegging across forbidden territories. During the production of *Gator*, an incident occurred in which some of Needham's beloved bottles of Coors were appropriated by a cleaning lady, and so the idea struck the stuntman for a good-natured, rip-roaring yarn involving the transport of contraband beer. Needham turned in a handwritten script to Reynolds, who called it "one of the worst ever" yet saw the potential for fun in his friend's idea. Reynolds used his commercial clout to get Universal and its powerful executive, Lew Wasserman, on board with the project and with the notion of casting Jackie Gleason.

And with that, one of the great screen adversarial relationships was born when Gleason assumed the role of the Bandit's nemesis, Sheriff Buford T. Justice. Gleason, bumbling about with his beer belly and cigar, inhabits Justice and evokes every redneck sheriff archetype possible in his absurdist creation. As a cultural stereotype, Justice is an embrace of the benign nitwit Southern law enforcer, with such cartoonish exaggeration affording his profanity an inoffensive PG timidity. It is this kind of inspired lunacy that makes the picture so endearingly enjoyable, as it parlays its rebellious scofflaw attitude into an inoffensive, almost genial nature. Property, vehicles and perhaps Buford T. Justice's dignity may all endure absolute destruction throughout, but one is never in fear for the safety and wellbeing of the characters; the picture is entirely cartoon in construction and presentation. Unlike most action pictures, which very clearly define the hero and villain as "Good" and "Bad" to direct the audiences' moral compass and allegiance, here we can applaud in equal measure the titular duo despite their adversarial relationship on opposing sides of the law. We can salute the rapscallion Bandit for his recalcitrant ways and not feel any moral complications for cheering when he flouts the law, while conversely we can laugh at Justice's constabulary foibles, political incorrectness and the wild comic abandon that Gleason brings to the role.

The legacy of *Smokey and the Bandit* is that of an enduring entertainment, marking the moment that Reynolds went from movie star to film icon. Two enjoyable theatrical sequels followed: *Smokey and the Bandit II* proved another massive box office success while the largely Reynolds-less *Smokey and the Bandit Part 3* bombed. When asked on the French film show *Cinéma Cinémas* if he tried to have fun on films where the script is less than impressive, Reynolds considered the chemistry and camaraderie of the actors on screen to translate to a thrilling, good-time vicarious adventure for the audience. "Yes, you try to have fun," Reynolds affirmed. "You hope that if you have a good enough time, the audience will too, which I think is probably the secret to *Cannonball* and *Smokey and the Bandit*. I mean, we were having such a good time that nobody was listening to the words. If you listened to those words, you'd throw up, you know."[4]

Rarely revered as a director as much as he was as a stuntman, Needham made films that were among the most financially successful and popular of their period, the most notable being this, his debut. Honoring Needham at the 2012 Governors Awards ceremony at which he won an honorary award, Quentin Tarantino praised *Smokey and the Bandit* as

> one of the most enjoyable first-directed features ever made, I mean really, to this day it completely holds up, a magnificent movie of action and comedy; Burt Reynolds at his highest as far as his persona was concerned. But also, and this is really important: a true Southern movie, a real Southern movie, not a Hollywood Southern movie, a real Southern movie which understood the South in a really, really lovely way.[5]

According to legend, Alfred Hitchcock was also a great admirer of the Bandit's escapades, a rumor confirmed as true by director Sacha Gervasi: "Patricia [Hitchcock] told the story that every Wednesday he would screen films on the lot in his office. The last one he screened before he died was his favorite film of the past few years": *Smokey and the Bandit*.[6]

The Master of Suspense, and several million others, can't be wrong.

Notes

1. "The Bandit: Burt and crew talk about Hal Needham Recorded 2016," uploaded by Ron Swett, July 14, 2018, https://www.youtube.com/watch?v=nbhk7lL4yhU.

2. Burt Reynolds, *But Enough About Me* (London: Blink Publishing, 2015), p. 180.

3. Brock Yates, *Cannonball! World's Greatest Outlaw Road Race* (Minnesota: Motorbooks International, 2003), p. 175.

4. "Cinéma Cinémas–Burt Reynolds—1987," uploaded by Thomas Boujut, October 9, 2012, https://www.youtube.com/watch?v=6-jEoqhXKYE.

5. "Quentin Tarantino honors Hal Needham at the 2012 Governors Awards," uploaded by Oscars, December 2, 2012, https://www.youtube.com/watch?v=-JsYTFukcgw.

6. Tim Robey, "Alfred Hitchcock biopic: Dial M for Mischief," *The Telegraph*, February 6, 2013, http://www.telegraph.co.uk/culture/film/film-news/9839836/Alfred-Hitchcock-biopic-Dial-M-for-mischief.html.

Semi-Tough

(1977)

"There comes a point in a man's life when he's got to think about something other than fuckin' and football."—Billy Clyde Puckett

Burt Reynolds and Kris Kristofferson play best friends and Miami pro football teammates Billy Clyde Puckett and Marvin "Shake" Tiller. They share an apartment with and affections for Barbara Jane Bookman (Jill Clayburgh), the beautiful daughter of their team's owner. In the battle for her attention, Shake's philosophical bohemia wins over Billy Clyde's rustic cowboy charms. Both men are media darlings, with Shake shilling personal hygiene products on TV while Billy Clyde is being wooed by a distinguished publisher to write a book about his experiences as a sports star. "No sensationalism. Nothing cheap, we're not that kind of house," says the eager editor. "We want the real truth, Billy Clyde, like what drugs the players take and how games are really fixed, the influence of the Mafia…. We know that there are gay football players, but who do they like to do it with? And are there more homosexuals on the offense or the defense?"

Marvin "Shake" Tiller (Kris Kristofferson) has second thoughts about marriage while Billy Clyde Puckett (Reynolds) is more than willing to take his place in *Semi-Tough* (1977).

"Defense," Puckett says. "You're allowed to use your hands on defense, gives you a better chance to grope somebody."

Billy Clyde has become disillusioned with the life of a sportsman and tires of playing second fiddle to Shake in the affections of Barbara. With Barbara spellbound by Shake's shaggy spirituality and dreamy demeanor, Billy Clyde decides to enlist in Friedrich Bismark's B.E.A.T. (Bismark Earthwalk Action Training) seminar to discover his sensitive side and gain an insight into winning Barbara's heart. This is the opportunity for director Michael Ritchie to engage the film's central comedic device of satirizing then-fashionable counter-cultural New Age self-help fads such as Werner Erhard's controversial Erhard Seminars Training ("est").

To please the Reynolds cinematic universe, the team for which Shake and Billy Clyde play was changed from the novel's original New York Giants to a Miami team. The picture differs from the source novel in several additional ways, notably the central love triangle, which is not consummated prior to the film's narrative. *Semi-Tough* is a ribald and sexually liberated romantic comedy which alternately functions as sports movie and social satire. The physical act of the sporting event takes a backseat to director Ritchie's focus on where the game has gone as regards the ancillary industries that support the sporting industry. It is not a picture about plays and tactics, or even winning and losing (apart from matters of the heart), it is about the crass, the commercial and the consciousness.

Ritchie rose to prominence during the American New Wave with lauded, confrontational and socially aware, if not commercially viable, works such as *Downhill Racer* (1969), *The Candidate*, *Prime Cut* (both 1972) and *Smile* (1975). He soon settled into a more aesthetically conventional style of filmmaking that conformed to the classical, nay *invisible*, filmmaking practice that major studios prefer. The result of this shift in style and sensibility saw a more streamlined aesthetic and increased box office receipts for the likes of *The Bad News Bears* (1976) and *Semi-Tough*; but if Ritchie willingly eschewed arthouse and critical credibility in favor of embracing a studio craftsman's career, not all of his endeavors worked accordingly and the remunerative success was not to last. He embarked on a series of ill-received major studio pictures *The Island* (1980), *Student Bodies* (1981), and *The Survivors* (1983), though he did strike gold in the 1980s with his Chevy Chase comedy *Fletch* (1985), which remains beloved enough to be considered a classic of its genre. Further star vehicles with Goldie Hawn (*Wildcats*, 1986), Eddie Murphy (*The Golden Child*, 1986) and Dan Aykroyd (*The Couch Trip*, 1988) disappointed audiences and critics alike.

In the aftermath of *Smokey and the Bandit*'s mammoth success, Reynolds was set to start filming his love letter to stunt professionals, *Hooper*, though ill health and other circumstances forced the project to be shelved for a year and *Semi-Tough* instead became his next box office success. One can't help but feel Reynolds was sending up his own public persona in Billy Clyde's Gene Autry–quoting, tabloid-courting pretty boy athlete, and perhaps in allusion to Reynolds' infamous *Cosmopolitan* spread, Kristofferson gets to parody a nude photo shoot. Not for the first time, Reynolds uses nostalgia for the art and culture of a bygone era as a device for his characters to retreat into. Gene Autry's songs are heard as a surrogate narration in place of Billy Clyde's emotional stoicism. In fact, the film is wonderfully scored by Autry's country balladry, while posters of his great B-westerns (*The Singing Cowboy*, 1936; *Night Stage to Galveston*, 1952; *On Top of Old Smoky*, 1953) adorn the walls of Billy Clyde's room; Autry is to Billy Clyde what Humphrey Bogart is to Detective

Phil Gaines in *Hustle*. While Billy Clyde's lack of sophistication could be the object of satire, and is quite often the subject of the film's many humorous moments, the filmmakers are sufficiently fond of the character not to make him a complete buffoon: Reynolds' down-to-earth practicality and charming earthiness allows the audience to root for Billy Clyde in his quest for Barbara's love. *Semi-Tough* was another success for Reynolds, now reaching the zenith of his remarkable prosperity and popularity, which makes it all the more astounding that Reynolds' next picture would be a daring gamble, especially for an actor whose success traded on his image as an indestructible, virile, good-time everyman.

The End
(1978)

"Forgive me, Dave, for I have sinned."—Wendell Lawson

In a move that would baffle most of Reynolds' fans and critics, the success of *Smokey and the Bandit* did not lead to more high-octane road pictures in the same vein—those would come in a couple of years. Instead, the star took a risky sidestep into some rather dark and interesting territory.

The End is a comedy in which real estate man Wendell "Sonny" Lawson is diagnosed with a terminal blood disease and, rather than endure a slow, agonizing death, he decides to kill himself. When that suicide attempt fails, he is committed to a mental institution where he meets schizophrenic patient Marlon Borunki (Dom DeLuise), with whom he hatches a plan for his demise. Sonny tries to make peace with the women in his life, with whom he has great difficulty maintaining a solid relationship, including his daughter Julie

Marlon Borunki (Dom DeLuise) isn't going to break his promise to help Sonny Lawson (Reynolds) meet his demise, even after Sonny changes his mind, in *The End* (1977).

(Kristy McNichol), his ex-wife Jessica (Joanne Woodward) and needy girlfriend Mary Ellen (Sally Field). All are unaware of Sonny's plans for self-destruction, not that it would matter to Jessica anyway, as their estrangement is due to Sonny's 200 indiscretions. Receiving no support from Jessica, Sonny is further insulted when Jessica's new beau turns out to be one of the young students to whom she teaches English. But as Sonny's suicide attempts fail in hilarious ineptitude, he slowly begins to appreciate his mortal coil and makes a final plea to God to let him live. Unfortunately for Sonny, Marlon has become a loyal friend and has promised to carry out the assignment given to him.

The film was originally written by Jerry Belson as a Woody Allen vehicle, and one can certainly see how the character of Sonny could be applied to Allen's nebbish hypochondriac. But whereas Allen's creation might solicit his own sense of impending doom, he would rarely follow through on bringing about his own demise in the manner of Reynolds' rendering of Sonny. The script had been making the Hollywood rounds for seven years due to the subject matter being considered too much of a commercial risk, but with Reynolds interested, it had box office potential. The star brought it to his friend Lawrence Gordon, who had previously produced the Walter Hill boxing drama *Hard Times* (1975). With Gordon on board, Reynolds approached the studios, where his star power afforded him some leverage when pitching *The End*. Warner Bros. made the wise move of offering to finance the picture on the condition that Reynolds would make two more traditionally mainstream products as part of the deal. One of those was already signed and sealed as a "go" picture with the studio, *Hooper*, on which Gordon returned as producer. With the relatively low budget of *The End*, Warner Bros. had invested wisely in financing the picture, as the promise of further Reynolds blockbusters was as good a guarantee of major returns as anything.

For Reynolds, the deal would be sweetened further with his studio bestowing upon him that most coveted of privileges: creative control. Reynolds decided to use some of his hard-earned influence to not only choose to star in something out of left field, but to produce (with an investment of $1 million, half of what he was earning per picture at the time) and to direct it as well. This level of interest (artistic, executive and financial) ensured total authority over the project. "Finally I decided to do something similar to what Sylvester Stallone did with *Rocky*," Reynolds said. "I bought the script, produced it and directed it, as well as being featured in it. The picture could surprise a lot of people who think I can only do limited things."[1]

Having been in various near-fatal situations that brought him close to the white light, Reynolds felt that only he could play the role of Sonny Lawson with the sincerity and absolute pitch black humor required for the picture. Having worked solidly on film productions for over a decade, the workaholic actor's health began to deteriorate. He became prone to health scares on film sets and in meetings, not to mention contracting serious diseases from hazardous location shoots (such as that on *Operation C.I.A.*), which led to much gossipy speculation as to the cause. Ultimately, Reynolds received a diagnosis of hypoglycemia and Tietze's Syndrome. However, after so many health scares, Reynolds parlayed his gallows humor into *The End* and the gamble paid off for all concerned. He brought the picture in on time and under budget and it eventually grossed $40 million on its $3.7 million budget. Not bad for a story about a dying man attempting to commit suicide.

Ever the active film historian using his considerable influence for the entertainment of himself and movie lovers, Reynolds' casting of Golden Age stars Pat O'Brien and Myrna Loy was a wonderful gesture of appreciation to Hollywood's great actors of yore. O'Brien said of Reynolds' skill behind the camera,

> It was a complete revelation. I knew Burt, but I did not know the extent of his directorial ability. He has a very inventive mind and he never raises his voice. He's kind.... I marveled every day watching him. He had so many different types of personalities to direct: young people, middle-aged, and the old codgers like me. I've never had an experience quite like it.[2]

Dom DeLuise was privileged with the funniest lines of the film as paranoid schizophrenic Marlon, a man committed for strangling his father—"He was so Polish!" He said of Reynolds, "I trusted that director on *The End* more than any director I've ever worked with.... He's marvelous. He's spontaneous.... He is a gentle, understanding, extremely talented director."[3]

The End remains a significant and laudable departure for Reynolds and he has a unique way with deadpan comedy that makes him eminently watchable and very funny, especially when delivering such lines as "I didn't know I was sick, I just thought I found a new way to lose weight: throwing up." Indeed, some very fine verbal comedy appears throughout the picture, as in the scene in which Jessica, the supposed teacher, speaks a mangled mix of pidgin French, Italian and Spanish to her young Latin lover, to whom the only language is that of amore. The gallows humor of the picture could be a potentially depressing prospect were it not for the sharp writing and the game performances from all concerned. From the pessimistic consultations with his doctor to following the funeral cortege of a stranger and having the reflection of a crucifix mark his forehead as he sits and watches, *The End* is one of Reynolds' funniest pictures, displaying his keen understanding of great comic timing. In the lead-up to the best line in the picture, Sonny decides to have his first confession with a priest in decades, but instead of seeking absolution with the gravitas one would expect, he is met with a fresh-faced and eager young priest who insists that Sonny call him "Dave" instead of "Father." The payoff is the hilarious line, "Forgive me, Dave, for I have sinned." It is because of moments like these that one can easily forgive the morbidity of the themes and tone of *The End*.

Notes

1. Bernhardt J. Hurwood, *Burt Reynolds* (New York: Quick Fox, 1970), p. 92.
2. Sylvia Safran Resnick, *Burt Reynolds* (London: W.H. Allen, 1983), p. 206.
3. Dianna Whitely, *Burt Reynolds: Portrait of a Superstar* (New York: Grossett & Dunlap, 1979), p 104–105.

Hooper
(1978)

> "I'm gonna find the guy who invented Xylocaine and kiss his ass on Hollywood and Vine!"—Sonny Hooper

Sonny Hooper (Reynolds), "World's Greatest Stuntman," is shooting an elaborate action picture called *The Spy Who Laughed at Danger*, on which he is the stunt double for the film's star, Adam West. After a long time at the top, Sonny's body is starting to feel the strain of all those years of punishment, but to Sonny and his fans, showing signs of slowing down would run counter to his image as an invincible daredevil. Sonny's girlfriend Gwen Doyle (Sally Field) is concerned; she has seen the debilitating effects of such work in her father, Jocko Doyle (Brian Keith), a revered stuntman whom Sonny has replaced at the industry's top guy. Like Jocko, health issues are forcing Sonny's reign as the industry's preeminent stuntman to near its end, and he is relying heavily on painkillers to get by. Sonny witnesses an amazing stunt at a charity event performed by skillful up-and-comer Delmore Shidski, or "Ski" (Jan Michael Vincent). The two men become firm friends after a brawl in a local tavern and begin working together. Their bond is founded on mutual respect and friendly rivalry; their challenges become increasingly dangerous in a bid to outdo one another. Sonny's back has taken too much of a beating over the years and he is under orders from his doctor to quit before he is left paralyzed. But then the director of *The Spy Who Laughed at Danger*, Roger Deal (Robert Klein), is convinced by Ski to change the film's climax and have a car traveling at high speed leap a gorge. Sonny agrees on the condition that it is a rocket-powered vehicle, having Ski accompany him, and being paid $100,000, essentially a retirement fund. Such a stunt could either prove his ultimate triumph as a performer or could see him bowing out in a fatal blaze of glory.

Directed by the actual greatest stuntman in the movies, Hal Needham, *Hooper* is a fine tribute to those who sacrifice limb after limb for our entertainment and for the good of studio stockholders. Nobody knew that world like Needham, and the character of Sonny

Stuntman Sonny Hooper (Reynolds) risks life and limb for the movies in *Hooper* (1978).

Hooper could be seen as an amalgam of the greats of their profession: Jock Mahoney, Yakima Canutt and of course Needham. Much of Hooper's experiences relate directly to Reynolds and Needham's prior work. The major car stunt at the end of the picture is similar to that of Needham's automobile leap in *White Lightning* which seriously injured and nearly killed him when doubling for Reynolds. A tagline on the film's poster read "Ain't nobody can fly a car like Hooper!" Well, truth be told, ain't nobody can fly a car like Hal Needham. Many movies-about-movies have been released since, but as of 1978 *Hooper* was in the minority of pictures about the unsung stunters who make the stars look good. Brian Keith's character Jocko Doyle is a close sketch of Sally Field's real-life stepfather and legendary stuntman Jock Mahoney; Mahoney's blood daughter (Field's stepsister) Princess O'Mahoney appears in the picture as Wanda.

Doyle is an old master of the stunt world who has been replaced in an industry increasingly reliant upon more daring and dangerous stunt work that only the young and fit can handle, and he has resorted to medicating himself through alcohol. "You oughta drink more," Jocko tells Sonny. "Nothing hurts when you're numb." Jocko is an image of what potentially lies ahead for Sonny, crippled with pain and debilitated with self-medication, watching enviously as the next Young Turks reap the benefits of their brief stint at the top. As with many athletes, Sonny is over the hill at a relatively young age (his mid–40s), and Ski's presence can't help but remind Sonny that his time is up.

Following the mammoth success of Universal's *Smokey and the Bandit*, Warner Bros.

Gwen (Sally Field) tries to convince Sonny (Reynolds) to twice about performing a very risky stunt in *Hooper* (1978).

president Ted Ashley offered Reynolds $1 million for their very own definitive Burt Reynolds product, which was to be *Hooper*. However, health issues brought on by hypoglycemia meant a delay in starting the picture on schedule and so it was put on hold for a year while Reynolds got back in good health. In the meantime, he starred in the football industry satire *Semi-Tough* and directed, produced and starred in *The End*. *Hooper*'s summer 1978 release proved another huge draw for Reynolds' considerable fan base and a coup for Warner Bros., grossing more than ten times its $6 million budget. The picture was well received enough as to engender a spectacular turnaround of opinion of Reynolds from *New Yorker* film critic David Denby, who wrote:

> I took my time seeing the new Burt Reynolds picture, *Hooper*, because I hated his previous collaboration with director Hal Needham, the phenomenally successful *Smokey and the Bandit*, and because Reynolds has never been big box office in New York. Mea culpa mea maxima culpa. A raucous celebration of the childish daring of Hollywood stunt men, *Hooper* is one of the most entertaining films of the year, and if New York doesn't respond to it with the same enthusiasm as the provinces, then New York has become a snobbishly provincial movie town.[1]

Where Denby initially went wrong was to presume *Hooper* to be just another car crash spectacular from the Burt brand. It is a picture of far more weight and pathos than *Smokey and the Bandit*, even if it does share the same surface spirit of fun and adventure. *Hooper* is actually more in the tradition of backstage showbiz pictures, and *Singin' in the Rain* (1952) aside, these were rarely considered lucrative box office attractions. The intertextual formalism of these kinds of pictures doesn't always apply to a mainstream aesthetic which functions on invisibility and illusion through artifice. If you break through the fourth wall and put on display the mechanics of filmmaking, you risk depicting the neuroses and the fragility of those behind the scenes, as well as inviting complex self-reflexive considerations of the very act of watching movies. Many films in this canon, such as *The Last Movie* (Dennis Hopper, 1971), *Day for Night* (François Truffaut, 1973), *Day of the Locust* (John Schlesinger, 1975) and *Living in Oblivion* (Tom DiCillo, 1995) depict ego, money, pressure and dwindling sanity as ingredients for a precarious film production.

Sonny has become addicted to Percodan pills and shots of Xylocaine to suppress the pain those years of stunts are now bringing about. We witness how this kind of lifestyle impacts upon the friends and family of those willing to risk their life for the movies. But *Hooper* is good-natured enough and provides enough superficial fun as to not dwell excessively upon the more troubling aspects of the lifestyle of stuntmen. It is sufficiently dramatic and candid about the lives of those involved for us to truly care about the characters. There are several comedic set pieces which play into the kind of consequence-free cartoon violence that *Smokey and the Bandit*, *The Cannonball Run* and the likes of Clint Eastwood's *Every Which Way but Loose* (1978) and *Any Which Way You Can* (1980) used to great success. Bodies are flung through windows, bottles are smashed over heads, punches are landed, and yet everybody comes away unscathed; buddies, in fact. After one such bar brawl between the picture's stunt unit and a boisterous off-duty SWAT team, hands are shook, backs are patted and soon Sonny has everyone back to his place for a party, drinking and viewing old stunt reels (including one from *Deliverance*).

The picture is also notable as the third screen collaboration of Reynolds and Field, and their chemistry here is much more endearing and alive than their awkward, neurotic relationship depicted in *The End*. Perhaps given the personally relevant nature of much of

Hooper's narrative and characters, both actors appear to be truly invested in their material and it is here more than any other film that we truly sense the spark of chemistry that existed between the pair in real life. There is a tangible sense of fun, warmth, intimacy and genuine love here, more than most onscreen-offscreen relationships.

Note

1. David Denby, "Movies: Hoopla," *New York Magazine*, 28 August 1978, p. 94.

Starting Over

(1979)

"Can I call if I get happy?"—Phil Potter

Phil Potter (Burt Reynolds), is a New York travel writer whose wife Jessica (Candice Bergen) has seemingly outgrown their humble life with her ambitions to be a pop star. Phil is patient and caring; too kind, for example, to tell Jessica she is an awful singer. His passivity is finally brought to its limit when Jessica reveals she is seeing another man, Neil, the kind of man who signs his letters "Evermore." Potter moves out of their stylish Manhattan apartment to a cold water Boston apartment, where he attempts to rebuild his life while accepting the charity and well-meaning platitudes of his brother Mickey and sister-in-law Marva. At their home, Phil is immediately showered with prosaic words of wisdom. "Phil, this could be the best thing to happen to you," Marva says. "It could be very exciting…. The possibilities for growth and self-awareness, getting to know yourself, could be the most wonderfully happy, even thrilling experience!" Phil's loneliness is exacerbated in his grim new dwelling, and he ends up eagerly calling his brother at all hours of the morning to arrange the next day's dinner. As Phil exits a bus in a quiet suburban neighborhood, a timid young woman gets off at the same stop. The two walk in the same direction, with Phil trailing a little behind as the woman scurries along. Director Alan J. Pakula's camera privileges the woman to heighten her anxiety; then the woman whirls around on Phil and screams, "Get the fuck away from me! I've got a knife. I'll cut your fucking balls off, so help me!" Frozen in bewilderment, Phil remains static as the woman flees.

When Phil arrives at his brother's house, Micky informs him that their friend Marilyn Holmberg (Jill Clayburgh) was just attacked by a pervert. Phil is introduced to Marilyn, wrapped in blankets by the fire, comforted by Marva. And so the "pervert" meets his "victim"; much embarrassment ensues. It turns out that Micky and Marva had invited Phil and Marilyn as a blind date. Phil begins to set up a new life for himself, obtaining a part-time job teaching, taking part in a workshop for divorced men, and throwing himself back onto the singles scene. Phil endures a date with an overbearing single mother, Marie (Mary Kay Place), but when she sings Jessica's hit single, Phil plans on making his exit, but not before Marie corners him in an elevator after a duck dinner date. As the unfortunate dates come and go, he begins to fall for Marilyn, but complications arise when Jessica arrives back on his doorstep, now a pop star and attempting to win back Phil's affections with a deliriously out-of-tune rendition of her new song "Better Than Ever." Phil is torn between returning to his comfortable but passionless old life with Jessica and remaining on course with an uncertain but exciting future with Marilyn.

Starting Over is a brilliantly written, extremely funny romantic picture. With its floundering male protagonist uprooted from his comfortable domestic life, the picture plays into the social-cultural mood of the era's "divorce pictures" and male melodramas such as *Kramer vs. Kramer* (Robert Benton, 1979), *Author! Author!* (Arthur Hiller, 1982) and *Mr. Mom* (Stan Dragoti, 1983). In the opening scene, Phil, freshly scorned by the female species, abandons any chivalry that may have existed before his heart was broken. Leaving his apartment building, just as a dog tries to snatch clothes from his hastily prepared suitcase, a Yellow Cab handily pulls to the sidewalk; when a fur-coated lady loaded down with her shopping spree makes a break for the cab, we think Phil performs an act of selflessness by opening the door for her to enter. "Thank you," the woman says, just as Phil jumps into the cab, vowing "Not any more!" Pakula has returned to the examination of male-female relationship dynamics in his genre-hopping career, in pictures as varied as *Klute* (1971), *See You in the Morning* (1989) and *Presumed Innocent* (1990), works which would suggest the director has a particular distrust of the institution of marriage and suspicious of the very nature of monogamy. But in *Starting Over,* the director has some fun with his preoccupation.

One of the recurring narrative features is a divorced men's workshop which shares the same church space as that of the divorced women's group who meet afterwards. Despite the holy setting, there is no harmony between the sexes. In one darkly hilarious sequence, masterfully maneuvered by Sven Nykvist's circling camera, a 72-year-old member of the men's club laments a lifetime of monogamy and loyalty to a wife who left him on their 43rd wedding anniversary: "She said there were no surprises left," he says. Nykist captures a parade of meek, emasculated men, each countenance a portrait of dread as the old man

Phil Potter (Reynolds, cross-legged) joins the divorced men's workshop in *Starting Over* (1979).

tells of the inclination of elderly women to attach themselves to single older men: "You have no idea how many women want you as you're getting old; how many liver-spotted female hands reach out to squeeze the last drops from your body as they go about living longer than we do." The man's ghastly intonation culminates with the doom-laden toll of the church bells, announcing not only a damning reminder of the once-sacrosanct vows of marriage, but more immediately, the arrival of the divorced women's group. The two groups reach an impasse on the stairs, only for the men to yield and cower aside to let the procession of females march past.

In an era of sophisticated, urbane and very fine romantic comedies such as *The Goodbye Girl* (Herbert Ross, 1977), *Same Time Next Year* (Robert Mulligan, 1977) and *Manhattan* (Woody Allen, 1979), *Starting Over* is among the very best of the decade. It's gorgeously shot by Nykvist, erstwhile Ingmar Bergman and future Woody Allen cinematographer, who shrouds the film in a richly textured, warm decor that feels natural and unobtrusive, which contrasts exquisitely with the cold, harsh Boston winter outside. A master of natural lighting, Nykvist often illuminates the scene with the light available in the diegetic space of the scene: candles, a fireplace, etc. Nykvist's evocative formalism functions on two levels: capturing a more pessimistic mood to suit the dark comedy of the picture, but also embellishing the comforting sense of home and family that Micky and Marva supply Phil with in his dark hour.

Like many of its contemporaries, the picture is a rumination not just on lost love, but finding it again. The central irony of Reynolds being cast as a loser in love surely tickled many, but according to the actor, *Starting Over* is the closest thing to the real Burt Reynolds ever depicted on film. When the script came to his attention, he wasted little time in soliciting the interest of its director. "Pakula wanted one of those serious New York actors in the role, but I desperately wanted it for myself," Reynolds says. "My agent Sue Mengers thought I was nuts. 'You can't play a guy who can't get a date,' she said. I finally got a meeting with Pakula … he was polite and not about to make any offers. So I simply asked for a shot."[1]

The director was skeptical, informing Reynolds that his public image as a debauched, decadent Casanova was in contrast with the role of a man who struggles with the opposite sex. In essence: How could Burt Reynolds be believable as a man as beige and modest as Phil Potter? "I've played a lot of parts," Reynolds told Pakula, "but I've never played me. And this is me."[2] Pakula screen-tested Reynolds, an act not normally requested of major stars of such commercial caliber, and the actor won the role. According to Reynolds, "When we started the movie I told Alan that people were going to say he took a hell of a chance casting me. Actually, he couldn't lose though, because if I turned out well, he would get the credit. If I was really terrible, he could always say that the studio made him use me."[3] Despite the fact that Reynolds won the role and wholly embraced the opportunity of breaking stereotype and expectation, insecurities remained as he was resigned to the fact that Pakula was a perfectionist who had doubts about casting the star. But the director persevered and allowed Reynolds to deliver one of his finest performances with the pathos of a man in true existential crisis.

Jill Clayburgh was perfectly cast as Marilyn. The wonderful actress embodied a progressive, perhaps feminist ideal of the time. Phil and Marilyn's awkward introduction is a wonderful piece of narrative economy which informs us as to the type of person Marilyn is: needy, insecure, vulnerable, but vigilante. Clayburgh embodied the burgeoning sexual, intellectual and social liberties of the post-counterculture era. Throughout her career, Clayburgh craftily parlayed her well-bred, educated Upper East Side bohemia to the screen in such substantial pictures as *Semi-Tough* (Michael Ritchie, 1977), *An Unmarried Woman* (Paul Mazursky, 1978), *La Luna* (Bernardo Bertolucci, 1979), *It's My Turn* (Claudia Weill, 1980) and *Shy People* (Andrei Konchalovsky, 1987). The film's two supporting actresses both garnered Academy Award nominations, Best Actress (Jill Clayburgh) and Best Supporting Actress (Candice Bergen). Neither took home the prize, as Sally Field won for *Norma Rae* in the former category, while Meryl Streep reigned supreme in the latter for *Kramer vs. Kramer*. James L. Brooks and Dan Wakefield should have at least been nominated for their script, adapted from Wakefield's novel, but they had to compete with the socio-political heavy hitters of the year that included *Apocalypse Now*, *La Cage Aux Folles* and *Kramer vs. Kramer*.

The most obvious snub, however, was Burt Reynolds for Best Actor. Despite his terrific performance in the picture, it seems as though Hollywood, or at least the members of the Academy, refused to reward an actor who so thoroughly relished his fame, wealth and the act of acting. Though overlooked by the Academy, Reynolds was Golden Globe-nominated for "Best Actor in a Motion Picture—Musical or Comedy." He lost out to Peter Sellers for *Being There*.

Notes

1. Burt Reynolds, *My Life: Burt Reynolds* (Great Britain: Hodder & Stoughton, 1994), p. 229.
2. *Ibid.*, p. 230.
3. Sylvia Safran Resnick, *Burt Reynolds* (London: W.H. Allen, 1983), p. 174.

Rough Cut
(1980)

"I'm not imitating Tony Curtis, I'm imitating Cary Grant!"—Jack Rhodes

Burt Reynolds plays Jack Rhodes, a gentleman jewel thief who moves in the upper circles of British high society and aristocracy. He is considering bowing out of his criminal game while ahead of the law. Beautiful socialite Gillian Bromley (Lesley-Anne Down) convinces him to pull off one last major heist worth £30 million in uncut diamonds. Smitten by her power and grace, Rhodes is unaware that Bromley is being manipulated by corrupt Scotland Yard Chief Inspector Cyril Willis (David Niven); Willis plans on a grand retirement and is coercing Bromley with a threat of prosecution to recruit Rhodes to assist in the diamond heist. The business of burglary is compromised when affairs of the heart enter the fray, as Rhodes and Bromley become romantically entwined, leading to Bromley revealing Willis' role in the master plan.

When one of the great directors of Hollywood action pictures teams up with the greatest action star of the period, you expect fireworks. *Rough Cut* instead gives us soggy kindling. One of the myriad problems with the picture is its glossy, elegant facade; a creaky, old-fashioned classical Hollywood aesthetic which sits perfectly well with the refinement of Downs and Niven, but feels far too delicate for someone of Reynolds' edgy energy and anarchic spirit. Regardless, Reynolds takes the opportunity to indulge in a character that is part tribute to his hero Cary Grant, allowing the star to channel his dormant debonair flair as the charming crook resplendent in haute couture. Reynolds' introduction in the picture even allows him to showcase his impression of Grant, whom Bromley mistakes for Tony Curtis. Reynolds stepped up to craft Rhodes as required: elegantly rugged, witty and handsome, but the stagnant material lets him down.

Don Siegel, so brilliant a genre chameleon, whether working in horror (*Invasion of the Body Snatchers*, 1956), action (*Dirty Harry*, 1971), western (*The Shootist*, 1976) or espionage (*Telefon*, 1977), flounders with this conventional and lethargic material. It comes as no surprise that the production of *Rough Cut* was as convoluted as the plot of the picture. Siegel and producer Daniel Merrick feuded to the point that the renowned director was fired and replaced by a series of filmmakers including Blake Edwards, who was also fired and replaced by Peter R. Hunt. Drafting Hunt, a director of variable pedigree (*On Her Majesty's Secret Service*, 1969; *Shout at the Devil*, 1976; *Wild Geese II*, 1985; *Assassination*, 1986) into the situation proved disastrous. Stuntman Vic Armstrong recalled the mess: "When Reynolds heard about it, he said, 'The only reason I'm doing this fucking film is because of Siegel. Get him back.'"[1]

And so Siegel was duly reinstated. Reynolds further exercised his power of approval and brought in Hal Needham to direct second unit, which would instill some much needed life into the stodgy caper picture. Armstrong recalls his first impressions of an ostentatious Needham upon arrival in England: "He had gold dripping all over him. He had gold chains and medallions of the movies he'd directed, and how many millions they'd earned, which was a huge amount, on his belt."[2] With Needham on the crew, the picture benefits from the legendary stuntman's instinct for intricate and exciting action, executed particularly well in the climactic airport jewel switch.

Up to four endings were shot for *Rough Cut*, with six screenwriters coming and going along the way. Original screenwriter Larry Gelbart (*Oh God!*, 1977; *Tootsie*, 1982) was so dismayed with the final cut that he is credited under the pseudonym Francis Burns. Lawsuits and arbitrations flew for a variety of discrepancies, including one in which the Directors Guild of America fought in Hunt's corner against Merrick and Paramount when the sacked director claimed his salary. When the picture wrapped, Merrick was also sued by David Niven, the actor dismayed at the cuts made to his character and to his name being relegated to third billing behind Reynolds and Down. The case was settled out of court, resulting in Niven winning $125,000 in damages—"Not bad money for being shafted,"[3] according to Niven. But while the production may have been a mess and the picture itself less than the sum of its parts, Reynolds left an indelible impression upon his distinguished co-star: "I would love to make every picture with Burt Reynolds—if that were possible,"[4] Niven said. Unfortunately, the two stars were never given the opportunity of a more agreeable picture to work on together, and so *Rough Cut* remains a curious relic which teases with what could have been.

Notes

1. Vic Armstrong with Robert Sellers, *The True Adventures of the World's Greatest Stuntman: My Life as Indiana Jones, James Bond, Superman and Other Movie Heroes* (London: Titan Books, 2011) [n.p.].

2. *Ibid.*
3. Michael Munn, *David Niven: The Man Behind the Balloon* (London: JR Books, 2009) [n.p.].
4. *Ibid.*

Smokey and the Bandit II

(1980)

"I'm the only guy in the world who could drink up a Trans-Am."—The Bandit

Like the original *Smokey and the Bandit*, this sequel opens with Little Enos (Paul Williams) and Big Enos Burdette (Pat McCormick) conniving to transport a shipment across the country for their personal amusement and financial gain. Big Enos is running for governor of Texas as a conservative and tries to make a name for himself by delivering a special crate from Miami to the Republican Party Convention in Dallas, and there's only two men for the job: Cledus "Snowman" Snow (Jerry Reed) and Bo "The Bandit" Darville (Reynolds). The Bandit is whiling away his days as an alcoholic, lounging around a flophouse motel in the shadow of his former celebrity and wallowing in self-pity. ("Do you want a picture of me? They're only fifty cents!" he asks sadly.) Frog (Sally Field) has rekindled her romance with Junior Justice and is walking down the aisle only to be interrupted by Cledus looking for help in sobering up Bo. With Frog fleeing the Justice clan once again, Buford and Junior hit the road as the titular Smokey in hot pursuit of the Bandit. Making life more difficult for Bo & Co. is the revelation that that their cargo contains a pregnant elephant named Charlotte, and the logistics of transporting such comes with its own comic possibilities.

How do you follow one of the biggest box office successes of all time? Well, if you are

Bandit blows down his house of Buds with a burp in *Smokey and the Bandit II* (1981).

director Hal Needham, repeat it note for note, and so the director replicates his hugely popular 1977 original slavishly. And yet there isn't anywhere near as much affection for *Smokey and the Bandit II*, which is a shame because this picture is often just as much fun as the first. However, despite the majority of the 1977 cast returning and with the script hitting all the right beats, there is a notable change in chemistry between Reynolds and Sally Field. Where previously there was an electric cuteness between the two, obviously sparked by their burgeoning real-life relationship, here their tone is charged with drama, antagonism and tough love. When Frog chides Bo for refusing to grow up and take responsibility for his life, the scene is effective though perhaps for all the wrong reasons, as it feels all too real and relevant, knowing that the Reynolds-Field relationship ended around the time of the film's production. "You're hooked. You're a fame junkie," she chides. "They might as well lock you up and give you intravenous feedings of *People* magazine and *National Enquirer* headlines. And if you're a real good boy, they'll give you an occasional *Tonight Show* enema!"

Dom DeLuise is the main addition to this sequel, playing Frederico "Doc" Carlucci, a gynecologist of questionable repute, with typically wild abandon, rendering his Italian stereotype to absurd proportions of cliché. He's rarely without a glass of wine and a plate of pasta no matter the situation. Meanwhile, Jackie Gleason returns and receives even more screen time here, playing not just one but three roles: Sheriff Buford T. Justice, Gaylord Justice and Reginald Van Justice. The Great One delivers a relentless assault of funny one-liners in between repeating his famous "sumbitch" catchphrase. A recurring gag is that the apoplectic Justice is fitted with a mobile blood pressure monitor which is constantly set off when irked by, well, everyone. One of those to relentlessly alert Justice's "haemo-guage" often is Junior, as Gleason and Henry continue their touching but abrasive father-son relationship, in which Daddy Justice is brutally caustic as ever. "Hey, Daddy, look at that big, ugly alligator!" says Junior, to which Buford replies, "That reminds me, I gotta call your mamma tonight."

 Buford T. Justice (Jackie Gleason) and Junior Justice (Mike Henry) are left at the altar once again in *Smokey and the Bandit II* (1981).

Smokey and the Bandit II is a thoroughly enjoyable, undemanding picture. If one single shot sums up the entire affair, it is Bo's unflattering introduction: a drunken burp directly into the camera. It speaks volumes about the overall personality and tone of the picture: lowbrow, rude, rambunctious, and in-your-face, but we wouldn't want a *Smokey and the Bandit* picture any other way. Aside from the awkward references to Reynolds' life, which makes it feel as though we are voyeuristically listening in on a couple's argument, *Smokey and the Bandit II* is littered with in-jokes referencing Reynolds' previous work and cultural iconography. The seedy "Gator Motel" is a nod to the star's iconic character Gator McClusky, and when Bo reveals he released a record which tanked, he laments the failure as being "the wrong selection of material: 'The Bandit Sings Cole Porter.'" Of course, Reynolds did experience his own failed attempt at singing from the Cole Porter songbook in Peter Bogdanovich's *At Long Last Love*.

The Cannonball Run

(1981)

"Don't think for a minute that we in Washington don't appreciate your Mothers' March to ban the sale of colored toilet paper to help reduce irritation of the rectum!"—Arthur J. Foyt

An ensemble road comedy of epic proportions, *The Cannonball Run* is the story of an illegal cross-country race which begins in Connecticut, takes in the Midwest and finishes in Southern California. Amongst the many racers who line up to punch their clock cards before proceeding west is J.J. McLure (Reynolds) and his road partner Victor Prinzi (Dom DeLuise), traveling in an ambulance which is actually a modified 1978 Dodge Sportsman B-200 van. Their chief rivals for the prize money: shifty gamblers Jamie Blake (Dean Martin) and Morris Fenderbaum (Sammy Davis Jr.), who disguise themselves as priests yet undermine their own diversion tactics by driving an indiscreet Ferrari 308 GTS. Another contestant is Seymour Goldfarb Jr., delusional playboy heir to the Goldfarb Girdles empire, who is under the illusion that he is playboy actor Roger Moore. In one of the film's many self-referential gags, Goldfarb is actually played by Roger Moore. The race is being observed by Arthur J. Foyt (George Furth) of the Safety Enforcement Unit, who seeks to shut down the race on environmental grounds. Foyt is accompanied by photographer and nature-lover Pamela Glover (Farrah Fawcett).

The Cannonball Run is based on a real-life coast-to-coast race, the Cannonball Baker Sea-to-Shining-Sea Memorial Trophy Dash (aka Cannonball Run). It took place on several occasions throughout the 1970s, flouting highway laws at every opportunity. The Cannonball Run race was the brainchild of automotive journalist and future Motorsports Hall of Fame honoree Brock Yates, who was inspired by the work of Edwin G "Cannonball" Baker and conceived the race partly in protest to the 55 MPH speed limit being rolled out across America at the time. The race inspired several pictures, including *The Gumball Rally* (1976), *Cannonball* (1976), and of course, *The Cannonball Run*. One of those who took part in the 1979 race was Hal Needham, the famed Hollywood stuntman turned hugely successful filmmaker. He drove a Dodge Sportsman B-200, a modified ambulance kitted out with a Chrysler HEMI 90-gallon

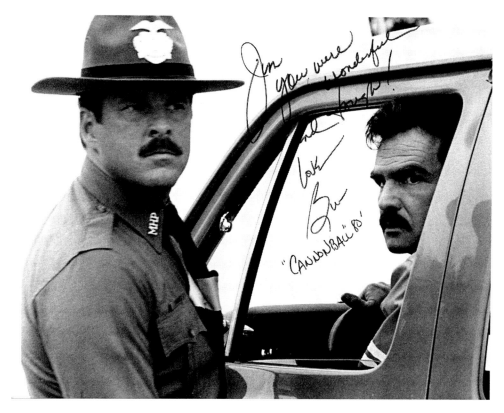

C. James Lewis and Reynolds filming a scene for *The Cannonball Run* (1981) (photograph courtesy C. James Lewis Collection).

engine which gave out somewhere in California before he could reach the end of the line. Needham's passenger for the journey was Yates. As the two petrolheads became firm friends, they began a brief but successful screenwriting partnership which produced this picture specifically based on their exploits, as well as *Smokey and the Bandit II*.[1] Yates even appears in here as the organizer of the event, seen boosting the morale of the assembled drivers as they embark upon the race: "You are certainly the most distinguished group of highway scofflaws and degenerates ever gathered together in one place."

The picture was produced by Golden Harvest, a titan of Hong Kong cinema. Its cofounders, Raymond Chow and Leonard Ho, created stars such as Bruce Lee and Jackie Chan, and brought with them to Hollywood their formula for a fresh, kinetic kind of action cinema with the likes of *Enter the Dragon* (1973). The success of their entering into partnership with Hollywood power players was staggering as *The Cannonball Run*, with its plethora of stars and budget of $16 million, saw the return of a whopping $168 million in worldwide grosses,[2] making Reynolds' $5 million salary a justified investment. Ten years later, Golden Harvest scored even bigger with *Teenage Mutant Ninja Turtles* (Steve Barron, 1990), which raked in over $200 million worldwide on a $13.5 million budget. *The Cannonball Run* also gave Golden Harvest an opportunity to market their own indigenous talent, and placed Jackie Chan amongst the myriad American performers in his very first Hollywood screen appearance. It was a fine introduction for Chan, who became a hugely

Jill Rivers (Tara Buckman) and Marcie Thatcher (Adrienne Barbeau) unzip for the wrong kind of traffic cop in *The Cannonball Run* (1981).

popular box office draw in America as well as internationally with films like *Rumble in the Bronx* (1996), *Rush Hour* (1998) and *Shanghai Noon* (2000).

Academy Award–winning producer Al Ruddy (*The Godfather*, 1972; *The Longest Yard*, 1974) initially put the project together as a Steve McQueen vehicle. McQueen, however, was ailing and unable to take on such a physically demanding production. A major name would be required to appease Golden Harvest and one name that more than met the criteria was Burt Reynolds. Ruddy's previous association with Reynolds must surely have appeased the suits at Golden Harvest, as *The Longest Yard* accumulated a staggering $43 million on an estimated budget of $2.9 million. And so Reynolds broke Hollywood records when he received $5 million (plus a percentage of box office receipts), one-third of the film's $16 million budget, for five weeks of fun shooting *The Cannonball Run* in Georgia.

With Reynolds came a number of performers who were close to the actor's heart but who had been out of the limelight for some time. After James Garner and Don Rickles turned down the roles of Blake and Fenderbaum, Rat Pack members Dean Martin and Sammy Davis Jr. stepped in. Neither had starred in a motion picture in several years; Martin had starred in the largely forgotten crime drama *Mr. Ricco* in 1975, while Davis appeared in the similarly ignored western *Gone with the West*, also 1975. Loni Anderson, then a television star via her role in *WKRP in Cincinnati*, was considered for the part of Pamela Glover. But the role eventually went to Farrah Fawcett, another actress awaiting casting in a successful picture, having starred in a string of financial failures following her departure from *Charlie's Angels*. Perhaps the most inspired piece of casting is that of western mainstay Jack Elam as the grotesque Dr. Nicolas Van Helsing, a "doctor of proctology and other assorted tendencies" and "graduate of the University of Rangoon, as well as assorted night classes at the Knoxville, Tennessee, College of Faith Healing." The good doctor is taken on the ride in McLure's ambulance to keep Glover sedate with his impressive hypodermic needle with which Van Helsing also regularly self-medicates. It didn't matter that some of the co-stars hadn't been lucrative for some time, as Reynolds' name on the marquee was enough to guarantee at least some kind of return on investment.

The picture's skittish sense of humor is typified by the inclusion of Roger Moore sending up as far as is legally possible his turn as James Bond. By 1981, Moore had appeared as Ian Fleming's superspy in four Bond pictures, but as he had always considered his performance as Bond somewhat playful in the first place, he felt no need to satirize it further and initially declined the offer of appearing in the picture; it would take a meeting with Needham to convince Moore of his comedic potential. Needham envisioned Moore's character as having delusions of living as James Bond, but Moore relented, suggesting, "I won't send up Bond, but I'll tell you what I would do…. I would send up Roger Moore…. I'd love to play someone who thought he was Roger Moore, particularly if I had a name like Seymour Goldfarb and a mother played by Molly Picon."[3] Moore thought Needham merely humored him with an "Okay," but then the *Cannonball Run* script arrived on Moore's doorstep complete with the character of Seymour Goldfarb Jr., a delusional millionaire philanderer who imagines he is Roger Moore, drives an Aston Martin, is seen with a different gorgeous woman in every scene, and features a mother to be played by Yiddish theater icon Molly Picon. Needham delivered.

The Cannonball Run plays like a live-action version of Hanna-Barbera's *Wacky Races*, an anarchic cartoon that unspools in such a casual manner that it feels more like you're eavesdropping on a party of friends having a good time. As with most Needham pictures (*Hooper* excepted), plot and character take the proverbial back seat to gags and stunts. While pictures such as *The End*, *Semi-Tough* and *Starting Over* paid dividends for Reynolds personally and aesthetically, it seemed as though he could rarely please critics with these substantive roles in respectable productions, so the star was just as well to cash in on a lark. And he did just that with *The Cannonball Run*. As with *Smokey and the Bandit*, Reynolds distilled a story of civil disobedience and served it up as an easily digestible, eminently profitable and supremely entertaining slice of Hollywood entertainment.

Notes

1. Gareth Owen, "The Cannonball Run Collector's Booklet," DVD Supplement, *The Cannonball Run*, Fortune Star Media, 2010.

2. Michael Curtin, *Playing to the World's Biggest Audience: The Globalization of Chinese Film and TV* (California: University of California Press, 2007), p. 54.

3. Roger Moore with Gareth Owen, *My Word Is My Bond: The Autobiography* (London: Michael O'Mara Books, 2008), p. 238.

Paternity

(1981)

"I'm a man who has everything: no wife, no kids, no house, no mortgage."
—Buddy Evans

It seems as though Buddy Evans (Reynolds) has it all. He has a successful career as the manager of Madison Square Garden and leads the comfortable life of a bachelor in a luxurious apartment. But Buddy's buddies, Larry and Kurt (Norman Fell and Paul Dooley), remind him that something is indeed missing. No, not a woman, but a child ("There's nothing to say that Buddy Evans was here!"). Buddy is in his mid–40s and as the years roll by he yearns to be a father; but the committed playboy has never found the right woman. Rather than going through the dating and mating game, he decides to interview a procession of women in order to find the ideal surrogate mother.

An ideal candidate has been right under his nose all along: Maggie (Beverly D'Angelo), a waitress at his local restaurant, struggles to make ends meet while aspiring to be a classical musician. The $50,000 being offered by Buddy would help her realize her dream of studying music in Paris. For Buddy, this is strictly an emotionless business transaction and Maggie is quite happy with that arrangement, but we are well aware of the generic registers of the romantic comedy and await the expected courtship to follow between Buddy and Maggie.

Paternity was director David Steinberg's filmmaking debut. He was a noted comedian before Reynolds sought him out to helm the picture and together their comedic sensibilities worked exquisitely. Reynolds parlays his excellent comic timing and physical mannerisms into one of the most likable performances of his career, rendering Buddy as a genuinely warm, witty guy who is successful without being a shark or a cynic.

The picture proved to be the last of the run of sophisticated adult comedies in which Reynolds drew upon his sensitivity and humility—*Semi-Tough*, *Starting Over*, *The End*—and it was the actor's real-life persona that intrigued Steinberg the most. "The Burt Reynolds that I love most and admire more than any other Burt Reynolds is the one he displays when he hosts *The Tonight Show*," Steinberg said. "[F]or *Paternity*, I told him to be that person, the person he has never been in any film."[1]

Paternity is a pleasant and predictable comedy, but it does have some subtle post-feminist satire to keep things sharp and topical. When Kurt walks past a beautiful woman on the street, he comments to Larry that she is a "pretty girl," to which Larry sarcastically replies, "We don't say 'pretty' any more. That's sexist. Now we say, 'She's got good bone structure.'" The guileless Kurt then pays a compliment to a pretty restaurant waitress: "I like your bone structure!" Later, in a very funny montage sequence, Buddy sets out to find an appropriate surrogate mother for his child and we meet some of his ex-girlfriends, including a tough butcher whose skills at extracting animal organs reminds Buddy of just why it didn't work out between them.

The picture is unfairly overlooked in the realm of 1980s romantic comedies. It offers an alternative view of the domestic terrain as seen from a paternal perspective, devoting its narrative to a man's longing for single parenthood. But as we never actually spend time with the much sought-after child (the film's ends upon the birth), *Paternity* rarely gets into heavier dramatic territory *à la Kramer vs. Kramer* (Robert Benton, 1979), *Author! Author!* (Arthur Hiller, 1982) and *Mr. Mom* (Stan Dragoti, 1983). These pictures depict the multiple struggles of single parenthood from the male viewpoint, but *Paternity* stays very much within the optimistic fantasy of fatherhood without actually showing the hardship and heartbreak of such responsibility. Reynolds expressed his desire to be a father openly and often, and *Paternity* is his most definitive cinematic declaration of such. Buddy's professional life and playboy ways are far too complicated for him to accept full domestic responsibilities as a single father; his relationship with Maggie, which presents a culture clash as well as an age gap, feels rather too convenient and conventional an outcome. As Maggie's water breaks and she goes into labor, Buddy proposes marriage and she accepts. In the end, Buddy gets to have his child, gain a wife and maintain his professional success. Does that mean that Maggie gives up her dream of studying music in order to become Buddy's domestic goddess? Such a question is never answered or addressed as the film ends on the potential for domiciliary bliss, the film designed for light consumption with its genial nature and hilarious set-pieces. Charlie Peters' breezy script was executed with levity and sensitivity while the picture was handsomely produced by Lawrence Gordon and Hank Moonjean, who deliver a slick love letter to New York City with its elegant use of the Big Apple's iconic locations.

Note

1. Nancy Streebeck, *The Films of Burt Reynolds* (New York: Citadel Press, 1982), p. 100.

Sharky's Machine
(1981)

"I'm gonna pull the chain on you, pal. And you wanna know why? 'Cause you're fucking up my city. 'Cause you're walking all over people like you own them. And you wanna know the worst part? You're from out of state."—Sgt. Tom Sharky

Sgt. Tom Sharky (Reynolds) is a tough Atlanta narcotics cop, known on the streets as "the man with the smiling eyes." After an uncover drug sting goes wrong and members of the public are wounded in a shootout, he is demoted to the vice squad and busted down to the department's hellhole basement office. Soon Sharky becomes embroiled in a web of intrigue after the routine arrest of a hooker leads to her implicating a crime syndicate and political power players in the operation of a high-class prostitution ring. Sharky and his "machine"—Papa (Brian Keith), Arch (Bernie Casey), Nosh (Richard Libertini)—set up a surveillance operation tracing the movements of expensive escort Dominoe (Rachel Ward) and uncover the shady involvement of the prospective governor of Georgia, Hotchkins (Earl Holliman). A politician of dubious repute, Hotchkins has been seeing and supporting Dominoe, but their liaison is complicated as the beauty is also the object of desire of her feared pimp, Victor (Vittorio Gassman). Dominoe has been under Victor's control since childhood and she feels it is time to break free of his gainful slavery. This doesn't sit well with the gangster, who dispatches his sociopathic enforcer brother, Billy Score (played insidiously by Henry Silva), to eliminate Dominoe. Billy manages to slip past surveillance and make his way to her apartment, firing a shot through the front door just as it is answered. But Dominoe isn't home; her friend Tiffany has been killed by Billy. With Victor assuming that Dominoe is dead, Sharky offers her refuge while he manipulates the situation to his advantage to bring down the kingpin, the corrupt politician and their entire empire.

Several years before *Sharky's Machine* went into production, Burt Reynolds made the fateful decision to introduce Clint Eastwood to a book called *The Outlaw Josey Wales*, which Eastwood made into a brilliant motion picture in 1976. As a return favor, Eastwood introduced Reynolds to William Diehl's 1978 book by Sharky's Machine, who sent him a copy and noted its potential as a "Dirty Harry in Atlanta" type of property. Orion Pictures and Warner Bros bought the film rights to Diehl's novel as a vehicle for Reynolds to direct and star in, granting him creative control over the project.

Reynolds as Sgt. Tom Sharky in *Sharky's Machine* (1981).

One of the elements of Diehl's novel that attracted Reynolds was its similarity to Otto Preminger's masterful *Laura* (1944), a film noir which Reynolds fervently admired. Indeed, Reynolds strips back Diehl's globe-trotting World War II backstory, confining it to the bustling metropolis of Atlanta; the picture retains the political corruption though relegates it to a subplot, focusing primarily on what one could term the "Laura Narrative." Though worlds apart in context and milieu, the central themes and even specific scenarios of *Laura* are replicated or paid homage to by Reynolds. Note the similarities: an elusive woman of mystery is the object of desire among a trio of admirers of variable motives; said woman is assumed dead in a gun attack on her home, but the actual victim was somebody else of similar form and figure; the woman turns up alive, troubling those who initiated her murder while enabling police to successfully bring the fiend to justice. Even the method and tool utilized by the murderer is transposed to the contemporary film: a fatal double-barrel shotgun blast through the front door of the target's home, disfiguring the victim enough to cause confusion in identifying the body.

With a supportive studio affording their chief artist autonomy, Reynolds assembled a cast and crew of considerable talent and pedigree. In a moment of great discovery, he hired English actress Rachel Ward for the crucial role of Dominoe. Having appeared in two minor horror films, *Night School* (Ken Hughes, 1981) and *The Final Terror* (Andrew Davis, 1981), Ward auditioned for what would be an enormous opportunity for any new actress: the female lead of the new Burt Reynolds picture. "As soon as I saw her," Reynolds says, "I told myself, 'If this girl can talk, she's got the part.'"[1]

Ward's introduction onscreen in *Sharky's Machine* is true to the tradition of memorable film noir femme fatales. As with Lana Turner in *The Postman Always Rings Twice* (Tay Garnett, 1946), we meet Dominoe legs first. The camera's slow reveal suggests a seductive and potentially dangerous temptress, playful with her powerful sexuality and ability to hypnotize men. Ward was subsequently nominated for the "New Star of the Year" award at the 39th Golden Globes for her portrayal of Dominoe.

Sharky's Machine is an excellent, gripping crime thriller in the mold of distinctive police pictures such as *Dirty Harry* (1971), *McQ* (1974) and *The Gauntlet* (1977). It also distinguishes itself by virtue of its exotic off–Hollywood setting of Atlanta, far from the familiar concrete confines of New York, Los Angeles and San Francisco. *Sharky's Machine* deserves plaudits for the brilliantly composed photography of acclaimed cinematographer William A. Fraker. Responsible for some of the most eye-catching *mise-en-scéne* of New Hollywood cinema (Roman Polanski's *Rosemary's Baby*, Peter Yates' *Bullitt*, Richard Brooks' *Looking for Mr. Goodbar*), Fraker makes extensive use of sharply designed structural configurations

Shooting *Sharky's Machine* (1981): left to right, cinematographer William Fraker, first assistant cameraman Keith Peterman and actors Reynolds, Earl Holliman and C. James Lewis (photograph courtesy C. James Lewis Collection).

within his framing; at times his interiors mirror the architectural landscape of downtown Atlanta. Fraker's aesthetic is understated but powerfully utilized, though Reynolds reins in any formal excesses that might make the film too obvious an exercise in film style. It remains gritty enough to support the sordid underworld plot, but for those with an eye for framing and composition, *Sharky's Machine* is a rewarding experience.

Camera operator Nick McLean Sr., whose résumé reads like a history of great American cinema of the 1970s and 1980s, helped establish the picture's distinctive aesthetic with his kinetic camerawork and memorable aerial photography. McLean's time on *Sharky's Machine* proved to be a fortuitous experience, as his fearless and stellar work here captured the attention of his boss; considerably impressed with McLean's style and work ethic, Reynolds decided to promote his camera operator to full cinematographer on an upcoming picture. McLean soon found out that Reynolds stayed true to his word as within months of finishing *Sharky's Machine* he received a script for a picture called *Stroker Ace*. Reynolds had McLean shoot some test footage of Loni Anderson—"he was really testing me,"[2] says McLean—and the star was confident that he had found the right man to shoot the rambunctious car-racing picture. And so in 1983, McLean shot *Stroker Ace*, his first work as cinematographer, and from there he enjoyed a major career shooting pictures for the likes of Sylvester Stallone, Steven Spielberg, Richard Donner, Mel Brooks and many more, culminating in his acclaimed cinematography on the hugely popular television sitcom *Friends*. "*Sharky's Machine* was a terrific film to work on, it really made my career," McLean said. "Burt was the #1 star in the world at the time, there was plenty of money, and the studio wasn't bugging us, we were left alone to make the movie we wanted to make."[3]

Notes

1. Burt Reynolds, *My Life: Burt Reynolds* (Great Britain: Hodder & Stoughton, 1994), p. 241.
2. Nick McLean Sr., *interview with author*, Skype, January 15, 2018.
3. *Ibid.*

An Interview with Rachel Ward

Australian actress Rachel Ward began her modeling career in the late 1970s as a cover girl for major fashion magazines including *Vogue* and *Cosmopolitan*. Then she began getting TV work in the U.S., promoting cosmetic brands such as Revlon. In the early '80s, she ventured into film work and will be recognizable to horror film buffs from Ken Hughes' *Night School* and Andrew Davis' *The Final Terror*. But it was Burt Reynolds' intensive search for the female lead and subsequent casting of Ward in *Sharky's Machine* that proved fortuitous for the budding actress and brought her to national attention. High-profile film roles would ensue for Ward throughout the 1980s with her casting in Carl Reiner's *Dead Men Don't Wear Plaid*, Taylor Hackford's *Against All Odds* and the acclaimed ABC miniseries *The Thorn Birds*. Ward later retreated from mainstream Hollywood pictures and while intermittently appearing in television films such as *Johnson County War* (also starring Reynolds), she has emerged in recent times as a prolific, award-winning filmmaker in her homeland, working behind the camera on Australian television productions as well as writing-directing theatrical features such as *Beautiful Kate*.

Wayne: *What do you recall of landing the role of Dominoe?*

Rachel: I remember the very first mention of *Sharky's Machine*. My agent was sending me to play the lead opposite Burt Reynolds! I was quite new to Hollywood and I had at that point done two small horror films. One of those was called *The Final Terror*, which we

Rachel Ward as Dominoe in *Sharky's Machine* (1981).

shot up in Oregon City, California, and co-starred Daryl Hannah. After we finished that film, I heard my agent was sending me to audition for *Sharky's Machine*. I said to my agent, "You're crazy, I'm not going to get the lead opposite Burt Reynolds!" I guess that was a typical woman, thinking they are less than, rather than more than, what they are capable of, and my agent said, "Well, think of it like this: It has to be an unknown actress because the character disappears ten minutes into the movie, and if it was a big star you'd know that she was coming back." So, it became a role for an unknown. Every young actress wanting a leg-up in the industry was up for that part. So I realized I did have a shot if they were looking for an unknown actress.

How did the audition go?

I was doing an awful lot of auditions at the time and they can take an enormous amount out of you; you need to have a realistic hope of getting the audition and that you're aiming for the right level. I did a very good audition with the woman who was casting [Terry Liebling] and I remember feeling very good about it. Then word came back that I was on a short list and it was down to two girls. Burt was already in Atlanta doing pre-production and the two girls were going to be flown to Atlanta to audition with him. So I flew to Atlanta and as I was checking into my hotel room, my girlfriend rang me from New York and she said, "Well, you'll never guess who was here with me and who has just come from Atlanta," and it was a girl that I grew up with in England called Clio Goldsmith, who had been making films in Rome. Burt had been scanning the globe for his Dominoe and the two women he chose had been childhood friends, yet had careers in two different places. So it turned out that it came down to me and Clio and I remember standing in the kitchen of a small apartment that I was sharing with Daryl Hannah in Studio City when my agent gave me the call to tell me I'd gotten the role. It was pretty damn exciting; I knew my career had shifted into another gear immediately. Burt gave me an opportunity which afforded me a really nice career for the next couple of years.

Given that Burt was the world's biggest box office star at that time, I imagine it was a fascinating period to be in close proximity to him.

He definitely carried that star persona but in a very agreeable way. You felt how much everybody on the set really liked him; he was never rude to anyone; he never shouted at anyone … they adored him! I wasn't particularly familiar with his work; I mean, he hadn't been a pin-up of mine, nor had I been to see any of his films, because they seemed to appeal to a very male audience. But when I met him, I found that he was very charming. He was a lot older than me and had a lot of experience, so I definitely felt quite a considerable power imbalance there. But he was very much a gentleman and was very nurturing and very protective of me. He sort of set me up as well, he found me a business manager and when we finished the picture, he had fitted my incredibly hot apartment in Studio City with air conditioning units. He was very kind in doing little things he could for up-and-coming people.

Given the number of actors who appear recurrently in his films, I get the impression he created a family atmosphere on set.

He did always have a coterie of friends around him; he had Charles Durning on the film, Henry Silva, Earl Holliman, all of whom he had worked with a few times, and he had these makeup guys and wardrobe people who were always on the set. He had a house down in South Carolina and on the weekends we sometimes stayed there and I remember one time we went white water rafting. He made everything like a wonderful adventure for us all. Burt was very comfortable around people, he was godlike, and he had this big swath of people around him all the time. He was very charismatic. I definitely had a big crush on him when we were shooting.

Was he a playful kind of director?

I remember there was a scene where I had to laugh spontaneously, and his character was watching me through the telescope and falling in love with me; the scene called for me to be playing the piano and he wanted me to laugh. So when I was doing the scene, as I was playing the piano, he had a recording of a toilet flushing set up so that when I put my hands on the keys you would hear the sound of the flushing. It was so silly and ridiculous but I did laugh and he got that on film. He went out of his way to get what he needed from his actors. Laughing spontaneously is one of the hardest things to do as an actor and so he knew how to help, because he was an actor too. I suppose he knew how much encouragement was needed, how much approval was needed, so he was always incredibly kind.

The film is extremely stylish and very well constructed.

I do remember the scene at the door to the apartment, when he's pretending to work as an electrician, and that fabulous low shot of me from his perspective. It is a very stylishly done piece of direction.

That is a very film noir, femme fatale type of introduction to your character. It's very seductive, a little bit dangerous, but done with a twinkle in the eye.

Burt knew his stuff; he knew his film history and what he wanted to recreate. I guess it was fun for him, he was kind of a Svengali sort of figure, because I was so green and he was able to create his fantasy woman in a way. He was quite particular about what he wanted to get.

How so?

He loved my English accent; he didn't want me to have an American accent. If I improvised at all, he was very particular about what he liked, what he didn't like, and what I didn't like. I could definitely feel a difference between an American sensibility and an

English sensibility; I was leaning toward teasing his character, bringing in some irony to it, but he was very keen to keep Dominoe sweet. It was a bit of an English-American sensibility clash. Not too much, it's just a general observation about when you have to go work in another culture, you're always aware of that. American cinema likes to sell sweetness, or something less-complicated, and so whatever slight irony or cynicism I wanted to bring to the film was out the window, he wanted me to be playing lovely.

Was it ever an issue on set?

I remember I laughed at him; he's writing that poem at the window and I thought, "Oh, that's a bit corny," and I laughed at him. So he was a little bit nervous about me laughing at him—Sharky, not Burt—so there was a little argy-bargy as he didn't want me to mock the character too much. This is a moment where he's opening his heart but my instinct was just to laugh and mock him for it. Burt is very protective and inclusive.

Despite his sense of humor, I get the impression of utmost sincerity in his work. No matter what role Burt is playing, there is a sense of the real Burt on the screen. Having worked with him and gotten to know him, how true is this?

He always plays Burt Reynolds. People underestimate how difficult that is, because you have to be incredibly sure of your own persona and the particular appeal of that persona. He knew who his audience was and what their expectations of a Burt Reynolds picture were; and he knew how to win, how to be strong, and how to be courageous. I think at that time Burt was ready to move on from the car movies, which were so popular. He was very focused on directing. And even though *Sharky's Machine* wasn't as huge a success as some of his past films, it was a different genre for him and I think he did fine. I got very good reviews and so did Burt. When it came to acting, he was very unpretentious; he was very un-method, he just wanted you to be real. He wasn't mucking around, he cast people who were right for the roles. He would never talk to you about the background of the character or anything that particular. As long as you were present with him in the scene, that's all he wanted.

How do you feel about Sharky's Machine, *looking back on it almost four decades later?*

It was a time in Hollywood when the options available to pretty girls were these kinds of roles, the "sexy prostitute with a heart of gold" kind of thing. I had some great opportunities for a girl at that time but it was not something I wanted to repeat. Particularly being a European, I was always going to be cast as a fantasy, and that is pretty limited, it runs out quickly as an actor. But I think within those limitations that *Sharky's Machine* is as good as it got. On other films like *Against All Odds*, I felt quite cheapened—I was always in a bathing suit and there was a lot of emphasis on my breasts, and on *Dead Men Don't Wear Plaid* I also played "the girl." But Burt respectfully refused to exploit me or my body, even in scenes such as the striptease sequence with Vittorio Gassman and even with the fact I was playing a prostitute, I never felt cheapened, I was respected and well-photographed. Burt just wanted me to be beautiful and be appealing. On *Against All Odds,* I felt like I was selling sex and not romance, it was always "put the bathing suit on!" Burt didn't do that, on *Sharky's Machine* he wasn't selling sex, he was selling romance.

I think the romantic side of Burt Reynolds is under-appreciated. Look at that run of great romantic films he made from the mid–70s to mid–80s, such great chemistry with his female co-stars…

And he loved those girls that he worked with; he loved Dolly Parton and Candice Bergen. He had such great relationships with these people, really tremendous friendships, and he always liked to work with his friends. So you see that on the screen.

You seem to value the time you spent working with him.

We finished *Sharky's Machine* on great terms. I ended up meeting Clint Eastwood with him … he had that coterie of people that he would have around to his house where we'd all get together, have dinner, and he would run movies. I was a part of that for a couple of months after we finished shooting the film. He was definitely very helpful with my onward career. I did an audition for *Dead Men Don't Wear Plaid* and it was that very good audition which got me the role in the film, but it would have been like Burt to ring up Carl Reiner and put in a nice word. I'm very grateful for the opportunity that I was given. Do I sit and look at these films and think about them? No, never. It was male fantasy stuff which was done well and served me well. I've certainly no gripe about it. *Sharky's Machine* enabled me to have an acting career; it gave me that leg up.

The Best Little Whorehouse in Texas

(1982)

"Boys, I got myself a pretty good bullshit detector, and I can tell when somebody's peeing on my boots and telling me it's a rainstorm."—Ed Earl Dodd

The Chicken Ranch, a rural brothel, caters to the lonely males of Gilbert, Texas. Run by Miss Mona (Dolly Parton) and honoring old-fashioned hospitality, it operates with impunity as it counts among its loyal customers the local sheriff, Ed Earl Dodd (Burt Reynolds). Ed Earl and Mona are in love, but that doesn't get in the way of business. While the cherished whorehouse may be immune from law enforcement, it does become the target of tabloid television reporter and moral crusader, Melvin P. Thorpe (Dom DeLuise). Thorpe is out to expose the impure activities of the Chicken Ranch and enflame a movement of moral outrage designed to bring down the establishment. The town is shamed in the national media for being associated with such seedy goings-on. This places Ed Earl in a difficult situation, having to adhere to his duties and appeal to Mona to shut down, at least while the press is stoking social and political fires with the issue. Ed Earl is annoyed to find Mona has still been operating discreetly when she is subject to a sting operation by Thorpe, drawing much shame and embarrassment to the town and to Ed Earl as sheriff. Despite Ed Earl's best efforts to appeal to the governor (Charles Durning), who is under fierce pressure from his electorate to close the Chicken Ranch, Mona has to cease trading and shut the doors of the Chicken Ranch, leaving many of the working girls with nowhere to go.

The Best Little Whorehouse in Texas is based on the Broadway play of the same name, which was inspired by a series of articles published in a 1974 issue of *Playboy* magazine regarding the exploits of Houston television reporter Marvin Zindler. On August 3, 1973,

Zindler brought about the closing of a La Grange bordello known as the Chicken Ranch. Zindler led an exposé on potentially illicit activity there, which in turn made the KTRK-TV reporter a local celebrity and led to him being profiled in Hugh Hefner's influential publication. This national attention led to the event being turned into literary, musical, and cinematic adaptations. In the picture, Zindler is portrayed as media personality Melvin P. Thorpe, in a brilliantly exaggerated satire by Dom DeLuise.

Dolly Parton is the perfect screen foil for Reynolds, with her genial, good-humored nature on a par with that of her co-star. Reynolds apparently had his on his eye on Parton as a co-star since the mid–70s when he fancied her for a part in *W.W. and the Dixie Dancekings*. Despite her massive stardom, Parton brings an earnest humility to the character of Mona, an inherently decent soul who gives to charity with the proceeds of her prostitution outfit. Parton shows empathy for the characters and their economic milieu, humanizing them rather critiquing them. Parton said,

> This person, this lady, this madam, she is me because I am just full of life and love and energy for all kinds of people. Although I didn't own a whorehouse, if I had not been as fortunate as I am, who knows what I could have been.... I gave it a lot of thought and I talked to my folks about it and I saw it as a story about life, a way to show that these people have personalities; that these people have reasons for being what they are.[1]

Miss Mona (Dolly Parton) serenades her man in *The Best Little Whorehouse in Texas* (1982).

The theatrical element of *Best Little Whorehouse* meant a golden opportunity for Reynolds to flex his musical muscle. Despite having released an album in 1973, he had little occasion to sing on film in the past. Reynolds spent ten weeks working with a vocal coach, but despite the effort, the scene that would have proved a perfect showcase for his musical abilities was deleted from the theatrical cut of the picture. Reynolds sings "Where Stallions Run" (written by Parton for her co-star to perform) in a scene that was to appear after Earl and Mona's domestic fight following Thorpe's storming of the Chicken Ranch. In the heat of the fight, Mona insults Earl by saying, "You ain't never gonna be no more than you are right now: a chicken shit sheriff in a chicken shit town!" Wounded, Earl responds, "Maybe

Reynolds as Sheriff Ed Earl Dodd in *The Best Little Whorehouse in Texas* (1982).

you're right, but it's a hell of a lot better than being a whore." The scene leads to a tender moment in which Earl is seen wandering a vast plain in deep contemplation, lonely and hurt after his tense encounter with Mona.[2] In the theatrical cut, the scene is scored with the melody of "I Will Always Love You" but the beautifully shot scene only lasts roughly 30 seconds. The scene was fully reinstated for a rare cut of the film shown on U.S. television in the 1980s. To keep the running time at two hours, the song was substituted after cuts were made to the racier elements of the film. Camera operator Nick McLean Sr. recalled,

> At that time, Burt wasn't really considered a lightweight actor, he was known as an action star and that's what audiences really wanted. When we showed *The Best Little Whorehouse in Texas* at some test screening, people complained because they didn't want to see Burt singing and dancing. This meant that one of the scenes that had Burt singing in it got cut. … The song was called "Where Stallions Run" and Burt did a fantastic job with it, but the people spoke and the studio listened. It's a shame that song didn't make it into the final cut of the film. It's a beautiful scene.[3]

Another actor who was afforded the opportunity to dazzle audiences with his rarely displayed musical chops was Charles Durning. World War II veteran and skilled soft-shoe man Durning had been most visible as a character actor in the edgy pictures *Hi, Mom!* (Brian De Palma, 1970), *Dog Day Afternoon* (Sidney Lumet, 1975) and *Twilight's Last Gleaming* (Robert Aldrich, 1977), and in *Best Little Whorehouse* Reynolds finally found the ideal showcase for the actor's song and dance skills. Director Colin Higgins had Mickey Rooney in mind for the role of the governor, but Reynolds convinced him of the potential kudos that introducing the world to Durning's significant skills would bring. "I got Colin's ear one day," Reynolds said. "'You know, Colin, when the industry sees Mickey sing and dance up a storm, what's the surprise? He's been doing that since he was five! But now you take a fellow like Charles Durning, no one in the industry really knows what a great song and dance man he is … who do you think will get all the credit for that brilliant, offbeat casting? You!'"[4] More significant than kudos or credit for his director, Durning's performance earned him an Oscar nomination for Best Supporting Actor, the first of two consecutive nominations (the following year, Durning was shortlisted for his supporting role in Mel Brooks' *To Be or Not to Be*).

From a commercial perspective, an expensive musical film was a particular gamble for a studio at the time; recent entries in the genre such as *At Long Last Love* (Peter Bogdanovich, 1975), *Can't Stop the Music* (Nancy Walker, 1980), *One from the Heart* (Francis Ford Coppola, 1982) and *Yes, Giorgio!* (Franklin J. Schaffner, 1982) all failed to make a dent at the box office. However, Reynolds and Parton's presence provided Universal with marquee value assurance, and with some of Hollywood's top film technicians working behind the scenes, the film was guaranteed some industry prestige. Director Higgins was brought onto the picture at the suggestion of Parton, bringing with him significant critical and commercial pedigree after having written the acclaimed Hal Ashby picture *Harold and Maude* (1971)—a film much admired by Reynolds—and having directed *Foul Play* (1978), a clever homage to the films of Alfred Hitchcock. More significant, and perhaps even more reassuring to Universal was Higgins' previous film *9 to 5* (1980), a massive financial winner, earning over $100 million on a $10 million budget. That film also starred Parton, and so another Higgins-Parton picture was the perfect recipe for receipts. Higgins brought a lightness of touch to the comedy and an expert handling of the complicated musical production numbers. McLean recalls,

> Some really great people worked on *The Best Little Whorehouse in Texas*. Burt was at the top of his game, he was a box office guarantee at that point. Colin Higgins was a very good director, I liked him

a lot. William Fraker was the director of photography and he was one of the best in the business, he had an incredible eye and a masterful way with framing. I was the camera operator on the film and it was a lot of fun, but being that it was a musical, you had to have a lot of discipline and control. There are a lot of rehearsals and a lot of work involved for the dancers; as the cameraman, you just have to be sharp, watch them carefully and follow the choreography; the dancers pretty much always hit the same marks every time so you have to be on your game.[5]

Despite the smutty implications of the title, *Best Little Whorehouse* is a wholesome affair. With its two amiable and photogenic leads, it manages to be sexy without resorting to prurience; the picture's many displays of flesh suggest the carnal exploits enjoyed at the Chicken Ranch but rarely does it depict anything as salacious as actual sex. "I said I would like to see more of a romance," Parton recalls. "Wouldn't you feel like you wasted five dollars if you paid to see *Whorehouse* and you didn't see me and Burt kiss? I was makin' a joke, and I stuck to it—I'm not going to miss my chance to kiss Burt Reynolds. There ain't no way I'd do sex scenes. I'm talking about love scenes."[6]

The picture is so amiable and self-consciously Southern that one wonders if some of the dialect is deliberately affected to emphasize some kind of absurd, theatrical ideal of Southern charm and politeness, and there is no one better than Jim Nabors (as Deputy Fred) to introduce the picture in his own inimitably wholesome manner, such as in his opening narration in which he relates the background to the whorehouse and its odd name: "It wasn't always easy in them days to come up with hard cash. So, for a while, as the story goes, the girls begin accepting poultry in trade: one bird, one lay. And that's how the place got its name: the Chicken Ranch!" Only Nabors could deliver lines such as "She insisted that each girl check her gentlemen for the clap and wash him off with soap and warm water … Some of the fellas did think that was the best part!" with such guileless execution.

Notes

1. Dolly Parton, "The Making of the Film," DVD Supplement, *The Best Little Whorehouse in Texas*, Universal Pictures, 2001.
2. "Where Stallions Run—Burt Reynolds," YouTube, uploaded by Grinnygog1975, 20 August 2008, https://www.youtube.com/watch?v=DLMVi5UwQdU.
3. Nick McLean Sr., interviewed by author, Skype, January 15, 2018.
4. Burt Reynolds, *My Life: Burt Reynolds* (Great Britain: Hodder & Stoughton, 1994), p. 246.
5. Nick McLean Sr., *interview with author*, Skype, January 15, 2018.
6. Chet Flippo, "The Unsinkable Dolly Parton," *Rolling Stone*, December 11, 1980, https://www.rollingstone.com/music/music-country/the-unsinkable-dolly-parton-197779/.

Best Friends

(1982)

"That's great! That's perfect!! 'They moved into their dream house and dated happily ever after.'"—Richard Babson

The titular best friends of Norman Jewison's romantic comedy are Richard Babson (Reynolds) and Paula McCullen (Goldie Hawn), a pair of Hollywood screenwriters who are introduced to us as they struggle through a reading of their latest work, a steamy, cod–Tennessee Williams Southern soap opera with some particularly heavy-handed dialogue. Reynolds scores immediate laughs upon his deadpan first appearance, with Richard doing his best to channel some overwrought Dixieland melodrama: "Look, I'm your sister and I suppose I love you, but I'm having trouble working up sympathy for your unhappy childhood."

In these opening scenes, we get a glimpse into the dual domestic-professional lives of Richard and Paula: Things seem blissful as they are comfortably nestled away in their tastefully designed, sun-soaked Spanish-style villa. Paula playfully chides Richard for always creating generously bosomed female characters ("But I always make them suffer for it," he retorts), and director Jewison lulls us into the cozy, laidback West Coast vibe with some lounge crooning on the soundtrack. It's so evocative an introduction, you can almost taste the cocktails and canapés of a Hollywood brunch. The film soon takes satirical shots at hip West Coast culture, here represented by scene-stealing Ron Silver, who is excellent as egocentric producer Larry Weisman, the kind of Hollywood cretin who keeps a giant framed poster of Edward G. Robinson from *Little Caesar* displayed on the wall behind his desk as a means of subliminal intimidation and street credibility; the sort of square who sees himself as a hip hustler but in designer shorts and polo shirt, complete with crocheted sweater jauntily strewn over the shoulders. Weisman will also fabricate his child's illness to avoid a sporting lunch with an associate rather than admit he can't decide on which fashionable tennis shoe to wear. The reaction of Richard and Paula to Weisman's unscrupulous shyster suggests they are more than familiar with his brand of business.

In the kind of contrived dialogue that could only ever be spoken in a well-written Hollywood romance, against the backdrop of the illustrious Los Angeles skyline on their impossibly gorgeous Hollywood Hills balcony, Richard says to his partner, "Paula, there

Richard Babson (Reynolds) and Paula McCullen (Goldie Hawn) decide to give marriage a try in *Best Friends* (1982).

are some statements I want to make with my life, you're one of them. Living with you just says that you're my lover and my friend, it doesn't state that you're the woman I want to spend the rest of my life with; marriage makes that statement." Richard had it sweet, but then he had to go and mention the M-word. Paula is uncomfortable and doesn't want to talk about it, preserving the eternal youth that she feels marriage would put an end to: "I just keep thinking Life is in three stages: that you're born, you get married, and then you die," she says rather pessimistically. But then, they marry. Richard and Paula's honeymoon takes us on a road trip to meet each of their parents, visiting their respective homelands where we decipher the culture clash and contrast of the two families.

Echoing the rare Hollywood tradition of husband-wife screenwriting duos—such as Ruth Gordon and Garson Kanin; Henry and Phoebe Ephron—the film's script was written by what could be the authentic, semi-autobiographical version of Richard and Paula: Barry Levinson and his wife Valerie Curtin. The couple broke up around the time of the film's production, and perhaps that says a lot about Richard and Paula's relationship, but together Levinson and Curtin have perceptively crafted many great scenes of uncomfortable truth in relationships, of those with our significant others and with our family.

The script is largely affectionate towards the aging parents of the two characters, though it does occasionally veer towards satire. Paula's old-fashioned parents, Eleanor and Tim McCullen (Barnard Hughes and Jessica Tandy), reside in a comfortable middle-class Buffalo neighborhood. In contrast, Richard's parents, Tom and Ann Babson (Keenan Wynn and Audra Lindley), are depicted as vulgar Virginian condo-dwellers, bickering and uncouth. All parents are buffoonish creations, such as Ann, who takes Polaroid pictures at inappropriate moments, wanting to capture every moment for posterity. There is a sweet tone to these scenes with the parents, particularly when visiting the McCullens. Paula's traditional East Coast parents insist on the "kids" sleeping in separate bedrooms. Indeed, Paula can't bring herself to sleep with Richard in her old room anyway—"This isn't a room for sexual relations, this is a room for slumber parties!" With Richard alone in a separate room, Eleanor caringly tucks her new son-in-law into his bed or offers to wash his dirty underwear.

The McCullens are clueless and somewhat out of touch with their daughter's life, as seen when Eleanor mistakenly congratulates them on their new play, rather than their film. But this cluelessness isn't a lack of interest; their love is so great for their daughter that her success in Hollywood doesn't make a difference to them. Behind the absurdity of Eleanor's coddling of the two adults is genuine familial affection. There is a bittersweet truthfulness in the picture's depiction of one generation becoming aware that they are imminently replacing another, of seeing our parents become vulnerable to age and to illness. With her parents' various ailments, Paula endures a heightened awareness of their mortality and puts herself through phases of mourning for their imaginary demise. This is an insightful touch that says something about the closeness in Paula's family. She loves her parents so much that she much mentally prepares for her grief by fantasizing about their death.

In a picture where two successful middle-aged professionals are once again thrown into a domestic domain ruled by the parents, such a premise could have been the setup for more frivolous fun and frolics, but all involved play it subtle and sharp. Indeed, the casting of Reynolds and Hawn might suggest an altogether jauntier affair than what this relatively quiet domestic comedy achieves, but the actors tone down their considerable personalities to render the characters with a lived-in sense of history, as utterly believable in trading stinging barbs as they as they are sharing romantic gestures. Such huge personalities as that of Reynolds and Hawn could have created a disparity in the dynamic of the relationship, but neither jostles for control of the screen, Reynolds brings some of the same modest, endearing qualities and vulnerability that stood him in good stead for *Starting Over*. *Best Friends* may not be the kind of film on which Reynolds' loyal constituency was built; it is however a genre piece which serves him well as a performer. At the time, Hawn was coming off the huge success of *Private Benjamin* (Howard Zeiff, 1980) and *Foul Play* (Colin Higgins, 1978) and was commanding a hefty price tag of $3 million per film. Reynolds was already at his career zenith and receiving the same salary, and so the prospect of Reynolds and Hawn starring together meant potentially huge marquee value for Warner Bros. With the much-admired Norman Jewison producing and directing, the film carried a certain prestige quality.

"We had a good time making *Best Friends*," says actor and Reynolds' stunt-double C. James Lewis. "Norman Jewison was a great director and Jordan Cronenweth was our superb cinematographer. And then you have Burt and Goldie, who just had this great chemistry. We had some fun moments."[1] While on-set, Lewis witnessed some farcical goings-on to rival any of the on-screen comedy:

> We went to Buffalo, New York, to shoot so we could have some snow. Well, it never snowed. But it was freezing. One day we were at the train station in Buffalo, which is all marble and extremely cold in winter, and we were setting up a shot when an animal wrangler brought in pigeons that Norman wanted for the shot where Burt and Goldie walk through the train station. The birds were to flutter as the actors walk through the station, but the birds wouldn't fly because it was too cold. So they threw bird seed down and tried it again, the birds wouldn't fly. So Norman said, "Get rid of the damn birds!" and that's when he, Burt, Goldie and the first assistant director went off to talk about what to do with the shot. While that was happening, a few of us on the crew were trying to keep warm. Inside the train station they had set up chairs, furniture and a heater for us. Burt's brother Jimmy was there and he had a three-quarter–length down coat on and he was backed up to the space heater. So one of the guys on the crew noticed this and said, "Jimmy, if you don't get away from that heater you are going to catch on fire." And at that moment, Jimmy Reynolds caught on fire. The down comforter is basically like plastic, extremely flammable, so the flames just shot up off the back of Jimmy's head. So me and another person both got up, grabbed furniture blankets, and started beating on Jimmy to put out the fire. Just then the birds flew in panic and there were feathers everywhere; that's when Burt and Goldie walked in and saw all the commotion. The birds are going everywhere, they see us beating on Jimmy and Burt's in complete disbelief, his nostrils flaring, like "What's going on?!" And then Norman comes in and says, "I told you to get rid of the birds, not kill them!"—Norman thought we were killing the pigeons and Burt thought we were beating up his brother! There was smoke everywhere, feathers flying, and I'm like "Burt, Jimmy's on fire!" and you could see the wheels turning in Burt, he couldn't comprehend it in all in that moment, he was like "What?!" and I'm saying, "We're trying to put him out!" Meanwhile, Norman is panicking, "Oh god, who killed the birds? We're all going to jail!" If only we had a camera; what happened behind the scenes in that moment was like something out of a movie.[2]

Notes

1. C. James Lewis, *interview with author*, Skype, August 17, 2018.
2. *Ibid.*

Stroker Ace

(1983)

"Everyone loves me... I'm good looking."—Stroker

Stroker Ace, a champion NASCAR driver with authority issues, is left sponsor-less after a falling out with Zenon Oil boss, Jim Catty (Warren Stevens). A free agent, Stroker is courted by fried chicken king Clyde Torkel (Ned Beatty), whose sponsorship would see the champ become the new face of the Chicken Pit fast food franchise. However, in signing the phonebook-sized contract without reading the fine print, Stroker ends up humiliated, shilling Torkel's chicken in ridiculous commercials and at various public appearances. Looking for a swift exit, Stroker and his best friend, mechanic Lugs Harvey (Jim Nabors), struggle to craft a way out of the contract; Torkel is one step ahead and refuses to sack Stroker, binding him to his contractual obligations to compete in the important end-of-season championship race in the hope that Stroker's success will bring Chicken Pit to the masses.

Loni Anderson plays glamorous Chicken Pit advertising director Pembrook Feeney, who is assigned to Stroker's media campaign. Pembrook is a skilled professional whose work is constantly undermined by the prurient allusions of her colleagues in regard to her

Stroker dons the feathers in the fast lane in *Stroker Ace* (1983).

striking looks. A virgin, a teetotaler and a Sunday school teacher, Pembrook is a challenge for lady-killer Stroker; though naturally she falls for his effervescence.

In the interim since the wild success of *The Cannonball Run*, Burt Reynolds successfully shifted from his tough guy image to amorous lead in a series of romantic comedies, something his action hero contemporaries often failed to do. With *Paternity, Best Little Whorehouse* and *Best Friends,* Reynolds displayed skill in forging a likable hunk identity buoyed by his humility, attractiveness, screen magnetism and self-deprecating sense of humor. Yet while these romantic comedies made money, they didn't make *Cannonball Run* kind of money. *Smokey and the Bandit, Smokey and the Bandit II, Hooper* and *The Cannonball Run* were extraordinary successes, and so it seemed that Reynolds struck a formula for cinematic gold that would surely yield box office returns as long as the required ingredients were added: Burt front and center; Hal Needham directing; lunkhead sidekick; bumbling adversary, pretty ladies and vehicles, lots of vehicles. Another Reynolds-Needham collaboration would be inevitable and that film was to be *Stroker Ace*. The script was written by Needham and Hugh Wilson, the latter the creator of the Loni Anderson–starring *WKPR in Cincinnati* and future director of the hugely successful *Police Academy* (1984). *Police Academy* is a film with which *Stroker Ace* shares much of its comical styling as well as an actor: Bubba Smith. Needham and Wilson's script was based on William Neely's novel *Stand on It*, the fictional autobiography of a NASCAR driver called Stroker Ace.

Stroker Ace certainly isn't a film designed for critics and film historians to mine its script for meaning and poetics; it's a Hal Needham picture, and in movie terms that means

Cinematographer Nick McLean Sr. and director Hal Needham shooting a scene for *Stroker Ace* (1983) (photograph courtesy Nick McLean Collection).

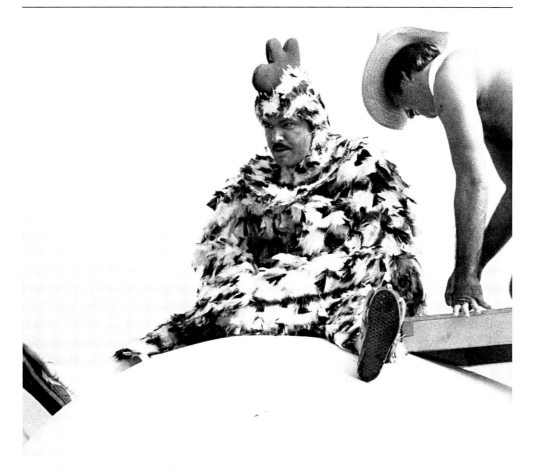

Reynolds and actor–stunt double C. James Lewis shooting a scene for *Stroker Ace* (1983) (photograph courtesy C. James Lewis Collection).

speed, stunts and smashes. The filmmaker's style is economical and unfussy; there are no particular artistic flourishes here, the focus is strictly on the informal atmosphere created with what feels like a bevy of friends and on the spectacular car racing sequences. Cinematographer Nick McLean Sr. recalls Needham's workmanlike approach to directing a major studio picture:

> Hal didn't care much about cinematography or editing or anything like that, he just wanted to get the action on film and let us do our own work and worry about those kinds of things. He didn't know much about that stuff anyway, he was a stuntman who lucked into directing because of his friendship with Burt. When I first met with Hal, it turned out we had some mutual friends so we got off to a good start. Hal was a tough cookie, I'll tell ya! He was a big stuntman in Hollywood, a genuine tough guy, the real deal, but he was very fair and he was real honest. If he didn't know something, he'd come to you and ask, but he knew what he was doing most of the time.[1]

C. James Lewis, who plays Aubrey James' crew chief, worked with the no-nonsense director on several films. According to Lewis,

> Hal Needham was not an actor's director. I went to him one time with an acting question and he said, "What the hell are you asking me for?! I don't know!" So I just said, "Okay, thank you," and I walked away thinking, "I asked you because you are the director." But if you were asking Hal about a stunt,

how to flip a car or make a jump, then that was fine with him; he was in his element with that kind of stuff; he was a real tough guy. I was glad to see Hal getting an Honorary Governors Award from the Academy in 2012. He finally got a statue. Hal was something else.[2]

The tale of Reynolds turning down James L. Brooks' *Terms of Endearment* to star in *Stroker Ace* is now the stuff of industry legend. It is interesting to speculate on what he could have brought to *Terms*, but his loyalty to his friend Needham remained firm. Reynolds perhaps never forgave himself for not postponing *Stroker Ace* to accommodate Brooks' schedule and often blamed the picture for being responsible for him losing much of his fanbase, but the star was often his own most vocal critic. Lewis said,

> *Stroker Ace* is an enjoyable picture and it was a lot of fun to make. I've talked to a lot of people down the years and they never have a bad word to say about it. They might love *Smokey and the Bandit* better, but when people love Burt Reynolds movies, they really do love them. I think that when his films got panned, it pained him inside. He might say, "I don't listen to the critics or care what they say," but deep down Burt was far too sensitive not to care; Burt had a tough exterior, but I feel that he would have been much happier had the critical notices been positive.[3]

Stroker Ace has occasional moments which reduce it to a ribald farce, which at times threaten to diminish the film's otherwise light heart and good nature. Anderson's wholesome bombshell Pembrook asserts her independence and professional resolve early on, only to end up in several bawdy scenes where she is subject to sleaze. If it isn't Torkel literally trying to bounce on top of her at a "meeting," it's the otherwise benign Stroker undressing her as she lay inebriated, though he ultimately refuses to take advantage. Pembrook scores a victory for decency by kicking the forceful Torkel square in the scrotum—"What's a scrotum?" Lugs asks ingenuously. If you can submit to *Stroker Ace*'s good-humored and tumultuous manner, it makes for an extremely entertaining Saturday matinee; the fistfights and vehicular carnage are tempered with a cartoonish lunacy that makes the film a fun and inconsequential filler in the Reynolds *oeuvre*. Further fun is also to be had during the blooper reel played over the end credits, most amusingly when Jerry Reed appears from behind Reynolds, who stands in full chicken body suit; as Reed teases the star, Reynolds issues him a stern whack of his wing.

Notes

1. Nick McLean Sr., *interview with author*, Skype, January 15, 2018.
2. C. James Lewis, *interview with author*, Skype, August 17, 2018.
3. *Ibid.*

The Man Who Loved Women

(1983)

"I love watching women. I love the way they walk, I love all the different shapes, the way they move."—David Fowler

Director Blake Edwards' *The Man Who Loved Women* opens with a funeral procession, all women, mourning the loss of a man who obviously made a great impact on the lives of many. An omniscient female narrator tells us, "All these women, they follow him even to the grave. How is it possible? Well, why not? They loved him very deeply; each in her own way—passionately, kindly—forever. What appears impossible is that there's no jealousy, no envy, no rage, not even cynicism. It may seem like a miracle but, well, I don't like miracles. I prefer to think it's something more simple; as simple as that he really and truly loved all these women ... and yes, me too."

The man mourned is David Fowler (Burt Reynolds) and the narration is by Marianna (Julie Andrews), one of the scores of women lined up to say goodbye to the greatest lover they have ever known. But Marianna knew him better than most; she was his psychiatrist. David presented himself to Marianna after being diagnosed with symptoms of anxiety and depression. His ennui is that of a tortured artist; he is a sculptor but there are days when all he can do is look but not create. He is uninspired to the point where he cannot even order from a restaurant menu because to choose is too great a challenge for his listless malaise. His appetite for the female form has become so voracious lately as to render him socially and sexually ineffective. To Marianna it is inertia; to David it is impotence. But a man as powerful and virile as he cannot fathom being at the mercy of such weakness. In backstory we learn David is sympathetic to prostitutes due to a boyhood of brothel bothering; he has what he says is "an enduring appreciation for the women of the street."

David loves women, and the only member of the opposite sex in close proximity who hasn't made his list of conquests is his assistant Nancy (Jennifer Edwards), a former hooker. David picked her up when cruising Sunset Boulevard; he wanted to save her, not seduce her. "I told her the truth about wanting to get her off the street, change her mind about being a whore. The rest of the truth was that I wanted her; that was the problem, I could have her, she was paid for, she was sleeping in my bed. If I did have her, what would her chances be then?" David's adoration for women is so absolute that the thoughts of all the women he will never meet are enough to morally cripple him. As he reveals his vulnera-

Psychiatrist Marianna (Julie Andrews) breaches her professional ethics as she becomes intimate with patient David Fowler (Reynolds) in *The Man Who Loved Woman* (1983).

bilities when recounting his life's story, Marianna is presented with a crisis of conscience and ethics, as she realizes that she is falling in love with this handsome and sensitive aesthete.

The Man Who Loved Woman is a remake of François Truffaut's 1977 French picture of the same name. For the most part, Edwards remains loyal to the original. There are some minor differences in the central character (named Morane in Truffaut's version, and played by Charles Denner), and some of those differences serve Reynolds well. While his David is existentially tormented, he still manages to float through the narrative on immense charm and refinement while remaining largely unthreatening. David's milieu is a privileged one and not the most relatable; he is far from the common man (an unusual position for Reynolds). Denner's Morane, with his more humble profession as an aerodynamics engineer, is presented as a more desperate character; at times he can be sleazy and demanding in his pursuit of the women he adores. One character device wisely not carried over into the remake is Morane's seven a.m. wakeup call during which he obsesses over an operator whom he calls Aurore, having named her such after she refuses to disclose her name. Morane almost cancels his subscription to the phone service when a male employee awakens him one morning instead of Aurore. "To be woken up by a man is unbearable," Morane says. Morane's compulsions, sexual promiscuity and single-minded pursuit of the female form is depicted with just the right amount of sincerity by Denner and amusement from Truffaut that the character, and the film, can function unscathed from a contemptuous politically correct feminist reading that such a narrative could invite.

Similarly, a character such as David could easily be misinterpreted as shallow and misogynistic; the script requires us to sympathize with a man vacuous enough to fall in love with a pair of legs first and their owner later, a man whose only solace is found between said legs; there are more than enough lingering shots of long lady limbs. But Reynolds renders David as eminently endearing as well as believably in anguish. David believes that the physical form of a woman is as aesthetically profound as the form of a sculpture or other equal to any work of art and this is a characteristic lacking in Truffaut's depiction of Moran, whose obsession feels grounded in something less aesthetic and more prurient.

Fowler is presented as a fashionable West Coast artist with New Age sensibilities and a propensity for introspection, and is attempting to reconcile his boorish ways of the past; we accept that this soulful artist's heart is pure, if anguished, and that his sexual amorality is indeed a psychological flaw and not something more directly salacious. The flashback method in Truffaut's picture is introduced when Morane decides to document his history of women in what is ostensibly a book of love, but here David recounts his own memories of amore to Marianne, which is a neat device for the two of them to become increasingly intimate. The clinical setting also engenders further sympathy for David as a man genuinely in conflict with himself and with his lost connection to his mother. As a child, David was a defender of his mother's virtue, having been teased for the many male admirers she had accrued as a beautiful woman.

One of the film's most distinctive elements is Edwards' sophisticated formal film style. The elegant production design of Roger Maus and tastefully composed cinematography of Haskell Wexler are informed with the same devotion to geometric composition and share a similarly vivid color palette as David's beloved Ron Davis abstract art collection. Wexler's camerawork proceeds in a hazy dreamlike state; the heightened colors and intricate framing takes us out of the traditional Hollywood romantic comedy and into something altogether more artful and aesthetically interesting. Several of the various Abstract artworks that enrich the picture's *mise-en-scéne* are actually the work of Edwards, who was an amateur sculptor.[1]

C. James Lewis, who plays Lt. Cranzano, has appeared in several Blake Edwards pictures including *City Heat*, *Sunset* and *A Fine Mess*. He recalls a poignant moment:

> *The Man Who Loved Women* was the first film I worked with Blake on; he was such a special man. I will never forget one day when I was walking through the set when Blake and Julie [Andrews] stepped out of his trailer with these two adorable little Vietnamese girls. I knew Blake's daughter from a previous marriage, Jennifer Edwards, but I hadn't met these two little girls before. But as I was on my way somewhere, Blake called me and said, "Jimmy, come over here!" and so I went over and bid Miss Andrews a fair greeting and said to Blake "Yes, sir?" and he said to me, "You see these two little girls? If anyone ever asks you why you went to Vietnam, here are two reasons." I couldn't even talk, I just said "Thank you, sir." Those two little girls were adopted from Vietnam by Blake and Julie. I didn't know that beforehand, but Blake just floored me when he said that. That meant the world to me, I treasure that moment.[2]

Notes

1. David Ng, "The Art of Blake Edwards," *Los Angeles Times*, January 17, 2009, https://latimesblogs.latimes.com/culturemonster/2009/01/blake-edwards-a.html
2. C. James Lewis, *interview with author*, Skype, August 17, 2018.

Cannonball Run II

(1984)

"I have a weakness for blondes and women without mustaches."—Sheik Abdul ben Falafel

As if letting its audience know that they in for much of the same as before, *Cannonball Run II* opens with its familiar credit sequence, that of a white Lamborghini Countach roaring through sun-kissed desert highways to the strains of Ray Stevens' invigorating theme song "Cannonball." Sheik Abdul ben Falafel (Jamie Farr) sponsors another cross-country race to appease his father, King Abdul ben Falafel (Ricardo Montalban). Having lost the first time round, the sheik vies for first place when his father orders him to "emblazon the Falafel name as the fastest in the world." In the race to win the $1 million prize, Falafel is once again joined by a host of famous and familiar faces: welcome back J.J. McClure (Reynolds) and sidekick Victor Prinzi (Dom DeLuise), once again competing alongside Blake (Dean Martin) and Fenderbaum (Sammy Davis Jr.). Blake and Fenderbaum aren't just speeding for prize money, they have goons trailing after them for money owed. The pair are in debt to sleazy Don Don Canneloni (Charles Nelson Reilly), while Don Don is in arrears with mob boss Hymie Kaplan (Telly Savalas). After Blake and Fenderbaum are bailed out by Falafel, Don Don decides to kidnap and extort cash from the ostentatious sheik. Banding together to save the sheik, the various racing teams descend upon Don Don's bolthole of Pinto Ranch, where a climactic showdown of brawn and brawling ensues.

Victor Prinzi (Dom DeLuise) and J.J. McClure (Reynolds) prepare to hit the road once again in *Cannonball Run II* **(1984).**

Other returning *Cannonball Run* veterans include Jackie Chan, Mel Tillis and the hilarious Jack Elam, while new additions to the series include Montalban, Savalas, Marilu Henner, Shirley MacLaine, Frank Sinatra and Tony Danza. In an inspired piece of casting, three actors from *The Godfather*, Alex Rocco, Abe Vigoda and Michael V. Gazzo, appear in a very funny parody of their roles in Francis Ford Coppola's classic gangster picture. Notable by his absence, however, is Roger Moore as girdle giant Seymour Goldfarb Jr. Any temptations Moore may have had to reprise the role were dashed in the aftermath of a stunt gone disastrously wrong, a horrific automobile accident on the set of the original picture which left one of his co-stars, Heidi von Beltz, quadriplegic. Aside from feeling the self-referential send-up of himself had run its course, far more off-putting was the devastating circumstances of von Beltz's accident, as Moore recalled that "the end of shooting of the first film was tarnished for me when my last on-screen female companion was seriously injured in a car crash when a stunt double was brought in to complete a driving sequence with her and lost control. It rather upset me, to be honest."[1]

As with the first picture, *Cannonball Run II* is constructed of a series of humorous sketches, allowing the various performers a moment to display their comedic talent in rotation. Doug McClure gets a few laughs as the blonde-haired and blue-eyed dolt, a former actor and now servant to the sheik; his job is to gratefully receive abuse destined for his masters. ("A thousand thanks," he says as King Abdul delivers another slap across his face.) One of the picture's funniest scenes sees J.J., Prinzi and Fenderbaum resplendent in harem drag as they infiltrate Don Don's ranch in the guise of a performing trio, dancing to the Supremes' Motown classic "Stop in the Name of Love" which leads to Don Don making them an offer of lifetime contracts at the Pinto Club. The scene is worth watching just for the normally stoic Henry Silva's hysterical facial reactions. In fact, the goons are given the best material in the picture, as their send-up of gangster movie characters and clichés is particularly delightful. Cinematographer Nick McLean replicates Gordon Willis' chiaroscuro lighting from *The Godfather* for a scene in which Don Canneloni strokes a dead cat and laments (in Brando-esque mumbling) his position of power: "And now the Rigatonis, the Tortellinis, the Fettuchinis and even the Raviolis are bigger than we are. And why?" High interests, acid rain, Japanese imports and "none of the above" are all answers put forward by his bumbling cronies; "Gee, boss, if I knew there was gonna be a test, I would've studied." It is lowbrow and unsophisticated, but it works.

Cannonball Run II was seen as the nadir of director Hal Needham's series of vehicular farces, which had run their course with both Reynolds and his audience. Critical opinions were never a concern to the studios as these films made significant returns regardless, but it was evident that particular disdain was reserved for this outing. Roger Ebert declared, "*Cannonball Run II* is one of the laziest insults to the intelligence of moviegoers that I can remember. Sheer arrogance made it," and he threw shade on the cast, calling it "a roll call of shame."[2] Critics were not alone in voicing disappointment in the picture: "I think *Cannonball Run II* is probably the weakest picture from that whole period of cars and stunts movies," said *Cannonball Run* actor-stuntman C. James Lewis. "The quality just became a little weaker on that film…."[3] Cinematographer McLean somewhat more sanguine, recalled the good times and good friends:

> The scripts on films like *Stroker Ace* and *Cannonball Run II* weren't real good, but you overlook that because of who else is working on the picture and because you know that making the film is going to

Cinematographer Nick McLean Sr. (white t-shirt and cap) with Dean Martin (in police uniform) and crew between takes on the set of *Cannonball Run II* (1984) (photograph courtesy Nick McLean Collection).

be a lot of fun. I like to do my own aerial photography and there was plenty of aerial work called for here, so I was happy to go to work on *Cannonball Run II*.[4]

Cannonball Run II will be remembered for being the final big-screen collaboration of Rat Pack members Sammy Davis Jr., Dean Martin and Frank Sinatra. The Chairman of the Board, however, didn't have time to revel in the fun on set, preferring to turn up early, film his scenes and leave. McLean remembered a humble icon:

> We rehearsed the scene that features Frank Sinatra for a whole day before he arrived on the set. Hal wanted to get that perfect, so we went through it with a second team, mapped out exactly what the shots were going to be so that when Frank came in, we were ready to roll. We were told that none of us were to talk to Frank and all that kind of thing, so everybody was panicky of him, but when Frank arrived on set he was terrific, a very friendly guy, and would have no problem talking to people. He was there at the coffee truck first thing in the morning and we were done by noon. Hal had a helicopter for Frank so that when he was done with the scene, he was out of there. Shirley MacLaine, who was also in the film, would hang around when Frank was on the set, she was like a groupie, she'd be standing behind cameras just watching us filming the scene so she could be in the same room as Frank, which was kind of cute.[5]

Needham's typically unpretentious style of filmmaking contributes to the breezy nature of the production; his skill in constructing stunt sequences suited such a picture which lives or dies according to the competency of its action set pieces. McLean said,

> I did a couple of pictures with Hal and by the end of *Cannonball Run II* we were very good buddies. The great thing about working on a Hal Needham picture was, you didn't have to work long hours because Hal didn't like to work too hard. He would come in very well prepared, had all his homework done, and didn't trifle too much; he just didn't want to work too many hours … ten hours at the most. He wanted to get it done and get out of there. With movies like *Stroker Ace* and *Cannonball Run II*, the stunts were our main concern, and once we got that right, that was our job done.[6]

"When people see my movies, I want to get their adrenaline flowing," Needham said. "If I don't, I haven't done my job."[7] And Needham certainly got the job done on *Cannonball Run II*, which despite its unenviable critical legacy is essentially a replica of the first picture in the best sense of the comparison. *Cannonball Run II* isn't a picture which makes allusion to art, or even to storytelling, it is a sketch show punctuated by car stunts, populated by extremely likable entertainers having fun together. The episodic nature of the narrative structure can make it feel rambling and directionless, but like the original picture, this sequel works as a supreme piece of anarchic cartoon entertainment. According to McLean,

> There were some tough moments, it was hot as hell in Arizona. In fact, one of the days we were filming out there was considered one of the hottest days on record, it was around 118 degrees, and it was the scene where the plane comes in on the blacktop. We were losing crew like crazy; they were dropping like flies because of the intensity of the heat. But it was a great experience, and like I say, because Hal was directing, the hours were good, and it was a really fun experience. When all those guys got together, there was no ego, we were all just there having a good time and a lot of laughs.[8]

Notes

1. Roger Moore with Gareth Owen, *My Word Is My Bond: The Autobiography* (London: Michael O'Mara Books, 2008), p. 239.

2. Roger Ebert, "Cannonball Run II," *The Chicago Sun-Times*, January 1, 1984, https://www.rogerebert.com/reviews/cannonball-run-ii-1984.

3. C. James Lewis, *interview with author*, Skype, August 17, 2018.

4. Nick McLean Sr., *interview with author*, Skype, January 15, 2018.

5. *Ibid.*

6. *Ibid.*

7. Hal Needham, *Stuntman!: My Car-Crashing, Plane-Jumping, Bone-Breaking, Death-Defying Hollywood Life* (New York, Boston, London: Little, Brown and Company, 2011) [n.p.].

8. McLean, *interview with author*, Skype, January 15, 2018.

City Heat

(1984)

"Look, do me a favor, don't save my life any more!"—Mike Murphy

It's 1933 and Kansas City is being torn apart by a fierce rivalry between gangsters Leon Coll (Tony Lo Bianco) and Primo Pitt (Rip Torn). Only two men can restore some order to the streets, Lt. Speer (Clint Eastwood) and Mike Murphy, P.I. (Reynolds). Speer has a love-hate relationship with Murphy, his partner when Murphy was a cop. When Diehl Smith, P.I. (Richard Roundtree), is thrown from a window to his death by Pitt's goons, Speer and Murphy reluctantly join forces to crack down on mob bosses and corrupt city officials. They take us on a thrilling journey through an evocative period world of decadent jazz clubs and seamy gin joints.

For Warner Bros. and for audiences of 1984, *City Heat* should have been a golden ticket: two of the biggest stars on the planet, Reynolds and Eastwood, starring side by side in a raucous crime picture directed by an auteur filmmaker, Blake Edwards. But there was a fly in the ointment.

Edwards wrote a script entitled *Kansas City Blues* which attracted the interest of Reynolds and Eastwood; the pair had been itching to work together. Edwards was set to direct the picture and was in the comfortable position of a pay-or-play deal, in that he would receive his full directing salary whether he made the film or not; in the end, he didn't direct and he did get paid. With the addition of Reynolds and Eastwood came suggested edits to Edwards' script, and the writer balked; it got to the point where the script was no longer resembled the one that Edwards had nurtured: "They gave me a lot of money and told me I was off my own picture, and then I watched them chop off its hands and its feet and make it into this monster. And it was my brainchild they were mutilating."[1]

There had also been pre-production clashes, which apparently included Eastwood objecting to some of Edwards' requirements, such as a chauffeur service delivering him from his home in Santa Monica to the Warner Bros. Burbank studios. "Unfortunately, the first meeting between Clint and Blake fared only slightly better than that of Custer and Geronimo," Reynolds recalled. "Both are close friends of mine, but as soon as Blake brought out lunch—caviar and champagne—I knew my beer and pretzels buddy was going to fly south on this one."[2] After that awkward meeting, Edwards didn't last long on the film. With the picture now operating under an Eastwood regime, Edwards was replaced by Richard Benjamin, a familiar face as an actor, but who had only previously directed two films, *My Favorite Year* (1982) and *Racing with the Moon* (1984). Benjamin was evidently a talented actor, but as a director he was, most crucially, malleable under Eastwood's instruction.

Left to right: Reynolds, Clint Eastwood, Madeline Kahn, Jane Alexander, unidentified woman and C. James Lewis on the set of *City Heat* (1984) (photograph courtesy C. James Lewis Collection).

Ultimately, Edwards chose to dissociate himself from the project and used the pseudonym Sam O. Brown for his screenwriting credit.

There was an element of regret when Edwards exited the production. "I was dying to work with Blake Edwards," said cinematographer Nick McLean Sr. "He used to live right by me in Malibu and one day his daughter came up to me on the beach and said, 'You know, Daddy wants you to shoot his next film,' and, boy, don't think I wasn't excited. Then when I learned Blake was off the picture, I was kind of upset, but I wanted to do the film anyway."[3] Actor C. James Lewis, who plays Irene Cara's discourteous suitor, remembered the tumultuous shift in personnel:

> Blake Edwards was just so smooth; he wasn't up, he wasn't down, just smooth; he worked with such an open hand and surrounded himself with the best people, the same way Burt Reynolds did and the way Clint Eastwood did. But the three of them together just didn't work out. *City Heat* was originally named *Kansas City Blues* and Blake was going to direct it, that was the plan, but then there were disagreements and Clint stepped in. Clint wielded a lot of power, and has done for a long time. Warner Bros co-produced the film with the Malpaso Company, which is Clint's production company, and they have always had a tight relationship, so Clint got to choose the director, Richard Benjamin. Clint and Burt had an agreement where they got to choose certain people who they wanted to work on the film; Clint got to choose the key grip, Burt got to pick the cinematographer. So Burt brought in Nick McLean to shoot the film.[4]

"Here's what happened on that film…" says McLean. "Something went wrong between Blake and Clint, they just didn't click, and so Clint wanted to bring Richard Benjamin in to direct it. Richard is a great guy but he wasn't the best director of all time, so Clint essentially ran the show. Clint was the guy that we all went to for putting the film together and for how it was going to look."[5]

Lewis confirms McLean's assertion that the true author of *City Heat* was indeed its powerful star: "Richard Benjamin was in over his head, he was just a figurehead; Clint Eastwood really directed that movie."[6] McLean continued, "Burt was sick for much of the picture, he was around but he really wasn't doing too well because he was involved in a stunt that went wrong on the set. He was supposed to get hit with a dummy breakaway chair but the stunt guy picked up a real steel chair and whacked Burt across the face with it, and so he ended up with severe jaw problems after that. It was a really bad incident and it screwed Burt for a couple of years."[7] The impact of the chair hitting Reynolds full force across the head was so fierce that it left the actor in shock but, maintaining his old athlete's stamina, he shook off the incident and continued filming. But subsequent headaches and jaw pain ultimately led to the diagnosis of a fracture of the temporo-mandibular joint. TMJ disorders can be one of the most painful, with symptoms of nausea and disorientation, as well as restricted movement. Reynolds' inability to eat solid food meant sudden and alarming weight loss, and he dropped to around 140 pounds from his regular weight of just over 200. Reynolds looked ill, leading to scurrilous and disparaging remarks in the tabloid press and amongst some of the actor's supposedly closest associates. Reynolds: "The injury not only affected the rest of the picture but in many ways altered my life forever. It was an accident."[8]

City Heat is a stunningly rendered homage to the aesthetics of film noir and the gangster pictures of the 1940s, with McLean photographing some of the richest images of his career. Lewis said, "It's a great thing that Burt brought Nick in to shoot *City Heat*, because it is a beautiful looking film, and that is entirely thanks to Nick McLean. The film is perhaps a little too campy for my taste—I would have preferred something a little more serious—but it is truly a visually stunning picture."[9] McLean enthused,

> Clint knows filmmaking like nobody else. He was great to work with, just terrific. He allowed me to do some of my best work on that picture. He liked being in the shadows and being framed in the dark. We actually keyed Clint from the back! His key light wasn't in front of him, it was at the back and he would just turn his head a little bit to pick up the side light. We'd three-quarter backlight him so that the light just kind of slid off his face. He'd say things like, "Don't worry about it, I've been doing this for 50 years, I'll find the light!" and "It's okay, the audience knows who I am."[10]

Despite the stunning photography and the presence of two major stars at the top of their game, the film struggles to find a suitable tone. Perhaps it is the very difference in personality of its two leads that contributes to the uneven mood. Eastwood, stoic and reserved, stalks his way through the film with the sobriety of his erstwhile Dirty Harry persona; meanwhile Reynolds is as convivial as always. Both leads bring diverging and contrasting traits to the picture, never truly reaching a tone that suits them both at the same time. Eastwood's comic reactions to action around him in several scenes feel forced and out of character, whereas it is entirely natural for Reynolds to mug and contort his features in pursuit of a laugh. As such, the spirit of the film is confused, at times dark and serious, then farcical and self-consciously aware. It never truly descends to outright parody, but there are comical scenes which undermine the script's dramatic qualities. *City Heat* is far from a bad film: The script is dense and busy enough to hold one's interest, the period setting is brilliantly realized and the photographic style is sumptuous and finely crafted, truly one of the great-looking pictures of the 1980s. While the film rarely feels like the satisfactory underworld melodrama that it wants to be, the myriad aesthetic qualities as well as the simple but powerful pleasure of seeing two of the greatest film stars of their generation share the screen make *City Heat* as easy a film to enjoy as much as it is an easy film to lament what could have been.

Notes

1. Julia Cameron, "Home Movie: Blake Edwards' Life is Autobiographical," *Chicago Tribune*, September 21, 1986, https://www.chicagotribune.com/news/ct-xpm-1986-09-21-8603100965-story.html
2. Burt Reynolds, *My Life: Burt Reynolds* (Great Britain: Hodder and Stoughton, 1994), pp. 261–271.
3. Nick McLean Sr., *interview with author*, Skype, January 15, 2018.
4. C. James Lewis, *interview with author*, Skype, August 17, 2018.
5. Nick McLean Sr., *interview with author*, Skype, January 15, 2018.
6. C. James Lewis, *interview with author*, Skype, August 17, 2018.
7. Nick McLean Sr., *interview with author*, Skype, January 15, 2018.
8. Reynolds, n.p.
9. C. James Lewis, *interview with author*, Skype, August 17, 2018.
10. Nick McLean Sr., *interview with author*, Skype, January 15, 2018.

Stick

(1985)

"I got a friend out in the Everglades; he's gas bubbles and gator bait."—Stick

Burt Reynolds plays Ernest "Stick" Stickley, a reformed criminal just released from prison and making his way back to his hometown of Miami. Riding a boxcar into the city, Stick leaps from the locomotive to his freedom, unaware that he has just jumped right back into the underworld that proved his initial downfall.

Stick is intent on reconnecting with his estranged daughter Katie (Tricia Leigh Fisher) and with his former cellmate Rainy (Jose Perez). The two men are barely reacquainted when Rainy convinces Stick to accompany him on an illicit drop-off, delivering on behalf of local gangster Chucky (Charles Durning). Stick reluctantly agrees and the pair travels deep into the Everglades, where they meet with a bagman and assassin named Moke (Dar Robinson). Moke works for drug kingpin Nestor (Castulo Guerra), Chucky's business rival. This drug deal turns into a fatal double-cross that sees Rainy killed and Stick fleeing for his life after killing some of Nestor's men in self-defense. Stick lies low, taking shelter with friend Luis (David Reynoso) and vowing to make Chucky pay the $5000 that Rainy was to be remunerated for the job. At the same time, Nestor blames Chucky for the loss of his men and insists that Chucky owes him a life in return. To enter the gangland inner circle, Stick stealthily plans an encounter with eccentric cigar-chomping playboy Barry (George Segal), a "wheeler-dealer type" associate of Chucky's who operates within the legitimate business world. Stick utilizes his car thievery skills to manipulate his way into the good graces of Barry, who doesn't realize he is being set up and hires the criminal as his personal driver. Stick's working class, streetwise attitude and rugged appeal beguiles the pretentious, the affluent and the decadent. Once ensconced in Miami high society, Stick uses Barry and his connections to get closer to Chucky. One of those who can help Stick in his quest for vengeance is a beautiful financial advisor named Kyle (Candice Bergen).

Reynolds' first directorial effort since his exceptional work on 1981's *Sharky's Machine*, *Stick* marks the star's return to southern noir. With its contemporary new wave score (complete with pounding electro drums), flashy editing and serio-comic tone, *Stick* seems to vie for the same kind of juxtaposition of action, humor and aesthetic pizzazz that brought success to *Beverly Hills Cop* (Martin Brest, 1984) and *48 Hrs* (Walter Hill, 1982). The picture is exceedingly enjoyable, despite the awkward melodrama of the wholly extraneous subplot involving Stick and his daughter Katie. Reynolds does a fine job of bringing Elmore Leonard's titular character to life, looking true to his written form, "like he was from another time: dustbowl farmer turned hobo." Reynolds' easy charm makes it impossible for him to be entirely dour or gruff, even when the script calls for gravity; when coupled with Richard Lawson's affable African-American chauffeur Cornell, the result is that both actors' geniality keeps the film in breezier territory, which can be troublesome when attempting to present a dark and dangerous world of dodgy dealings and vile antagonists. Such levity can undermine the more interesting shades of dark that the picture presents when it works best.

Charles Durning turns in a brilliantly grotesque rendering of drug-dependent gangster Chucky, resplendent in oversized Hawaiian shirts, ludicrous red fright wig and wild, ungroomed eyebrows. Chucky looks like he belongs at a carnival fairground rather than mixing with the bourgeois elements of Miami society. While Chucky perfectly fits within the picture's world of outsized, vividly crafted villains, George Segal's Barry is a risible, almost absurdly out of control creation that seems to have wandered on to the wrong film set. Just as Segal's daft performance threatens to run the picture off-course, Dar Robinson counters the lunacy by providing superb support as the albino assassin Moke. With his chalky pallor and piercing "bunny eyes," erstwhile stuntman Robinson brings an incredible sense of menace and a commanding screen presence as Moke. Credit where credit is due: The screen version of Moke is a far more intimidating figure than Leonard's literary version. While Robinson dons a lariat necklace with a black hat and waistcoat combo suggesting a wicked cowboy, Leonard's description of Moke in his novel conjures a less-imposing image: "The boy was a study, trying hard to effect the grungy look of a heavy-metal rock star, the headband, the illustrated disco shirt opened all the way."[1] One of cinema's most celebrated stuntmen, Robinson died the following year in an accident during the making of Richard Fleischer's *Million Dollar Mystery*.

Cinematographer Nick McLean Sr. recalled working with the revered Robinson:

> Burt loved stunt guys and he thought Dar would be good enough to get away with playing the main villain, but Dar wasn't really a very good actor. I mean, he looks great with the white hair and blue contact lenses, he really looks like a creepy villain, but they actually had to dub Dar's voice for Moke, because in real life Dar had a high, squeaky kind of voice. The studio liked everything about him except his voice, so they had to fix that in post-production. Every time you hear Moke talking, that's a voiceover.[2]

In an amazing feat of physical prowess and awesome stunt work, Robinson performed Moke's climactic high rise fall without the aid of green screen technology or back projection. "That was a terrific stunt and a great shot!" McLean enthused. He continued:

Burt really wanted to see him going down and to see the pool below, which meant you couldn't have a safety bag down there to catch his fall. So Dar figured out how to put a wire around his ankle that he hooked up to a cylinder which would slow him down by his feet before he hit the cement. It looks like a total freefall and he even manages to squeeze off a few rounds up at Burt as he's falling. It's looks amazing.[3]

Dar Robinson as villain Moke in *Stick* (1985).

McLean was responsible for the film's stunning photography, a rich style which nicely juxtaposes the glossy world of urban high-rises and pristine, white-washed mansions with the seamy underworld environs and rural danger zones. He elaborated:

I had a great time shooting *Stick*. At that point, Burt and I had this rapport where we knew what the other was thinking and trusted each other's ideas. We did those opening helicopter shots of Burt in the boxcar on the first day of shooting. That is actually Burt jumping out of the moving boxcar. I said

Cinematographer Nick McLean Sr. and actress Candice Bergen have a laugh between takes on *Stick* (1985) (photograph courtesy Nick McLean Collection).

to him, "Don't you want to leave that until the last day of shooting?" because it was really a tough stunt, it required the character to jump out of that boxcar and go down about 20 feet. He could have seriously injured himself. But Burt said, "Let's just go for it!" He loved doing his own stuff.[4]

Some of McLean's richest and most textured work from throughout his collaborations with Reynolds appears in *Stick*. Witness the shootout in the Everglades, which starts out as a grim, gray affair but after the gunfire and mayhem ensue, the image takes on a sumptuous twilight quality. McLean's dynamic camerawork during the well-staged action sequences are captured by an exciting mix of aerial photography and a roving tracking camera which takes us through the claustrophobic and cavernous cane field. "Those are some of the most beautiful shots in the movie," said McLean. "But they just happened; we were quick and efficient enough to get them on film without ever anticipating how the light would change as it did. Those shots weren't pre-planned or part of an overall design for the film, we just saw how the sky was developing as the sun was setting so we set up some cameras, had the actors ready to go, and we got it. That was all legitimate, no CGI or anything."[5]

While those particular shots were achieved with ease and skill, other setups for the scene proved somewhat more challenging. Reynolds' stunt double on the picture, C. James Lewis, recalled the hair-raising activities involved in filming the memorable sequence:

In that scene, there's a van with Burt in it and a car with the bad guys following behind; Burt gets out, empties the jerry can, waits for the guys to come in and lights it. Well, I drove the van, suited up, and had my game face on. The special effects guys dug two 15-foot-long trenches about a foot wide and they poured gasoline in there. Then they scored the roof of the van and loaded it with explosives. They said, "Okay, here's what we're going to do: Jimmy, you're going to drive in and there's shots flying; you

Reynolds (left) and stunt double C. James Lewis discuss a scene on the set of *Stick* (1985) (photograph courtesy C. James Lewis Collection).

stop the van and jump out, grab the jerry can, spread it around and you're going to run to this safe place"—a hole they dug for me—when it happens these stunt guys will be blown backwards and then you start running away as the field becomes engulfed in flames."[6]

So here's the problem: They are shooting from two helicopters, one of which has Burt and Nick in it, and there are also cameras on the ground. They loaded the film in the magazine and didn't test fire; you gotta bump it to make sure it works. They get ready to shoot, they call action, and then … nothing. I'm sitting in a hole full of gas, and the vapors are filling the air. I'm breathing fumes! I'm thinking that if this thing blows up and I'm breathing in fumes, I'm going to come out of here like a human torch with fire coming out of my ass! So I started sneaking away out of that hole. Now I'm coated in gasoline, I can smell it, I can feel it, and I can taste it. Well, I got a little scared, I admit it. There are only two things that I'm afraid of in this life: fire and my first ex-wife. Anyway, there was air getting through that cane field but there's no breeze; I feel like I'm saturated. So then I can hear, "Roll cameras! Action! Action, Jimmy!" When that explosion went off, the hood of that van went 85 feet in the air and damn near hit the helicopter, that's how much they packed that van. It was like Dante's Inferno. I started running and I was afraid to breath in the fumes, so I'm running and I'm holding my breath, which was a mistake but I didn't want to suck in fumes and burn my lungs. I'm not lying to you, there were animals escaping that cane field along with me; rats as big as dogs, snakes, all fleeing that inferno right with me. As I'm running, I'm thinking to myself that I'm not going to get out. I eventually got to an irrigation ditch and I reminded myself what I had to do for the shot, which was I'm going to jump over that ditch, roll through the jump and then I'm going to look back at the fire. Well, what happened was, I jumped the ditch but because I was holding my breath I didn't have enough in me to make the jump, I ended up hitting the other side of the ditch head-on. It was like Wile E. Coyote: I hit it hard and slid down in slow-motion. Burt asked Nick if he thought I was all right and Nick said, "I think he's acting," but Burt said, "I never told him to do that, I told him to jump, roll, look back and go!" Well, Nick says, "You know what? I think that boy is out." Burt told the pilot to land the helicopter and he hopped out and ran over to the ditch and helped pull me out and asked if I was okay and I said, "I don't think so, my head really hurts." The cane field is ablaze, I'm injured, and I'm being helped into a helicopter. It was like Vietnam, I had a flashback to the war! When Burt asked me if I was okay, I told him I was sorry for messing up the shot, and he said, "Buddy, it looked good until you hit the ditch and passed out."[7]

Reynolds had a very near-miss of his own. In the confrontation between Stick and Moke, an accident occurred that nearly cost Reynolds his eyesight. The problem happened when Moke fires his weapon after being thrown out of the van by Stick. The gun being used by Robinson in the scene was a large caliber weapon and when the actor fired it, a blank hit Reynolds directly in the eye and knocked him out. Luckily, Lewis and McLean were both standing nearby and ran to Reynolds' aid.

Nick and I jumped in the van immediately and we talked to him; he said, "I'm hit, I can't see!" We told him not to move and we got the nurse in. Nick told them to clear out the helicopter and I never seen anybody move so fast as the two camera assistants out of the back of that helicopter. We threw Burt in and took off. Thankfully, being that we were shooting down in the 'Glades, the helicopter screamed over to Miami and within 20 minutes Burt was at one of the best eye institutes in America, which happens to be in Miami. They got Burt straight in to surgery, pulled that piece of wadding out and saved his sight. The doctor said that getting Burt there as quick as we did was the only thing that saved his eyesight.[8]

Despite such dedication in making the best possible adaptation of Elmore Leonard's novel, critiques of the picture were harsh and Reynolds fought an uphill battle with Universal over the picture's final cut. The screenplay is credited to Leonard and co-writer Joseph Stinson, the latter having also written the Reynolds-Eastwood double-header *City Heat*, but despite the author's involvement, Leonard biographer Paul Challen notes the author's disgruntled feelings towards the film: "To this day, the making of *Stick* into the film that was released in 1984 [*sic*] is one of the sorest points in Leonard's career…. Reynolds did just about everything wrong as he possibly could—the thing bears no resemblance to anything Leonard would ever dream of writing."[9] In fairness to Reynolds, not all of the blame can be placed on him. While the star's name was still of marquee value in the mid–1980s, creative autonomy eluded him on this picture. Reynolds engaged in a fierce struggle with Universal over the editing and content of the picture and the studio ultimately refused the cut of *Stick* that Reynolds turned in; executives demanded reshoots, additional action sequences, and an alternate ending to be filmed. Cinematographer McLean had already moved on to another film by the time the new material was ordered, and his replacement was Fred Koenekamp (*Patton, Billy Jack, The Towering Inferno*). Koenekamp was a cinematographer of more traditional Hollywood style, somewhat in opposition to McLean's maverick European influence. "The guy they brought in had a completely different style to me; his aesthetic came from the old studio system." McLean said. "There's about 20 minutes worth of additional footage in there that I didn't shoot and it's obvious because it's totally not my style of filming. The way he shot those scenes are not are what I would have done there at all. It's unfortunate but those kinds of things happen and it's out of your control."[10]

Intriguingly, an alternative cut of *Stick* was broadcast on British television in the late 1980s; this was most likely Reynolds' initial version of the picture. The theatrical cut absolves Kyle from iniquitous involvement, free for her and Stick to literally drive off into the sunset and resume their romance. But the televised cut includes what was to be Reynolds' intended finale set in Chucky's Grove Towers apartment, where Kyle is implicated in the initial doublecross. We see Stick arriving to the building as Kyle and Chucky are scheming and arguing; Moke then appears, leading to a verbal and physical scuffle which results in the villain's spectacular fall. The picture ends there without any romantic resolution between Kyle and Stick. This climax makes far more sense structurally; the theatrical version of the scene is edited awkwardly to have Kyle excluded from the scene entirely, having Moke hold the ailing Chucky's medication hostage just as Stick elliptically appears on the balcony out of thin air. The opening scene from the televised cut of the film also gives us an idea of how Reynolds initially wanted the picture scored. The theatrical version has a typical 1980s synthesizer score by Joseph Conlan and Barry De Vorzon, and it is a brilliant one at that; however, the televised cut indicates that Reynolds wanted a rootsier musical palette, as the opening credit sequence contains a country ballad, rather than Conlan and De Vorzon's pulsating electronic music. Another victim of the picture's reshuffling was *Ghostbusters* and *Pretty in Pink* actress Annie Potts, who was cast in the film as a movie studio executive, but her scenes were excised for the theatrical cut while the character of Stick's daughter Katie was shoehorned into the narrative. "I wanted to make that movie as soon as I read the book. I respected Leonard's work," Reynolds recalled. "I turned in my cut of the picture and truly thought I had made a good film. Word got back to me quickly that the people in the Black Tower wanted a few changes."[11]

With that, Universal pulled the movie from its release schedule and Reynolds went about shooting the additional material. "I gave up on the film. I didn't fight them. I let them get the best of me…. When I reshot the film, I was just going through the motions. I'm not proud of what I did, but I take responsibility for my actions. All I can say—and this is not in way of a defense—is if you liked the first part of *Stick*, that's what I was trying to achieve throughout."[12]

Notes

1. Elmore Leonard, *Stick* (London: Phoenix, 2007), p. 10.
2. Nick McLean Sr., *interview with author*, Skype, January 15, 2018.

3. *Ibid.*

4. *Ibid.*

5. *Ibid.*

6. C. James Lewis, *interview with author*, Skype, August 17, 2018.

7. *Ibid.*

8. *Ibid.*

9. Paul Chalen, *Get Dutch!: A Biography of Elmore Leonard* (Toronto: ECW Press, 2000), p.105.

10. Nick McLean Sr., *interview with author*, Skype, January 15, 2018.

11. Craig Modderno, "Burt Reynolds is The Comeback Kid," *Los Angeles Times*, January 04, 1987, http://articles.latimes.com/1987–01-04/entertainment/ca-1803_1_burt-reynolds/4.

12. *Ibid.*

An Interview
with Michael D. O'Shea

Michael D. O'Shea is an Emmy-winning cinematographer and recipient of the 2011 Television Career Achievement Award from the American Society of Cinematographers. He began his career as a camera operator in the mid–1960s on shows such as *Daktari*, *Gunsmoke* and *Death Valley Days* before a big break into major motion pictures came in the form of Nick McLean Sr. and Burt Reynolds. Acclaimed cinematographer McLean had

Camera operator Mike O'Shea (at the camera) and cinematographer Nick McLean Sr. (right) on set of *Cannonball Run II* (1984) (photograph courtesy Nick McLean Collection).

been considered one of the great camera operators of the 1970s, shooting some of the most revered maverick films of the New Hollywood movement with legendary cinematographers such as Vilmos Zsigmond, Conrad Hall and William Fraker. When tasked with shooting the stunt and gag-filled action comedy *Cannonball Run II*, McLean was on the lookout for a hot new cameraman who he could trust to deliver a dynamic style for the frenetic picture, and he was keeping watch on one particular camera operator who caught his eye. *Cannonball Run II* proved a major boon to O'Shea's career and led to a series of collaborations with McLean, including *City Heat, Stick, The Goonies, Short Circuit, Twice in a Lifetime, Spaceballs* and *Mac & Me*. After making his mark as a camera operator, O'Shea became a noted cinematographer, working on several Mel Brooks films (*Robin Hood: Men in Tights, Dracula: Dead and Loving It*) as well as shooting the major television shows *Chicago Hope, CSI: Miami* and *Bones*.

Wayne: *How did your professional association with Burt Reynolds come about?*

Michael: Well, it all came about because of Nick McLean, who has been a very close friend of mine ever since he called me up one day to ask me if I would be his camera operator on *Cannonball Run II*. I knew of his fantastic career, about how good Nick was, and I knew all of the great films that he worked on. So I was amazed when I found out he was keeping an eye on me and watching my work closely.

Do you recall how it felt being asked to work on this film? I imagine there must have been a lot of expectation and excitement around Cannonball Run II.

It was an unbelievable experience for me. I was a camera operator on a TV show at the time and one day Nick called to the set to speak to me. I had only met him a couple of times socially beforehand, but that day it felt like we knew each other forever. Then some time later I got a phone call from him telling me he was going to shoot *Cannonball Run II* and wanted to know if I would be his camera operator. Nick had shot *Stroker Ace* and *Staying Alive* and he was considered one of the really great cameramen in the business, so this was a huge opportunity for me. I thought he was looking for me to work the second or third camera, but he said, "No, I want you on the A camera." I couldn't believe it, it was such an honor to be considered for this important job by Nick McLean.

It must have been a lot of pressure working on this major picture for the biggest movie star in the world.

I actually worked with Burt prior to this, on *Smokey and the Bandit II*, where I worked the extra cameras, but this was a different situation, I was now the main guy working the A camera. Being there with both Nick and Burt was a special experience. I was really able to observe how they worked so well together when I came onto *Cannonball Run II* and it was a special kind of relationship, you could feel both the friendship and the sense of trust between them.

What was it about their relationship that made it such a rich and prolific one?

Some of their greatest work can be seen in the films they did together and I was there to witness how well they worked with each other. They had both been great football players in the past and I think that provided a solid foundation for them; then Burt had seen what a great cameraman Nick was when they worked together on *Sharky's Machine* and that led to Burt moving Nick up to cinematographer on *Stroker Ace*. Burt knew what he wanted and Nick knew how to get it. The friendship that is there between them translated into this amazing work on the screen. You could see these two guys really loved each other and being around that kind of relationship on the set really made going to work every day such an enjoyable thing. Nick was the cinematographer on *City Heat* and he knew exactly how to shoot Burt and Clint [Eastwood], his lighting and compositions serve the story so brilliantly, it is phenomenal work. *City Heat* showed everyone what Nick was capable of achieving and just after that film we went to Fort Lauderdale, Florida, to shoot *Stick*. Nick was cinematographer on that again but this time Burt was not only starring in it but he was directing it as well. God, what an experience that was! To be able to go to that environment every day with these two amazing guys, Burt Reynolds and Nick McLean, set me on a path that I'm still on today, and it's a path that I have been on for over 35 years. It was not only the quality of work that we did that made it so special, but they made it fun. They made it feel like a family and I can't thank them enough for that.

Stick is one of my favorite Burt Reynolds films. What made it such a special experience for you?

Stick was so beautifully made, and it is because of that collaboration of Burt and Nick, how they both understood the script and how their ideas gelled together. I don't mean to sound corny, but watching the two of them working on something was like watching a ballet, because they trusted each other so much and shared all of these great ideas. That's a major thing in this industry: Directors need to be able to trust their cinematographer's instincts. You can tell Burt trusted Nick every inch of the way because the work is right there on the screen. As complicated as shooting the movie could get sometimes, the both of those guys made my job as easy as possible because they are so professional and know exactly what they want. What a team Burt Reynolds and Nick McLean made.

Burt endured some difficulties around this time, following his accident on the set of City Heat *and then facing battles with Universal over the production of* Stick. *Did that stuff ever affect his work as director on the set of the film?*

Burt was only ever a gentleman. Burt Reynolds is a man; a real, honest man. He's human, so he has good days and he has other days where he didn't feel so good, but no matter what, Burt Reynolds always treated people with respect. I will never forget the humility and respect he had for people, and the decent way that he treated my family when they came to visit the set, and he did it in such an unassuming way.

Burt was at the absolute top of the game as a director, as an actor, as a star, he was the #1 box office guy in the world, but he was also one of the most loyal people in Hollywood. Nothing changed in Burt as he became this huge star. He made you feel so welcome. My mom and dad, along with my sister and my wife, came down to visit me in Fort Lauderdale as we were filming *Stick* because I had been gone for a long time; back then, Burt owned a dinner theater out in Jupiter and the first thing Burt did was ask me, "Would your mom and dad like to go out to the theater to have dinner and see a play?" I said, "Are you kidding, Burt?" and he said, "No, it will all be on me! You go with your mom and dad and have a good time." So we all went out to his playhouse and had a great time and a very nice dinner. That's the kind of guy Burt Reynolds was. It was about family. If my mom and dad were on the set, he made sure to come over and speak to them, he really made them feel welcome and feel part of his own extended family. So when you see any negative stuff being written about Burt Reynolds, they are wrong. Burt Reynolds changed my life. My mom and dad taught me how to treat people right, but Burt Reynolds and Nick McLean also taught me to how be kind and to respect people throughout your career.

It sounds like shooting Stick *was a great experience for you.*

Oh, it was a great time. I even got to momentarily bask in the glory of looking like Burt Reynolds because back when we were shooting *Stick* I had a big black mustache, so Burt and I resembled each other. There were always big crowds of people around the locations because we were shooting it in Burt's part of the country and they love him there; a couple of times when I would be walking to the set, or getting to the camera, people would be waving at me and saying, "There he is!" thinking I was Burt. I never thought I looked that good but I just said "What the hell" and I would have a lot of fun with that and wave back, especially at the pretty girls. It was very funny, I would never go up and talk to them because I'd be busted straight away, so I would wave from a distance and they would get all excited thinking Burt Reynolds was saying hello.

You continued on with an amazing career, shooting the high-profile films **Extreme Prejudice***,* **The Lost Boys***,* **The 'Burbs** *and* **The Naked Gun***. Had the opportunity arose, would you have worked with Burt again?*

I would have loved to work with Burt again and I actually did get the opportunity. I was asked to go and work with him on another film but unfortunately I wasn't able to do it because I was already signed on to do another picture. I was really sorry I couldn't do it.

Do you recall which film that was?

It was a picture Burt was doing in Las Vegas called *Heat*. I got a call from the production manager: "Burt Reynolds said to get you up here as soon as you can." Do you know what that meant to me? It meant everything. "Burt Reynolds wants you here." That was unbelievable to hear. I was still only a camera operator at that point, so can you imagine how important it was that the biggest movie star in the world specifically requested me? There was some kind of trouble going on with the production of the film and I was to replace somebody else but unfortunately I was away on this other film and I couldn't do it. But I am so thankful for having worked on those pictures that I did with Burt, I only have good things to say of my experience of being around him.

Having worked with Burt on those several occasions, films in very different genres, what in your opinion makes Burt Reynolds such a magnetic screen presence?

Firstly, Burt is a terrific actor. He really brings everything he has to a role. I always liked his work, but this magnitude of personality and charisma that we witness on screen I later found is how he really is as a person. That man could be as dramatic in a serious role or as funny in a comedy as any other actor and pull it off; he can be very deep or very funny, but mostly, Burt Reynolds is very *real*. He translated all of those great qualities of his personality to the screen and I think that is why so many people love him, because he is being absolutely genuine. What you see is what you get. And as you say, I worked with him several times and across different genres—comedy, drama, action—so I've seen him work in different styles of filmmaking that require different types of performances of him, and each time he brings himself and he aces the role every time. That's who Burt is. That's my story and I'll stick to that forever. Burt Reynolds is a good man to the core. He is about family and friendship and he makes you feel that you are part of his life. He even made my mother and father feel like that, and this was when he was at the height of his fame, yet he still had time and warmth for everybody. That all made my job easier, and for me that job came with a lot of pressure because I was operating the camera for one of, if not *the* top cinematographer in the business, who himself was previously the top camera operator in Hollywood, and I was doing it with the biggest movie star in the world. Burt made things comfortable and fun, when he walked onto the set, he was your friend and I have always considered him a friend ever since.

Heat

(1986)

"I've been knocked down, blown up, lied to, shit on, shot at. I'm not a virgin except in my heart. Nothing surprises me any more except what people do to each other. I'm a licensed pilot, I lectured on economics at Yale, and I can memorize the front page of *The New York Times* in five minutes and read it back to you in five weeks. I was National Golden Gloves champion three years in a row and I'm fluent in four languages and.... I lie a lot."—Nick Escalante

Set in the neon glow of a seedy Las Vegas, *Heat* tells the story of Nick Escalante (Reynolds) a former soldier of fortune and now a kind of protection agent with a heart of gold. When his prostitute friend Holly (Karen Young) is brutally beaten by young mobster Danny DeMarco (Neill Barry), he demands that she be paid $20,000. Holly flees Las Vegas with half the money after leaving the other half to Escalante, who is saving up $100,000 to move to Venice, Italy, and live comfortably—the $100,000 will be his "fuck you money." The $10,000 left to him by Holly burns a hole in his pocket, however, as Escalante is a former compulsive gambler; he is also well-connected and doesn't fear the wrath of the undisciplined DeMarco, who has set out on a path of revenge against Holly's avenging angel. Meanwhile, the central story sees Escalante solicited by a meek but wealthy young businessman named Cyrus Kinnick (Peter MacNicol), who wishes to avail himself of Escalante's advertised services as a "chaperone" under the guise of needing protection as he gambles big in the casinos. But what the kid really requires is a figure of masculinity to teach him how to be a man, to be coached into being a more physically capable and emotionally assertive person. To convince Escalante of his independence, the financial whiz kid claims to have made millions of dollars. Such braggodocio fails to impress Escalante but he still agress to spend time Kinnick winning and losing some money. The pair's relationship takes on a father-son dynamic, only with bloody noses as part of the bonding ritual. Escalante is emotionally rattled when Kinnick is assassinated by DeMarco's goons, the student having tried in earnest to protect his teacher and friend.

Heat should have been hot, because this picture started out with some serious pedigree: venerated New Hollywood auteur Robert Altman to direct a screenplay by the Oscar-winning William Goldman based on his own 1985 novel, starring Burt Reynolds and produced by Elliott Kastner (*Where Eagles Dare, 92 in the Shade, Breakheart Pass, The Missouri Breaks*). What went wrong?

The idea of a Reynolds-Altman vehicle had been gestating as far back as 1969, when Altman wanted Reynolds for *MASH*, but the actor was recuperating from the illness he picked up filming in filthy waters on *Operation C.I.A.* Altman left *Heat* a couple of days before cameras were due to roll, and so the vacancy was filled by acclaimed producer-director Dick Richards. Richards had directed the previous Kastner

Nick Escalante (Reynolds) surveys the Las Vegas Strip in *Heat* (1986).

productions *Farewell My Lovely* (1975) and *Death Valley* (1982) and produced Sydney Pollack's massively successful *Tootsie* (1982), for which he received an Academy Award nomination. Reynolds was wary, having heard of the numerous fistfights the director had been involved in on various film shoots, sarcastically pointing out, "Three pictures, four punchouts. Sounded lovely to me."[1] At the loss of Altman and facing a potential production shutdown, Kastner insisted upon Richards. Reynolds was vocal in his criticism of Richards from the get-go: "Sweet to the producer, he criticized extras, verbally abused crew members, and took advantage of others in all kinds of bully ways.... I hated his type, and told him so."[2]

Things came to a head over a disagreement on how Peter MacNicol's death scene should be filmed. After some moments of bravado and finger-jabbing between the two, Reynolds knocked his director out cold. Soon after, Richards was involved in another on-set collision, only this time it was with the cold hard ground rather than Reynolds' fist: The director fell from a crane truck. Emerging from the multiple fracases with head injuries and a lawyer in tow, Richards successfully sued Reynolds, the punch ultimately costing the actor half a million dollars.

The incident made filmmakers wary of Reynolds' volatility. "I was suddenly perceived as a crazy, moody mental case,"[3] the actor said. Noted screenwriter Tom Mankiewicz (*Superman: The Movie, Ladyhawke, Dragnet*) recalled a meeting with Reynolds for a prospective project, an encounter that left Mankiewicz somewhat unnerved at the prospect of working with the troubled star, after Reynolds recounted the tale of him landing Richards onto a crap table with a single punch. "I thought, oh, fuck, I'm going to Miami with this guy. It was like a house of horrors. It was unbelievable. Then there was a rumor that Burt had AIDS. He didn't have AIDS. But something was wrong. I thought, I'm trapped in the fucking funhouse here."[4] In any case, the project never materialized.

After the skirmishes, television director Jerry Jameson (who had previously worked with Reynolds on *Dan August* and later on *B.L. Stryker*) was brought in to get the production back on schedule, as was trusted cinematographer Nick McLean Sr., who Reynolds could rely on as a professional and as a personal ally. McLean's work with Reynolds is always daring and interesting, and here he was in charge of the second unit photography while James A. Contner (*Cruising, Nighthawks, Jaws 3-D*) was the chief cinematographer. As such, *Heat* is a terrific looking picture. McLean recalled the tense situation:

> The producers of *Heat* called me up and said, "Burt just decked the director. Get up here quick and help finish this thing!" So I went in and shot some of it with Jerry Jameson, who was brought in to finish off directing it. I was told the original director was giving Burt a hard time; he allegedly started poking Burt in the chest and Burt just decked him. Burt doesn't do too well with people giving him crap. They kept the original cinematographer on the first unit but I went and shot the second unit work. I was there for maybe two weeks of work, but really I was there to support and pal around with Burt.[5]

The camerawork impresses in the opening scene: Escalante enters as a lecherous barfly and attempts to pick up a beautiful woman; her weakling date Osgood (Wendell Burton) enters the fray and supposedly beats up Escalante. Of course this scenario turns out to be a complete ruse; in the following scene, we see Osgood pay Escalante for his help in making the woman believe he has the testosterone and gallantry of a real man. During the fisitcuffs, where Escalante rips a toupee from Osgood's head in an effort to further emasculate him, the camera takes on an unusual subjective perspective, cutting between both characters' viewpoints and intimately positioning the viewer directly in the middle of the two sparring characters. This places us directly within the conflict and further establishes the taller Escalante's authority in the unfolding situation while positioning Osgood as the physically inferior of the two. The camerawork takes full advantage of the colors that Las Vegas offers in the exterior scenes; some of the best shots in the picture occur during Escalante and Kinnick's rooftop conversation overlooking the Strip.

The qualities of *Heat*, and they are numerous, have been irrevocably lost among the pejorative dialogue that exists on the film. There is indeed a struggle to juggle the picture's parallel plots which wrestle for your interest and this is perhaps owed to the fact that *Heat* has no definitive author. As a result, the tone and direction is inconsistent. At some points it feels very much like a serious crime drama, and other times a generic action thriller. The marketing campaign made the picture look much more explosive than it really is; the end product is actually a quiet neo-noir study of a flawed man with a mysterious background, constantly dragged back into the underworld that he yearns to leave behind. The tale offers the kinds of redemptive opportunities for its cynical, hard-edged hero as the best of film noir does, and it occasionally makes for an interesting sort of masculine melodrama. Here is a man turning his back on the violent past and dreaming of a tasteful life in Venice. He is playful and tender with children, and maintains platonic friendships with women; the closest thing he has in his life to male companionship is Kinnick, but then that relationship is founded on violence. Violence always finds its way back to Escalante. Masculinity in crises is a theme that runs throughout the film. Kinnick's entire reason for hiring Escalante is so he will be taught how to use violence to protect himself; in the end, no amount of learned fisticuffs protect him from the hail of bullets from the machine gun that mows him down. Reynolds plays the role of Nick Escalante not with the merry, cavalier demeanor of old, but with the kind of resigned, world-weary detachment that would inform his performances in *Malone* and *Physical Evidence*. As in *Malone*, Reynolds is an erstwhile man of violence looking to leave behind the life of force, to retreat to some idyllic land to seek tranquility and become a man of peace.

Goldman's script has some wit and some great lines that add a hard-boiled quality to the language of these shady underworld characters. "When a guy has a name for his cock, you know he's not playing with the full deck," is how Holly neatly describes the preening gangster DeMarco. Goldman has remained tight-lipped on the production of *Heat*, and perhaps for good reason; the picture is only afforded one line of recognition in Goldman's books on screenwriting; he once noted, "The reason you will not learn more about this baby in these pages is simple: to my knowledge, lawsuits are still flying."[6] This speaks to the unfortunate legacy of contention that *Heat* has sparked amongst those involved.

Notes

1. Burt Reynolds, *My Life: Burt Reynolds* (Great Britain: Hodder & Stoughton, 1994), p. 284.
2. *Ibid.*
3. *Ibid*, p. 286.
4. Nick McLean Sr., *interview with author*, Skype, January 15, 2018.
5. Tom Manciewicz and Robert Crane, *My Life as a Mankiewicz: An Insider's Journey Through Hollywood* (Kentucky: University of Kentucky Press, 2012), p. 320.
6. William Goldman, *Which Lie Did I Tell?: More Adventures in the Screen Trade* (New York: Pantheon Books, 2000), p. 50.

Malone

(1987)

"I decided not to have a master any more."—Richard Malone

In this tough action thriller, Reynolds steps into the well-worn boots of a shadowy Vietnam vet-turned-CIA man, Richard Malone. Malone has tired of the trigger and is defecting from agency life as a covert assassin for the government to seek a more peaceful existence, but he soon makes the mistake of straying into a dilapidated ghost town nestled within a scenic Oregon valley. The town is run by a powerful right-wing zealot and property developer, Charles V. Delaney (Cliff Robertson). Delaney and his enforcers are using heavy-handed tactics to buy, nay muscle, out local residents and businesses in order to establish his own private playground for his burgeoning paramilitary organization. With his army, he plans on gaining enough momentum to overthrow government, or in Delaney's own words: "You might say I'm in the survivor business. I encourage people to fight for their rights like our forefathers."

When Malone rolls his '69 Ford Mustang to the nearest service station after breaking down, he discovers a town living in fear of the evil tycoon. The hospitable station owner Paul Barlow (Scott Wilson) and his daughter Jo (Cynthia Gibb) endear themselves to Malone by inviting him to stay with them while waiting a few days for the necessary auto parts to arrive in order to repair Malone's car. Malone witnesses the malevolence leveled at the few remaining citizens of the town, including the killing of a farmer who didn't sell to Delaney quick enough. When the Barlows are intimidated, Malone utilizes his military training to protect his hosts. Malone is quietly anticipating the repercussions of his company

Reynolds as the title role of *Malone* (1987).

desertion and he carries himself with an almost fatalist demeanor: "You know too much … one of the first things you taught me is that nobody just walks away," warns Lauren Hutton's C.I.A. spook, Jamey. And sure enough, Jamey is "entrusted" with erasing the company's wandering rogue liability. But Malone and Jamey are more than mere colleagues, they are part-time lovers.

Throughout the 1980s, Hollywood was lucratively dealing with the hangover from the Vietnam War, prolifically exploiting the conflict and the emotional fallout to a great degree in many films, from Academy Award winners to grindhouse B-movies. For every serious attempt addressing the theme such as *First Blood* (Ted Kotcheff, 1982), *Uncommon Valour* (Ted Kotcheff, 1983), *Gardens of Stone* (Francis Ford Coppola, 1987), *In Country* (Norman Jewison, 1989) and *Born on the Fourth of July* (Oliver Stone, 1989), there are absurdist orgies of violence in the vein of *The Exterminator* (1980), *Missing in Action* (Joseph Zito, 1984) and of course, *Rambo: First Blood Part II* (George P. Cosmatos, 1985). In almost all of the pictures, the protagonist was damaged goods, wandering "back in the world." *Malone* is the kind of decent espionage action picture that filled shelf space in video stores of the mid– to late–'80s, films like *Assassination* (Peter R. Hunt), *Lone Wolf McQuade* (Steve Carver, 1983), *Commando* (Mark L. Lester, 1985) and *Wanted: Dead or Alive* (Gary Sherman, 1988). These films used somewhat serious scenarios involving U.S. government covert operations and subversive activities as a generic function for essentially silly shoot-'em-up pictures.

Director Harley Cokeliss was an odd choice for *Malone*, having made some interesting short art films for the BBC in the 1970s before notable work as second unit director on the *Star Wars* sequel *The Empire Strikes Back* (Irvin Kershner, 1980). His other work includes the early Ray Winstone drama *That Summer!* (1979) and the John Carpenter–scripted *Black Moon Rising* (1986). Cokeliss handles the action efficiently and constructs some nice set pieces, including a tense barber shop showdown between Malone and Tracey Walter's foolhardy Calvin Bollard.

The director frames Reynolds in such a manner as to privilege his commanding, iconic presence, often shooting the actor from below, tilting the camera up and affording him as towering a presence as the Oregon mountain peaks that encase the action. Cliff Robertson makes for a fine villain and appropriately amplifies Delaney's patriotic fervor and megalomania to fever pitch—"playing God in this valley"—a turn nicely contrasted with Reynolds' sober reserve. Delaney (quite obviously drawn from aspects of controversial political activist Lyndon LaRouche) holds weekend conferences to enlist rich sympathizers into his Sacred Covenant for Leadership Training in his American Cause, even quoting from Thomas Jefferson in his induction speeches: "The tree of freedom must be nourished from time to time with blood from its patriots." When Malone finally confronts Delaney at his heavily fortified enclave, Delaney reiterates his political rhetoric.

Malone is, in a word, *Shane*. As with George Stevens' classic 1953 western, this picture plays on the myth of the hard-won homestead being threatened by tyrannical industrialists, until a handsome, mysterious stranger arrives in town to keep the wolves at bay. The heart of the picture is the familial relationship that develops between Malone and Jo, with Cynthia Gibb playing the Brandon DeWilde character; even her name Jo is an obvious nod to DeWilde's Joey. Their relationship largely mirrors that of Alan Ladd and DeWilde in the earlier film, though complicating matters are some awkward allusions to Jo's prurient interest in Malone. Although these sentiments are entirely unreciprocated from Malone, the lusting gestures of the teenager toward the 50-year-old stranger may make some a little queasy. In contrast to his charming, jocular personality of previous pictures, the Burt Reynolds of the 1980s presented a more stoic, thoughtful persona; his frontier avenger of integrity and empathy is a sober response to the hyper-masculine feats of cartoon carnage that Sylvester Stallone and Arnold Schwarzenegger were serving up in the period.

While Reynolds made certain studios hundreds of millions in revenue, the health

Delaney (Cliff Robertson) and Madrid (Alex Diakun) plan their misdeeds in the name of patriotism in *Malone* (1987).

rumors that plagued the actor meant the phone didn't ring as much as it used to. But some power players still valued the name "Burt Reynolds" and what it meant to audiences. According to Reynolds,

> There were studios that didn't call which I naively thought I had a relationship with. I thought they were my friends. I know [Orion president] Mike Medavoy still cares about me and wanted me to do *Malone* for his company. He also must think my name or presence means something in a picture because I'm getting $3 million for *Malone*. It's funny, but I've never found any civilians in the past two years who made me feel alienated from them. The only alienation I've felt has been through the industry.[1]

Malone is hardly the recipe for career rejuvenation that Reynolds craved in the 1980s, but it is a slick, economical and finely executed piece of work, one which offers Reynolds a chance to hone his hardened image for the era; he has rarely been as reserved and unflappable as in this tough picture. Despite the narrative and thematic similarities, the mood and tone of *Malone* are less in the tradition of the sentimental, elegiac *Shane* and more in line with the violent late-era westerns *Hang 'Em High* (Ted Post, 1968), *Valdez Is Coming* (Edwin Sherwin, 1971) and *Lawman* (Michael Winner, 1971).

Note

1. Craig Modderno, "Burt Reynolds is The Comeback Kid," *Los Angeles Times*, January 04, 1987, http://articles.latimes.com/1987–01-04/entertainment/ca-1803_1_burt-reynolds/4.

Rent-a-Cop

(1988)

> "I like the '60s. Life was simpler back then; all you had to worry about was trying to get laid for the first time."—Tony Church

Disgraced Chicago policeman Tony Church (Reynolds) is the only survivor of a drug bust-turned-massacre in a downtown hotel. In the botched undercover sting, Church and his men were set upon by a masked and heavily armed individual who could potentially be identified by a prostitute who was turning tricks in a neighboring room. The killer is named Dancer (James Remar), an ex-cop who is now an enforcer for a major drug kingpin. The prostitute is the feisty, good-natured Della Roberts (Liza Minnelli), who is unfortunate enough to have mistakenly knocked on Dancer's door on her way to work. In the aftermath of the massacre, Church has a bust-up with his superior, Lt. Wiser (John P. Ryan), who blames Church for blowing months of surveillance and undercover work. Church is fired and finds humiliating temporary work as a department store detective (the film's awful title refers to this). In one amusing scene, we see Church dressing up in a white beard and fat suit as Santa Claus to trail creeps around the perfume stands. At this embarrassing moment, Church is offered a lifeline when Della wants to hire him as her bodyguard (Dancer has made several attempts on her life). Church reluctantly accepts the assignment and the two become unlikely partners in law and in love, uncovering a link from the hotel slaughter to

Tony Church (Reynolds) is relegated to department store detective just in time for the Christmas season in *Rent-a-Cop* (1988).

Della's madam, Beth Cooper (Dionne Warwick): Beth runs a high-class prostitution ring, and on her books are some of Chicago's social and political power players.

Rent-a-Cop features a distinguished supporting cast. Remar is of particular note for his chilling portrayal of Dancer, so-called for his interest and skill in the performing arts. Remar had already played a burgeoning hoofer in William Friedkin's *Cruising* (1980) and here his lithe figure and graceful movements allow for an intriguing contrast with his more pugnacious demeanor and threatening visage. Elsewhere, Reynolds regulars include Bernie Casey as Church's former colleague and Robby Benson as a fresh-faced greenhorn detective staking Church's apartment out rather ineptly. Benson recalled,

> I got a phone from Burt Reynolds asking if I'd go to Italy with him and be in his film. He said he'd send the script over immediately…. Burt was one of the greatest friends anyone could have, but this was just … awful! And it took place in Chicago in the dead of winter. I had no idea where the romance of making a film in Italy came from, but it wasn't anywhere on the pages…. I reread the script at a turtle's pace trying not to miss anything. Chicago. Chicago. Chicago. And the script wasn't getting any better.[1]

Benson was to find out that to save money, the production shot interior scenes at the famed Cinecitta Studios in Rome with a mostly Italian crew. Exteriors were filmed in chilly Chicago, and the picture makes sure you know it, capturing the city's iconic architecture and landmarks, as well as having Church stand under a huge neon "Chicago" sign, to dispel all doubt as to the location.

It's a European co-production; a mix of sensibilities and feeling of dislocation may be the reasons the picture feels unlike any standard Hollywood action thriller of the period. This wasn't the first time director Jerry London used well-regarded Italian crew on one of his productions. The picture's eminent cinematographer, the Academy Award–nominated Guiseppe Rotunno, had previously shot London's 1983 war picture *The Scarlet and the Black*. Rotunno also shot many of Federico Fellini's films, including one of the great Italian director's most visually stunning works, *Fellini Satyricon* (1969). He also worked with other

Italian masters such as Vittorio De Sica and Luciano Visconti before making his mark in Hollywood. Just as the New Hollywood filmmakers were influenced by the European masters in their work, they also sought out the very craftsmen who cultivated the European style they so loved, and so maverick American filmmakers hired Rotunno to shoot the likes of *Carnal Knowledge* (Mike Nichols, 1971), *China 9, Liberty 37* (Monte Hellman, 1979), *All That Jazz* (Bob Fosse, 1979) and *Popeye* (Robert Altman, 1980). The cinematographer had come from crafting highly artistic, often expressionistic *mise-en-scéne* for some of the most lauded of international directors, though his approach to *Rent-a-Cop* is much less stylized than, say, his work on Fellini's rich tableaus. It is perhaps Rotunno's reluctance to adopt a heightened, flashier style that the film doesn't feel immediately visually striking in the typical manner of an '80s action thriller. The photography is more subtle, making sparse use of color which is often sourced from neon lights to infuse the otherwise flat palette of the cold Chicago exteriors. It is with the bright, busy interiors that Rotunno really gets to craft some rich and intricate compositions.

Adding to the picture's prestigious pedigree is celebrated composer Jerry Goldsmith, whose fine score informs the film with a romantic, reflective and melancholic tone, but one which is often at odds with the farcical humor and the scenes of destruction. Goldsmith's solo trumpet piece, which is essentially Church's theme, is a haunting and graceful cue, before transposing into a grander and altogether more bombastic, heroic piece. Goldsmith's music gives this slight action thriller the gravitas of a weightier, classier picture, adding to the overall off-kilter quality inherent. Jerry London, a prolific and Emmy-winning TV director, made his feature debut here. He and editor Robert Lawrence crafted action sequences that pulse with a Peckinpah-esque sense of rhythm, at once brutal and balletic.

Despite aesthetic touches such as these, the plot of *Rent-a-Cop* is purely mechanical. There is nothing to the narrative that a seasoned cop thriller viewer won't guess well in advance of the film's predictable conclusion. This is by-the-numbers genre filmmaking, so in that case the film must provide us with good performances and/or interesting aesthetic construction to keep it stimulating. In that regard, the picture does hold up reasonably well: It works as a scant but entertaining slice of genre filmmaking, but it failed to find an audience. London was optimistic of his star's commercial appeal but didn't anticipate the cool indifference with which the picture would be met. "[Burt's] last couple of pictures were dark movies," the director said. "Audiences didn't come out of theaters with that warm glow that Burt can give. I think this film will do it. Everyone says Burt hasn't been better in years."[2]

Rent-a-Cop reunites Reynolds and Minnelli 12 years after their co-starring efforts in *Lucky Lady*; the chemistry between the pair keeps this film eminently watchable. Della's garrulous nature (or *joie de vivre*, as she calls it), contrasts nicely with Church's stoicism and irascibility. While Reynolds tries his best to be solemn and humorless, Minnelli works overtime to bring a sense of fun to their scenes. She is a delightful screen presence, bringing her unique beauty, street glamour (all gaudy fake fur, heavy makeup, high heels) and a sense of manic pixie girl whimsy to the film's otherwise gritty, cold and hard-edged diegetic world.

While these two actors are a decent double act, they make for a less-convincing romantic couple. Minnelli brings such a likable wide-eyed optimism and innocence to Della that it sits in stark contrast to Reynolds' resigned, world-weary rendering of Church, so much that it is hard to believe that one would ever dare consider the other a suitable mate. Fortunately, the pair does not jump into bed post-haste: Writers Charles Shryack and Michael Blodgett give Church and his charge plenty of time to develop their attraction to each other. In the end, we accept their union because we want to believe it, not because it makes perfect sense. Ultimately, it feels as though Reynolds is restrained from bringing too much of his persona to the picture, reining in as much humor and life—*his joie de vivre*—as possible in order to render Church as a curmudgeonly masculine figure, a man from another era, ensconced in his own world of beer, baseball and 1960s records.

With Reynolds still able to command a $3 million payday, stakes were high. Opening in January 1988, the picture's competition that month included *The Couch Trip* (Michael Ritchie), *For Keeps* (John G. Avildsen) and *Return of the Living Dead II* (Ken Wiederhorn); up against such teen-oriented fare, the U.S. box office returns for *Rent-a-Cop* were weak, only $295,000, evidence of Reynolds' diminishing box office clout. For the first time in decades, it seemed as though the star was alienated from the cinema-going youth audience who were making the likes of Jason Vorhees (*Friday the 13th*), Freddy Krueger (*A Nightmare on Elm Street*) and John Rambo (*First Blood*) the reigning box office kings. It perhaps hasn't helped the film's reputation that both Reynolds and Minnelli were nominated by the 1988 Golden Raspberry Awards for Worst Actor and Worst Actress, respectively. Minnelli won.

Notes

1. Robby Benson, *I'm Not Dead…. Yet* (United States of America: Valor Editions, 2012) [n.p.].
2. Ivor Davis, "Reynolds Seeks Rebirth in New Year, New Film," *The Sun Senitnel*, January 19, 1988, http://articles.sun-sentinel.com/1988–01–19/features/8801040739_1_burt-reynolds-rent-a-cop-liza-minnelli.

Switching Channels
(1988)

"Gain some fat; we'll make you a movie critic!"—John L. Sullivan IV

After the commercial failure of Reynolds' action pictures *Heat* and *Rent-a-Cop*, the star returned to the big screen with this frothy romantic comedy, his first light material in a number of years.

Reynolds is John L. Sullivan IV, cynical manager of a cable news station, and Kathleen Turner is his ex-wife and star reporter Christy Colleran. She's engaged to egotistical airhead Blaine Bingham (Christopher Reeve), a sporting goods manufacturer. As Colleran's boss, Sullivan is still within close enough daily proximity of his ex-wife to feel something is salvageable, but the younger, richer Bingham, resplendent in ice-tipped hair, virility and wealth, dazzles Colleran by offering her a new life in New York. Sullivan attempts to hold onto Colleran and assigns her to cover the impending execution of murderer Ike Rosco (Henry Gibson) in vulgar "live execution"–style reportage. Rosco's escape is a huge media event. While the three main players go to war on the battlefield of courtship, there is some sharp political satire courtesy of Ned Beatty's corrupt, buffoonish D.A., who uses the execution as a political platform for his own gain.

Switching Channels is ostensibly an update of Lewis Milestone's 1931 newspaper comedy *The Front Page*, itself based on the Broadway play of the same name by Ben Hecht and Charles MacArthur. Director Ted Kotcheff's modern version retains its Chicago setting but adds a twist or two, taking the story out of the newspaper office and into a 1980s television newsroom, once again switching the gender of the lead role from male to female (as it was in the first remake *His Girl Friday*) and including the very contemporary dilemma of having the careerist reporter being made to choose between marriage and work. In a role originally designated for Michael Caine (who bowed out due to scheduling conflicts with *Jaws 4: The Revenge*), Reynolds plays the Walter Burns character made famous by Adolphe Menjou, while Kathleen Turner tackles the firebrand "Hildy" Johnson role immortalized by Pat O'Brien. As with "Hildy" in *The Front Page*, Colleran uses her new partner and potential for a metropolitan life to spite her boss, though *Switching Channels* introduces the added complication of an ill-fated marriage to their relationship history.

Kotcheff was in the unenviable position of remaking a story which had been successful in four prior incarnations: the original stage production; the 1931 film version; the highly regarded Howard Hawks' 1940 remake *His Girl Friday*; and another 1974 reboot, directed by Billy Wilder and starring Jack Lemmon and Walter Matthau. He recalled:

> Perhaps as a defense mechanism, I did not have any of the three previous movies in mind when I made *Switching Channels*, nor did I watch them again to prepare. But, perhaps I should have…. Comedies, I learned from making *Switching Channels* and *Fun with Dick and Jane*, are very fragile pieces of art … they work, or they don't…. I have never been fond of remakes or sequels … but I felt *The Front Page* could be updated to the world of television news. The Elizabethan dramatists continually borrowed plots and used them to their own ends, and that was what I wanted to do in this case.[1]

Kathleen Turner gets aggressive as ambitious reporter Christy Colleran in *Switching Channels* (1988) as an undentified colleague looks on.

Given the pedigree, acclaim and love for the three prior films, it was to be expected that critics would shoot arrows at Kotcheff's efforts. Sure enough, anyone expecting verbal fireworks of the Cary Grant-Rosalind Russell variety are left sorely wanting. Reynolds and Turner certainly don't lack the bite and snark so crucial to their fiery relationship, but there's a lack of sexual and romantic chemistry that is the spine of all versions of the text. Perhaps the snide underbelly of the performances are a result of genuine tension between the two stars. Turner was unhappy with the casting of Reynolds in place of Michael Caine. "I think my most unhappy film experience was *Switching Channels*," Turner admits, "the only one I ever chose to do for the money, which is probably why I was so unhappy."[2] Turner and Caine spent several weeks rehearsing the crucially witty repartee between the lead couple, who are supposed to have known each other for 15 years, married for over a decade and are able to finish each others' sentences. "Burt came into a group that was already working together and knew each other, so he might have felt a little bit like an outsider,"[3] Turner speculates.

Christopher Reeve gets to expand upon Ralph Bellamy's milquetoast insurance man Bruce Baldwin from *His Girl Friday*, bringing broad blonde bimbo brashness to bear for Baldwin's boring bumpkin. The choice of Reeve to appear as a man who suffers acrophobia might seem a little too on-the-nose a gag given his position in film history as the definitive Superman; even Reeve failed to see the trait as little more than a one-note joke, despite the phobia being written into the script prior to his casting. One scene which amplifies the ironic comedy sees Bingham suffering a panic attack in a glass elevator when it jams while ascending through a shopping mall. "Everyone assured me this would be hysterically funny,"[4] says Reeve, who was deeply dissatisfied with the production.

Commercially speaking, *Switching Channels* proved a blow to Reeve's rep as a profitable leading man. He reminisced:

> Before I knew what was happening, I had signed a contract and found myself on location in Toronto making a fool of myself. To make matters worse, after two weeks of filming with Kathleen, we learned that Michael Caine would not be able to join us…. Burt Reynolds was brought in to replace him. Unfortunately he and Kathleen couldn't stand each other, so I had to take on the added burden of being a referee.[5]

The financial performance of *Switching Channels* perhaps wasn't helped by the recent release of the very well-received *Broadcast News* (James L. Brooks, 1987) which offered a much more authentic look at the lives and loves of those under the pressure of the newsroom. Other than the contemporary setting, there is nothing particularly current about *Switching Channels*. It misses an opportunity to satirize the hyperbolic nature of its cable television milieu and the inflated egos that orchestrate and administrate it. As a remake of a remake, the picture feels bound to the conventions of source material that was many decades old, dating back to the 1920s. It merely transposes the story to the modern day but without the cynical bite of Lewis Milestone's darkly humorous depiction of jaundiced reporters. Though there are many absurdist and often very funny observations on the profession and ethics of journalism, which can be traced back to the earliest adaptation of the text, the film ultimately settles for the standard conflict-resolution formula of the domestic romantic comedy, i.e., which man will she choose?

Despite the regret of its makers and damaged reputation as an expensive misfire, the film is nowhere near as bad as could be expected. There are some fine visual gags, such as the lunchtime meeting between the three leads in which the restaurant serves lunch in a boxing ring, a nice metaphorical gag relating the physical sparring of the pugilists in the squared circle to that of the verbal sparring within the love triangle. Ned Beatty's crass politician provides many funny one-liners: "Ladies and gentlemen, welcome to the first execution open to the free uncensored public … you wouldn't see that in Russia!" In an amusing opening montage, we are introduced to Colleran as the kind of ambitious reporter who will get in the line of fire at a police raid, correspond from rain-drenched marathons, and referee televised political debates. Turner was ideally cast—brash, sexy, confident, witty, and with an accent that can oscillate from middle-class mid–American to mid–Atlantic, evoking the linguistic styling of Carole Lombard and Bette Davis. Reynolds, too, knew perfectly well how to play this material. Reynolds, a big fan of Old Hollywood comedians such as Cary Grant, is very capable of parlaying his quick wit, roguish charm, and great sense of irony to the proceedings, bringing the required sophistication to the verbose comedy.

Notes

1. Ted Kotcheff with Josh Young, *Director's Cut: My Life in Film* (Toronto: ECW Press, 2017), [n.p.].
2. Kathleen Turner and Gloria Feldt, *Send Yourself Roses: My Life, Loves and Leading Roles* (Great Britain: Headline Publishing Group, 2008), p. 155.
3. *Ibid.*
4. Christopher Reeve, *Still Me* (London: Arrow Books, 1999), p. 228.
5. *Ibid.*

Physical Evidence
(1989)

"I think his jockstrap is moldy, do you want to look into that?"—Joe Paris

Physical Evidence begins with the darkly humorous scenario of a man about to commit suicide by diving off Boston's Tobin Bridge only to discover the body of a gangland victim already hanging there. When the curious man reaches for the body, he slips and ends up suspended over the Mystic River crying for help, having developed an instant appreciation for life. The film rarely comes up to anything so playful or deliriously manic in the following 90 minutes.

The next scene introduces us to boozehound ex-cop Joe Paris (Reynolds), who is rudely awoken by two detectives looking to speak to him in connection with the death of a shady nightclub owner, Jake Farley (the corpse from the bridge). Farley, "like Nixon," recorded every conversation in his office for the purpose of building dossiers of dirt on associates from both sides of the law, and one of those on tape is Paris. The cops find evidence in Paris' apartment, including a bloody shirt that carries both his DNA and that of Farley's. The trouble for Paris is that he blacked out from drinking the previous night and doesn't remember a thing. With the help of ambitious public defender Jenny Hudson (Theresa Russell), Paris pieces together the activities from that fateful night.

Cue a procession of legal thriller clichés executed with zero sense of style or cinematic dexterity. Homicide, check; green lawyer looking to prove herself, check; cross-examination

Ex-cop Joe Paris (Reynolds) is out to clear his name in *Physical Evidence* (1989).

second act centerpiece, check; investigation of red-herring suspect, check; lawyer-client conflict of interest, check; questionable juror selection, check; and finally, the restoration of trust between previously untrusting lawyer and client, check. Aesthetically, the picture is unexciting, looking more like a work destined for television rather than the major star vehicle destined for the silver screen that it is, or was supposed to be. There are some neat elliptical editing tricks to keep the narrative moving along briskly, but other than that there is nothing here to suggest a serious investment in filmic flair to bring this turgid plot to life. The cinematography is the work of John A. Alonzo, an often brilliant director of photography (*Chinatown*, 1974; *Black Sunday*, 1976; *Scarface*, 1983; *Internal Affairs*, 1990), but his work here is flat and uninspired.

With the picture's tantalizing premise of a man waking up after a blackout and becoming the chief suspect in a murder, *Physical Evidence* could have been an intriguing paranoia thriller in the mold of Michael Crichton's superior *Coma* (1978) or producer Martin Ransohoff's *Jagged Edge* (1985). But tension and drama are thin on the ground here. *Physical Evidence* was actually conceived as a sequel to Ransohoff's hit for Columbia, but apparently the script didn't pass muster with studio chief executive David Puttnam. The problem that *Physical Evidence* faced from the beginning was its very design to be a sequel to a hit film for a studio whose boss despised the very notion of sequels. Despite Columbia having released massive, franchise-spawning hits such as *Ghostbusters* (Ivan Reitman, 1984) and *The Karate Kid* (John G. Avildsen, 1984) just prior to his takeover as chairman, Puttnam had no interest in capitalizing on name recognition. So regardless of the positive reviews and generous box office take of *Jagged Edge*, a sequel would run counter to Puttnam's noble determination to produce small-scale, high-quality art films with the industrial clout of a major studio.

Producer Ransohoff re-structured his property as a standalone picture and star vehicle. In the end, Columbia handled domestic and Canadian distribution, while the British company Rank Film Distributors, which had previous affiliations with Ransohoff, looked after foreign sales. Perhaps Ransohoff thought that Reynolds' name as a brand would make a lucrative substitute for the *Jagged Edge* connection, and while it is true that the star delivered the kind of hard-boiled performance his fans adore, the producer may not have figured on Reynolds' co-stars underperforming.

Physical Evidence contains none of the erotic charge that bolstered *Jagged Edge*, and the major problem of such is the limp chemistry between Reynolds and Russell. At no stage do we believe in the romantic attraction between the two, which supposedly blossoms against the tension of some disingenuous culture clash animosity that resolves itself as Joe ditches the slovenly clothing, the cigarettes and cans of Budweiser to appease the clean-living bourgeois siren. Paris represents the working class ne'er-do-well who defies the odds to end up in the arms of an upwardly mobile yuppie go-getter. Reynolds was rarely placed in a romantic pairing as dull and unbelievable as this one with Russell. Knowing Russell's erstwhile screen credentials, it's hard to reconcile such tame, almost vague femininity that the actress displays here as Hudson with the fiery, daring sexuality of her edgier work elsewhere: *Bad Timing* (Nicolas Roeg, 1983), *Black Widow* (Bob Rafelson, 1988), *Track 29* (Nicolas Roeg, 1988). The line readings between Reynolds and Russell are delivered with such a lack of conviction that one could interpret a sense of, at worst, animosity between the actors, and at best, a difficulty in believing their own lines.

Hudson, like many other characters, is ill-defined and underdeveloped. Aside from displaying little tangible passion for the man she is supposed to be falling in love with, we see nothing to suggest what it is that makes her a successful careerist. Most people think she is incapable of having justice prevail and Paris exonerated, and who could blame them? Where one would expect steely determination and a brass neck, Hudson plays petulance and disregards sound advice in favor of arrogantly following her own ill-judged instincts.

It isn't just Hudson who lacks clear definition; supporting characters are woven in and out of the unfolding mystery with teasing backstories but are left massively underdeveloped, with motives left unclear and relationships unexplained. One such half-drawn character is the sympathizing cop who tries to aid Joe. We know he feels strongly about the bad reputation police have to endure and he sees Joe's battles as something he can crusade against, but why such allegiance to Joe and his plight? How about the queasy brother-sister relationship between Matt and Amy Farley (Tom O'Brien and Angie McNab), with its curiously incestuous undertones? The Farley siblings are rarely seen not pawing each other and displaying an unusually intimate bond. Nothing further is mentioned about the physical or emotional dependency of this relationship, typical of this picture's confused, unspecific direction. Ultimately, *Physical Evidence* is rarely exciting enough to qualify it as a decent thriller, while it fails miserably as a romantic drama.

Breaking In

(1989)

"You've got larceny in your blood, kid. I knew that first time I saw you."—Ernie Mullins

Breaking In, perhaps unsurprisingly, opens with a burglary: Mike (Casey Siemaszko) enters a middle-class suburban property and is helping himself to a plate of leftovers and cold beer when he is confronted by a distinguished older cat burglar (Reynolds) *also* in the midst of robbing the house. The elder gentleman (who genuinely seems gentle) is Ernie, a career criminal whose cover has just been blown by the prowling Mike, who says he doesn't steal money, preferring instead to rifle through utility bills and help himself to the contents of the fridge. Mike struggles to eke out a living working legit at Bob's Tire and Body garage and is beguiled by Ernie's seeming professionalism. Ernie calls Mike to meet so he can split the proceeds from the safe: "I'd rather have a partner than a witness." Despite Ernie's impression of Mike as some "wacko that goes creeping around people's houses for the thrill of it," he offers to take the kid on some big jobs. Ernie teaches Mike the varying codes of underworld ethics, including how to live a frugal life so as not to draw attention to one's criminal deeds. The partnership serves Ernie well in being able to pull off greater heists and therefore reap greater financial rewards. But Mike is reckless with his loot, quitting his day job, spending lavishly, and therefore drawing the attention of the FBI.

By the end of the 1980s, the diminishing box office returns of Reynolds' increasingly routine action pictures dictated that audiences were tiring of such offerings. The actor, too, had evidently begun to avoid the tough guy roles that maintained his star throughout the decade. Having taken the unpredictable leap into outright comedy with *Switching Channels*, Reynolds would make anothering surprising foray into the world of independent film, working with the highly regarded Scottish director Bill Forsyth, who made his name with the much-loved *Gregory's Girls* (1981) and the critically lauded *Local Hero* (1983) and was here making his second American feature film following 1987's *Housekeeping*. For *Breaking In*, Forsythe originally had veteran character actor John Mahoney in mind for the character of Ernie, but working with Hollywood producer Harry Gittes and his fellow investors at

Partners in crime Mike (Casey Siemaszko) and Ernie (Reynolds) say farewell in *Breaking In* (1989).

Act III Communications meant conceding to Hollywood demands and casting a major star in the lead. While Mahoney could certainly have brought a sense of subtle anonymity and working class dignity to the character, another choice of Forsyth's proved to appease the producers' demand for marquee name value. Burt Reynolds' A-list box office clout made him an agreeable name to the producers.

Here, Reynolds is subtle, quiet and unassuming, delicately balancing humor and sincerity. Ernie, guarded and cynical, will not be ruined if his affection for the kid isn't reciprocated, he has had many people come and go in his life as a criminal and so he will move on regardless, though not without caring for the kid in the meantime. When Mike is imprisoned and takes the rap for crimes committed by Ernie, the elder larcenist pays off mobsters to take care of Mike during his stay in prison. Despite Ernie's return to, presumably, the solitary life, looking after Mike's well-being gives the film a touching conclusion.

In his most acclaimed work, *Local Hero* (1983), Forsyth saw his lonely, unsatisfied oil company executive, Mac (Peter Riegert), experience a personal journey of contentment and satisfaction with a foreign land—Scotland—and its people on a routine buying expedition for his company, only to return home to his luxury apartment just as lonely as when he left, just as Ernie walks away from the incarcerated Mike as lonely a man as he was before he met him. Ernie's time spent with Mike leaves an indelible impression on his life just as Mac achieved some kind of personal renaissance through his encounter with the mythic Scottish village of Furness; whatever Ernie saw in the disorganized and undisciplined kid to take him on as a partner in crime and friend in life, Mike's imprisonment ends the potential for something more meaningful to come of their brief dalliance.

The picture is sustained by an intelligent script from John Sayles (*The Return of the Secaucus Seven, Matewan, City of Hope*) which retains numerable qualities to make this an enchanting and often melancholy journey into male bonhomie. A master of low-key, intelligent adult cinema, Sayles wrote a script that wisely avoids mawkish sentimentality, though there are some genuine moments of pathos. Sayles and Forsyth crafted a love story between two men lacking a sense of familial security, stability and comfort. Ernie sees in young Mike the potential to not only to make more money as a two-man team, but with whom he creates a bond that will fill the void in his life, that Mike will act son to Ernie's surrogate father, and vice versa. But Mike is not the brightest bulb. While Ernie sees the opportunity of the new partnership to not only be rewarded in a financial sense, but in an emotional one too, the young apprentice seizes upon the working relationship as a path to upward mobility in the most juvenile and irresponsible manner. The discipline of the older thief is lost on the new blood as we witness Mike spend his newfound fortune on gaudy excesses (the car, the apartment, the prostitutes), while Ernie remains modestly housed in a working class neighborhood by the airport, happy to while away his evenings playing poker within the low-rung criminal fraternity and to contently ignore the airplane noise.

Breaking In is a quiet, beautiful piece of work, one of the most understated and underrated in the Reynolds catalogue. The picture closed out the 27th New York Film Festival in 1989 and was favorably received, with special praise going to Reynolds' mature performance. Vincent Canby said that the picture "has a lot of the appeal of a 1949 Oldsmobile convertible that still looks almost new and drives like a dream, if none too fast. Speed is not of the essence here…. Mr. Reynolds has not appeared more fit—nor has he given a more accomplished performance—in a very long time."[1] Peter Travers noted the esteemed company that Reynolds was keeping and the benefits of such, considering him "an actor who's been squandering his talent and our time on beefcake baloney.... Forsyth and Sayles have liberated the actor in Reynolds from the smirking blowhard. Burt proves himself a world-class charmer."[2]

Filming *Breaking In* proved a memorable experience for Reynolds, as 16 years after he plaintively asked God to consider him worthy to be a father on his song "A Room for a Boy Never Used," the question was finally answered. While on location in Oregon, the star received a call informing him that he and his wife Loni Anderson were now the proud parents of their first and only child via adoptive mother. On August 28, Quinton Reynolds was born, so named after noted *Collier's Weekly* journalist and war correspondent Quentin Reynolds, as well as in reference to Burt's turn as Quint on *Gunsmoke*.

Notes

1. Vincent Canby, "Film Festival; 'Breaking In,' Crime Primer Features Burt Reynolds," *New York Times*, October 9, 1989, https://www.nytimes.com/1989/10/09/movies/film-festival-breaking-in-crime-primer-features-burt-reynolds.html.

2. Peter Travers, "Breaking In," *Rolling Stone*, October 19, 1989, https://www.rollingstone.com/movies/reviews/breaking-in-19891013.

An Interview with Bill Forsyth

Bill Forsyth is one of Scotland's most acclaimed and beloved filmmakers. After the low-budget debut *That Sinking Feeling*, the director went on to greater financial success and widespread acclaim with his charming romantic coming-of-age film, *Gregory's Girl*, and the offbeat comedy *Comfort and Joy*. His next film *Local Hero* marked a commercial progression for the director, featuring a cast of Hollywood heavyweights including Burt Lancaster and supported with a popular soundtrack by Dire Straits singer-guitarist Mark Knopfler. In 1987, Forsyth directed his first American film, *Housekeeping*, a well-received dramatic comedy starring Christine Lahti. His next project saw him collaborating with another major Hollywood Burt: Reynolds.

Wayne: *Considering your prior work,* Breaking In *seems like an unusual choice of film at first glance. What was it about John Sayles' script that attracted you to the material?*

Bill: What attracted me to the material was that it played against any notion of glamorizing crime or exploiting it for pure entertainment. It explored the notion that a life of crime was at the end of the day a matter of dogged work and discipline and knowledge acquired; just like any other human pursuit. This struck me as having great human and comedic potential as a movie. And it also had its own native sense of authenticity. So I was very much interested.

Did Sayles approach you with his script?

I was actually approached by the producer Harry Gittes, who was developing the project with Act III Communications Productions, a company run by TV veteran and legend

Norman Lear. Then the script that I was given to read was indeed an old script of John Sayles.' John is a prolific writer with many, many scripts under his belt. I believe he had written this one at least ten or so years previously. So I met with John in New York, and over a beer we had a good and practical conversation. It reached a very straightforward accommodation. We were both independent filmmakers looking to get a result; John would get a long dormant script into production, earning him some income, and getting the script onto the screen, and I would get the chance to make one more film, and also earn some income. That's what makes the wheels go round. We recognized one another as birds of a feather. John was happy for me to personally develop the script some more; firstly to dust off the slightly dated feel, and secondly, to enable me to put my own personal stamp on the material.

How much leeway did you have over script changes and casting choices?

The production company was on occasion a little anxious about some of my choices as a director during the production. This is only natural as a situation. It happens all the time. They want to make a movie exploiting marginal characters, but they want these characters to be unthreatening and appealing at the same time. For instance, the producers were a little anxious when they made a visit to the set to discover that I had concocted a fairly stark and bleak setting for the boarding room of Casey's character Mike. He was after all a marginal character socially, a porch creeper, as I think Ernie labeled him. So one of the producers suggested I might lighten things by decorating the kid's room with model airplanes, to suggest that he might have a hobby … a lighter backstory God forbid. I desisted. Also, there was some tension and anxious phone calls when it came to the details of Mike's prison term when he was sentenced in court. I think I had written 14 years in the script. The producers figured that the co-star of their film didn't deserve this, although it stood as the mandatory amount for Robbery with Explosives. They figured around three would be plenty. So I filmed the actor playing the judge pronouncing every number between seven and twenty years, so that we had room for discussion in the long fraught days of post-production. I can't remember the final outcome.

Burt Reynolds was coming off a series of violent action pictures. Just how did he end up in the Pacific Northwest playing a sexagenarian crook in a quiet, modestly budgeted crime drama?

We came to casting Burt Reynolds in a slightly roundabout way. My own first instincts were to cast a completely unknown actor, or at least an actor who wasn't recognized in any way as an A-list player. My reasons were that the character Ernie had, as a matter of discipline and sacrifice, reduced his own life to almost monk-like proportions. He lived in a state that could only be called beyond modest; he didn't even find any joy in spending the occasional cash riches that his job delivered; he lived in a miserable tract house right under an airport flight path. He seemed intent on punishing himself in advance for his social misdemeanors; he even denied himself the rewards and comforts of a family life. In short, he had created for himself a life of jail time, except on the outside. Ernie didn't have to go to jail; he was already there.

So I presume Burt wasn't your first choice?

He was not. I had in fact found an actor that fitted the bill; at that time he was almost a complete unknown in terms of film, but a terrific character actor, someone who could easily portray my notion of Ernie as a house mouse, rarely seeing the daylight. This was John

Mahoney, many, many years before *Frasier*. But of course none of this reasoning appealed to the producers! I was just a crazy foreigner who didn't know the rules! This was true.

Was Burt was your choice or was there insistence from the producers to hire someone of his prominence?

Burt was my own personal choice, that's a fact; he was my first choice from the box office "names" on offer. Even though I came up with his name, there was a bit of an issue about asking Burt to play a character older than his real self. It is always a decisive moment for an actor when he has to make this crossover decision. Burt, I feel, handled it very well. It was his choice to give his character a limp. It worked. I'm an old guy myself now, and at some point of every day I find myself doing the "Ernie hobble" involuntarily; and at that moment I silently offer Burt a tribute … he taught me how to hobble through old age with a bit of a swagger. I learned at the feet of a master.

There is sense of chemistry between Burt and Casey Siemaszko, which feels entirely natural. Did you guys spend much time ironing out their relationship in rehearsal?

We didn't spend much time in rehearsal mode, so far as I recall. Burt and Casey were two thorough professionals. They turned up on set with the performance. We weren't setting out to "find" these characters in the course of a shooting day. We three already knew who they were. So the shooting process was one of just finessing what we already knew should take place. I never was a filmmaker who was interested in my actors "finding" the characters for me in a creative way. In an interpretive way, yes; but creatively the characters were already there in the written script. Most actors are in tune with this situation. The movie set is not the place to go about "finding" a character.

Burt has such a huge screen personality which audiences recognize immediately and often expect of him. Did he adjust to the more humble qualities of Ernie immediately?

Burt stepped out of line only once. I caught him in the act. During rehearsals for one of the heists, he turned up his coat collar in a rather "cool" Sharky way. He saw my reaction to this, and before I'd crossed the floor to talk to him he'd already come up with the excuse that he was doing this to hide his identity. He knew at once I didn't buy that and soon desisted. Burt only made one wrong move, so far as I'm concerned: by hiring a telephone stripper to turn up on set on the day of my birthday. I'm a low-key kind of person and it was an embarrassing situation. She kept asking me to look at her as she did her thing. I couldn't oblige.

Coming as you do from low-budget independent British cinema, how did you find this new landscape of working with Hollywood stars such as Burt Reynolds, Burt Lancaster, Robin Williams, etc.?

I always did find it easy, satisfying and indeed pleasurable to work with A-list folk like Burt and Burt and Robin and the rest; to my mind, an accomplished actor is an accomplished actor. Whether he/she is also a star is in most ways an afterthought. For all concerned, the process and satisfaction of the work itself is the key to the exercise. We all turn up in the morning with the same goal in mind and my working relationship with Burt Reynolds was a pretty conventional one so far as a commercial movie is concerned. We'd block out scenes with the camera and put the characters' situation together as we did so. I started my filmmaking career with 16-year-old kids in Glasgow, Scotland, and at the end of the day Burt Lancaster or Burt Reynolds never did ask any more of me than 16-year-old

Dougie Sannachan or Billy Greenlees demanded in 1978. Burt was as good and loyal (to the work in hand) a pro as I ever had the pleasure to work with.

Looking back on Breaking In *30 years later, how do you regard this particular foray into Hollywood filmmaking?*

I will admit that *Breaking In* was a noted non-event commercially. I never ever did make much headway in finding a mainstream audience in America or anywhere else. I just don't speak the language of American popular cinema, and never did feel the need or desire to do so. It strikes me that I only ever did make the one movie over and over again; and *Breaking In* was one of the run, and I consider it as good or as bad as its stablemates.

All Dogs Go to Heaven

(1989)

"You know, goodbyes aren't forever."—Charles B. Barkin

In a canine-run New Orleans underworld of 1939, shifty German Shepherd Charles B. Barkin (Reynolds) and his cohort in crime Itchy Itchiford (Dom DeLuise) break free of the dog pound to return to their home turf where Barkin and bulldog business partner Carface Caruthers rule with an iron paw. A deal to part ways and split the profits of a casino operation that they run together goes awry when Barkin is double-crossed and killed by Caruthers. Barkin ascends undeservedly to Heaven, where an angel named Annabelle tells the dog that his time on Earth expired when a gold watch timing his life has stopped. Barkin refuses to accept his wings, a halo or any such fate and steals the watch to set it back. While he is returning to the Earthly plain Barkin is warned that once he leaves Heaven, he will never be allowed to return. Facing eternal damnation, Barkin has a chance to redeem himself when he begrudgingly befriends an orphan girl named Anne-Marie. The little girl is kidnapped by Caruthers because her ability to converse with animals offers the kingpin potentially lucrative connections to racing fixes. Anne-Marie is rescued by Barkin and Itchiford, but they are not entirely noble in their efforts, thinking the young girl will be of financial benefit to them also. Despite Barkin's best efforts, a deep bond grows between the forlorn youngster and her two new pals. When Anne-Marie is put in further jeopardy by the dastardly Caruthers, Barkin is killed (again) saving her, thus earning his halo and allowed to escape the hellish lake of fire and return to Heaven.

If an animated Don Bluth picture seems like an oddity at this point in a retrospective of Burt Reynolds' career, it is actually more relevant than it may seem at first glance. Not only is Reynolds flanked by regular co-stars Dom DeLuise (providing his third voice for a Bluth production), Charles Nelson Reilly and Loni Anderson, but the theme at the heart of the picture—rogue male becomes surrogate father figure to a child—is a recurring theme throughout the Reynolds *oeuvre*, playing into the paternal yearning at the heart of many of his pictures. *All Dogs* is stunningly crafted, hand-drawn by Bluth's team of animators when the company was based in Ireland in the late 1980s, but the biggest draw of the film is the snappy dialogue largely improvised by Reynolds and DeLuise, and the sheer hilarity of Reilly's neurotic, incompetent gangster mongrel Killer.

The character of Charles B. Barkin was written with Reynolds in mind and the con dog has the same kind of mischievous rogue qualities that Reynolds harnessed in his live-action pictures. Unlike most animated films up to that point, where each actor recorded their dialogue by reciting lines in isolation, Reynolds and DeLuise performed in the studio together, often riffing and improvising with each other, adding that genuine Reynolds-DeLuise bonhomie to the picture.

For a children's picture of fleeting running time, there is an awful lot to consume here. The pathos of the picture, as well its dark humor, is complex enough to make it a perfectly consumable product to an adult audience. Unlike your average contemporary children's production which is most likely to coddle its audience with innocuous benignity, *All Dogs Go to Heaven* unleashes a torrent of underworld iniquity: drinking, gambling, floozies and demons from hell collecting for the Lake of Fire. And did I mention the poverty, death and illness? All of this would be disturbing if it weren't for Reynolds and DeLuise's natural, good-natured chemistry which keeps the picture alive when it threatens to get bogged down in its murky over-plotting and sinister characters. And even if the grim setting of jazz-age New Orleans provides *All Dogs Go to Heaven* with a suitably sinful setting, it only serves to contrast nicely with the celestial imagery and to heighten the fairy tale feel-good factor at the the film's heart.

Former Disney artist turned animation mogul Bluth made a name for himself with the troubled *The Secret of NIMH* (1982) and with two successful Steven Spielberg collaborations, *An American Tail* (1986) and *The Land Before Time* (1988). While those pictures were made for and distributed by major Hollywood studios and production companies (MGM, Universal, Amblin), *All Dogs* would be co-financed and distributed by an arthouse enterprise, Goldcrest Films, as the first in a three-picture deal worth $70 million.[1] Goldcrest had occasionally enjoyed great successes with the award-winning pictures *Chariots of Fire* (1981), *Gandhi* (1982) and *The Killing Fields* (1984) while achieving smaller returns on more modest productions throughout the decade; their costly period films *Revolution* (1985), *The Mission* (1986), *Absolute Beginners* (1986) and *Matewan* (1987) all tanked. *All Dogs* represented a potential leap toward more mainstream product and made twice its $13 million budget in domestic receipts. However, Bluth's next film *Rock-a-Doodle* failed at the box office and forced the Sullivan Bluth Studios into liquidation, ending the partnership.

Notes

1. John Cawley, "The Animated Films of Don Bluth: At Home in Ireland," http://www.cataroo.com/DBireland.html

Modern Love

(1990)

"Take good care of my Billie, or I will break you into 10,000 little pieces."—Col. Frank Parker

Greg (Robby Benson), a South Carolina PR man in the entertainment business, has been in love with the female form since his birth. In a very funny opening montage narrated by the character, Greg's lustful awakening was set in motion with the offering of his mother's breast; he was a lover scorned at the tender age of one and from there we witness his failed attempts at amore from childhood right up to his contemporary adulthood. This opening scene sets the film up nicely and it soon develops a delightfully quirky tone that is hard to define, and one that proves inconsistent. After ditching his ditzy white trash girlfriend in a fit of anxiety over a false alarm pregnancy, Greg meets the charming and whimsical urologist Billie ("the only doctor in the universe on food stamps") who in an act of professional sabotage and self-imposed poverty yearns to be a stand-up comedian rather than a physician. Kooky before it became a fashionable trait in the late '90s, Billie is the kind of wonder woman seen so often in romantic comedies that privilege moping males and their myopic malaise; a funky free spirit who whirls into the lives of boorish, boring men like Greg and take them on a magical journey of impromptu dancing, impossibly romantic gestures and eccentric humor. That is before real life comes crashing down upon them in the guise of marriage, mortgage and maternity. When Greg and Billie fall in love, he immediately declares his interest in having children. Opposing religious ideals (Jewish vs. Catholic) underscore a divide in familial relations between the in-laws.

Now married, Greg and Billie settle down into domestic lethargy, and so too does the picture's sense of humor and energy. In fact, for a romantic comedy with pretentions of whimsy and wistfulness, *Modern Love* becomes quite dark and doesn't exactly make much of a case for the quiet life being the ideal life. Greg has outbursts and moments that reveal him to be something of a precious and shallow man-child, petty and immature; we're never quite sure if Greg is in love with the idea of being in love, or harbors genuine feelings for his wife. At one point, after the honeymoon has ended, Greg is even given a monologue in which he says he misses the feeling of being in love, alluding to a sense of dissatisfaction with his lot once the initial excitement of courtship has subsided. By now both Greg and the film have become fairly miserable. When his mother-in-law Evelyn (Rue McLanahan) tells Greg, on her deathbed, not to stop having fun, it seems too little too late. *Modern Love* treads very similar ground as John Hughes' superior *She's Having a Baby*, an earlier film that ruminates on the same themes (young couple facing life changes and adult responsibilities; parents of opposing social status; accepting domesticity, etc.) in a similar manner, as with the elliptical leaps into fantasy sequences, montage editing and surrealist humor. However, where Hughes was a master of pathos, Benson never truly stirs the soul with his worthy ideas, many of which are left unexplored, particularly that of the culture clash that threatens any semblance of familial harmony: His strictly Jewish, hers devoutly Catholic. While much is made of Greg's dismissal of Evelyn's helping hand with the newborn, little to nothing is made of what could have been an interesting relationship between Greg and his father-in-law, Col. Frank Parker (Burt Reynolds). "I will break you into 10,000 pieces," the colonel threatens, before issuing a sincere kiss of affection. It is this kind of uneven storytelling and tone that marks the picture as something of a missed opportunity, and it's not for the lack of good ingredients.

To many Reynolds fans, Robby Benson's boyish good looks and quirky acting style will recall moments such as the hilarious confession scene from *The End* ("Bless me, Dave, for I have sinned") or his grisly demise in *Lucky Lady*, but by 1990 Benson was in full auteur filmmaker mode with this whimsical dramatic comedy in which he starred as well as wrote, produced and directed—not to mention composed music for. *Modern Love* was shot on location in Columbia, South Carolina, in the spring of 1989 and was independently produced and distributed by Triumph Films. Benson made the picture while teaching filmmaking at the University of South Carolina and wisely used the locality and its residents, with many of Benson's students actively involved in the production by providing themselves for bit parts, as crew members and on-set assistants. The economy of such independent means and methods allowed the filmmakers to spend a fraction of what it would have cost to make the picture in Hollywood. Joining Benson onscreen are his real life wife, Karla DeVito, and their daughter Lyric as his onscreen wife and daughter respectively.

Modern Love is obviously a deeply personal picture for those behind its creation, which is something that makes the film's inherent flaws all the more disappointing. Reynolds' presence is most welcome in the few scenes that he appears, cutting a distinguished figure of calm and poise amidst the cartoonish anarchy; the actor generously took time away from shooting *B.L. Stryker* to appear in his friend's picture. "Burt lost money on this one," Benson told *People* magazine in 1990, referring to the actor being paid scale salary of $398. "He spent $10,000 out of pocket to bus his own people for his days on location."[1] Reynolds said:

> The problem with Robby is, he's almost too good to be true. He really is that sweet and vulnerable. He had a great career and then made some films that didn't work, and he got blamed. That's Hollywood. It eats people alive. So he decided to get out of town for a while, and he is a wonderful teacher. And Karla is stunning, bloody wonderful in the picture too—and she'd never been before the cameras in her life.[2]

DeVito, erstwhile stage actress, is indeed buoyant and lovely; while Rue McClanahan's southern belle mother-in-law and Reynolds' stern but caring army psychologist father-in-law are terrific together. If the picture doesn't work quite so well as a comedy, it works superbly in its moments of quiet drama. McLanahan's death scene, and Reynolds performance in it, is staged with grace and poignancy, as are some of Benson and DeVito's more tender moments, far away from the penis jokes and hyper-parenting. Perhaps their finest time onscreen together occurs in the final scene, in which Benson extends tenderness and goodwill towards his family, something tragically missing throughout much of the picture.

Notes

1. Jim Jerome, "Kissing Hollywood Life Goodbye, Robby Benson and Karla Devito Flee to South Carolina to Make Modern Love," *People*, May 28, 1990, https://people.com/archive/kissing-hollywood-life-goodbye-robby-benson-and-karla-devito-flee-to-south-carolina-to-make-modern-love-vol-33-no-21/
2. *Ibid.*

B.L. Stryker

(TV Series, ABC, 1989–1990)

"Watch out, criminals. B.L. Stryker, one-time pride of the New Orleans Police Department, is on the case again."—Oz Jackson

B.L. Stryker is an ex-member of the New Orleans Police Department. His particular brand of justice as a cop was meted out with a heavy hand, resulting in him being reprimanded and disgraced. These days Stryker ekes out a low-rent career as a West Palm Beach private detective while living on a grubby houseboat with his two parrots. Stryker is within close enough proximity to the seedier element of Miami's high society for him to maintain a busy schedule with his agency, Stryker Investigations, the day-to-day operations of which are run by quirky free spirit secretary Lynda Lennox (Dana Kaminsky). Stryker is occasionally assisted by his best friend Oz Jackson (Ossie Davis); once a world-famous pugilist, he now keeps the disorganized and volatile Stryker on an even keel with his sage wisdom. Rita Moreno plays Kimberly, Stryker's ex-wife, and there isn't much love lost between them (Stryker: "I've got cold sores nicer than her!"). Kimberly is now a Palm Beach socialite after having moved on to increasingly wealthier suitors in the years since she divorced Stryker; husband number five is septuagenarian multi-millionaire Clayton Baskin (Abe Vigoda). Despite the acrimony between Stryker and Kimberly, there is always a distinct air of sexual chemistry between the two.

In the series' opening installment "The Dancer's Touch," Stryker is on the trail of a serial rapist and killer targeting young bourgeois Miami women. This case troubles Stryker because he must identify with the attacker in order to get an insight into his motives and actions; it was this psychological skill that afflicted Stryker's mental health and drove him to increased aggression while at the New Orleans Police Department and got him booted out of the force.

Reynolds and Julianne Moore play adversaries in the *B.L. Stryker* film *High Rise* (1990).

B.L Stryker was part of ABC's Mystery Movie package, which included three other shows competing for the audience's attention: *Gideon Oliver*, *Kojak* and *Columbo*. While *B.L. Stryker*s were essentially TV movies which would air every fourth week of the month in the U.S., several of them, including "Blind Chess" and "Blues for Buder," were re-packaged as individual films in Europe. The Season One Episode Four entry "Auntie Sue" was sold as the standalone film *Dirty Diamonds* in the UK and Ireland VHS rental market. These were distributed by CIC Video for Universal Pictures to satisfy the demand for feature films starring Reynolds. Despite being designated as straight-to-video product, which normally indicates weaker content, the quality of production and the considerable star power of these *B.L. Stryker* films far exceeded the usual standard of video premieres.

As Reynolds had done in past film work, he cast genuine Hollywood royalty as guest stars: Douglas Fairbanks Jr., Maureen Stapleton, Harry Carey Jr., Doug McClure and Ricardo Montalban. "Burt always brought in the best," said cinematographer and director Nick McLean Sr. He continued:

> On "High Rise," I had Ricardo Montalban, who was incredible. What a great guy he was. Burt told me to work it into the story that the air conditioner goes off in the building, which would mean Ricardo would have to get his shirt off, and he did! Ricardo was about 65 years old and he looked amazing! He was such a good performer, you would never have known he was a cripple; look closely at his walk; he has to fake that so it looks normal. He was in an accident with a horse and it mangled his leg up and when he's not on the set, he limps like crazy. And then there was Julianne Moore, who played Ricardo's sidekick. She went on to become a big star. I had never heard of her by that time, but of course she had never heard of me either. And Rita Moreno, who won an Oscar, an Emmy, two Tony Awards … when she was on *B.L. Stryker*, she said, "I've done all that work and won all those awards and still can't get hired anywhere!" She's 85 years old today and still looks amazing. And Ossie Davis: I have a picture of him here on my desk, he was probably my favorite guy of all time, he was the greatest, a phenomenal guy.[1]

Reynolds also offered recurring roles to some other familiar faces from his *oeuvre*, including Alfie Wise as Stryker's wealthy computer wiz neighbor (and constant source of ridicule) Oliver Wardell, and C. James Lewis as Officer Cartrude. Lewis' association with Reynolds goes back to the late '70s, when the Vietnam veteran and former Sheriff's Department pilot enrolled in the Burt Reynolds Institute for Theatre Training. Throughout the early '80s, Lewis acted in several Reynolds pictures while also performing as the star's stand-in, due to their similar physical appearance. However, by the mid–80s, Lewis found himself at a career crossroads. He said:

> By about 1987, things slowed down for me and I had to make a decision. I was either going to remain a stand-in and be pigeonholed or I needed to just hold out and be an actor. I got some work, I was in *Punch Line* with Sally Field and Tom Hanks, I was in *Sunset* with Bruce Willis and *A Fine Mess* with Ted Danson. Then I got a call from Nick McLean, whom I had worked with on several pictures, and he said, "We're going to Florida to do *B.L. Stryker*. Will you come down and work as Video Assist? And I think Burt wants to talk to you as well." And I said, "Well, I can't run the video and be a stand-in as well," and Nick told me it was bigger than that. So I talked to Mr. Reynolds and he told me he had a great part for me. It was the recurring role of Officer Cartrude, a uniformed Palm Beach police sergeant. And Michael O'Smith was going to be the chief of police, and I knew Michael from Burt's theater. What an actor! After the first year of *B.L. Stryker*, I bought my own house, one that I still live in today, and I decided that this was going to be my home.[2]

Aesthetically, *B.L. Stryker* is a tour de force. Each episode is the work of considerable film-making talent. Some episodes were directed by Reynolds veterans Hal Needham and Jerry

Cinematographer Nick McLean Sr. filming an aerial stunt with Reynolds on *B.L. Stryker* (1990) (photograph courtesy Nick McLean Collection).

Jameson. The stylish pilot film "The Dancer's Touch" is exemplary of the show's highly artistic aesthetic as it is directed by erstwhile cinematographer William Fraker (*Fade In, Gator, The Best Little Whorehouse in Texas, Sharky's Machine*) and shot by McLean. With two of Hollywood's best cameramen crafting the visual world of *B.L. Stryker*, the show was only ever going to be visually stunning. McLean's stylish photography heightens the unsettling mood of "The Dancer's Touch" by utilizing darkness and shadows, which contrasts equisitely with the searing brightness of the daytime exteriors of West Palm Beach. McLean remained as the cinematographer for the entire series, except for the episode which he directed, "High Rise." In relinquishing cinematography duties while directing "High Rise," McLean brought in Reynolds regular Bobby Byrne. Having worked with Reynolds previously on *Smokey and the Bandit*, *Hooper* and *The End*, Byrne was already a trusted member of the Reynolds stock company and McLean felt comfortable with him taking the reins.

With the show containing plenty of stunt work and intricately staged set pieces, Reynolds felt assured in having McLean aboard; the cinematographer had established a stellar reputation in Hollywood as one of the go-to cameramen for the best in aerial and stunt photography. His skill and efficiency not only meant some spectacular footage being captured but also reassured Reynolds that he wouldn't have to perform a difficult or dangerous stunt too many times before a printable take was in the can. According to McLean,

> I made it as easy on Burt as I could. In "High Rise," for example, Stryker spends some time in a mask and jumpsuit, so I figured he could have a stunt double fill in and allow Burt to take a couple of days off. You couldn't see if it was Burt or not, so there was no need to have him in there. I know Burt didn't want to work that hard anyway so he was happy that I managed to get him some time off.

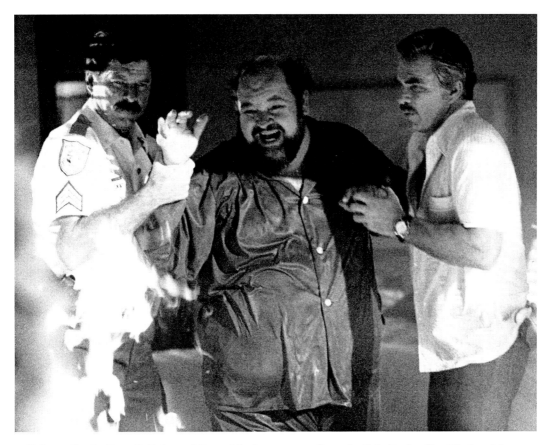

C. James Lewis, Dom DeLuise and Reynolds shoot a scene from the *B.L. Stryker* film *Die Laughing* (1990) (photograph courtesy C. James Lewis Collection).

As I was the cinematographer on all of *B.L. Stryker*, it meant that I was able to work closely with Burt and pay attention to how he directed his episodes, so I learned a lot from him and knew what was required of me when it came time to direct my own one. Directing is pretty tough, I can tell you that every single question on the set comes to you, the buck stops here. But I got a lot of accolades for doing it from a lot of people. Universal didn't originally want me directing "High Rise" but they ended up loving it and wanted me to do more.[3]

Unfortunately for all concerned, ABC failed to renew the show for a third season. But there were better times ahead in the world of television for Reynolds and his trusted collaborators. McLean said,

The plan was that if *B.L. Stryker* got picked up for another season, I was going to be directing every other episode, but then the show was cancelled. It's a shame because *B.L. Stryker* was a one-of-a-kind deal for television. It had an amazing cast, we had those great Old Hollywood legends appearing in some episodes and then we also had these really talented up-and-coming actors like Neil Patrick Harris, Julianne Moore, Kristy Swanson and Michael Chiklis, who all went on to have huge careers. The show looks spectacular too. It doesn't feel like you are watching a TV series because we shot them like they were theatrical movies; some of Hollywood's best were making them, people who would normally work on major motion pictures. It was all shot on location, which gave it a different look and feel from your usual television production. It was great working in Florida; Burt is revered down there, everybody loves him. But the good times came to an end when we got word that the studio wasn't going to be renewing it for the third season. It was disappointing for a little while, but it wasn't long before we were back working with Burt again, this time on *Evening Shade*, which lasted four seasons and was a huge success.[4]

Notes

1. Nick McLean Sr., *interview with author*, Skype, January 15, 2018.
2. C. James Lewis, *interview with author*, Skype, August 17, 2018.
3. Nick McLean Sr., *interview with author*, Skype, January 15, 2018.
4. *Ibid.*

Evening Shade
(TV Series, CBS, 1990–1994)

"My wife isn't speaking to me, I got a football team that can't play football, I've got an assistant coach that stains wood, I've got a son who doesn't want to get his face hurt, I've got another son whose feet stink and he sucks money out of people's pockets, a friend who gave me a gyp vasectomy, and a naked woman stalking me all over town. I think I'll just go home and get under the bed."— Wood Newton

As the '90s dawned and just as Burt Reynolds' marquee value had diminished following a run of badly received pictures, the actor found a more welcoming home in the medium of television. *B.L. Stryker* had featured some of Reynolds' best work of the period but the series was dropped from Universal's production slate after its second season; this wasn't the first time Reynolds endured cancellation of television shows, as *Hawk* and *Dan August* were also unceremoniously dropped. Despite the demise of *B.L. Stryker*, Reynolds immediately set up home over at CBS for another excursion into small-screen storytelling, with a genteel sitcom called *Evening Shade*.

Evening Shade is an old-fashioned entertainment in the best sense. Its warmth, humor, sentiments, optimism and empathy for human frailty, foible and foolishness are cut from the same cloth as the works of Frank Capra. Reynolds plays Wood Newton, a former Pittsburgh Steelers football hero who retired early after incurring an injury and is now coaching an incompetent high school team in Evening Shade, Arkansas. Wood's wife Ava (Marilu Henner) is the working mother of their three (soon to be four) children: Taylor, Molly and Will. In the first episode, Ava announces that she is expecting another child. The idea doesn't sit comfortably with Ava's professional commitments and ambitions as a lawyer and soon-to-be district attorney. Wood, it seems, is the victim of a botched vasectomy. Ava's father Evan Evans is the local captain of industry and the owner of the town's newspaper, and has something of a grudging kinship with Wood ever since Ava married Wood when she was 18, a fact which has irked Evan ever since. Other friends and family members in the Newtons' lives include Evan's girlfriend and local stripper Fontana Beausoleil (Linda Gehringer), Ava's cantankerous Aunt Frieda (Elizabeth Ashley), comically un-athletic physical education coach Herman Stiles (Michael Jeter), Wood's friend and physician Harlan Eldridge (Charles Durning), Harlan's ebullient wife Merleen (Ann Wedgeworth) and bar owner (as well as show narrator) Ponder Blue (Ossie Davis). Davis' opening and closing narration has a hint of Rod Serling about it: It never indicates that we're entering another

Reynolds (left) as Wood Newton and Hal Holbrook as his father-in-law Evan Evans in *Evening Shade* (1990).

dimension, but it feels as though the town of Evening Shade is very much an autonomous world of its own. It is a nostalgic fiction that harbors only the purest of souls, even if they are incompetent doctors, uncouth strippers and football coaches with a shameful losing streak. It is as though Reynolds and the show's creators had envisioned an idyllic version of small town Americana, a town without prejudice, without class or cultural contrasts. In the Christmas episode of Season One, Wood tires of his bickering family and the materialist source of their ire; he decides that they don't deserve the many gifts awaiting them under their tree, and asks where the local hard luck family lives so he can make their Christmas a better one. It is this kind of noble spirit that fuels the show and its characters.

Evening Shade is the product of Linda Bloodworth-Thomason, creator of *Lime Street* (1985, ABC) and *Designing Women* (1986–1993, CBS). She and her husband Harry Thomason were as well known for their high-profile friendship with Bill and Hilary Clinton, having worked with the them in the years prior to Bill's time as commander in chief. According to actor–camera assistant C. James Lewis,

> One day when we were shooting *Evening Shade* I was walking through the stage door and the phone was ringing; the phones don't actually ring, they have a little flashing light in case the cameras are rolling. Now, it wasn't my job to be answering this phone, but there was nobody around, no PA, no AD, so I said, "What the hell…" and just picked it up and said, "Stage 11. Jimmy Lewis, how may I help you?" and this woman on the other end said, "Please stand by for the president." Now I'm thinking this a joke and then suddenly Bill Clinton comes on the phone and says, "Hey, Harry!" President Clinton was looking for Harry Thomason; Harry and his wife Linda Bloodworth-Thomason were our executive producers, and Harry often directed episodes as well. So I said to Mr. Clinton, "Mr. President, Harry is just setting up a shot but I'll go get him as quickly as possible," and he said, "Oh thank you, that's very nice of you." So I took off running and found Harry and he looked at me, probably thinking the building is on fire or something, and I said, "Harry, President Clinton is on the phone looking for you!" and Harry said, "Tell him I'll be there in a minute." I'm standing there thinking, "I can't tell the president of the United States to wait a minute; I might not be alive tomorrow!" So I got on the phone and said, "Mr. President, Harry is walking to the phone right as we speak."[1]

Reynolds directed many of the episodes, and also drafted in other filmmakers and actors whom he had worked with in the past to direct (David Steinberg, Robby Benson, James Hampton). Other past collaborators of Reynolds returned, including cinematographer Nick McLean Sr., who was brought in at Reynolds' request as the show's director of photography. Reynolds convinced McLean to make the transition into television after maintaining a stellar career shooting for the big screen.

Somewhat reluctantly, McLean acquiesced after he considered the major breaks Reynolds had afforded him, as well as considering their friendship. "I really didn't want to do *Evening Shade*," he admits. "I had no interest in shooting episodic television. But *Evening Shade* became the first sitcom that I worked on and I did it only because Burt had asked me. Burt had done so much for my career that I thought 'To hell with it…' and I think I ended up shooting over 100 episodes."[2] McLean was given more leeway on the visual style of the show than most network sitcoms were usually allowed. However, with Reynolds executive producing, the star's influence was felt behind as well as in front of the camera. McLean said,

> Burt had a lot creative control over *Evening Shade*. I had brought the Steadicam into *Evening Shade*, which was never done before on a sitcom. If I wanted to make something look real stylized, Burt was behind me 100 percent, he'd just say "Do it!" and "If it takes longer to set up, then it takes longer." It was very liberating to have such freedom on a TV show. Burt directed a lot of the episodes and the producers, the Thomasons, pretty much left him alone; they knew the show would sell as a Burt Reynolds product

so they left us to do our thing and I could try just about anything I wanted. Burt actually spent a lot of time in the editing room on *Evening Shade*; he really helped construct the episodes in the editing.[3]

All the elements were present for a classic Reynolds vehicle: the Southern setting; a coterie of familiar faces; a football context; and an opportunity to display the comedic, romantic and dramatic traits of his considerable talents. There was a natural chemistry on display which kept the show a witty and lively affair, and despite its deliberate contrivances (such as the townsfolk gathering and singing "Amazing Grace" outside the hospital where Ava is suffering childbirth complications), the camaraderie and funny tradeoffs between the characters bristled with warmth and wit. In one of the finest episodes, "Gambler Anonymous," Kenny Rogers guest starred as an old pal of Wood's who lands in Arkansas for airplane maintenance. Rogers is invited over for some steak and a $20 bottle of wine, which of course surprises Wood's family and one by one, the Newtons' friends arrive, agog at the superstar in the living room. Just how does the country music legend know Wood? Well, Wood used to furnish Rogers with football tickets when he played for the Pittsburgh Steelers, until Terry Bradshaw came along and got him better tickets; the recurring joke being Wood's grievance with hotshot Bradshaw. To finish out the episode Rogers serenades the Newton assembly with a rendition of "Twenty Years Ago," a song from his 1986 album "They Don't Make Them Like They Used To." The song was written by, among others, Arkansas songwriter Wood Newton, whom Reynolds' *Evening Shade* character may or may not be named after. A tender moment of reflection and longing, it perhaps sums up the entire intention of the show, which is that the minute moments of family and friendship, those we take for granted, are those we will miss the most when life gets that bit more complicated. The show invited us into the lives of the residents of Evening Shade and invited us to share their moments with them.

After a commercially treacherous first season during which the show came in at number 49 in the Nielsen ratings, it skyrocketed with acclaim from the television industry and viewers. Nominations for its creators and cast boosted the show's profile, leading to a spike in viewership and a peak ranking of number 15 on the Nielsen charts. Throughout its four-season run, Reynolds was honored with a Golden Globe, an Emmy and a Q Award for Best Actor for his performance as Wood Newton.

Notes

1. C. James Lewis, *interview with author*, Skype, August 17, 2018.
2. Nick McLean Sr., *interview with author*, Skype, January 15, 2018.
3. *Ibid.*

Cop and a Half

(1993)

"We do not have a love-hate relationship. We have a hate-hate relationship."
—Nick McKenna

Reynolds plays gruff Tampa law enforcement veteran Nick McKenna, who is placed in charge of gangland murder witness Devon Butler (Norman D. Golden II). A police pop culture enthusiast, Devon is well aware of terms such as quid pro quo—"one hand washes the other"—learned from one of his beloved television cop shows. The youngster duly applies his knowledge of police procedure to his advantage, demanding to be treated as an acting officer for a week in exchange for handing over the vital evidence needed by McKenna to bust mob boss Vinnie Fountain (Ray Sharkey). Devon gets to taste life on the police force, questioning suspects and performing traffic duty, in which he learns discretionary tactics on when to let a violation slide and when to act; with Devon on duty, most people are safe going a couple of miles over the limit, unless you are his school principal, and then it's time to book him. Devon isn't lying when he says, "I'm your worst nightmare: an eight-year-old with a badge!" As a child brought up on a steady diet of TV cop shows, he relishes the love-hate relationship that he expects; he fails to see Nick's belligerence and intolerance as anything other than par for the course of being a great cop duo. And where does Devon get this lingo? "Prime time!" he says.

Nick is the kind of loner maverick that audiences became familiar with throughout cop cinema of the '70s and '80s. He is burnt out, cynical, pessimistic. His colleague asks Devon, who aspires to be just like Nick, "Why do you want to be a cop? Look at this guy! Raggedy-ass clothes, 20-year-old car, bad back, bad marriage, bad attitude … son, does that sound like any kind of life for anybody?" But these are the very qualities that Devon holds dear in his vision of the ideal cop, right down to Nick's questionable snakeskin footwear: "Nice pair of boots, Nick. I have to get me a pair of those!" Devon enthuses. Staying true to tradition and clichés so beloved of Devon, Nick's gruff demeanor and reluctance to partner up is blamed on the old chestnut: His partner was killed and he blames himself. Nick also doesn't have very much time for kids, and has all the right reasons for such a mindset: "You can't have any fun with a kid. You can't take him to a bar! He has one drink and he falls off the stool."

Cop and a Half was part of the series of contrived crime comedies that were a fixture of the late '80s and early '90s American cinematic milieu, alongside *K-9* (Rod Daniel, 1989),

Devon Butler (Norman D. Golden II) is everyone's worst nightmare, an eight-year-old with a badge, in *Cop and a Half* (1993).

Kindergarten Cop (Ivan Reitman, 1990), *Stop! Or My Mom Will Shoot* (Roger Spottiswoode, 1992) and *Cops and Robbersons* (Michael Ritchie, 1994). The film also continues another Hollywood tradition of the era: A reluctant father figure finds himself in a situation in which he must embrace previously dormant paternal instincts; an element of this trope is that these narratives often place professional, white-collar, middle-class men into the unpaid workforce of the domestic domain, as seen in *Mr. Mom* (Stan Dragoti, 1983), *Three Men and a Baby* (Leonard Nimoy, 1987), *Parenthood* (Ron Howard, 1989) and the Reynolds film *Paternity* (David Steinberg, 1981). It could be said that it's a cynical, patriarchal post-feminist construct to depict the mothers of these films as absent or unengaged with their responsibility, their careers often of more concern than the child and therefore the onus of responsibility is placed upon the man, comically of course. For these men, parenting, domestic chores and emotional engagement with children (those not of their intellectual level or cultural and social standing) is indeed an endurance test. It's out of their nature and character, and so the arc of these films must see the protagonist overcome the fear of embracing their paternal instincts.

Of course, the heart of *Cop and a Half* is the emotional bond between the fatherless Devon and the dependent-less and responsibility-free Nick conquering any hesitations he has in embracing their burgeoning relationship. It is an old-fashioned, and some may say clichéd model, but the sentiment is sweet and the picture harmless. Reynolds, as always, seems at ease with his young charge, playing their relationship as reluctant for as long as possible until the budding chemistry gives way to genuine love. It may be perhaps the most unlikely cop duo since Clint Eastwood and Tyne Daly shared a patrol car in the *Dirty Harry* picture *The Enforcer*. But Reynolds and young Norman D. Golden II make for an amusingly mismatched pair in this jolly affair.

Cop and a Half was directed with professionalism by Henry Winkler. While this is strictly commercial studio filmmaking by the book, it has goodwill to burn and fun to boot. The picture is largely played as a live action Saturday morning cartoon; the violence is slapstick and the villains are bumbling and largely benign, right down to the bizarre creation that is Vinnie Fountain, played by an ailing Ray Sharkey. Dogged by rumors of being stricken with AIDS, Sharkey strenuously denied the allegations of ill health until months before his death in 1993 from complications associated with the virus. Sharkey's performance, as strange as many other elements of this film, works perfectly; the actor amplifies the knowingly bizarre contrivance of Vinnie Fountain as some anachronistic antiquity, who croons 1950s ballads in slickly high-coiffed hair while commanding the utmost fear and respect from his crew. Fountain and his goons are largely played for laughs like a motley crew of Hanna-Barbera gangsters, a live action Anthill Mob, and that is just fine for a picture this anarchic. And if anyone was ever in doubt, the picture ends with Devon resplendent in his own pair of snakeskin boots.

The Man from Left Field
(Made-for-Television, 1993)

"He's not a ghost. I've seen him before ... he came from left field."—Beau Prinzi

The Indiantown Indians is a little league baseball team down on its luck. It's comprised of kids from the wrong side of town, a group of working class youngsters living with poverty, abuse, deadbeat dads and single mothers. "Just once I'd like to play on a field where the bases aren't tin cans and the mound isn't a stack of old newspapers!" one player says in reference to their impoverished milieu. The kids are anxious to recruit a coach in order to make the league and their last attempt is dashed when Mr. Bates, a drunken Wednesday night bowler (the closest thing to a sporting adult they can muster), chews them out for interrupting his hangover.

Hope comes in the form of the eponymous man from left field, a wandering amnesiac, ragged and disheveled, watching ominously from the dugout. Despite a taciturn demeanor that should send them running back to Mr. Bates, "The Man"—who they call Jackie Robinson in reference to the famous Major League player—imparts wisdom and knowledge, mentoring the disadvantaged kids with his insights into the game: "He's crowding the plate. Throw it at him and then he'll think you're trying to hit him, and throw three straight strikes."

Jackie soon makes a difference to the boys' lives in many ways, not to mention making an impression on Beau's beautiful mother Nancy Lee (Reba McIntyre). Tackling scumbag boyfriends and abusive parents, Jackie becomes a surrogate father figure off the field; in one sweet scene, he introduces the kids to the birds and the bees in perhaps the most innocent way imaginable: taking them to a movie theater for a screening Howard Hughes' once-controversial *The Outlaw* (1943), where the boys are introduced to the smoldering sexuality of Jane Russell. Jackie takes exception to the abuse administered upon player Bam Block (Adam Cronin) by his brutish, alcoholic father. Jackie visits Mr. Block and dishes out some tough justice. Another player, J.C., traumatized at losing his beloved grandfather and sole guardian, runs away and almost succumbs to a watery doom in a nearby river, only to be saved by Jackie. In the midst of all this drama, Jackie experiences a frightening flashback to major events from his past and realizes how and why he lost touch with the reality of his life.

While Burt Reynolds was enjoying a blossoming career on television with *Evening Shade*, American cinema was undergoing a shift in aesthetics and economics. A new movement was bubbling under the surface of the mainstream, one which would eventually though briefly rival the studio system. The 1989 release of Steven Soderbergh's *Sex, Lies, and Videotape* engendered an interest in low-budget alternative pictures from a new breed of young auteur. Its financial success ($36 million return on a $1 million budget) piqued the curiosity of the studios and the uneasy relationship between risqué left-field content and corporate executive mentality reached its commercial apex with Quentin Tarantino's *Pulp Fiction* in 1995. Burt Reynolds was eventually embraced by this indie community, but between Bill Forsyth's *Breaking In* and his fantastic supporting role in Alexander Payne's daring satire *Citizen Ruth*, Reynolds lost some of his cinematic capital when it came to leading roles in big-budget studio pictures. *B.L. Stryker* came and went in two seasons and then *Evening Shade* was broadcast to great success, but Reynolds' big-screen appearances were limited to voiceover work in *All Dogs Go to Heaven*, a supporting role in Robby Benson's *Modern Love*, a cameo in Robert Altman's *The Player*, a guest appearance in *Beverly Hills 90210*, and co-starring in a TV movie vehicle for country singer Randy Travis, *Wind in the Wire*. Reynolds' sole major cinematic work was *Cop and a Half*, a film which made money but did little to make Reynolds a relevant film star in the 1990s. With most appreciation of Reynolds at this time coming from television audiences, it was probably a wise a move to focus on feature-length television pictures such as *The Man from Left Field*. It was directed by Reynolds, produced by Renée Valente (the casting director responsible securing Reynolds his early starring role in *Hawk*), shot by Nick McLean Sr., scored by Bobby Goldsboro, and returns to the themes of familial yearning and surrogate patriarchy that had continued to interest its star, thus leaving little doubt that the film is entirely a Burt Reynolds project. McLean said,

> Most of *The Man from Left Field* was done on Burt's ranch that he owned down in Jupiter, Florida. It really was some ranch. We did several movies and a lot of *B.L. Stryker* there. We had two or three soundstages on it, there was a landing strip—Burt had his own plane and helicopter—he had thoroughbred horses there, he even built the baseball field that you see in the picture on the ranch, he had about 300 acres there. That's the luxury of being the #1 movie star in the world for five years in a row. When you have your own landing strip on your property, you know you've made it![1]

One of the film's greatest assets is McLean's presence behind the camera, as his luscious cinematography lifts it out of its made-for-TV limitations, though McLean is quick to credit his boss:

> Some of the best shots in that movie were Burt's idea, those beautiful landscape shots and the sunset scenes where he is walking across the countryside in silhouette, they were all his idea. He'd come back from shooting at the end of the day and say, "God, I saw this great sunset," and we'd take the camera back there the next night hoping for a similar sunset. So that really lush photography you see in there was really more Burt's idea than mine, we'd just go and capture it as best we could. On a TV movie, you pretty much light it the same way and execute your camera moves the same way. The only difference is the quality of the image; you don't get that great widescreen, CinemaScope type look that a theatrical film offers.[2]

The Man from Left Field is unlikely to make anyone's list of favorite Burt Reynolds films, but as a sensitive, inspirational melodrama, it works very well, thanks in no small part to the well-crafted photographic style and Reynolds' obvious empathy for his struggling characters. And in the grand Reynolds tradition of casting former sporting heroes, Joe Theismann, former Toronto Argonauts and Washington Redskins quarterback, appears as the coach of the Indiantown Indians' rivals.

Notes

1. Nick McLean Sr., *interview with author*, Skype, January 15, 2018.
2. *Ibid.*

The Maddening
(1995)

> "You're gonna hear his name three more times, and that's the last time you will ever hear his name again. Arthur, Arthur…. Arthur!"—Roy Scudder

Cassie Osbourne (Mia Sara) is the frustrated housewife of engineer David Osbourne (Brian Wimmer). Cassie and their young daughter Samantha think that David's frequent business trips have become too much of a priority for him. David is working on a multi-million dollar contract in the Catskills and is under strict orders and the threat of losing his job if he refuses to be on-site as required, and so he takes another trip away only to come home to an empty house and some of his clothes being boiled on the stove. Cassie and Samantha have taken flight to her sister Joanne in Tampa, but along the way things take a sinister turn. Pulling in at an isolated gas station run by a former athlete, Roy Scudder (Burt Reynolds), the attendants admire Cassie's classic vehicle while Roy manipulates the engine for it to break down. Roy then suggests a shortcut to Tampa that will shave off an hour's traveling time. Eager to move on from the sleazy environs, Cassie sets off only for the car to fail, as planned, just as Roy arrives to help, offering to tow the car to his place in the remote Florida countryside.

Cassie is introduced to Roy's wife Georgina (Angie Dickinson), who is suffering from grief and some kind of post-traumatic ailment ever since the suspicious death of her baby boy Arthur. It is suggested that since the death of their child, the Scudder family has lived with twisted delusions. When Cassie and Samantha arrive, they are drawn into the sick mentality of the Scudder clan, with Georgina under the illusion that the Osbourne mother and daughter are her sister and niece. Almost immediately this supposed sanctuary becomes a house of malevolence, with Samantha taunted and bullied by the Scudder daughter Jill, while Cassie is locked in an upstairs bedroom where she will be beaten and raped. Roy's sadistic streak is triggered upon witnessing apparitions of his deceased father, a semi-invalid tyrant who envied his son's youthful fitness, just as his son was embarrassed by his father's physical imperfections. Parallel to this, David frantically searches for his family, while he too is being tracked by slovenly bumbling detective Chicky Ross (Josh Mostel), who, having been misinformed by the Osbournes' nosy neighbor, suspects that David is responsible for the missing mother and daughter. According to Andrew Neiderman's source novel, both David and Cassie have lost their parents and this is the source of their longing to be together as much as possible, as well as to be present for their only child. Had this idea been presented in the film version, it would have given some legitimacy to the sub-textual theme of parental dysfunction, innocence lost, and absent familial emotions. However, the picture is more concerned with the surface narrative and tonal registers of the horror genre; it is not particularly concerned with the nuances of the psychological or social elements that could have been mined.

After Reynolds made a detour into mainstream family-friendly films with *All Dogs Go to Heaven*, *Cop and a Half* and *The Man from Left Field*, few fans anticipated that his next move would be down a slippery road to a rural hellhole, a descent into *The Maddening*. Fitting Neiderman's description of Roy as "tanned dark by the sun … his features could be called handsome: sharp and angular," the film's script would have little use for Reynolds' natural charisma as it calls for menace and sheer brutality on the villain's part; although the actor's warmth does come in handy early on when deceiving Cassie at the gas station with his seemingly benign local hospitality. Reynolds' formidable physical stature, still potent and strong in his mid–50s, benefits his performance as the imposing psychopath.

As is typical on a Reynolds picture, former colleagues and co-stars appear. *Sam Whiskey*'s Angie Dickinson plays Roy's mentally unstable wife, while Angela Bomford appears as prying neighbor Mrs. Plummer; Bomford can be seen in the *B.L. Stryker* episode

"The King of Jazz." Cinematographer Nick McLean once again brings much of his distinctive style to the picture, perhaps the most accomplished and memorable aspect of the production. He recalled:

> Once I got the feel for the story, I knew what kind of lighting would suit it best, which was minimal lighting but stylishly used. We spent a lot of time shooting in that house and there was a lot of night shooting, which meant we could control the lighting and really craft the look of it, and so what you have is a very moody, dark picture. It's really kind of a horror film, which translated to me as a lot of shadows and high contrast lighting. I actually tried to use as little lighting as I could. One of the reasons the lighting on *The Maddening* is so good is because I had this gaffer called Danny Eccleston, who I had also worked with on *B.L. Stryker*, and who had a tremendous command of the light. That's why this film and *B.L. Stryker* look as good as they do, because I used Danny and he was terrific.[1]

The Maddening was partly shot on Reynolds' own West Jupiter, Florida, ranch, previously owned by infamous gangster Al Capone. Reynolds bought the land in 1968. While the actor owned it, the ranch variably functioned as an animal feed store, a country and western radio station, a petting farm, his own sanctuary and, in later years, a movie studio. McLean continued:

> A lot of the film was shot out at Burt's ranch but the main house location was actually a neighboring property. Danny Huston came down and we got in Burt's helicopter and scouted the areas. As we were looking down, we spotted this interesting-looking house about a mile from Burt's ranch but we kept going, we shopped around all day and looked at a million houses. But we ended up going back to the first house that stood out and that's where we shot it. It was right there in Jupiter, Florida. Burt knew the people who owned the house so it worked out pretty easy.[2]

The film harks back to "fear of the country, beware the rural family" texts such as *Deliverance*, *The Texas Chain Saw Massacre*, *Two Thousand Maniacs*, *Spider Baby*, *Death Trap* and *Straw Dogs*. Given its release into the more controlled censorship climate of the mid–1990s, *The Maddening* was never going to be as truly violent and confrontational as the 1970s pictures of similar theme, nor would the slick contemporary aesthetics of the era allow the film to wallow in the sleazy atmosphere that it so desperately needs. The film feels too muted, too much a product of its low-budget straight-to-video restrictions and commercial requirements for it to realize its potential as a truly shocking piece of work. That said, there are some nasty moments throughout, such as the nail-peeling incident which would make your average broken nail feel like a Christmas present any day of the week. *The Maddening* is a solid Southern gothic thriller but one which didn't resonate very well with audiences. McLean recalled:

> I don't know what happened to that movie or why it didn't do better. I don't think it did real good and I believe not too many people saw it. I don't think I even saw the entire finished film. All the elements were there for a good movie. Burt had total control and he could have wielded it if he wanted to, but he and the director Danny Huston got along good and Burt was at a stage in his life where he just wanted to act. So Burt was happy to leave Danny alone to do his thing there. I enjoyed working on it. We shot it really quick and I liked working with Danny, I liked him a lot. We actually spent most of the time talking about his dad, John Huston. Who wouldn't?[3]

Notes

1. Nick McLean Sr., *interview with author*, Skype, January 15, 2018.
2. *Ibid.*
3. *Ibid.*

Citizen Ruth

(1996)

"You want me to send a message? I ain't no fucking telegram, bitch!"—Ruth Stoops

Laura Dern is outstanding in the lead role of Ruth Stoops, a white trash delinquent and frequent guest at the local police station due to her glue-sniffing and aerosol-inhaling. Upon being arrested after another chemical blackout, Ruth learns she is pregnant. Her previous four children have been taken out of her custody and so the presiding judge makes her an unusual and morally questionable offer: abort the fetus and she will evade felony charges. Normally Ruth ends up slapped with a misdemeanor charge, but this time it is escalated to felony as she is considered to have recklessly endangered her unborn child, the child she never knew she was carrying.

At the jail, Ruth meets a group of pro-life protestors who had been taken in for causing disruption at a local abortion clinic; they include Norm and Gail Stoney (Kurtwood Smith and Mary Kay Place), advocates of Christian conservative family values. The Stoneys take Ruth into their home to live alongside their son Tony (Sebastian Anzaldo III) and their secretly wayward daughter Cheryl (Alicia Witt). When Ruth rebels against their propagandistic pro-life onslaught and escapes Norm's sleazier tendencies, she becomes the cipher of a radical pro-choice opposition force headed by a lesbian couple, Diane (Swoosie Kurtz) and her manipulative cohort Rachel (Kelly Preston). Macho security for the liberals is provided by Vietnam veteran Harlan (M.C. Gainey) and his gang of sympathetic bikers. Ruth becomes a lower-class project for these warring moral and political factions. On one side we have the Stoneys: lower-middle class store workers and traditional conservative Republicans; on the other side, countercultural, alternative-lifestyle intellectuals, figures of a professional or artistic class far removed from the orthodox conformity of the middle–American pro-life camp. The Stoneys decide to call in the big guns, summoning the head of the Baby Savers ministry, Blaine Gibbons (Reynolds). Hilariously, a child named Eric who was previously saved by Blaine at an "abortuary" picket line is now his rather hands-on teenage personal assistant, at Blaine's beck and call to dress, massage and meet his demands. Blaine sees the only option to keep Ruth on their side is to furnish her with $30,000 to bring the unborn child to term. When the pro-choice gang gets wind of this, they make a counter offer for her to abort said child. A bidding war for Ruth's allegiance ensues while Blaine's old nemesis, Jessica Weiss (Tippi Hedren), is flown in to give some political gravitas to the pro-choice campaigners.

Now a political football tossed between the two sides, Ruth refuses the dogma of both and plays them off against each other to her advantage, as best her limited intelligence will allow, even after she suffers a miscarriage unbeknownst to her supposed supporters on both sides. Ruth leads a deeply unattractive lifestyle, but it is her life to style as she sees fit. No matter what iniquitous squalor awaits, we must cheer her moment of independence as the two opposing forces continue to battle over an entity that no longer exists. If the picture takes on any side, it is Ruth's own choice, identifying with no one else's philosophy other than her own, even if that philosophy is the pursuit of self-destruction via deadbeat boyfriends and chemical dependency. Amidst the frenzy of political rhetoric, it is liberating

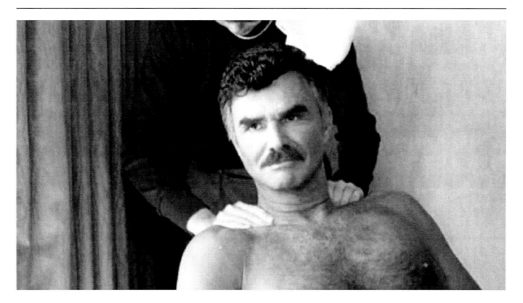

The sleazy Blaine Gibbons (Reynolds) gets a rubdown from the young man he saved from an "abortuary" many years ago in *Citizen Ruth* **(1996).**

that the picture presents its anti-heroine as flagrantly apathetic to anything remotely partisan in this contentious discourse. Indeed, one of the best things about *Citizen Ruth* is that it refuses to take a political stance on either side; Alexander Payne is an equal opportunity satirist, sparing neither rabid, radical liberals nor the conformist, God-fearing Republicans. No matter what side enters the fray, it will ultimately end up obliterated by Payne's coruscating comedy. Ultimately, Ruth refuses to placate either side and continues on with life on her own terms, as degrading and unseemly as it may appear to most people. Despite all the grandstanding and sloganeering from both sides, with their wails of "freedom" and "liberty," in the end they only seek to limit Ruth's privileges as a grown adult woman with a mind of her own, no matter how dysfunctional that mind may be. The cult of pro-choice advocates is depicted to be just as buffoonish as the ritualistic pro-life camp.

Citizen Ruth was never going to be a commercial contender to rival the blockbusters released at the same time, with such innocuous fare as *Jerry Maguire*, *The Preacher's Wife* and *Mars Attacks!* appealing more widely to audiences. Box office receipts for *Citizen Ruth* were dire, the picture's domestic takings stalling at a little over $285,000, perhaps a warning sign to other filmmakers of the perils of handling hot political potatoes, even if your film stars Laura Dern and Burt Reynolds. *Citizen Ruth* provides all the material possible to ignite some fierce and lively debate on the thorny issue of abortion, calculated to offend all in its blanket takedown of everybody who takes a stand. In the end, few people had the opportunity to be offended. The death knell for *Citizen Ruth* was its lackluster release from distributor Miramax, meaning those willing to engage in the film's controversial narrative had barely a chance to see it. Such studio apathy made the film's own director aghast. "I didn't get one single protest letter from *Citizen Ruth*, not one," Payne said in reflection of the film's paltry release, while also comparing the more conservative, perhaps apathetic political rhetoric of '90s cinema to the virulence of the important films of the New Hollywood era: "I hope that we are entering an age where films throw grenades, where they question, don't just support the status quo, because that's what we used to have in the '70s, throwing grenades."[1]

It was only a matter of time before Reynolds and his iconic film career would be embraced by a new generation of filmmakers, those who perhaps experienced his great works of the 1970s as eager young film students and movie buffs. Paul Thomas Anderson was credited with affording Reynolds the platform for an official Hollywood revival with *Boogie Nights*, but before that it was Payne who saw major potential in the star for his provocative satire. *Citizen Ruth* did lend Reynolds some credibility in Park City, Utah: He received a standing ovation from an adoring crowd after a screening of the picture at the Sundance Film Festival. "I used to be a big movie star," Burt proclaimed as he addressed the audience, "I hear the '70s are back … and I just want to say it's a whole new ball game."[2] And with that, the Sundance audience erupted in cheers for the returning icon. It could be that Reynolds represented the cinema of the 1970s New Hollywood era that the Young Turk indie filmmakers of the 1990s embraced, the era of the auteur filmmaker where the major studios produced quality product, artfully achieved and with a sociopolitical conscience. The independent movement of the early '90s saw some of that New Hollywood resolve revived; the quality films of directors Alison Anders, Tom DiCillo, Hal Hartley, Todd Haynes, Robert Rodriguez, David O. Russell, Quentin Tarantino *et al.* heralded a new kind of maverick American Cinema. At a certain point these indie films crossed into the mainstream, seeing some of their directors flirting briefly with major studios while others wholly embraced and remained within the commercial milieu for the long haul. The Burt Reynolds of the 1970s was a figurehead of both acceptable mainstream success and edgier left-field material, and directors Paul Thomas Anderson, Bill Bennett, Clive Fleury, Danny Huston, Alexander Payne and others gave the actor a chance to indulge in characters he wasn't used to playing, characters of questionable morality in stories that privileged themes and ideas over stunts and action. Here, Reynolds provides the perfect amount of absurdist caricature to his pampered moral mouthpiece, complimenting the elastic physical comedy of the long-limbed Dern and the cartoonish mugging of their co-stars.

Notes

1. Peter Biskind, *Down and Dirty Pictures* (Great Britain: Bloomsbury Publishing, 2004), p. 242.
2. Lynn Hirschberg, "Deliverance," *The New York Times*, June 16, 1996, https://www.nytimes.com/1996/06/16/magazine/deliverance.html.

Striptease

(1996)

"You never covered yourself in Vaseline? You don't know what you're missing…."
—Congressman David Dilbeck

Striptease, based on the 1993 Carl Hiaasen novel, tells the story of Erin Grant (Demi Moore), a single working mother battling for custody of her daughter against her petty criminal ex-husband, Darrell (Robert Patrick). Erin works the pole at the Eager Beaver strip club. Her most ardent fan, Republican Congressman David Dilbeck (Reynolds), causes a commotion and public relations nightmare after a bachelor party reveler gets touchy-feely with Erin; Dilbeck breaks camouflage and rushes the stage to smash a bottle of champagne over the offending individual's head and is recognized by another fan of Erin's. As the politician is up for re-election, the fan proceeds to blackmail Dilbeck, pressuring him to persuade a judge to swing Erin's custody battle in her favor, lest the media find out about the scuffle of sleaze. The fan ends up "a floater" in a Florida swamp, which happens to be where vacationing Dade County police officer Al Garcia (Armand Assante) is trying to enjoy some downtime. Cue a murder investigation, political intrigue, sugar industry subterfuge, and bare breasts ... lots of bare breasts.

Striptease is neither a provocative erotic drama nor thought-provoking feminist tract; it is a lark, a political satire masquerading as social justice polemic. The heightened absurdities of the performances all feel right for the satirical tone—all except that of Demi Moore. She plays the film entirely sober while those around her seem to be in on the joke and the general silliness of the enterprise. As politically liberating as the picture may have felt to its star and its filmmakers, the lovingly photographed glimpses of torrid flesh not only fail to arouse in any sense of the word, but they completely undermine any suggestion that *Striptease* is doing a service for independent women. The only service this picture provides is plenty of farcical material for Democrats to laugh at a Republican buffoon caricature, which it admittedly does rather well. Salacious scandals in the political realm were part of the national conversation around the time of the production and it duly takes aim at the hypocrisy of our supposedly genial statesmen.

Reynolds is brilliant as the disgraceful, unethical though likable Congressman, playing the character with such gleeful abandon that his scenes are a comic masterwork in and of themselves. There are too many wonderful scenes of Dilbeck to mention, all of which show-

case Reynolds' comic abilities in full flight, unafraid to make himself look foolish in search of humor whilst retaining immense charm. Even when we are fully aware of his character's more nefarious demeanor and rapscallion ways, Reynolds gives Dilbeck the necessary gravitas when he is required to give speeches on family values, only minutes after parading around his Presidential Suite hotel room decadently covered in Vaseline—"I can feel it squishing between my toes."

A mainstream product with the potential commercial caliber of *Striptease* came around at the right time for Reynolds. Having

Congressman David Dilbeck (Reynolds) is resplendent in cowboy hat, waistcoat and Vaseline in *Striptease* (1996).

gone through various financial difficulties due to ill-fated investments, plus his costly divorce, Reynolds had begun venturing into the world of straight-to-video and independent films. *Striptrease* presented the actor with the opportunity of a major cinema release. Like any jobbing actor, Reynolds took a flight to Florida to audition for the film in front of skeptical director Andrew Bregman and producer Mike Lobell, who both imagined Gene Hackman as their ideal Dilbeck. Hackman turned them down. After auditioning, Reynolds won the role. "I knew I could play him," Reynolds says. "I could make him likable and dangerous. There are very few people who can do that. I always played likable and dangerous. I had a persona. Unfortunately my persona became bigger than my acting."[1]

The picture's fashionable porno chic and liberated sexual mores allow Erin to bring a certain amount of class and taste to the muddied moral waters of her profession. By turning her striptease into performance art, Erin, and the audience, can live with the work. However, her manager Orly (Jerry Grayson) is dismayed at the aesthetically sound tendencies of her show, even chiding her choice of musical accompaniment: Annie Lennox. As Erin embraces what limited artistic expression can be derived from disrobing in front of strange men for money, the film posits the notion that stripping can be a noble profession if given room to be appropriately aestheticized. Of course, with Moore starring as Erin, the character is instantly given a more glamorous quality. She is perfectly and naturally formed, while some of her colleagues are artificially accentuated; she is an independent woman, while others have no other way of making a living; she is artistic, while her colleagues are unrefined. Erin is adored, particularly by the men in her life, such as her manager Orly and club bouncer Shad (Ving Rhames), who protect and nurture her as detective Garcia does. Shad will threaten death by power drill to anyone who dares refer to Erin as a stripper rather than as a dancer. In other words, Erin is not a victim nor is she exploited. She has more than her share of willing patriarchal bodyguards and supporters to protect her from the parade of deadbeat husbands, unscrupulous politicians and lecherous in-laws.

Moore had come off a trio of steamy commercial hits—*Indecent Proposal* (Adrian Lyne, 1993), *Disclosure* (Barry Levinson, 1994) and *The Scarlet Letter* (Roland Joffe, 1995)—and seemed poised to be something of a contemporary Jean Harlow, her casting immediately heralding some kind of cinematic sins to follow. The prime marketing tool for the picture was Moore's body itself, as all variations of the poster artwork featured the actress in various stages of undress or complete undress. While Moore is daring and edgy enough to give the picture some volatile sex appeal, her classical beauty, manicured features and tasteful aesthetics make the seedy world of strip joints seem somewhat less improper, too Hollywood. Director Bergman, producer Rob Reiner, Warner Brothers and Columbia Studios—all major industry players—evidently thought Moore attractive enough to make this a viable project based on her provocative iconography, but perhaps overestimated her ability to carry the film on a performance level.

Regardless, *Striptease* was a hit, though it was a colossal bomb with critics. Many singled out Moore as the chief issue with the film. "[T]he movie is unwisely built as a vehicle for Moore, an actress with no humor, manic or otherwise," wrote *The Washington Post* reviewer, who concluded that the supporting cast "is a fine chunk of talent as well and manages to steal most of the scenes from the wooden Moore."[2] Roger Ebert noted, "[A]ll of the characters are hilarious except for Demi Moore's…. The movie's fatal flaw is to treat her like a plucky Sally Field heroine. That throws a wet blanket over the rest of the party."[3]

There is, however, enough good material in *Striptease* to enjoy, despite Moore's miscasting and the mismarketing of the picture as a controversial erotic drama. The picture is neither erotic nor sexually provocative; it is, however, a funny political satire, particularly great as Reynolds shines (literally) with his parody of the uncouth Republican politician. The picture is punctuated with nicely shot, well-edited dance sequences in which the choreography of Moore's dancing combined with Annie Lennox's pop music works on a purely visceral level.

Notes

1. Lynn Hirschberg, "Deliverance," *The New York Times*, June 16, 1996, https://www.nytimes.com/1996/06/16/magazine/deliverance.html.

2. Eric Brace, "Striptease: Burt Reynolds Outstrips Moore," *The Washington Post*, June 28, 1996, https://www.washingtonpost.com/archive/lifestyle/1996/06/28/striptease-reynolds-outstrips-moore/28794142–1672–4f3b-a119–4e8ec6efdf1e/?noredirect=on&utm_term=.198c69f18657.

3. Roger Ebert, "Striptease," *Chicago Sun-Times*, June 28, 1996, https://www.rogerebert.com/reviews/striptease-1996.

Frankenstein and Me

(1996)

"It's what I've always wanted to do: to paint my dreams on a silver screen."
—Les Williams

Set in a small town in the Mojave Desert in 1970, the charming *Frankenstein and Me* focuses on Earl Williams (Jamieson Boulanger), a 12-year-old horror obsessive who daydreams of bringing Frankenstein's Monster back to life. None of this sits well with his strict teacher, Mrs. Perdue (Louise Fletcher), or his hard-working mother Judy (Miriam Cyr). His predilection for the fantastical finds a more sympathetic supporter in his father Les (Reynolds). Les was once a dreamer himself, a failed actor who gave up on his dreams too early; he even issues Earl and his brother Larry copies of *Famous Monsters of Filmland*. The Williams kids, along with their friend Kenny (Ryan Gosling), sneak out on Halloween night to catch a drive-in screening of *Night of the Living Dead* but are busted by a local cop and marched home. Along the way, Earl receives some devastating news: Les has had a heart attack. Not long after the kids arrive at the hospital, Les dies. With his father gone, Earl is bereft of the one person in the world who understood his passion and validated it. Judy, a staunch pragmatist, cruelly uses Les' failures in life as a warning to Earl that "dreaming doesn't pay the bills" and forces him to focus even more on his schoolwork, despite already good report cards. When a carnival arrives in town, Earl visits it to view the body of the purported real-life Frankenstein's Monster, bought by the carnival in Budapest in 1948 and traveling with the show ever since. Earl's fascination is satisfied even further when he sees the monster's coffin failling from a truck while the carnival is moving out of town. With the possibility of having a dream realized, Earl puts it down to destiny and decides to load the coffin onto his father's truck and haul it to a gothic-looking mining shack where he fancies bringing the body back to life.

Earl's immersion into the world of horror keeps him young while his teacher and mother force the real world prematurely upon him with derision. Mrs. Purdue, complete with 1950s conservative attire and sense of moral panic, makes the case to a judge that Earl be sent to a reform school so that other kids are safe from the child's "sick sensibilities." Only then does Judy become an advocate for Earl's interests and support him against the prig Purdue. When you are 12, the excitement of a surreptitious

Les Williams (Reynolds) calls the shots as a director in Heaven in *Frankenstein and Me* (1996).

screening of *Night of the Living Dead* should indeed be more important than thinking about making ends meet. Earl and Larry's devotion to the fantastical also functions as a portal of escape: When Larry is bedridden in hospital with a throat problem, Earl takes his mind away from the malaise and into a fanciful world of monsters and vampires.

The straight-to-video production values and mild children's horror give *Frankenstein and Me* the feel of an extended episode of *Goosebumps* or *Eerie Indiana*. It is a polite entertainment that would appeal to any young horror fan, nicely capturing the wonders of film frights for an innocent youth. It astutely details a deep father-son bond cut short and ruminates on the notion that something seen as trivial to other people—a love of horror movies—can actually be the glue that binds a relationship, be it familial or friendly, and provide the fertile ground for a bond to develop into something deep and meaningful. Les may have failed in the pursuit of his dreams, but he is not bitter. His life taking an alternative direction resulted in his creation of a loving family. Reynolds gives a performance of nuance and sensitivity, rendering Les as a decent man of love and compassion, that which makes his loss so devastating to his children, and the audience. With his own inclination to dream and love of movies, Les was much more than a father to Earl and Larry, he was their friend. In a deeply poignant climactic scene, Earl daydreams of filming a horror picture, only to hear a familiar voice yell "Cut!" It is Les, who is bestowed with a heavenly glow and looks resplendent in his directors' chair. Though imagined, the moment allows Earl a sense of closure to say goodbye to his father in a manner befitting them both, in the pursuit of making monster movie magic and engaging in the shared passion that brought them close together.

Mad Dog Time

(1996)

"Who would've thought it, our Vic a paranoid schizophrenic. All this time I thought he was just a putz!"—Ben London

Mad Dog Time opens with an ominous voiceover that somewhat awkwardly declares, "On the other side of the cosmos, in deep space, a parallel universe was born: Nick's World. It was joyful, it was … full of joy. Nick's World was goddamn fuckin' full of joy!" And just what is this Nick's World? It's a milieu of swanky art deco nightclubs and well-attired gangsters such as Ben London (Gabriel Byrne) and Mickey Holliday (Jeff Goldblum). Mickey, a refined hoodlum, finds himself in the complicated situation of being involved with not one but two femme fatale bombshells, Grace Everly (Diane Lane) and her sister Rita (Ellen Barkin). The problem is not that he is in love with a pair of sisters, but Grace is the moll of the elusive Vic (Richard Dreyfuss), a feared gangster who also happens to be Mickey's boss. Vic's arrival is imminent, having taken a leave of absence as kingpin while undergoing psychiatric treatment for schizophrenia. While he rested in his diminished capacity, various other factions have been quarrelling over territorial control. Vic's return causes much upset among the city's warring mob bosses.

This is where the colorfully named criminal avatars such as Jules Flamingo (Gregory Hines) drop in, say hi, and wave goodbye, figuratively of course. A parade of great cinematic faces, including Billy Drago, Michael J. Pollard and Henry Silva come and go; even British punk rocker Billy Idol appears as foul-mouthed gangland rival Lee Turner, who is introduced and then efficiently dispatched. In another baffling moment, Paul Anka arrives on stage crooning "My Way," the iconic song that Anka wrote for Frank Sinatra in 1969. So far, so bizarre; but Anka is joined by the grimacing, off-key Ben for the rendition, which leads to the egomaniacal hood being dispatched, presumably for crimes against music. Meanwhile, Reynolds is wasted on this material and barely afforded the time to flesh out his menacing hoodlum, Jacky Johnson. We do, however, get an opportunity to once again see Reynolds briefly pitted against his former *Sharky's Machine* foe Henry Silva, who as always is a maniacal and unique screen presence.

It becomes clear pretty quickly that the presence of all these actors is for mere window dressing, paraded for fleeting recognition only to be dispatched unceremoniously in a series of contrived set pieces which generally take place when rival goons have a showdown while sitting at tables facing each other. With such arbitrary instances of mayhem, no time or investment is given to these people, which is especially surprising given the casting of "name" actors. A procession of celebrities cannot substitute for an actual coherent narrative. Director-writer Larry Bishop's script is full of bizarre, quasi-philosophical hard-boiled dialogue which makes the picture very hard to digest. Byrne's performance as Ben London is supposed to be eccentric but he comes across as obnoxious, particularly so as Byrne is given the most egregious dialogue, such as "Vic does not want you dead any more, but God does," "I'm a practicing Ben Buddhist" and the classic "I think your best bet is to tell him he's killed you already, and hope that he believes you." The picture's absurd, idiosyncratic humor distances us from any real engagement in the characters and their story. As such, *Mad Dog Time* is a celluloid vessel completely devoid of any sense of drama or pathos. The picture is pure artifice and the smoking gun evidence of its superficial regard to character is their homophonic names: Vic, Mick and Nick. The filmmakers actually believe that rhyming such names constitutes a sense of humor. Consider such lines: "Vic is a sick prick, Mick," and "You mean Jake pulled a Nick trick?" or "Micky, meet Nicky!" Yes, this is the kind of picture where this substitutes for actual comedy.

It must be acknowledged that *Mad Dog Time* is handsomely rendered and nicely photographed; Nick's World is a chic and timeless netherworld populated by stylish criminals and stunning showgirls. However, such grand design is wasted as the setting for such a dismal, inexplicable exercise in ego inflation that must have been pitched thusly: four men sit in a room spouting over-written dialogue and then shoot each other. Repeat *ad nauseam*.

Raven
(1996)

"Compassion? Oh, I took that in night school. I failed it!"—Jerome Katz

Jerome "Raven" Katz is the tough leader of a mercenary team on assignment in Bosnia to obtain a Soviet satellite decoder. The team is sacrificed by a group of corrupt C.I.A. officials who plan on handing over the device to the Iranians. Raven has better plans: to sell it on the black market for $50 million. Fellow soldier Martin Grant (Matt Battaglia) wants to return the device to the company before quitting for peaceful civilian life: "I said I'm getting out, not selling out!" But Raven refuses to relinquish the goods, leading to a mid-flight punch-up between the former comrades, resulting in their pilot getting shot and the helicopter crashing into a lake. Grant survives and is later seen leading a regular life, haunted by his experiences in Bosnia, while the C.I.A. men responsible for the betrayal are now Senators wielding their influence through the corridors of power in Washington. Thought to be dead, Raven returns to seek revenge on those who hoodwinked him into the death trap.

Director Russell Solberg was a Hollywood stuntman and occasional filmmaker, mainly dealing in television work such as episodes of *Renegade*, and with the intermittent straight-to-video action picture (*Payback*, 1991; *Forced to Kill*, 1994). Here Solberg delivered a satisfyingly routine revenge fantasy that works as a cheap, no-frills thriller, indistinguishable from the director's previous two pictures only for the presence of its major star. Reynolds had two major studio releases either side of the video premiere of this picture, *Striptease* and *Boogie Nights*, both of which catapulted him back into the national consciousness. The picture also marked the first major role for Matt Battaglia, a graduate of the Burt Reynolds Institute for Theater Training who had minor roles in *B.L. Stryker* and *Evening Shade* and went on to star in a series of pictures with Reynolds. A former linebacker for the Philadelphia Eagles, Battaglia has a commanding physical presence, ideal for the hero of an action adventure such as this. His stoic reserve is in perfect contrast to Reynolds' garrulous general.

Aesthetically, there isn't much to admire about the picture, but it does entertain as a vehicle for Reynolds as a tough, wise-cracking angel of vengeance. "I'd shoot you in the belly, but it'd take about five years to reach your heart," Raven menacingly affirms to one of his huskier victims. And despite the lower profile of the project, the star was at least able to enjoy some autonomy on the project, a privilege which may have softened the blow of having to accept material well below his standard. "I've changed every word of mine in the film," he told a *New York Times* reporter during filming. "It's a part I can play…. It's my part, my persona. And if you play a pink flamingo, you can play one for life, if it's a hit." When Reynolds wielded his considerable control and declared to producer Stu Segall that he had indeed altered the script. Segall conferred free rein to Reynolds with the satisfying reminder, "That's okay…you're the star!"[1] That he truly was.

Note

1. Lynn Hirschberg, "Deliverance," *The New York Times*, June 16, 1996, https://www.nytimes.com/1996/06/16/magazine/deliverance.html

The Cherokee Kid
(Made-for-Television, 1996)

> "This right here is a Bowie Knife; Jim gave it to me a long time ago. You take that, go on out there and kill yourself a critter; make a blankie out of it!"
> —Otter Bob

The Cherokee Kid opens with a showdown on a dusty western street. The titular Kid is engaged in a duel with the Undertaker (Gregory Hines). When it comes time to draw, the Undertaker proves to be faster. As the Kid is felled, the story winds back and proceeds in flashback form. We learn that the Cherokee Kid is actually Isaiah Turner, a youngster from a hardworking farming family who becomes a legend in the Oklahoma Territories for fighting off the industrialists forcing homesteaders to sell their land dirt cheap. Turner vowed vengeance after his family was gunned down by powerful railroad tycoon Cyrus B. Bloomington (James Coburn), who declares, "Nobody can stand in the way of progress!" Eighteen years later, the Kid's hunger for vengeance remains undiminished and he takes off on a "magnificent quest." He consistently bungles his opportunity for retribution, not knowing a thing about gun slinging, though he does later become proficient in the use of throwing knives and axes thanks to his burgeoning friendship with Otter Bob (*the* Otter Bob?!), a grizzly mountain man and noble savage, played by Reynolds. A friendship blossoms between the pair despite the Kid's loquaciousness and Bob's stoicism; in essence, they complete each other. Otter Bob introduces the Kid to the ways of the rugged West: how to catch and skin an animal, and how to drink whiskey. After Otter Bob meets an early demise thanks to merciless tracker Frank Bonner (Mark Pellegrino), the Kid befriends another legendary figure, Nat Love aka Deadwood Dick ("a man of such character; a man of such … cojones!"), played by Ernie Hudson. Just like Otter Bob, Love gives the Kid a taste of manhood by introducing him to the outlaw way of life, which the Kid takes to rather well as exemplified by his bank robbing skills. With Bloomington poised for governorship, whereby he could control the land and its people and remain untouchable by law, the Kid sets out to attract the attention of the tycoon by robbing his banks. The Kid makes the papers and raises the ire of Bloomington, who is forced to hire the deadliest gun in the west, the Undertaker, to take care of his problem. And so the film comes full circle as the Cherokee Kid meets the Undertaker for a high noon showdown on main street of Larabee, Texas.

The Cherokee Kid exists in that brief window of Hollywood history where comedian Sinbad was something of a big deal and a marquee name. In the same year that *Cherokee Kid* premiered on HBO as one of their original productions, Sinbad was also appearing on the big screen in the festive Arnold Schwarzenegger picture *Jingle All the Way*. Sinbad is an engaging and likable presence, ideal for such light material, while Reynolds too plays Otter Bob as an absurdist creation, right to his dying word. The veteran actors here, Reynolds and Coburn, ham it up and bring some Hollywood glamour to the otherwise cheap and cheerful product. Successful television director Paris Barclay keeps any overt cinematic style to a minimum as the picture rarely betrays its small screen origin. Harmless and inoffensive, this is cartoon cowboy stuff that plays with the conventions of the American western picture for laughs; the plot is purely by-the-numbers and exists merely as a vessel to deliver Sinbad to his audience. The comedian gets to unload a series of one-liners, wave a Derringer around and generally play cowboy for 90 minutes. As contemporary comedy westerns go, it is no *¡Three Amigos!*, but it can certainly sit alongside also-rans such as *Lightning Jack* and *Shanghai Noon*.

Meet Wally Sparks
(1997)

"I hate Wally Sparks!"—Governor Floyd Preston

Wally Sparks is a character that Rodney Dangerfield was born to play. A self-important, flippant, attention-obsessed tabloid talk show host, Sparks is a vulgar amalgamation of Morton Downey Jr., Jerry Springer and Roseanne Barr (all of whom appear here as themselves), whose brand of politically incorrect hosting is causing an exodus of viewers and is straining relations with network management. Reynolds plays network head Larry Spencer, a handsome and powerful executive complete with fawning sycophant executive underling Alan Miller (Eamonn Roche). In an effort to boost ratings, Sparks' producer Sandy Gallo (Debi Mazar) concocts a plan to air a show in which the presenter interviews his fiercest and most vocal opponent: the governor of Georgia, Floyd Preston (David Ogden Stiers). If pulled off correctly, this coup could make Sparks' show more appealing to conservative viewers and boost ratings. Preston's malcontent son Robby invites Sparks to a reception at the Governor's Mansion, where Sparks fakes an injury and temporarily ingratiates himself into the Preston household. Will the outlandish entertainer and the stuffy politician make up and become friends by picture's end? Is there any doubt?

In a picture of such lowbrow aspirations, there's little to applaud other than the amusing performances and Dangerfield's very funny one-liners. Reynolds is excellent in his brief screen time, shooting down his toady sidekick at every opportunity with his keen bullshit detector. The potential for a searing satire on the daytime talk show arena is squandered in favor of a tired narrative that focuses on the strained relationship between Sparks and Preston, two men of opposing moral and political divides who grudgingly come to respect and perhaps even love one another. Such mawkish sentimentality sits in contrast with Dangerfield's caustic, uncompromising sense of humor. Director and erstwhile actor Peter Baldwin assembled the film in a thoroughly workmanlike fashion with a minimum of style. *Meet Wally Sparks* is a missed opportunity, but remains an entertaining time-waster.

Bean

(1997)

"Bean, are you presently on any medication? You certainly could use some."
—Lt. Brutus

Bean (Rowan Atkinson), a bumbling man-child, works as a security guard at London's Royal National Gallery. He is entirely inept even at the most basic element of his job: to stay awake and protect the paintings. The gallery's board of executives, unable to fire Bean, decide to send him to America to oversee the acquisition of the James McNeil Whistler painting *Arrangement in Gray and Black No. 1* (aka *Whistler's Mother*) at the Grierson Art Gallery in Los Angeles. The painting was purchased and donated to the gallery by a generous patron of the arts, Gen. Newton (Reynolds). Grierson curator David Langley (Peter MacNicol) mistakes Bean for an important art professor and invites the foreigner into his home for the duration of the visit. Langley's residence more closely resembles an obscure art instillation than an actual home, while his more traditional wife and children endure a strained relationship with their unusual guest. The film follows Bean's attempts to navigate the Los Angeles way of life, skate through his appointment to the Grierson Gallery, and ultimately endear himself to his hosts.

When British comedy star Atkinson brought his small screen creation Mr. Bean to the big screen in 1997, few would have thought that the uniquely English humor of the silent comic series would have translated into the spectacular box office returns accrued in its theatrical run. With Richard Curtis (*Four Weddings and a Funeral*, 1994; *Notting Hill*, 1999; *Love Actually*, 2003) co-writing and UK comedy star Mel Smith (*Morons from Outer Space*, 1985; *The Princess Bride*, 1987; *Wilt*, 1989) directing, *Bean* contains the right pedigree to produce the goods. It certainly delivered in financial terms, if not entirely in laughs. Atkinson's Jacques Tati–esque shenanigans boded well in short bursts on television screens in its initial programming throughout the mid–90s, but an 80-minute cinematic treatment means the silent character must attempt at least some verbal engagement with those around him, as well as to actually become involved in a feature-length narrative. While Bean's absurdist escapades were funny in the confined space and humble environs of the television sitcom, the character is left floundering on film. MacNicol carries the story on his own unique comic sensibilities, ably assisted by the delightful Pamela Reed as his burdened and rather sensible wife Alison.

Amidst a distinguished cast that includes Sir John Mills and Harris Yulin, Reynolds' appearance as Gen. Newton briefly lends the film further Hollywood star power. The name Newton evokes Reynolds' character Wood Newton from *Evening Shade*, though there is nothing to suggest this was an intentional reference or in-joke. Another allusion to the star's screen past is the presence of Peter MacNicol, Reynolds' co-star in the 1986 thriller *Heat*. In that picture they made a fine screen duo, a pairing of contrasting physical and moral stature; here they aren't afforded any moments to once again display such chemistry.

Boogie Nights

(1977)

"I've got a feeling there's something wonderful in those jeans waiting to come out."—Jack Horner

Boogie Night welcomes us into the heady environs of the San Fernando Valley of 1977, the world of Jack Horner (Reynolds), a successful director of adult films, and his coterie of actors, technicians and wannabes. These lost souls are Jack's "family," and for a few of them it is a much better life than that at home. Among Jack's loyal friends are Amber Waves (Julianne Moore), a porn actress engaged in custody proceedings with her husband, and Rollergirl (Heather Graham), the eager starlet whose quirk of never taking off her skates (even for sex) has earned her the unique handle. Jack is taken by the youthful beauty and considerable bulge in the trousers of nightclub busboy Eddie Adams (Mark Wahlberg) and offers to audition the kid for work in his films. After a successful romp with Rollergirl (the aforementioned "audition"), Eddie gets the job and soon finds he is valued in the world of porn, going on to considerable acclaim as a formidable screen talent. But "Eddie Adams" is no name for a star, but "Dirk Diggler" is a name that not even the searing bulbs of a marquee could handle; "so bright and sharp," Eddie says of his new appellation, "that the sign, it just blows up because the name is so powerful." And with that, Jack gives his blessings and a star is born.

From here, *Boogie Nights* skillfully traces the hedonistic days of disco, depicting the late '70s as an endless summer of parties and porn, when filmmakers like Jack had some dignity and pride in their product before video took porn from the big screens of seedy grindhouse movie theaters to the sordid back-store video shelves. For a film immersed in the world of pornography, *Boogie Nights* is far from salacious; rather, Anderson takes us on a backstage tour of the industry and its more clinical requirements, such as the funding of an adult picture, as Jack explains, "You got your camera, you got your film, you got your lights, you got your synching, you got your editing, you got your lab. Before you turn around, you've spent maybe $25,000 or $30,000." The sex depicted on screen is clinically shot, often viewed through the lens of cinematographer Kurt Longjohn (Ricky

Kurt Longjohn (Ricky Jay) and Jack Horner (Reynolds) film a scene in *Boogie Nights* (1997).

Jay) while love scenes are left to the imagination. Of course, the good times cannot be celebrated forever, as cheap drugs and cheap porn derail the industry from decadence to depravity. The film becomes most brilliant as the third act takes us out of the frivolous, decadent '70s and brings us into the '80s literally with a bang, and some brain matter. Anderson details the move of shooting adult pictures on film to the burgeoning, cost-effective format of VHS. Cameraman Longjohn, a cinematic purist of sorts, urges the already reluctant Jack to resist shooting on video, but the way of the future prevails much to the misfortune of Horner and his clan of actors. As the porn industry shifts to murkier territory, with an influx of more tawdry product and willing participants, Eddie, Roller-girl, Amber and the others drift into a pit of despair that brings them closer to drug dependency and prostitution.

Director Paul Thomas Anderson signals his maverick sensibilities right from the opening frames of *Boogie Nights*, a picture with such studious devotion to the culture of American cinema of the 1970s that it immediately draws parallels with the filmmakers of that era. The narrative sweep, ensemble casting and procession of characters invites comparisons to Robert Altman epics such as *Nashville*, while its unflinching trek into the sordid underbelly of society evokes Paul Schrader's work. The film contains an intricately choreographed single-take Steadicam shot, and not only that but Anderson sets out his stall and achieves it immediately, introducing all the major characters of the picture within the space of the first three minutes in a virtuosic display of film style. Indeed, *Boogie Nights* is a sophisticated piece of work, boldly declaring Anderson's skill as a storyteller and pop-culture scholar.

One of the greatest elements of the production is the exquisitely compiled soundtrack, taking in everything from the '70s disco of the Emotions' "Best of My Love" to the polished '80s New Wave of Nena's "99 Red Balloons" and the best of the era's radio rock.

At the time of making the picture, Anderson issued his thoughts on working with Reynolds:

> He's a great actor and a great guy, so those two things ... once you sort of get past the fact that he's an icon and it's Burt Reynolds standing in front of you, you just look at the two basic things, which are "Is he a good man?" and "Is he a good actor?" and he is those two things. And he's wonderful. He had a lot to offer and a lot to bring to it.[1]

While *Citizen Ruth* and *Striptease* once again brought Reynolds to the attention of critics, *Boogie Nights* can be credited with bringing the star back into the Hollywood mainstream and into the hearts of a new generation of film fans. This picture brought the star long-overdue critical accolades and approbation, that which he had not received since the height of *Evening Shade*; he was Oscar-nominated (Best Supporting Actor) but lost to Robin Williams for *Good Will Hunting*. While the Oscar may have eluded him, Reynolds did win a Golden Globe, a Golden Satellite Award and various film critics' association awards. No doubt about it, Reynolds is outstanding here, but he had something of a difficult relationship with *Boogie Nights* over the years, having initially found the character of Jack Horner distasteful for various reasons. When Anderson called Reynolds to ask him to play the part, the actor told the director that glamorizing porn was not a good idea and that he wanted no part of it, "*Boogie Nights* revived my career, but I did my best not to do it," Reynolds said. "But he kept calling. And I kept turning him down."[2] Reynolds soon embraced the idea of playing a character he had no respect for as an acting challenge, and achieved this by exploring a theme that has interested him throughout his entire career: family. "I searched for something positive in him: a sense of humor, a desire to do good work even though deep down he knew it wasn't appreciated. I began to think of *Boogie Nights* as family saga, with Jack as the father figure."[3]

Boogie Nights is loaded with ideas on the familial malaise. The characters that populate the picture find in the porn world a familial connection that has eluded them in their real nuclear family life. The model of middle-class stability fails them when they don't meet social expectations, such as achieving high school grades or having a respectable job, and they end up the recipients of parental and legal retribution. In the reversal of familial roles, we see that the suburban ideal has broken down for these people; physical and verbal abuse, taunting and undermining are part of the everyday culture of domesticity that is supposed to be their sanctuary.

One of the more troubling characters is not at all active in the porn industry but is a symbol of "good people": a domesticated wife and mother. That character is the Adams matriarch, played by Joanna Gleason. She is cold and cruel to her husband, who attempts affection with her only to be rebuked and humiliated, but she is outright abusive to Eddie, scolding him as a loser for his waywardness and lack of academic ambition. She tears down the posters of film and music icons from his wall in a fit of anger, provoking her otherwise mild-mannered son to near-aggression, all while his passive father ignores the conflict. It is with his porn family that Eddie finds love and acceptance, where substituting for his tyrannical mother is Amber, who engenders their intimate bond via sex, both on the set of their pornography films and in private. Amber simultaneously craves and coddles her surrogate son's body and that is one of the few notions of perversion that the picture offers us regarding the side effects of one's immersion into the porn lifestyle. Amber similarly embraces a mothering role to Rollergirl, but instead of an exchange of sex, their familial bond is solidified by sharing mirrors of cocaine.

Boogie Nights is an ambitious, multi-layered parable depicting a corrupt vision of the American Dream. The fun and frivolity of the first half of the picture gives way to the downside of such a lifestyle. Eddie's ego gets the better of him with the help of narcotic dependency; Amber loses custody of her child after the judge hears about the inappropriate environment that Amber could be exposing her child to; Rollergirl beats up a boorish reveler who recognizes her from porn tapes and from school. Even peripheral characters meet an unfortunate fate, such as Jack's assistant director Little Bill Thompson (William H. Macy), who shoots his wife and then himself after she repeatedly cuckolds him with younger, muscular men; producer Col. James (Robert Ridgely) ends up in prison after being caught in possession of illegal pornographic images.

And despite all of this tragedy, somehow *Boogie Nights* remains a rare piece of work that draws us into such a steamy and seamy milieu only to leave us feeling like we've just witnessed a tale of great human positivity and empathy. With Reynolds' in the role of Jack Horner, de facto patriarch of the *Boogie Nights* family, the story has a solid figure of decency and dignity, and when the picture occasionally errs on the satirical, Reynolds remains the film's emotional and moral anchor. But despite the plaudits, the awards, and the acclaim, Reynolds looked back upon his much-lauded role with typically wry sarcasm: "*Boogie Nights* changed things around for me. It gave me an audience I hadn't had before: people who go to Sting concerts."[4]

Notes

1. Paul Thomas Anderson, "Interview," DVD Supplement, *Boogie Nights*, Entertainment in Video, 1999.
2. Burt Reynolds, *But Enough About Me* (London: Blink Publishing, 2015), p. 216–217.
3. *Ibid.*, p. 217
4. Gayle MacDonald, "Still Slim. Still Gorgeous. Still Burt," *The Globe and Mail*, December 3, 2001, https://www.theglobeandmail.com/arts/still-slim-still-gorgeous-still-burt/article4157114/.

Big City Blues

(1997)

"What's important is that they're all men frogs on a night out looking for women frogs, a real hetero thing!"—Babs

Set across one eventful Miami night, *Big City Blues* is comprised of a multi-strand narrative structure that ties three exclusive storylines and a trio of couples together for the final act. Connors and Hudson (Reynolds and William Forsythe) are hitmen, while Angela (Georgina Cates) is a prostitute with modeling ambitions who meets aspiring rock star Walter (Balthazer Getty) on her quest to find her elusive doppelganger, whom she believes keeps crossing her path. Angela's lookalike, Marsha, is the intended target of Connors and Hudson. Angela is almost murdered in a case of mistaken identity but is saved when her ringing pager displays the phone number of a gangland boss (her regular john) which scares off his goons. Ayre Gross and Giancarlo Esposito play partying transvestites Babs and Georgie, respectively; their drug dealer Chrissie has upset Connors and Hudson's boss, leading to a showdown in which all six characters end up in a violent confrontation.

Director Clive Fleury emerged from some of Australian television's most recognizable productions (*Neighbours, Sons and Daughters, Home and Away*) and a background in documentary filmmaking (*The Call of the Frock, Turning Music into Gold, Funny Girls*) before making his foray into feature film production with *Fatal Past* (1993) and *Tunnel Vision* (1994). Those expecting a routine genre picture may be disappointed as *Big City Blues* is no ordinary picture; at first glance it may feel derivative of the kind of quirky crime picture of the era but Fleury soon reveals his own distinctly unorthodox style in which he tempers the picture's tense, gritty crime drama with dollops of absurdist comedy and a heavy dose of surrealism. Whether it is a cartoonish Santa Claus sitting in gridlocked traffic, a garish Amphibian party, or the day-glo gender reassignment operation anxiety dream of a transsexual, nothing is too uncanny for this picture. Once you can submit to the idiosyncratic charm of *Big City Blues* you will find a cheeky, perverse sense of humor that belies the plot's more sober elements and it is very easy to become beguiled by the picture's unique modus operandi.

In one hilarious sequence, Connors ends up as the next sacrifice of a blood cult operating in the basement of leader Kyle's parents' house. Just as a semi-nude, S&M clad Connors is about to "get the chicken," the cult leader's mother enters and inquires if the boys would like some supper. While the picture's avant-garde style and elliptical leaps of narrative serve it best, there are occasional touches of pathos which allow for some moments of humanity amongst the more unconventional flavors of the production; Georgie's existential malaise as a transsexual-in-transition and his affectionate relationship with Babs affords the film some emotional gravity.

Throughout American cinema of the 1990s, the crime picture received a resurgence of interest, led by the critical and cultural approbation of Quentin Tarantino's *Reservoir Dogs* (1992) and the commercial success of his follow-up *Pulp Fiction* (1994). Suddenly the arthouse crime picture became a thing and with a thriving indie film industry behind them, pictures such as Hal Hartley's *Amateur*, Jack Baran's *Destiny Turns on the Radio*, Alan Taylor's *Palookaville* and John Dahl's *Red Rock West* paid homage to the great history of stylish U.S. and European crime pictures. These hip, edgy productions are often marked with a distinct sense of irony and an almost academic knowledge of the history of the genre. Sure enough, *Big City Blues* opens brilliantly with an expertly fashioned homage to the French New Wave and to the casual criminals of Jean Luc Godard and François Truffaut, tastefully shot in rich black-and-white in the immediate handheld style of the Nouvelle Vague masters. It's a remarkable start to a picture which is extremely difficult to describe according to any standard generic registers; it turns out the art film we're watching is being exhibited in a theater and watched by the sharply dressed Connors, who leaves the cinema and meets up with his younger associate, Hudson. In their conversation, Connors wistfully remarks on the dearth of subtitles in the badly dubbed imports of foreign films. It is this kind of self-referential cinematic commentary that was a major component of the '90s indie crime drama. *Big City Blues* is sharply aware of its own uniqueness and it may take a viewer with a similar kind of pop-cultural literacy to truly appreciate the qualities of Fleury's picture.

An Interview with Clive Fleury

Filmmaker Clive Fleury began his career in television in the 1980s, directing episodes of Australia's most popular TV shows of the time. He is also credited with co-creating the massively popular Australian soap opera *Home and Away*. In the early 1990s, he moved into feature film production; his first was the steamy drama *Fatal Past* (1993). After finishing his second feature, the Patsy Kensit thriller *Tunnel Vision* (1995), Fleury decided to make a picture in the United States. That film would be *Big City Blues*, starring Burt Reynolds.

Wayne: Big City Blues *is a very original kind of film. can you tell me about the genesis of it?*

Clive: I wrote the script for *Big City Blues* when I was still in Australia. Later on, I went to America to make *Tunnel Vision*, and after that I decided to stay. While I was here, I was able to raise the cash to make the film with a company called Storm Entertainment. They had a list of people who they thought would make the picture immediately financeable and one of them was Burt Reynolds. So I approached his then-manager who came back and said, "No, not interested," and I thought that was the end of that. Just as we assumed that there was no hope of getting Burt on board, we ended up hearing from his assistant, who contacted us to say that Burt found the script and really wanted to do it. So I met with Burt at a hotel in Bel Air to discuss it, well, *tried* to discuss it as there was a rogue piano player who kept playing really loud, and when we raised our voices so we could hear each other, the piano player would hit the keys even louder.

Burt was on board after that. I actually lived close to his good friend Hal Needham, who directed him on many pictures, and one day I decided I would call and tell him I was about to work with Burt and ask him some questions. Hal and Burt loved each other, they were great friends. Hal told me that Burt likes to believe that he's not really an actor, which was kind of hard for me to understand being that I was about to direct him as an actor, but I understood what Hal was saying.

What did you take Hal to mean?

Having now worked with him, I guess that Burt would probably be too embarrassed to admit that he does love acting, because I have seen the amount of time and skill he puts into giving the best performance possible. What Hal meant is that Burt has never been able to reconcile with his love of acting because he never considered it a manly job or a masculine profession, probably because of the makeup and that side of it, or probably because it stands in contrast to the blue collar environment that he grew up around. That's probably why he loves doing stunts; he comes from a football background and the stunt work is as close to that as you can get. But I think he genuinely does love just doing the work. It's not as if he needs the money. He might not be as wealthy as he once was, but he could easily sit at home in his big house in Jupiter, never make another film again, and still live very well. But he chooses to work and also continues to teach acting, which he has been doing for decades.

Reynolds and director Clive Fleury on the set of *Big City Blues* (1997) (photograph courtesy Clive Fleury Collection).

Burt would spend pretty much all of the film in the company of his partner in crime, played by William Forsythe, and given their screen time together the chemistry needed to be absolutely right between the two actors. How did you go about casting Forsythe?

I met with William Forsythe at a hotel in Hollywood and I remember it being a strange meeting because William told me that he felt he had to do the film because of a dream that he had in which he was acting in a crime picture with Burt Reynolds. As strange as it sounds, it got my attention. William is a fantastic, intense actor and as you say the chemistry was important; William and Burt got on very well together. I think it is partially attributable to the fact that William has a very hot temper, as Burt has been similarly known to have, and when Burt witnessed him in an argument with someone, I think he saw a bit of a kindred spirit. I remember Burt saying, "Hey, he makes me look good!"

So how did you find working with Burt?

Burt likes to be directed, he trusts his director. He doesn't just roll onto the set and do his own thing, he is methodical. One day I was occupied trying to work out a scene with the cinematographer and Burt came over and asked me to talk to him about the character and the scene so that he would know precisely what he was going to do when we were ready to roll. You have to remember that Burt is the product of the old studio system. He is extremely professional and knows exactly where his marks are and where the light will be.

As you say, he comes from the old studio system, and so how did he find his newfound place working in this milieu of independent productions and arthouse films?

Burt had just shot *Boogie Nights* and *Striptease* and he was going through some sort of revival. We shot *Big City Blues* before *Boogie Nights* was released and for Burt that was just another film; he didn't seem too convinced of its merits. I don't think he had gotten along very well with Paul Thomas Anderson and he had said to me that he thought it was going to be a major flop and be forgotten. I found him a pleasure to work with even if we clashed a little bit early on over the look of the character.

What was it about the character that instigated the clash?

There are some things Burt is edgy about and one of those is his appearance. Our costume designer was Patricia Field, who went on to become the costume designer on *Sex and the City*, and I remember when Burt came in for costuming he was wearing this big country and western type outfit and announced, "I'll be wearing this!" Well, it wasn't long before Patricia set about fixing that. He has his own makeup artist and the kind of pan makeup they were using isn't always appropriate for certain films, especially in certain light, it doesn't photograph very well or it tends to look obvious. He is very protective of this and you will never see him being photographed while his makeup is being applied. Another thing was his hair. Because his character is aged and weary, I wanted his hair to be gray, but famously Burt wears his hair dark black and didn't want to wear it gray.

So how did you both resolve it?

This is the kind of guy Burt is, one of the things that makes him special. At one of our first meetings on the production, Burt arrives at the office wearing a cowboy hat, completely obscuring his hair. He knew that I wanted him to have the gray hair, but he sat there throughout our whole conversation without ever referencing the hair or removing his cowboy hat. And I never brought it up either. I thought to myself, "This is a disaster. I'm never going to get him to change his hair." So as he was leaving the office, he turned around and took off the hat and there it was: the gray hair that I had wanted for the character, and he smiled and walked out. He got me! He was taking the piss out of me, waiting for me to say something and I never did. So he wore his hair the way I wanted it for the film.

Aside from the gray hair, there are some scenes in there that we're not used to seeing Burt take part in.

There were times when it was challenging for Burt; he was doing stuff he never had to do before. For the scene where he's captured and about to be tortured, we had him wandering around on set at all hours of the morning in that S&M outfit, which he wasn't too happy about. It didn't help that he was going through some problems at that time; there was his divorce, the failure of some of his business ventures, and he was working on *Striptease* where he wasn't getting along with Demi Moore. He was brought up through the studio system, became the biggest star in the world for several years consecutively and here he is working on this low-budget indie film with a very small trailer and working long hours at night. I really appreciate that he chose to work on my film and bring all that skill to the production, when he really didn't have to or need to.

What are your lasting impressions of Burt having worked with him on an intense shoot like this?

Burt did me a huge favor in taking on the role and being in my film. It was a 22-day shoot and we had Burt for 12 days, so we were running on a tight schedule and working a lot of night shoots, which can be tough. We couldn't go over the 12 days because the *Striptease* people had him under contract for any possible re-shoots and pick-up shots should they have been required. If Burt was in a two-shot, you really needed everything to go right and everybody to nail it within a maximum of three takes, because after three takes Burt's energy would just drop. You have to remember his age and the fact that these were very draining night shoots. He comes from that very professional style of studio film-making, whereas some of the younger actors could easily do 12 takes and keep going. Older actors like Burt don't have massive techniques, they just know what to do and get it done. It has to be difficult going from being the #1 movie star in the world to working on this small independent film. I think he was also seeing some of the guys that he came up with, people like Clint Eastwood, who were able to retain their popular appeal and power within the industry while his had declined somewhat…. I'm sure that has to affect you.

What do you consider to be the ingredients for Burt's appeal?

Burt is a very charming man, both on screen and on the set. When I worked with him, he was in his 60s and he was still very fit and well-built up top. He had these wide shoulders and was very muscular, so there's still an element of sex appeal to him. We shot the film in Miami which is Burt's stomping ground, and it turns out that everybody in Miami knows Burt Reynolds. It's testament to his appeal as a performer that everybody knows who he is, even people who might not be particular fans of his films, they'll still know immediately who Burt Reynolds is and will want to engage him.

Did you come across moments of this shooting on location in Miami?

Oh, definitely! When we filmed that sequence on the bridge at night, there were so many people around. All you could hear was people driving past and shouting, "Hi, Burt!" He is very well loved by people and the Teamsters especially loved him, they'll do anything to protect him. One night a couple of Cuban guys came around to the set and started causing trouble, but the Teamsters intervened and dealt with it because they said, "We'll protect Burt!" It's unfortunate that for many people he represents a specific era of movies and a certain kind of picture, generally they will associate him with those very successful action films like *The Cannonball Run* and *Smokey and the Bandit* and the image of him that comes with that. I also think that another reason Burt hasn't received the credit he is rightly due is because some people don't take him seriously because he makes it look so effortless, he makes this whole business of being a massive celebrity and successful actor look like it is just a lot of fun. But they don't see the time, effort and skill that go into bringing such a level of performance look effortless. You don't need a massive repertoire to be a movie star, but you do have to be comfortable in who you are, knowing your audience, and how to deliver what that audience wants from you. I don't think younger actors appreciate the kind of work Burt puts into it, they don't see the skill he utilizes in making it look so easy. Before I worked with him, I went to a theater to see a new film he was in and the film wasn't good at all and the audience did not like it, but whenever Burt appeared on screen you could feel the audience just jolt to attention, they absolutely hung on his every move and word; it was electric. As soon as Burt is present, the audience just erupts. That's a movie star!

Crazy Six
(1997)

"Just because you wear a cowboy hat doesn't mean you're from Texas."—Dakota

Crazy Six is a tough crime thriller shot on location in Bratislava and set in a dystopian alternate vision of Eastern Europe after the fall of Communism, a rundown cityscape bluntly named Crimeland. Rival crime kingpins Dirty Mao (Mario Van Peebles) and Raul (Ice-T) are engaged in a territorial dispute which is attracting heat from the law, including Dakota (Reynolds), an American detective on their trail. At the center of it all is the titular junkie, Crazy Six (Rob Lowe), and his beautiful girlfriend Anna (Ivana Milicevic), a drug addict turned lounge-singer.

Just like many major stars who end up jobbing in the world of straight-to-video cult movies, Reynolds eventually joined the long list of marquee names that have graced the work of prolific B-movie auteur Albert Pyun. Major stars Dennis Hopper, Kris Kristofferson, Jean Claude Van Damme, Steven Seagal, Charlie Sheen, Rutger Hauer, Jack Palance, Courteney Cox, Angelina Jolie, George Kennedy and many others have all worked with Pyun. While Pyun's films have most often been cheaply made and lacking in high production values, occasionally along comes a diamond in the rough. Moody, melancholy, musical and sumptuously shot, *Crazy Six* is a memorable and interesting picture for numerous reasons, most notably the unique aesthetic prowess of the piece. For a filmmaker not known for the cinematic traits of his productions, Pyun, along with editor Natasha Gjurokovic and cinematographer George Mooradian, here crafted a stunningly rich palette and hypnotic assembly of footage. Gjurokovic's editing doesn't so much cut as it glides and fades, in real time and in slow motion from one illusory shot to the next. Mooradian's lush framing is rich with its extremely stylized use of color, contrasting the harsh, uninviting exterior world with a heightened, iridescent interior production design which nicely underscores the gaudy seediness of Crimeland's lurid underworld.

Another element that Pyun manages brilliantly is the soundtrack, which consists mostly of songs performed by the character Anna and is a constant throughout the film, functioning as both diegetic "in the scene" source music and non-diegetic mood music crossing time and space within the narrative. The mood created by this abstract aestheticism is one of existential, almost surrealistic timbre. It is an unusual style for such artistic tendencies to carry a straight-to-video B-picture, particularly one rooted in the gritty urban milieu of crime and decay, but it works if at the expense of an actual story. Beyond the basic set-up of the narrative, Pyun rarely goes any further in explaining character backstories or even the reasons for their presence, which brings us to the picture's other notable aspect: the casting. Lowe, looking disheveled and uncharacteristically unattractive, isn't given a lot to do aside from look mournful and despondent, but he is surrounded by an abundance of sheer personality. Van Peebles and Ice-T exchange artillery and verbal onslaughts in their own heightened idiosyncratic manner while Reynolds enters the fray as Dakota, bringing with him an ambiguous, almost mythical American persona. Dakota is resplendent in cowboy hat and duster coat combo, equipped with the cynical barbs of a film noir detective: "Just because you wear a cowboy hat doesn't mean you're from Texas" is one such line.

Without the picture's distinctive visuals, spellbinding tone, and parade of wonderful character actors, there would be little of interest in its flimsy plot. It feels as though Pyun is trying a different formula for visual storytelling, privileging the graceful techniques of his editor and the elegant compositions of his cinematographer, while relying heavily on music in preference to dialogue. But given that the story is rooted in narrative genre film-making (the crime thriller), the more experimental and artistic elements of *Crazy Six* might not work for those who cling to the idea of strict codes of "invisible" filmmaking techniques and trusted generic registers; the picture discards established filmmaking and genre conventions to create its own unique personality. Anyone willing to lose themselves to the mood of *Crazy Six* may find the film a rewarding experience.

Universal Soldier II: Brothers in Arms and *Universal Soldier III: Unfinished Business*
(Made-for-Television, 1998)

"When Americans go to sleep at night, they like to know they're safe. They want to know there are people out there protecting them, people like us. They don't want to get letters saying their sons and daughters are missing in action, or wounded, or dead. That's why the Universal Soldier was perfect."—Gerald Risco

Universal Soldier II: Brothers in Arms and *Universal Soldier III: Unfinished Business* are sequels to Roland Emmerich's 1992 sci-fi action picture *Universal Soldier*. It starred Jean Claude Van Damme as Luc Devreaux aka GR-44, a soldier who was killed in combat during the Vietnam War in 1969 but whose body was resurrected in a covert biochemical military project. The UniSol program was a top secret operation tasked with creating an elite counter-terrorism unit which harvested and regenerated the bodies of dead soldiers as an unstoppable force in the battlefields of tomorrow. In 1998, the unit's cover was blown when GR-44 caused upset amongst the operation when he began to have visions of his past life, despite his memory having been erased. With recurring images of his last moments of life and the assistance of a brave journalist, Veronica Roberts (Chandra West), Luc begins to piece together his backstory and reach out to his long-lost family. With memory clearance being essential to their functions as the ideal killing machine, Luc's recall and subsequent rediscovery of his humanity renders him a failure, a danger to the program, and he must be eliminated.

Luc's mission to become human again sparks a fight for survival against the highest levels of government and is further complicated when the UniSol program is hijacked by a gang of mercenaries headed by the psychotic Dr. Otto Mazur (played with typical delirium and grinning menace by Gary Busey). Mazur is working under the orders of a mysterious government official who goes by the moniker of "Mentor" (Reynolds); he is ultimately revealed to be Gerald Risco, deputy director of the C.I.A.—the "GR" in the UniSol names are his initials. Risco is aggrieved that the UniSol budget has been slashed and decides to sell their skills on the illicit diamond and arms black market. Meanwhile, Luc and Veronica are a thorn in the company's side as their potential to leak the covert operation could prove a threat to national security. In the interim, Luc rediscovers his long-missing brother Eric, a fellow veteran of the Vietnam War and failed UniSol unit due to his bio-

Matt Battaglia plays Luc Devreaux, aka GR-44, in *Universal Soldier II: Brothers in Arms* (1998).

chemistry not being right for the program. Under the aegis of Dr. Walker (Richard McMillan), Eric's DNA is being used to clone and develop a replica of him that will be amenable to the UniSol program and help track down Luc and Veronica.

Both films pick up directly from Emmerich's original and are essentially cheaply made, Canadian-produced TV movies which don't have the artistic or financial clout behind them to approach the technical skill of the first picture. However, consumed in the context of their more modest means, both sequels are rather entertaining, bolstered by fantastic soundtracks which feature an array of Canadian alternative artists (Bif Naked, Wild Strawberries, Voivoid, Change of Heart). Former pro football player Matt Battaglia takes over the Van Damme role of Luc Devreaux and provides the right amount of naïve curiosity for the resurrected soldier rediscovering his humanity. The actor's impressive physique is also apt for playing the main hero of this hyper-violent action franchise. Reynolds' fans might be disappointed at his lack of presence in the former picture, playing most of it shot in silhouette as the director playfully teases the star's iconic image with recurrent shots of his lower face and extreme close-ups of his clearly recognizable mustache. In *Universal Soldier III: Unfinished Business*, Reynolds featured right from the beginning.

An Interview with Matt Battaglia

Actor-producer Matt Battaglia is one of many successful graduates of the Burt Reynolds Institute for Theater Training. A former linebacker for the Philadelphia Eagles with movie star good looks, Battaglia had the right physical appearance to become a screen action hero, often starring opposite his mentor and friend. He scored major roles in the films

Joshua Tree (Vic Armstrong, 1993), *Raven* (Russell Solberg, 1997), *Universal Soldier II: Brothers in Arms* and *Universal Soldier III: Unfinished Business* (both Jeff Woolnough, 1998) while also managing a prolific career in television, being cast on *B.L. Stryker, Evening Shade, 21 Jump Street, Baywatch, Twin Peaks, Friends, Days of Our Lives, Queer as Folk, The Big Bang Theory, True Detective* and many more. In 2009, Battaglia produced the critically acclaimed and Golden Globe–nominated war picture *Brothers*, directed by renowned Irish filmmaker Jim Sheridan. More recently, the actor was seen in Kenneth Branagh's blockbuster *Thor*.

Wayne: *Like many other actors who have gone on to have great careers, you came through Burt Reynolds' acting institute. How did that opportunity come about for you?*

Matt: You know, I have a different perspective on this as I've actually known Burt Reynolds since I was a child. Burt and my father [Carmen Battaglia] were roommates in college and remained friends throughout their lives. Burt was around a lot when I was young.

Seven-year-old Matt Battaglia and family friend Reynolds on the set of *Deliverance* (1972) (photograph courtesy Matt Battaglia Collection).

Did being so close to this famous film actor inspire your decision to become an actor and get into show business yourself?

Not at all. When I was a kid and he was around us, I never knew him as an actor. I didn't know Burt Reynolds the celebrity or Burt Reynolds the movie star, I knew Burt my father's friend; to me he was Uncle Burt. He used to send us Christmas cards and he used to stay at our house in Atlanta, it was a place for him to keep out of the prying public eye and the media, because this was around the time of *Deliverance*, when he was becoming this huge star. He would come and stay at our house instead of going to a hotel. It was a safe place for him. I remember when I was about seven years old going to the premiere of *The Longest Yard.* I had no idea what was going on or what it was all about, but I remember seeing Uncle Burt on that big screen and realizing that it is what he did. You know, instead of leaving that premiere wanting to be an actor, I left wanting to be a football player. I was an All-American middle linebacker at the University of Louisville and then a professional football player in the NFL with the Philadelphia Eagles, but my career ended early with a broken neck bone. I was this massive, muscle-bound athlete, I wasn't a natural fit for acting but Burt convinced me to give acting a try. So he took me in at his acting institute.

How did you adapt to this new environment?

It was a complete culture shock. I wasn't used to tapping into my emotions, which you have to do to be a good actor. The only emotions I was used to working with were anger and rage, so this was a whole new ball game. It was tough for me, because you have to allow yourself to be judged and to be vulnerable. But I fell in love with acting and that superseded any of my reservations about other elements of it that took me out of my comfort zone.

It must have been a huge deal for students to have such access to a major star and to have such hands-on training with a professional at the very heights of the acting profession.

For a lot of the kids at the school, it was huge to have Burt there and working with you. For me, it was Uncle Burt, so I didn't have as much reverence of him as a movie star as the other student actors; he was more familiar to me. But yes, Burt was extremely generous with his time and talent. He gave literally hundreds of students an opportunity to hone their craft and to audition for shows and movies that he worked on. I was in two of the *B.L. Stryker* movies and later I was in *Evening Shade*, but I got those roles by auditioning, which came through being at the Burt Reynolds Institute for Theater Training.

How did it feel going from a workshop scenario to being on set, being a paid professional actor with the lights and cameras on you?

I never felt nervous about being on set and in front of the cameras. I had already been on a public platform being a football player, I was used to being a public persona and being on TV in interviews and things like that. I ended up starring in several feature films with Burt.

Which were Raven *and two films in the* Universal Soldier *franchise.*

Yes, and they actually didn't start out as Burt Reynolds films.

I often thought that. Even though Burt is the face of those films, on the poster and video art, you are the star of the films.

And I was perfectly fine with that. Having Burt Reynolds' face on the poster will sell your film, more than my face would. That's how the business works. If you have a huge star in your film, even if they only have four lines in the movie, you use them to promote the film.

If those films weren't conceived as Burt Reynolds films, what brought the filmmakers to casting him?

How that came about was through the producers knowing I was close to Burt. They would ask me if I thought if he would be interested in appearing in the film and if I could reach out to him. I said, "Sure, all he can do is say no," so I called him and he agreed to come onboard.

The ending of Universal Soldier III: Unfinished Business *suggests a continuation of the series with Burt's character being resurrected as a UniSol. Was this a plan for the series?*

It was mentioned that we could continue the series with further installments, but unfortunately those discussions never went anywhere. Those two films were originally planned to be Showtime's first theatrical releases, but that didn't happen either and they premiered on TV like Showtime's usual productions. Both *Universal Soldier* films were shot simultaneously. There were days where we would shoot scenes for *Brother in Arms* and then go straight to shooting some scenes for *Unfinished Business*.

How did you find working with Burt in this professional capacity?

When you are on set with Burt, he just treats you like a fellow professional. He likes everyone to be prepared and know their lines. Once he is there with you, he is just another actor trying to do his best, he never threw his weight around like others in as high a position as he was in can do. He would never abuse that stature. The only time I would see him losing his cool or wielding his considerable power on the set would be if he saw someone being treated unfairly. For example, if a director or another person in a powerful position was going hard on someone unjustly, Burt would not tolerate it and would make his feelings known to the offending individual.

Did you keep in contact with Burt in his later years?

Unless you lived local in Jupiter, it was definitely harder to see him, because in his later life he became quite reclusive, and I don't mean that in a bad way, I mean that he became more selective about seeing people and being seen. You have to remember and put into context just how big a star this man was, and then consider just how much his star had diminished in the eyes of the public and in the film industry. Think of how hard it is for a one-hit wonder who gets a taste of success and fame and then loses it; now consider someone of Burt's magnitude and the level of success he achieved, of that power that he had, and then to have that taken away over time. It was incredibly tough.

Was he in a good place when you last spoke to him?

I last saw him several years ago and we talked about God and about growing old. I feel bad for the way his fortune was mishandled and how some people in his inner circle took advantage of him and his finances. He could be too generous and perhaps too trusting of people. I also tried to give him some advice on his property as I spend a great deal of time developing real estate, but I don't think he ever took my advice seriously, I think he always saw me as Matt the little kid, the same way I always looked up to him as Uncle Burt. But he ended up going down the route that I initially suggested to him, but not at my prompting.

Do you think Burt received a fair shake from the industry?

Since his passing, I've been thinking about how much of a shame it is that Burt was never honored by the Academy in his lifetime; he should have at least been recognized by the Governors Awards, something to acknowledge his immense body of work and contribution to the film industry. Be he wasn't. I'm friends with Loni Anderson and when I was talking to her recently, she told me how excited Burt was about going to work with Quentin Tarantino. When Burt got up on the day he died, he didn't know it would be his last day on this earth, I'm sure he was just looking forward to the new opportunities that awaited him and was excited that something great was on the horizon with this Tarantino film. I wish that he could have lived to see that through and to be accepted by audiences once again.

Given that you knew both sides of Burt, the public and the private, you have a unique perspective, so I'm curious to know, what in your opinion made him so beloved and so popular a screen star?

In his private life, he was so humble and so caring. He was a great friend and was just down to earth. In public, he was so funny and self-deprecating, when you saw him on TV talk shows throughout the '70s and '80s he was so likable, he never took himself too seriously and I think that endeared him to men and made him attractive to women. He had a great sense of fun. Other people like Robert De Niro and Al Pacino might have had the critics fawning over them, but Burt Reynolds had more men wanting to be like him and more women wanting to sleep with him than any other actor you can name. He was a tough, strong man, yet had an incredible vulnerability which also translated to the screen extremely well.

Hard Time Trilogy
(Made-for-Television, 1998)

"Everything and everybody runs down here in Paradise. Down here, you see, because we're at the bottom of the nation. It's the land of the beautiful people; also retirees and mermaids and fugitives and tourists, crazies, criminals and of course … cops!"—Logan McQueen

Eight years after the demise of *B.L. Stryker*, Burt Reynolds received the opportunity to star in another series of made-for-television films based on the exploits of a maverick ex-cop. This time he plays Detective Logan McQueen in the Hard Time trilogy: *Hard Time*, *The Premonition* and *Hostage Hotel*.

In the opening of *Hard Time*, McQueen and his partner Duffy (Charles Durning) are staking out a drug deal when the bag man is accosted by a street gang and robbed of his briefcase which contains $190,000 in drug money. McQueen and Duffy give chase, reaching an impasse in a dead-end alleyway and culminating in the death of one thief. His partner-in-crime, a glass-eyed hoodlum named Catarato Estevez (Paco Christian Pieto), flees the scene. Also missing from the alleyway is the briefcase and whoever is in possession of it must face the ire of its owner, feared narcotics kingpin Connie Martin (Robert Loggia). McQueen is framed for the alleyway shooting and faces eager legal eagles such as Leo

Detectives McQueen (Reynolds) and Duffy (Charles Durning) are on the case in *Hard Time* (1998).

Barker (Billy Dee Williams), who is ready to make a political point by prosecuting a cop who did wrong. The department fall guy, McQueen is imprisoned but soon escapes in an effort to clear his name. He uncovers a trail of corruption leading to those closest to him.

The second installment, *The Premonition*, features former Reynolds acting student Gigi Rice as well as Hollywood heavyweight Bruce Dern. It begins with McQueen back in prison having taken the fall for his partner Duffy's crime of fabricating evidence and stealing money. McQueen meets some death row cons, one of whom is the spiritual Sebastian (Roscoe Lee Browne), a man paying the price for killing the man who murdered his family. Sebastian's words of wisdom offer McQueen an insight into forgiveness, which will come into play when reconciling his own strained relationship with Duffy. Another prisoner in line for capital punishment is serial killer Winston (Dern), who claims to have visions of a serial bomber killing female lawyers. Winston offers to help police find the terrorist but he will only deal with one cop: McQueen. The catch is that McQueen must reach out to Winston's estranged daughter and help reconnect them before his execution.

In *Hostage Hotel*, McQueen mans a rescue mission to save Congressman Robert Sinclair (David Rasche) and his family from a deranged Vietnam veteran, Flynn (David Carradine), who has hijacked the hotel in which Sinclair was to deliver a speech. All of this probably wouldn't matter much to McQueen except his best friend, Duffy, is also taken hostage. Now it becomes personal. McQueen infiltrates the hotel to disarm the ruthless Flynn, who deduces that McQueen is also a Vietnam vet judging from his tactical skills. Both men utilize their experience from days in the battlefield trenches for a deadly showdown.

While the *Hard Time* trilogy falls far short of the *B.L. Stryker* films, a series which overflowed with abundant wit, style and aesthetic grace, there is something likable about the Logan McQueen saga. It is yet another cop series with Reynolds delivering a no-nonsense performance and gripping stories of a maverick cop vs. an unjust and often corrupt system. There is almost a feeling that we're viewing Dan August nearing his pension and gold watch. Visually the films look like they were made for TV, having been produced to premiere on TNT and brought to the screen with a minimum of aesthetic flourish, though they are exquisitely cast. Charles Durning clearly has a blast with his role of McQueen's comically irascible Irish partner Duffy, whose idea of combination dieting is to pair whiskey with beer … in the same glass. Despite his 75 years, he is a remarkably threatening and imposing figure; even with his large frame and limited mobility, Durning can rough house with muscle-bound gangsters with ease. Appearing as Connie Martin's menacing enforcers are former WWF wrestler "Rowdy" Roddy Piper and martial artist Gene LeBell. Mia Sara provides potential love interest as an attorney of steely determination and a penchant for taking down corrupt cops but who can't resist McQueen's considerable charm. Paco Christian Pieto also makes for a memorable screen villain as Catarato Estevez. His appearance marks a recurring motif of the Reynolds oeuvre: Reynolds' fascination for villains with physical abnormalities. McQueen refers to Catarato as "Milk Eye" due to his blank white glass eye, which reminds one of the various villains that Reynolds refers to as "Bunny Eyes" in both *Hustle* and *Stick*.

The Premonition contains some interesting ideas and is the most atmospheric of the series, more of an unnerving thriller than a routine police procedural. Dern is fascinating as the opera-loving Winston. Tensions remain between McQueen and Duffy, the latter drunk on alcohol and remorse over sacrificing his friendship with his partner. Their soured relationship allows for some tender moments between Reynolds and Durning. *Hostage Hotel* is the most action-oriented and visually kinetic of the trilogy, no surprise given its direction by Reynolds regular, Hal Needham. It is also, unfortunately, the least effective in terms of tone and atmosphere. This entry embraces a more formulaic standard of filming, a distinctly tele-visual one, lacking the more nuanced style of the previous two pictures. The action plods along with a routine, workmanlike efficiency but bears none of the visual kineticism and high energy of Needham's previous works.

The Hunter's Moon

(1999)

"My daddy used to tell me this world was where people go on their way to Hell, so when they get there the shock wouldn't be so bad. My momma said this world is a place where we learn to live right, so when we get to Heaven, we'll all be well practiced."—Turner

Turner (Keith Carradine), a nomadic World War I veteran, is exploring the wilds of Appalachia when he is faced with two choices: turn left for Rassenbach Landing or turn right for Samuels Mountain. Choosing the latter, Turner is about to enter his own private Heaven and Hell. While camped on the mountain, he meets a beautiful young woman named Flo. At first the pair quarrel, she accusing him of spying on her skinny-dipping, but after an antagonistic introduction the two begin to find each other attractive. The man who lays claim to the mountain is Clayton Samuels (Reynolds), the feared, feared bootlegger and oppressive patriarch of a backwoods family, father to Flo and slow-witted son Jackie Lee (Andrew Hawkes). To keep his daughter virtuous, a significant number of young suitors have disappeared at the hands of Clayton, buried in the wilds of Samuels Mountain. When Turner arrives at Clayton's local supply store, Clayton notices the distinct sexual tension between his daughter and the stranger; this displeases him. Clayton is also running moonshine for the corrupt Judge Tully (played by a gleefully intimidating Pat Hingle), an ogre of a man who abuses his authority for his own gain and harbors some dark family secrets that have consequences for the Samuels clan. The matriarch of the Samuels family is deceased, which means Flo has had to assume those duties. But no matter how much care Flo provides, her relationship with Clayton is fraught with distrust; she blames her father for working her mother to death, but the reason for Clayton's aggression is later revealed that Flo is actually Judge Tully's illegitimate daughter, the result of an illicit affair with Clayton's wife. Clayton sees new arrival Turner as a threat to his authority and to the power he wields over his daughter; for Flo to fall in love and lead a life of her own would be at the expense of life as Clayton's slave. So with Jackie Lee in tow, Clayton searches the mountain for Turner. Clayton has the hills rigged with traps, making it treacherous terrain for Turner, who must parlay his skills as a soldier to outsmart the wily Clayton.

The Hunter's Moon contains some of Reynolds' very best late-career work; it also happens to be one of his most unknown credits. The actor, so often lithe and graceful, stomps around the scenery like the agitated bear of a man that Clayton is, barely containing his rage with a seething, slow-burning menace and unnerving grin. Ann Wedgeworth appears as Clayton's mistress Borlene, a lonely older seductress who beds Jackie Lee when Clayton is unavailable for service. Keen Reynolds watchers will know the glamorous Wedgeworth as Merleen Eldridge from *Evening Shade*, as well her appearance as the femme fatale Helen Rainey in the 1966 *Hawk* episode "Death Comes Full Circle."

This represents Richard Weinman's sole credit as director. He previously produced another eerie backwoods tale, the brilliant *Pumpkinhead* (Stan Winston, 1988). Weinman does

Clayton Samuels (Reynolds) doesn't take too kindly to strangers in *The Hunter's Moon* (1999).

a fine job here, showing great discernment in his poetic use of music and photography. Cinematographer Suki Medencevic's work is exceptional, capturing the beauty of the rugged landscape tastefully while also imbuing the film stock with a retro photographic quality that renders the picture a living, breathing snapshot of the Prohibition era. The film's soundtrack is an exceptional compilation of traditional Appalachian ballads performed by acclaimed soprano Custer LaRue, accompanied by folk ensemble The Baltimore Consort. Weinman's rarely seen film did manage to gain some well-deserved recognition when it won the Festival Prize at the Long Island International Film Expo in 1999. Perhaps the film's greatest legacy is that it led to personal triumph for two of its stars, Keith Carradine and Hayley DuMond, whose palpable chemistry in the picture was not just good acting; the pair fell in love on set and married in 2006.

Pups
(1999)

"Let me get this straight. You want me to quit smoking because it's dangerous, but you are holding up a bank? Stop being such an asshole!"—Daniel Bender

Thirteen-year-olds Stevie (Cameron Van Hoy) and Rocky (Mischa Barton) have been dating for a few weeks but are already talking about having kids—"lots of kids"—and getting married. They are still children, on the cusp of puberty, but feeling very much like the weight of the world is on their shoulders. In the startling opening scene, Stevie flirts with the idea of hanging himself in his mother's bedroom before raiding her drawers unsuccessfully for something of value to steal and prying into her pornographic videotape collection. He finds a loaded .44 Magnum. Later that morning, while on their way to school, things take a serious turn when Stevie reveals to Rocky that he brought along the gun and has decided rather impulsively to rob the local bank. In pure amateur form, they hold up the bank but aren't quick enough out of there before a patrol call rolls up and the situation escalates to full-blown hostage crisis. Taken captive inside are the bank manager (David Alan Graf), tellers J.P. (James Gordon) and Rio (Susan Horton), customers Mr. Edwards (Ed Metzger) and Joy (Darling Narita) and a paraplegic, credited in the titles as Wheelchair Man (Adam Farrar).

Things are heating up outside as the FBI is called in, led by negotiator Daniel Bender (Burt Reynolds). The situation inside the bank is its own melting pot of tensions, anxieties and precarious relationships. Two military veterans, Mr. Edwards (of World War II) and Wheelchair Man (of the Gulf War) are at loggerheads in their own commentary of the proceedings. Edwards blames the post-counterculture generations for the apathy and waywardness of contemporary America's youth; he also feels disrespected for the perceived lack of recognition for what his generation went through in ensuring freedom and democracy. Wheelchair Man, who admits to suffering from Gulf War Syndrome, believes the couple is a symptom of a morally debased society but not the cause of it. Throw into the mix the nebbish bank manager, the kind of person who hides out in therapy rather than confront his demons, physical or psychological, and the whole affair proves to be far too much for the child captors to handle. Between dealing with pan-generational conflicts, political dis-illusionment and the varying degrees of neuroses of their detainees, Stevie and Rocky also have to contend with the more pressing issue of the country's media and law enforcement camped outside commanding their attention.

Reynolds brings the right amount of world-weariness to the role of Bender, but also gives him a sense of straight-talking pragmatism. While essentially coddling Stevie into submission, Bender is himself an absentee father to his own admiring daughter. Despite repeated calls from his wife, Bender refuses to talk to his child; in one sense he is right, given the situation at hand, but there is also an underlying sense that he is regularly distant with his family.

By 1999, it seemed that a whole new generation of filmmakers and audiences were beginning to appreciate the significant screen presence of Burt Reynolds. He would be cast by directors who were young enough to appreciate the sheer star wattage of the actor at the height of his career, but who were now old enough to appreciate the opportunity to cast him at a time when he was considerably more affordable. The crop of film school graduates who were now making waves on the U.S. independent movie scene were taking full advantage of what Reynolds could lend their film: name recognition, Hollywood glamour, a formidable screen occupancy that few actors of the era were capable of main-taining.

Coming at the tail end of the Generation-X era, *Pups* is very much a product of its time, tapping into the jaded, cynical youth culture that was satirized in Mike Judge's *Beavis and Butthead* (1993) and examined unflatteringly in *Kids* (Larry Clark, 1995), *The Doom Generation* (Gregg Araki, 1995) and *Gummo* (Harmony Korine, 1997). Like the protagonists of those films, Stevie and Rocky are very much products of late-80s, early-90s media culture. They are self-absorbed to the point of obsession, armed with an abundance of film and tel-evision knowledge which may seem arbitrary to some but which remains intelligence that helps shape their own worldview. In their unfortunate milieu of absentee parenting and emotional negligence, pop culture has filled the role of educator in the lives of these kids. Stevie and Rocky have great rapport, and despite their only recent coupling they seem to have a genuine affinity for each other. Cutely, the pair continues each other's sentences, though this is a contrived attribute ascribed to them from the workings of a witty and sharp screenwriter who is more advanced in age and pop-cultural awareness than our two pubes-cent lovers. The rapid fire dialogue, hip and abundant in movie references, allows their relationship an exclusive quality, their own kind of romantic dialect, even if it makes their dialogue often feel overwritten. Stevie constantly apes Travis Bickle's famous "You talkin' to me?" line while brandishing his pistol, viewing his and Rocky's exploits as part of the great cinematic tradition, especially when he catches sight of their activities on the news: "That's some Bonnie and Clyde shit! Did you ever see that movie?" For any youth of the late 1990s, there was only one media outlet to trust, as so Stevie and Rocky call upon pop-cultural touchstone MTV and its iconic news presenter Kurt Loder to capture their momen-tous social event, taking Dire Straits' famous refrain of "I want my MTV" to a whole new level.

Pups may be stylistically more subtle and restrained than Oliver Stone's *Natural Born Killers* (1994) and Tony Scott's *True Romance* (1993), two notable films that also provide discourse on young violent couples operating under the spell of the '90s explosion of media and pop-culture. But it still functions in a similar world which is shaped by the entertainment industries, particularly the visual media of film and television. For those of us familiar with the texts referenced throughout the film, this can act as narrative shorthand; we can identify and link to Stevie and Rocky the attributes of characters from works as varied as *Dog Day Afternoon*, *Taxi Driver*, *Bonnie and Clyde* and *Midnight Cowboy* and assign a certain kind of fate to the couple through their affinity and surface similarities to these characters. At one point, Stevie lies down in the middle of the road to appreciate the clear blue sky, and when a car stops to admonish the irresponsible and dangerous act, Stevie responds in his thick New York accent with "I'm layin' here!!!" which of course is a nod to Ratzo Rizzo. Van Hoy's aggression, diminutive stature and unbridled energy, coupled with his strong regional dialect, recall a young Al Pacino and Dustin Hoffman. Through years of little human contact and ease of access to adult media, these precocious kids talk with the kind of bluster that is beyond their tender years, with little knowledge or conviction behind the words they spout. In a moment of prurient bravado, Stevie asks Rocky (though with no actual intention), "Are you ready for me?" to which she replies equally sarcastically, "Oh yeah! Do me, baby!" before giggling and teasing each other. It is another case of their lives being dictated and directed by the fictional language which they fail to separate from reality.

In the midst of the bank robbery, Stevie casually asks Rocky to sexually please him orally: "Give me a blow job, just a little one!" When Kurt Loder asks Rocky the sincere question "What do think of Stevie?" her immaturity fails to grasp the true nature of the inquiry; her reply is "I like him, he's got a big one!" Director Ash Cohen seems to be intimating that the relentless exposure to pornography and violence has led to a distorted view of basic human communication for these youngsters. Despite seemingly comfortable middle-class environs, the absentee parenting, physically or emotionally, is alluded to as the root of Stevie and Rocky's psychological malaise. All of this social commentary and heavy thematic underscoring might seem too obvious and bludgeoning if it weren't for the sheer brilliance of the cast and the utter conviction of their performances. *Pups* is a raw, uncompromising piece of work featuring a stellar turn from Reynolds and two startling performances from the young co-stars. Cohen offers a perceptive insight into the blank philosophies of the youth culture caught between declining Generation X and the burgeoning millennial generation that they are on the cusp of defining.

The Stringer

(1999)

"'Woman saved by reporter.' You're a fucking hero. But I like you!"—Wolko Newby

Filo (Elie Semoun) is a French film student living in New York squalor with his exotic dancer girlfriend. To make ends meet and support their loving relationship, Filo takes a stringer job for the Wolko Newby News Service. As a stringer, Filo's freelance job is that of a paparazzi-style video journalist who races to the location of accident and emergency reports heard over the NYPD and EMS frequencies, speeding there in advance of the cops'

12-minute response time and filming any chaos he can. Filo then sells the footage to any disreputable media outlet with low enough ethical concerns to air the horrid material. At first Filo has a crisis of conscience and must decide which is more important, money or morals. Of course, given his dilapidated apartment dwelling and general milieu of poverty, money wins. "No one will like you when you do this job," says Wolko Newby (Reynolds), "but if you do the job right, you can make a lot of money," even if that money is split 50–50 with Wolko.

Cynical and manipulative, with his long silver ponytail, ever-present cigar smoldering from his lips, and female lapdog always straddling a nearby desk, Reynolds informs Wolko with an air of calm Machiavellian menace, knowing what buttons to push in order to make his minions do his bidding. Peppered around Wolko's gritty office are framed pictures of brutality, images of guns and famous moments of historical violence, such as Eddie Adams' iconic 1968 photograph "Saigon Execution," a lasting image from the Vietnam War. To keep Filo sweet, Wolko name drops some friends who are "high up in Warner Brothers" and who Wolko says have seen and enjoyed the film student's work. Following on from the manic energy and moral malaise of the brilliant *Pups*, Reynolds scores another hit with this picture which is yet another disturbing look at the obsessive nature of a sensationalist contemporary media.

Filo's filmic fantasies allowed director Klaus Biedermann to indulge in some nicely constructed moments of more artful distraction, temporarily taking us out of the dour milieu of the narrative, such as when Filo is charged with chasing a horse on the Brooklyn Bridge. The horse has been set free by its owner, an actress who has since committed suicide, and in the midst of pursuit Filo finds the poetry in the image of the elegant animal in full flight of independence. Of course, Wolko chastises Filo for thinking aesthetically and filming the horse rather than capturing footage of the actress in the throes of death. ("Those idiots that watch television don't give a shit about a horse!" Wolko admonishes.) Under Wolko's watch, Filo begins to become insensitive to society's ills, coldly watching abuse and conflict until he descends into absolute obsession with capturing the grisliest images he can find. In several instances Filo stumbles across the aftermath of robberies and automobile accidents, some of which contain fatalities while others are just about rescued by arriving authorities, including a security guard gunned down in a late-night supermarket robbery and a young woman kidnapped, bound and beaten. Disturbingly, Filo prolongs the agony of those in distress: Rather than alerting police or emergency services he hangs back and films. In a brilliant centerpiece, Filo films the suicide of a mentally unstable woman who performs a rendition of "Amazing Grace" in anticipation of her fatal leap, though not before acknowledging Filo directly through his lens and reaching into his soul. It is a moment to shake Filo, and the audience, to our core.

There have been many films that deal with the urban loner driven to madness, and Biedermann's film has an oppressively gloomy style to match the themes of moral and urban decay. *The Stringer* is a stylish piece of work and uses the camera to great effect, inviting us into Filo's subjective viewfinder and engendering a sleazy voyeuristic feeling in the viewer. As his camera lingers on the carnage and human suffering, the film can prove a distressing viewing experience, but there is an underlying melancholy to the picture and to Filo's existence that saves it from descending into an unpleasant experience.

Mystery, Alaska

(1999)

"Two things we've always had in Mystery: our dignity and our illusions. I suggest
we cling to both."—Judge Walter Burns

In the town of Mystery, Alaska, the Saturday hockey game on the local pond has long
been the center of the universe. Mystery is the kind of place where few people leave; a
Rockwellian paradise where those that do leave are considered outcasts for willingly escaping
such handsome and homely environs. However, the town's congenial way of life is being
threatened twofold: as the proposed location for a big-box budget supermarket, Price World,
and the imminent invasion of the New York Rangers.

Charles Danner (Hank Azaria) is one of those who did leave Mystery, for a career in
New York as a sports producer. When he publishes an article in *Sports Illustrated* championing
his hometown and its legendary hockey team, his approbation piques the interest of the major
leagues. The cunning producer seizes upon an opportunity for a novel promotional exhibition
bout between the New York Rangers and the Mystery team, to take place in his hometown.
Major news networks are attracted to the town to cover the story with a human interest angle,
and thus the media circus duly arrives in Mystery and begins pitching their absurd ideas of
how to craft their narrative. Television news reporter Janice Pettiboe (Beth Littleford) suggests
calling the team "The Mystery Eskimos" based on her marketing blurb of "'Eskimos on Ice:
The Strange Snowmen Who Play on the Lake.' We don't know who they are or what they are;
all we know is they have poor dental health and can skate like the wind." Naturally this doesn't
sit well with the locals, or the Inuit Native American residents.

Among those locals are Judge Walter Burns (Reynolds) and his wife Joanne (Judith Ivey);
Mayor Scott Pitcher (Colm Meaney) and his wife Mary Jane (Lolita Davidovich), who is
having a fling with team hunk Skank Marden (Ron Eldard); local lawyer Bailey Pruitt (Maury
Chaykin), and a hockey team's worth of additional characters. If there is a nominal hero and
lead character amongst the ensemble, it must be John Biebe (Russell Crowe). As sheriff of
the town and local sporting hero, Biebe embodies the rugged spirit of Mystery: tough, rough-
hewn, no-nonsense, but humble. However, with eager young players looking to move up the
ranks and former love rivals back in town, Biebe's idyllic existence is rattled.

Judge Burns, who Reynolds plays with dignity and grace, presides over the town's petty
squabbles and other frivolities, has never played in the Saturday game and is somewhat cynical
of the town's obsession with the sport, particularly so after his son has decided to forgo college
in favor of staying in the town to hone his hockey skills. When Burns is asked to take over
as coach in preparation for the match against the Rangers, he balks. Then his friend Bailey
dies of a heart attack while arguing for the game to continue when bureaucratic concerns
threaten it. Burns now feel it is only right to honor Bailey by assuming the role of coach and
taking the team as far as they can go. Hockey, and perhaps sports at large, is representative
here of the tough spirit and vigorous resolve of these isolated rural folk, and as such the film
doesn't merely provide hockey as a spectacle for sporting enthusiasts, it is the backdrop for
us to navigate the lives and petty idiosyncrasies of the residents of Mystery. While there, we

witness burgeoning youthful romance, midlife crises, indiscretions, complicated marriages … a parade of essential human behavior well-told and entertainingly executed.

The film's screenplay was handled by television writer-producer David E. Kelly (*L.A. Law*, *Picket Fences*) and actor-writer Sean O'Byrne (*Wiseguy*, *Timecop*). With such a pedigree, it is perhaps inevitable that the film contains the distinct quality of a finely arranged sitcom, right down to Jay Roach's clear and straightforward visual style. Roach had just come off of the first two highly stylized *Austin Powers* films and there is little sign here of such authorship; rather the director eschews overt stylization and instead focuses on the multitude of plots and attendant relationships, all of which is neatly tied up in the postgame finale. This is all predictable in the extreme and the game itself is ultimately inconsequential, an excuse to invite us into the town and get a glimpse into the lives of the colorful locals. Those people of Mystery, Alaska, make it a very pleasant stay.

Waterproof
(2000)

"There's not many a man who would get shot and then come visit the family responsible."—Chris Hardwick

Tyree Battle (April Grace) is a single working mother driving a taxi in inner city Washington, D.C., to make ends meet. Her 11-year-old son Thaniel has become difficult, running with a bad crowd and neglecting his studies, and one night gets himself into serious trouble: Playing hookey from school, he hangs out with two older thugs who rob a grocery store and force Thaniel to shoot the owner, Eli Zeal (Reynolds). Eli's wound in not fatal, though it is enough to cause horror and panic in Tyree. Eli has no family to take care of him and so Tyree calls her mother to expect their arrival and the threesome hits the road for the rural town of Waterproof, Louisiana. Eli understandably wants hospital treatment, but Tyree fears her son will be jailed for the serious offense and hopes that the tranquility of country life and stability of a familial structure will instill in her son a positive attitude. But the Battles are far from stable. While all are welcomed into the family home by mother Viola (Ja'net Dubois) and patriarch Sugar (Whitman Mayo), the house is home to unresolved emotional issues, particularly between Tyree and her brothers, the mentally challenged Natty Battle (Orlando Jones) and the bitter alcoholic "Brother Big" Battle (Anthony Lee). This journey south means a confrontation with demons of the past for Tyree, and a culture clash for her urbanite son Thaniel and the Jewish Eli. However, the welcoming environment of Waterproof and the embrace and faith of its people all aid in nursing the ailing Eli back to health.

Writer-director Barry Berman's *Waterproof* script provides a solid canvas for some coruscating familial drama, on which it sensitively draws its portrait of inter-generational conflict. The themes of faith and forgiveness might seem a little heavy-handed were it not for the thorough conviction of the actors involved, all of whom bring an incredibly dynamic display of acting craft.

April Grace is particularly noteworthy for her towering performance. She exhibits the required feelings of hurt, shame and guilt and grounds the film in its emotional reality, reminding us that this is no mere sightseeing tour of idyllic rural settings, but an emotive and soul-stirring journey into the heart of a broken family. Reynolds is particularly good when sharing the screen with veteran actor Whitman Mayo (*Sanford and Son, Hill Street Blues*); their pairing makes for a fine double act of old coots trading wisdom and knowledge on the front porch of the Battle home. As Eli convalesces, he comes to appreciate a way of life he never got to taste before, just as the experience is new for big city exile Tyree. For Reynolds, *Waterproof* is exemplary of the kind of substantial dramatic work that eluded him at the height of his success. Reynolds admitted,

> It was a part that no one would have offered me ten years ago. One, because I wasn't a good enough actor, they thought. Two, because why use me when there's a whole bunch of guys that age. The reason I wanted to do this picture is because of the script. It was very sweet; it was a real character piece. It was a real relationship picture.... I was anxious that I could show that I could do it.[1]

Berman recalled his first encounter with the star:

> Burt called me up and asked me what made me choose him for this script.... I said what I honestly thought, I thought that he was a much deeper talent than had been displayed in any of the movies he had done before.... This is the kind of script that just appeals to actors, it gives them a chance to really, really work. I was very fortunate to be able to get my script around to people who once they read it, said, "I'd sure like to be in it."[2]

"It's a wonderful screenplay," Reynolds said. "You have to start with the words. The words are the foundation of the house; if you don't have the words, the house topples over.... There were no small parts; they were all interesting parts.... It's the sign of a wonderful script when every part is good. Good actors are attracted to it because of that."[3]

The majority of *Waterproof* was shot in Wilmington, North Carolina, in the summer of 1998. Crucially, the filmmakers also managed to shoot on location in Waterproof, Louisiana, for three days for some exterior work to ground the film in its actual setting, which is richly rendered by cinematographer Stephen Thompson. Thompson captures the scintillating Southern heat and lush rural splendor. Adding to the authenticity of the piece is the use of Waterproof residents as well as members of the local church, who provided their services as extras and furnished music for the service sequences.

Notes

1. Burt Reynolds, "The Making of," DVD Supplement, *Waterproof*, Cloud Ten Pictures, 2001.
2. *Ibid.*
3. *Ibid.*

The Crew

(2000)

"Yeah, we were wise guys again, all right. Fast women, fast cars, fast watches, and a scuffle in a men's room over a broad."—Bobby Bartellmeo

Meet the crew: Bobby Bartellmeo (Ricahrd Dreyfuss), Joey "Bats" Pistella (Reynolds), Mike "The Brick" Donatelli (Dan Hedaya) and Tony "Mouth" Donata (Seymour Cassel). The film introduces these New Jersey hoods as a bunch of vital young mobsters living large in 1968 before cutting to 30 years later when we see the colorful bunch of goons retired from mob life and living out their twilight years in Miami. From their tired South Beach residential hotel, the Raj Mahal, the codgers spend their days on the front porch ogling passing bikini-clad women. This is the kind of place where a young couple on the property market asks the quartet if any old residents who had an ocean-view apartment have died recently. "Hang out, maybe you'll be the first to catch the smell," Bobby replies sarcastically. The crew is upset to learn that their beloved home is to become renovated to an upwardly mobile haven for yuppies and so they hatch a fake murder plot to occur at the hotel in order to scare away any potential city slickers ruining their modest dwellings with aspirations to boho chic and exorbitant rent rates. Luckily, the Brick works in a mortuary and so can access a corpse on a whim. Unluckily for them all, the corpse that Brick decides to defile is that of Luis Ventana, the father of drug lord Raul Ventana (Miguel Sandoval). When the ironically monikered Mouth reveals the whole scheme in post-coital confession to stripper Ferris (Jennifer Tilly), the four men become subject to her plan for them to kill her mother, Pepper Lowenstein (Lainie Kazan), or else she will spill all to the incensed Ventana son. Detectives Olivia Neal (Carrie-Anne Moss) and Steve Menteer (Jeremy Piven) are on the case, but there is more to Detective Neal's involvement than she realizes.

This is a Miami of clichés, a town of loud suits, fedoras, cigars, Latin music and of course some stereotypical movie gangster caricatures: the sensitive one, the sociopathic one, the artistic one, the quiet one. Even the villain of the piece, Raul Ventana, notes his own similarities to cinematic criminals: "Do you know what I am? A cliché; a laughing mob boss! Do you know what happens to clichés? They die!" Kazan's brash, bossy, bosomy Jersey Girl is a hoot as a hostage, Pepper sharing cold cuts and sodas with the entertaining company of Reynolds, Dreyfuss, Hedaya and Cassel.

With such a lineup, *The Crew* is an essential "geezer movie," that curious subgenre that brings together ensemble casts comprised of former leading men or leading ladies and has them create an elderly comic variation of their past selves. While most of this is fairly standard stuff, there is one particularly eccentric subplot: the strained relationship between Moss and Piven's detectives. Their history as former romantic partners allows for some bizarre moments, such as when Menteer indulges his fetish for his partner's feet and enjoys some creepy toe-sucking. Olivia's much admired feet are less welcome later when she learns that Menteer is secretly working for Ventana and delivers some appropriate kicks. Screenwriter Barry Fanaro's credits include a prolific stint as writer-producer on the excellent '80s sitcom *The Golden Girls*, and Fanaro certainly knows how to wring a geriatric joke dry. *The Crew* is in the tradition of Clint Eastwood's *Space Cowboys* (2000), and the genre isn't showing any signs of slowing down, with recent works such as Zach Braff's *Going in Style* (2017), Ron Shelton's *Just Getting Started* (2017) and Bill Holderman's *Book Club* (2018). At this stage in his career, Reynolds, and those looking to work with him, were determined to accept that the actor was no longer action hero material. And so, with *The Crew*, Reynolds embraced roles which afforded him the opportunity to reflect on his life and his career, films such as *The Last Producer*, *The Hollywood Sign*, *Deal* and *The Last Movie Star*.

Director Michael Dinner's film career began interestingly enough with the teen drama

Catholic Boys (1985) and the crime comedy *Off Beat* (1986) before he made a major commercial misstep with the equine disaster *Hot to Trot* (1988). Here Dinner creates a very funny movie punctuated with well-timed one-liners and gangster movie references; this is not a canvas for than anything resembling drama or pathos. In a very funny sequence which parodies *GoodFellas* (Martin Scorsese, 1990), a busboy takes the crew through the kitchens of a low-rent delicatessen, only to escort them out the back door to a rain-drenched alleyway after being tipped a meager dollar for prime seats. This is when *The Crew* works best, in acknowledgment of the genre that it sharply satirizes. Dinner has never been the kind of director to leave any distinctive authorial stamp on his work and *The Crew* occasionally feels much more in line with the work of the film's producer: successful director and erstwhile cinematographer, Barry Sonnenfeld (*The Addams Family*, 1991; *Get Shorty*, 1995; *Men in Black*, 1997). The picture certainly contains some of his trademark hyper-stylized, in-your-face camerawork and unique visual touches.

Gangster comedies were also in vogue at the turn of the millennium, with *Analyze This* (Harold Ramis, 1999) and *The Whole Nine Yards* (Jonathan Lynn, 2000) both making big returns. However, rather than making off with the box office loot, *The Crew* came up short, stalling at $13 million worldwide gross. Despite its failure, *The Crew* is a vast improvement over Reynolds and Dreyfuss' previous attempt at gangster satire, the execrable *Mad Dog Time*.

The Last Producer

(2000)

"I love the French because you are as good as your best work, in this country you're as good as your last work."—Sonny Wexler

For Sonny Wexler (Reynolds), Hollywood has changed. He used to be a film industry power player, a producer who drafted contracts with the top people. A rarity in the business, Sonny also appreciates the cinema of Italy and France, and he subscribes to the theories of Orson Welles: "The first shot in the picture is the most important shot in the picture." He has worked with the likes of Richard Brooks and Fred Zinnemann, names that mean something to many people but not to the current crop of young hotshot executives running the studios. After 40 years in the business, Sonny is one of the last of his breed still alive and active; at business meetings he evokes the McCarthy witch hunts, which perhaps only dates him even more in the eyes of younger potential investors.

Sonny seeks financing for a script he has optioned from an up-and-coming screenwriter, Bo Pomerantz (Sean Astin), a project that he thinks will get him back in the good graces of the film industry and which will be his lasting legacy; he thinks this film won't only rejuvenate his own finances but could help his prescription pill–addicted wife and struggling restaurant-owner daughter. But getting pitches heard is proving tough: Despite having once produced an Oscar-nominated picture, he is met with indifference and ignorance. Sonny's producing partner Syd Wolf (Charles Durning) is skeptical and would rather they enjoyed living in the glory of the old days than start all over again with the uncompromising new regime at the studios. "You've got two choices," Syd tells Sonny. "You can march in there with a rocket between your legs and cut yourself a deal; or you can go and tell him how brilliant he is, how fair he is, how honest he is and then lay down, spread your legs and he'll fuck you." Sonny may not spread his legs, but he is about to get fucked regardless. He may know all the old studio secretaries and security guards but Sonny is no longer appreciated by studio head Damon Black (Benjamin Bratt). Black is the kind of sleazeball who believes his own bullshit when he spouts lines like "Hollywood is the center of the universe; we're like our own religion or Catholicism, only we've reached more souls than Christ." He uses a persecution complex to justify his grandstanding, lying about a blue collar background when he is actually the son of a wealthy banker, even claiming to hang out in working class bars to give him an insight into the kinds of films that ordinary people really want to see. Ever the shark in a silver silk suit, Black attempts to cut Sonny out of the deal and secure the rights to the script directly from Bo, leaving Sonny with three days on this option to come up with the $50,000 required to purchase the script or end up losing out on a major deal. In his desperation, Sonny turns to some unsavory investors.

The Last Producer is very much a personal piece for Reynolds, and one can certainly sense his dismay at his place in the film industry of the new millennium. Sonny's frustration is clearly drawn from Reynolds' own fall from grace with the major studios and the satirical jabs at the flippancies of the industry are indeed stinging. Despite the critical observations of a corrupt industry and some genuine drama in the various familial subplots, it doesn't stop Reynolds from crafting a pleasant, approachable comedy. There are moments of self-pity, but Sonny's concerns aren't entirely selfish or egotistical, it is out of anxiety for his ailing family that he is motivated to make one final cinematic statement. Reynolds excels in these kinds of roles primarily due to the sincerity of his delivery; he is in the rare position of being at once one of the most recognizable and famous film stars of all time yet possesses a vulnerable underdog quality that you can't help but root for. Just as Sonny believes in his script, Reynolds too brings a sense of conviction to *The Last Producer* and here he is terrifically and hyperbolically supported by Rod Steiger as Sheri Gance, a rather shady ex-cop who helps Sonny deal with Armenian Mafia financiers and offers expert advice on gainful insurance fraud; Ganse sinisterly promises that he can take of anything ... *anything!* As in *The Hollywood Sign,* Steiger and Reynolds make a formidable screen duo, worlds

Two screen legends, Rod Steiger and Reynolds, share a tender moment in *The Last Producer* (2000).

apart in terms of acting style yet abundant in personality and presence, their chemistry obvious and immediate.

The Last Producer is beautifully shot by cinematographer Nick McLean Sr., who took full advantage of the rich canvas of Malibu and Hollywood exteriors as well as the Warner Brothers backlot. McLean made terrifically fluid use of the Steadicam to give an otherwise static comedy picture a sense of grace and immediacy:

> The location and exteriors played a big part in how I shot the film. Malibu has everything a cinematographer could want; it's got good, clear weather, sometimes a lot of fog, and a lot of colors with the ocean and the clear blue skies. It's a great palette to work with. Burt wanted me to use a lot of handheld camera on *The Last Producer*; he wanted it to have a light, airy feeling so he allowed me to try different things with the camera. There was no point in over-stylizing the film, because it is a bright comedy, but going handheld was indeed something new for that type of film because in the old days they didn't do much of that handheld stuff, especially on comedies. Once you knew how the scene was to play out, I could think of ideas of how I wanted to shoot it, he trusted my judgment. Working with Burt meant total freedom of ideas and expression.[1]

Note

1. Nick McLean Sr., *interview with author*, Skype, January 15, 2018.

Driven

(2001)

"Buckle up. It's going to be a bumpy ride!"—Cathy Heguy

Former hotshot driver Joe Tanto (Sylvester Stallone) is brought back to the track by paraplegic team owner Carl Henry (Reynolds) when his up-and-coming rookie Jimmy Bly (Kip Pardue) starts to lose form thanks to his greedy and overbearing brother-manager, Demille Bly (Robert Sean Leonard). Carl thinks Joe can mentor Jimmy to success and give the reigning champion Beau Brandenberg (Til Schweiger) a run for his money. Joe's tutelage doesn't sit well with Demille, who would much rather see his brother meeting and greeting the press and nurturing corporate sponsorship deals; this of course brings much pressure upon Jimmy while tension in the camp mounts.

Joe's ex-wife Cathy Heguy (Gina Gershon) has found love and lust in young stud driver Memo Moreno (Cristián de la Fuente), which further complicates Joe's return to the team. Hanger-on Sophia (Estelle Warren) betrays her Beau for Jimmy, which causes the rookie further consternation on the track; and then there's Lucretia Clan (Stacy Edwards), a journalist writing an article on the male dominance of the sport but who ends up in Joe's arms. And so our helmeted heroes engage in a battle for glory on the race track and on the field of love, as the rivaling, fervid passions for Women and Automobiles are both at stake in this glorified soap opera.

Stallone tried for several years to make *Driven* a "go picture" at several studios. That's when independent production company Franchise Pictures came in. Co-owned by businessman Elie Samaha and former actor Andrew Stevens, Franchise specialized in straight-to-video and made-for-cable genre pictures before hitting upon something big with the cult movie *The Boondock Saints* (1999). In the following years, Franchise nurtured relationships with major stars by expressing interest in producing their passion projects which had been languishing in development hell and turnaround; in other words: scripts sitting on shelves. Success was achieved in earnest with the Bruce Willis vehicle *The Whole Nine Yards* (Jonathan Lynn, 2000) but only failure was achieved with John Travolta's long-gestating *Battlefield Earth* (Roger Christian, 2000) and the unfortunate Kevin Costner crime caper *3000 Miles to Graceland* (Demian Lichtenstein, 2001).

Driven would prove similarly ill-fated; it had stiff competition in another petrol picture released around the same time, Rob Cohen's *The Fast and the Furious*. Cohen's film quadrupled its budget to take in over $200 million and spawned a billion-dollar franchise, while Harlin's picture failed to recoup its budget of $94 million, stalling at a worldwide gross of $54 million. As its producer, screenwriter and star, Stallone's commercial cachet perhaps suffered more than any other for the film's failure. It would take the one-two punch of the near-simultaneous *Rocky* and *Rambo* revivals for Stallone to regain his iconic leading man status and climb out of the less-salubrious milieu in which he briefly found himself churning out the likes of *Avenging Angelo* (Martyn Burke, 2002) and *Shade* (Damian Neiman, 2003).

Director Renny Harlin and Stallone had worked together previously on the excellent action adventure *Cliffhanger* (1993) but the results here are less thrilling. Stallone's script supplies plenty of earnest platitudes for Joe to spout as required to the apathetic Jimmy, but the off-track dramas are of little consequence in comparison to the vehicular action which takes precedence. Indeed, the paper-thin narrative is strung together with dazzling displays of film assembly, frenetically edited footage which allows the picture's indulgent two-hour running time to pass by at a swift pace. Harlin edited the picture in such a manner that even dramatic dialogue scenes are assembled as though they were high-octane action sequences. The camera roves, zooms—*constantly* zooms—and circles around the characters as the editor insistently cuts; shots barely have time to breathe or reveal their *mise-en-scéne* before we cut to another angle. It's a jarring style of editing but it does give the picture a nimble, restless momentum; sometimes hypnotic, sometimes irritating, but always zooming.

Despite the bland characterizations and empty dialogue, some of the set pieces truly are awe-inspiring, including an exciting chase sequence that begins with two prototype cars being stolen from an industry party. On the streets of Chicago they hurtle dangerously through the regular nighttime downtown traffic. In another scene imbued with the film's dynamic spirit, Memo, instructed by the conniving and irresponsible Cathy, vies for the lead in a race, and collides with Bly. Memo loses control, veers off the track and crashes into a lake upside down. As a minor character in the film, we are less likely to assume Memo will survive, which increases our anxiety as Jimmy and Beau join forces to rescue him. It is a brilliantly constructed piece of suspense cinema. In scenes like these, it is easy to appreciate Harlin's innovative camerawork and use of special effects, which puts the viewer right into the driver's seat and onto the track in a maelstrom of speed, thunder and flying debris. It all makes for a rare cinematic experience; we are aware that the picture we are watching is quite awful in most aspects, yet we can't help but appreciate the sheer spectacle on display, nor deny its superficial qualities. Evidently, shooting the film at actual major racing events meant that the film looks even more extravagant than it might otherwise, with thousands of racing enthusiasts filling the stands and allowing the logistical difficulties of filming staged racing sequences to be minimized. With its high-gloss techno sheen, hyper-stylized MTV editing, agitated, restless camerawork and pulsating rap-rock soundtrack, *Driven* feels very much like the relic of turn-of-the-millennium pop culture that it is.

With *Smokey and the Bandit*, *The Cannonball Run* and *Stroker Ace* in mind, Reynolds' presence here may feel to be paying homage to his own history in the realm of celluloid cars'n'carnage, but *Driven* bears only passing resemblance to those films in its spectacular stunt work. Reynolds went on to appear in a cameo in the 2001 German picture *Auf Herz und Nieren*, a crime caper produced by his *Driven* co-star Til Schweiger.

Tempted

(2001)

"Under these waters, under this weed, things lurk that you don't want to think about. You would get nightmares out of what's under here and that's what my town is built on. All of these buildings, this whole place is built on the swamp. Think about it, a whole town built on those dark, shitty, shifting waters. That's New Orleans. That's my world...."—Charlie LeBlanc

Reynolds plays Charlie Le Blanc, a nouveau riche construction tycoon who is diagnosed with a terminal brain disease. He is married to a beautiful, statuesque ex-model, Lilly (Saffron Burrows), but before Charlie leaves his fortune to the trophy wife he wants to test Lilly's loyalty and fidelity. Charlie offers one of his employees, a young carpenter and part-time law student, $50,000 to tempt Lilly into committing adultery. Thus begins the downward spiral of Jimmy Mulate (Peter Facinelli), with a free lunch and a hundred dollar bill. He struggles to pay his law school tuition with the minimum wages he earns on Charlie's construction sites; the upfront advance of $10,000 is enough for Jimmy to seriously consider the seduction of Lilly. In an extension of his paranoia, Charlie enlists the services of surveillance expert Byron Blades (George DiCenzo) to record Jimmy and Lilly's every move. Byron normally doesn't take on anything as disreputable as cheating spouse cases, but will make an exception "as a personal favor" to Charlie; Byron alludes to having engaged in deceptive industrial practices on behalf of Charlie in the past, giving us an insight into Charlie's darker side. Lilly initially rejects Jimmy's advances but soon becomes wise to her husband's scheme and decides to turn the tables on him, inviting young Jimmy into her home and into her bosom.

Jimmy denies that anything indecent took place, but Byron's surveillance tapes provide enough damning evidence to Charlie that his wife may not be worthy of the inheritance. Jimmy's life is further complicated when he is implicated in the murder of a governor's son when his friend, Ted (Eric Mabius), murders his ex-boyfriend in a jealous rage. Ted convinces Jimmy to help him dispose of the body by accusing the deceased of molesting under-age boys and willfully spreading deadly diseases to unaware sexual partners ("He gave a

Jimmy Mulate (Peter Facinelli) and Lilly LeBlanc (Saffron Burrow) heat things up in *Tempted* (2001).

14-year-old boy AIDS, he's a fucking murderer!"). As a budding law student, Jimmy should know better than to aid and abet a killer. In no time whatsoever, the cops are all over Jimmy, ruining his chances of an internship with lawyer David Crabbe (Michael Arata). In another twist sealing Jimmy's fate, Lilly seduces Crabbe and convinces him to destroy vital evidence that implicates her in the web of intrigue.

Tempted opens terrifically with a camera tracking directly through a sun-kissed, golden-hued Louisiana swampland before cutting and seamlessly continuing its tracking shot through the treacherous dry domain of the Big Heat. In the great tradition of film noir, the omniscient opening narration is that of a dead man, though we are yet to realize it. The voice is that of Charlie LeBlanc, introducing us to the dark and dangerous world of his New Orleans. From there, director Bill Bennett piles on one plot twist after another, keeping us attentive with surprising double-crosses and triple-crosses. Bennett wisely avoids assigning any one particular character with more virtue than the other; each character remains as morally questionable and ambiguous as the other, making it harder for us to guess what the outcome will be. Killing Charlie off as the third act gets underway is quite an ingenious move as we are left without our lead actor to guide us through to the end of the film, leaving it entirely open and unpredictable as to where the narrative will take us.

Burrows and Facinelli make a compelling screen duo; her: tall and powerful, icy and detached; him: boyish and somewhat mopish; their sex scenes are suitably steamy. Once

Lilly takes charge of the situation, she exudes a predatory and manipulative side which makes her a powerful adversary for anyone looking to conspire against her; she is a suitable heir to the throne of the foregone femme fatale. However, one of the best performances in the film is Mike Starr's brilliantly understated turn as Charlie's loyal assistant Dot Collins. Minding Charlie's affairs is Dot's calling in life and Starr plays the role with such nuanced menace and absolute devotion to his boss as to render him bone-chilling. Watch Starr's subtle, rage-fueled facial tics as he witnesses Charlie's embarrassment and humiliation when presented with video footage of his wife betraying him. Dot is the kind of guy willing to throw his loving wife under a bus to make Charlie feel better after such a devastating discovery: "I don't got them kind of problems; I can't relate. You know my old lady, Pooch, bless her heart, she makes a mean muffaletta, keeps a good home. About the only man looking to fuck her would be Ray Charles." When Dot later refuses the hearty breakfast served up by his wife, the scene is played almost entirely on Starr's face as Dot accepts his fatalist quest of vengeance for his beloved boss. There's a subtle tragi-comic delivery in his refusal of his wife's cooking as he strides out of the kitchen to certain doom.

With its themes of adultery, conspiracy, obsession and revenge, all set against a torrid Southern backdrop, *Tempted* makes for a fine erotic thriller. Indeed, the sultry New Orleans setting is a major boon to the film, allowing Bennett to create a world of stark contrast and atmosphere, taking us from the white-washed bourgeois mansions to the louche neon-lit streets of scurvy blues bars and jazz joints. Much credit must also go to cinematographer Tony Clark and composer David Bridie for their contributions to this incredibly stylish and brooding environment for our characters to put their Machiavellian schemes into operation.

An Interview with Bill Bennett

Acclaimed filmmaker Bill Bennett has directed some of the most highly regarded works in contemporary Australian cinema, with several pictures recognized and honored at prestigious film festivals around the world. *Backlash* (1986) and *Malpractice* (1989) were both invited to Un Certain Regard to be part of the official selection of the Cannes Film Festival, while his 1996 feature *Kiss or Kill* won seven Australian Film Institute awards, including Best Picture and Best Director. In the late 1990s, he brought his distinctive style to Hollywood and directed major studio star vehicles such as *Two If by Sea* starring Denis Leary and Sandra Bullock, and *Tempted*.

Wayne: Tempted *has a wonderfully twisted narrative, it feels very much part of the canon of film noir. Was this a conscious influence in making the film?*

Bill: Yes, I am a student of cinema and I do love the classic noir films but really it was just an idea that intrigued me, this story of a man who destroys what he has by not believing that he's good enough for what he has. As regards the narrative and characters, we actually didn't use a script, we improvised using a treatment.

That's fascinating. Is that something you do often?

I've made a number of films that were improvised, including *Backlash* and *Malpractice*. I come from a documentary background and essentially what I do is work with the actors around a treatment. The treatment is normally around 20 pages long with a scene-by-scene breakdown and which doesn't include dialogue. I always have a two-week rehearsal period and it's always on location and the idea is to bring the actors to a point of such intimate connection with their characters that the dialogue comes as a natural consequence of that. So they know what their reality is; they know who they are, their backstory and their backgrounds, every intimate detail of their characters.

Tempted **director Bill Bennett (photograph courtesy Bill Bennett Collection).**

What does rehearsing on location offer such a method of working?

Being on location is important because it instills in them a sense of place and a sense of geography which impacts on their character in a whole lot of different ways. It impacts on their speech, on their physical movements, their body language, every physical aspect of their character. What we'll do in rehearsal is go through the treatment and the scenes, look at each beat and find what is required of that beat, what's underneath that beat, always keeping it from the point of view of that particular character and what that character knows and doesn't know. The dialogue comes at the very end of all that. We don't run lines or discuss dialogue during the rehearsal process, it comes on the day when it's time to shoot. Normally, we get it in two or three takes, sometimes more but not often. The idea really comes from documentary filmmaking.

Was it that sense of dramatic urgency that you get from real-life situations that you wanted to bring to fiction filmmaking?

I was always a frustrated dramatist when I was making documentaries because I would be dealing with these real people and real situations, spending a lot of time with them beforehand researching them and getting to know them, and then I would see them interact with others in these very dramatic situations. I was always surprised that they would come out with something that I could never predict nor could ever write as a dramatist, and yet what they came out with was entirely consistent with what I knew of them as a character or as a person. I wanted to have that capacity with fictional drama, to work with smart actors who are able to build a real character and have their responses to situations come from their world view.

Do you find actors are, in general, open to this method of working?

Some are and some aren't. The ones that aren't I weed out. Burt, I discovered early on, is quite a traditionalist. He is a very clever actor, and a fine actor, but he likes control, and this whole process was an act of letting go of control.

And so he came around to this way of working?
He came around to it after a while. Once he did, he found it incredibly liberating.

Does this method not play to his sense of control in affording him the ability to improvise and therefore control the dialogue?
But he couldn't control the people around him.

I see. How did the three main players find working this way as a unit?
Every actor comes from a different background of training and way of working. My job as a director is to even all that out. This way of working is a very empowering process for an actor. When you get to a rehearsal, all the actors want to do is get up and rehearse lines, to which I say to them, "How can you rehearse lines if you don't know who your character is? All you're doing is making stuff up." This method is not about making stuff up, it's about finding the truth of the characters and the truth of the moment and you can't do that unless you know who your character is entirely and what the truths of the moment are, and that's what this process is all about. Usually what happens is that at the start of the process the actors love the idea of it, then they get into it and find it terrifying, but at the end of the shoot they say, "I do not want to work any way other than this. I've had such fun, and it's been amazing."

Burt brought a great vulnerability to the role, even though the character ultimately engages in a nefarious scheme.
Burt was a very interesting actor to work with. I mean, he's a movie star, a genuine movie star. When you walk down the street with Burt, cars stop, they will hang out windows and call out to him; they'll stop him to take pictures, they'll follow him down the street, even young girls. He'd often turn around to a young girl tugging at his shirt tails and say, "Hey, do you know how old I am?" The thing about Burt that amazed me is that he is a consummate professional; he did his research for the film by reading a crime fiction author called James Lee Burke. Burt really studied his work.

What made you consider Burt for the role in the first place?
We share the same agency and his name came up on a list, and I had always admired him as an actor and I just felt he was right for the role; it really was as simple as that. Working with Burt is not easy, he is demanding of a director and I understand why, because he has worked with some of the best directors in the world. With a film shot in this particular way where I have to be in control, we clashed a couple of times, but in the end he respected my vision and in the end he believed it was some of the best work he had ever done. He appeared on *The Actor's Studio* after the film and he mentioned that it was among his best work. I think that is true, I do think it is one of his best performances.

What instigated the clash? Direction over character, narrative, aesthetics?
Oh, we had a couple of little contretemps. One of them was about the way I wanted to shoot a stunt sequence, which was quite an unusual way to shoot such a sequence but it was within the style of the film. Burt arrived with storyboards about how he thought the stunt should be shot. You have to remember that Burt is one of the top stunt coordinators

in the world so he knows how to film stunts. When I ran through the set-ups, he disagreed and said, "That's not going to work!" But I was confident that my idea would work because it was within the style of the film.

How did you resolve the issue?

The way we settled it was that I said, "Burt, let's do this my way and what I'll do is show it to you on the video monitor and talk you through how it's going to be cut together," and that's what we did. He looked at the shots, understood how it was going to be edited and he said, "Yeah, okay."

Can you tell me about the release of the film?

Well, the film was actually held for about a year because of a very complicated technical issue. What happened was, we discovered a problem with the negative cutting that took us a year to get right.

That sounds like a nightmarish scenario for a filmmaker. What happened?

The cutting machine that we used was out by a couple of microns which meant that every single cut was slightly out, not so much that it was perceptible to the human eye but it wouldn't have passed a [Quality Control] test. So we had to rectify every single cut in the film, which meant doing a digital rectification, and digital work wasn't as advanced as it is now so it took a long time and cost a lot of money. But the problem was solved and the film premiered at the San Sebastian Film Festival as part of a gala retrospective of Burt's work and he was duly feted.

I would imagine that someone of Burt's star caliber would be used to wielding a lot of influence on the set. Around this time, he began to work with a lot of independent directors, a younger generation.

A lot of first-time directors don't know what they're doing and sometimes you'll have a more experienced actor like Burt trying to call the shots, but I am experienced, I have won awards all over the world from some of the most prestigious film festivals, so I knew what I was doing. The way I work as a director is that on one hand I relinquish control to the actors, I have to in order for them to bring me the performance that I'm looking for. But on the other hand, I have to smack their hand and say, "No, stay in your box! You don't own the character, I own the character. You don't own this film, I own this film." And that's not only with Burt, it happens with experienced actors and inexperienced actors. Burt's an intimidating person, he's a tough cookie, but I have to say I came away from making the film with an enormous regard for Burt.

What is it that makes you consider him so highly?

He is not only a consummate actor but a true professional; I was not at all expecting him to approach the film with the level of knowledge that he brought. He is one of these unique people like Clint Eastwood who have been major stars for four or five decades in a row, there aren't many people like that and what happens when you have people like that, who have been working at the level they are for such a long time, is that they know the business and they know how filmmaking works. They have an extraordinary understanding of how a set works and how movies are put together. Burt is a film historian and he is very serious about the theater. His knowledge and love of theater is testament to his ability and approach to the craft. You have got to be serious about acting to do that.

What do you consider to be the essential ingredients that make Burt such a magnetic screen presence, such a star?

That's such a hard question; you could ask that of any actor. If you saw some of these people in the street, you wouldn't stop and say there's anything special about them. When it comes down to it, there's an underlying truth to the person, an uncompromising truth of knowing who they are and what they want, and that is the case with Burt. He remained uncompromising throughout his career. Whenever you are uncompromising, you will attract detractors, because sometimes the choices you make aren't the choices other people want you to make, or what the viewers want you to make. You know, I feel the same as you, I don't think people have given Burt his due as a great actor. Burt makes it look so easy, but critics and the public don't understand the huge intelligence and craft that goes into a performance that looks effortless. Burt has that ability and it comes from 50 years in the business working alongside some of the best actors and directors that have ever walked the planet. I admire Burt for the taking the line that he has; he could have become the cheesy movie star but he never did, he remained an actor, and that's why I wanted to work with him.

Hotel

(2001)

> "We came to a group decision to cut the iambic pentameters, heptameters, archaisms in order to try and create a fast food McMalfi, as it were, that would be easily digestible and accessible even to Hollywood stars."—Bosola

A film crew descends upon Venice, Italy, to shoot a cinematic adaptation of John Webster's Jacobean tragedy *The Duchess of Malfi*, in the style of the Dogme 95 manifesto. The picture is being directed by the unruly, egomaniacal Welsh filmmaker Trent Stoken (Rhys Ifans) and produced by Jonathan Danderfine (David Schwimmer). The production is being filmed by a TV crew fronted by obnoxious presenter Charlee Boux (Salma Hayak); her banal and insistent line of questioning often triggers Stoken to explode on camera, which of course is great material for a tabloid TV program. Most of the action takes place in the art deco confines of the Hungaria Hotel, where the production is based during their stay in Venice and which functions as a breeding ground of eccentricity with its own cast of oddballs, such as the hotel's in-house tour guide (Julian Sands), who is also a text-quoting former classical actor. Stoken is not making a Webster adaptation of Merchant-Ivory sensibilities; in fact, he chastises his actors for daring to bring some semblance of class or literary awareness to the picture. When the actors playing Antonio and the duchess rehearse a seduction scene in the manner of a classical reading of the text, Stoken disparages them for their decorum and demands of Antonio, "I want you to fuck her like a criminal!" Elsewhere, screenwriter Bosola (Heathcote Williams) harshly criticizes the simplification of his script when an actor complains of the lack of poetry to the words, as it has been decided that they had to "cut the iambic pentameters, heptameters, archaisms in order to try and create a fast food McMalfi." Perhaps not surprisingly, Stoken is shot by an assassin during a production meeting, but rather than killing him, he is put into a coma in which he can still see and hear all around him but cannot move. Hilariously, when Stoken is gunned down, no member of his crew realizes what has happened, they merely think he has just taken to the ground in a moment of eccentric dissociation.

Hotel is a subversive and intriguing piece of avant garde filmmaking and perhaps a most unlikely film to feature in this overview of Reynolds' career. Here in the fleeting role as the Flamenco manager, Reynolds' screen time is minimal, no more than a couple of minutes, and he is given only one line of dialogue. There is an interesting moment in the documentary on the making of *Hotel* presented on the European DVD which captures a terse exchange between Reynolds and director Mike Figgis. For the actors who took part in the making of *Hotel*, there was a narrative structure in place but there was no script; improvisation was necessary and, due to the multi-camera format of filming, the actors had to be ready at all times in case of being caught in the lens at any given moment, requiring them to be constantly in-character and not to rely on cues. The personas assumed by the actors are entirely their own creations and they had to invent their own inter-relationships. In a cast meeting observed in the documentary, Reynolds very politely wonders if he will receive any form of character backstory and be informed of his relationship to any of the many other actors. Figgis essentially says no, which leads a quietly frustrated though considerably calm Reynolds to wonder how an actor can logically perform a scene with other actors and not have any context or subtext in relation to his character and that of his fellow performers.

Despite the high marquee value of the international ensemble cast, *Hotel* is niche in the extreme and belies standard critical evaluation as neither traditional narrative trajectory nor classical film grammar applies here. The formal experimentalism and complex visual language of the film makes it sometimes hard to distinguish whether the characters' actions are part of the "real" world or that of the film-within-the-film. Using split screen designs and various dimensions for framing the action, the film often has the feel of a cinematic collage, a motion picture art installation experimenting with unique variations on narrative storytelling techniques, as with its quad-screen style in which four scenes unfold simultaneously. Due to the lo-fi digital photography, the beauty of Venice is rarely exploited; rather the picture has a muted, unattractive, un-cinematic quality that adds to its unnerving tone, and it is hard not to be taken in by the eerie, hypnotic atmosphere that Figgis crafts.

Despite the faux-realism of the documentary style, there is no gesture of verisimilitude. In fact, there are hints of vampirism and other unnatural proceedings within the hotel. Supporting the macabre tone is the grisly detours into cannibalism as well as a predilection for salacious psychosexual imagery, though there is nothing at all erotic about unsettling moments such as the night-vision seduction of the comatose director by the lustful hotel maid; or the bizarre scene in which Antonio receives rough anal sex from the duchess, only for her to give birth to twin plastic babies immediately after her orgasm.

Throughout his career, Figgis has oscillated wildly from flagrantly commercial studio pictures which sometimes failed miserably on both financial and aesthetic levels (*Mr. Jones, Cold Creek Manor, One Night Stand*) while some are remarkably effective (*Internal Affairs,*

Liebestraum, Leaving Las Vegas). But to most of his admirers, he is most remarkable for his idiosyncratic auteur works *Time Code* and *Hotel*, pictures which are at the very least intriguingly assembled.

Hotel is an easy film to dislike. It is pretentious in the extreme and offers nothing of film tradition to its audience, but it is this very refusal to conform to any expectations where one may find something admirable. This self-reflexive picture works best as a dark satire aimed at the absurdities of film production and bloated ego, though the improvisatory nature of the performances vary in quality: Some feel natural with the actors at ease with this daring method, while others mug and grimace their way through the proceedings, coming across as amateurish and embarrassing. In Figgis' resolve to reinvent cinema as something elusive and less easily definable, perhaps even digestible, *Hotel* is an intriguing, challenging, if not entirely fulfilling, visual experience.

Keen eyes will note the presence of two of Reynolds' recent collaborators, Danny Huston (director of *The Maddening*) and Saffron Burrows (co-star of *Tempted*).

The Hollywood Sign
(2001)

"I thought I saw your filthy face during the service and I'm glad to say you look as outrageous as ever."—Floyd Benson

Tom Greener (Tom Berenger), Kage Mulligan (Reynolds) and Floyd Benson (Rod Steiger) are actors whose glory days have long since passed and are now juggling lives of little consequence. Greener has returned to Tinseltown looking for a way back into the industry following a stint in prison for a fraudulent film production deal; Mulligan is an alcoholic mourning his dead son and moribund career; and Benson, once a screen legend with awards to his name, now fits house alarms for a living. It is through this endeavor that Benson hatches a plan to strike it rich and fund a comeback film that will spark interest in their respective careers. One evening, while drinking and wistfully reminiscing upon their lost profession at the Hollywood sign, the three thespians discover the decomposing corpse of a man that Benson recognizes as an associate of a criminal outfit in whose mansion he recently installed a burglar alarm. "How do you know they're gangsters?" Greener asks. "They had the big Rolex watches, they had the gold chains around their neck, and they had crocodile shoes on!" replies Benson. Mulligan hilariously retorts, "That doesn't mean anything, Floyd. They could have been executives from Paramount!"

The boss of said outfit, Rodney di Giacomo (Al Sapienza), siphons millions from a Las Vegas casino via a screenwriter girlfriend, Paula Carver (Jacqueline Kim), who is "researching" a spec script that should break her into the big time, if only it weren't for the downbeat ending that has producers fretting over the script's commercial prospects. It turns out that Paula is also a failed industry vet and former colleague of Greener. Together with the troika, Paula helps secure a Hollywood comeback like no other and all they need is the cash to fund it. The quartet plans to infiltrate di Giacomo's decadent Hollywood Hills bolthole and purloin the casino cash for their own needs. In order to do so, Greener, Mulligan, and Benson must give the performance of their lives.

The Hollywood Sign has enough self-conscious references and in-jokes to keep it moving along amiably when the convoluted heist plot becomes too far-fetched. Both the picture's pathos and humor are delivered courtesy of Reynolds' introspective consideration of his own career. In one sequence, Mulligan tearfully watches himself in *Navajo Joe*, reflecting upon the youthful beauty and feats of physical virility the actor was once capable of. The intertextuality doesn't stop there. Another gag plays upon our familiarity with Reynolds' image and masculine persona, as the clean-shaven Mulligan uses a Reynolds-like thin mustache as a disguise only for him to rub it off by accident in a fit of anxiety. *The Hollywood Sign* is another of Reynolds' self-referential films about filmmaking, something which interested the actor as far back as *Fade In* and which he continued to indulge in with *Nickelodeon, Best Friends, Hooper, Boogie Nights, Hotel, The Last Producer* and *The Last Movie Star* (not to mention Mel Brooks' *Silent Movie* and Robert Altman's *The Player*). It's almost as if Reynolds himself was continually trying to understand the intricacies and fripperies of the industry that anointed him the most financially successful for five consecutive years, then relegated him to lesser roles. *Boogie Nights* and its disturbing portrayal of the darker side of the San Fernando Valley notwithstanding, it is with affection and bemusement that Reynolds' respective characters in these films are engaged with the movie business; *The Hollywood Sign*, for example, provides many funny moments for the cine-literate in the audience, such as when Mulligan announces, "I played a forensic expert on a Roger Corman movie.... I was very good!" or when Benson says he's going to star in the new David Lean picture, despite the British director being dead for ten years.

In 2001, Hollywood was still cashing in on *Pulp Fiction* and the kind of cynical black comedy crime capers that Tarantino's film inspired. These pictures offer violent criminals ironically pondering the culinary flaws and qualities of fast food—in this case, raw fish. That very contrast of benign and routine conversation mixed with moments of vicious carnage is one of the ingredients of this kind of American independent picture of the period, along with verbose and often digressive dialogue, brash amorality and a bratty disregard for character and narrative convention. These tropes can be found in films such as *Things to Do in Denver When You're Dead* (Gary Fleder, 1995), *2 Days in the Valley* (John Herzfeld, 1996), *8 Heads in a Duffel Bag* (Tom Schulman, 1997), *The Boondock Saints* (Troy Duffy, 1999) *et al.* Only Tom DiCillo's *Double Whammy* (2001) saw though the diminishing returns of this particular subgenre and satirized it to great effect. If it weren't for Reynolds' contemplative moments in the picture, *The Hollywood Sign* would be bereft of any kind of gravitas. Steiger plays it large and loud, going for the big laughs with his over-the-top gruff demeanor and strange, unclassifiable cadence, while Berenger is a suitably stoic hero. So it is left to Reynolds to import some compelling honesty, pathos and drama into a film otherwise bereft of those qualities.

It is perhaps no coincidence that Mulligan is the only well-drawn, sufficiently personable character in the film. More than once, it feels that we are less watching Kage Mulligan than we are watching actual Burt Reynolds.

Snapshots

(2002)

"You can only crap on one crapper at a time. I don't need an extra crapper."—Larry Goldberg

Aisha (Carmen Chaplin) is the somewhat spoiled and self-indulgent daughter of wealthy divorced parents. Against her mother Narma's (Julie Christie) wishes, Aisha takes a trip to Amsterdam, where the mother fears her precious daughter will be seduced into a den of iniquity. But Aisha seeks not decadent delights but profound artistic and spiritual enlightenment, and some less-neurotic human contact. Aisha finds what she is looking for in the form of an aging prostitute who works the red light district, and in elderly bookstore owner Larry Goldberg (Reynolds). Larry is a countercultural holdout of the 1960s, still listening to Jimi Hendrix and believing he can change the world with his rustic emporium of literature. There is a subplot concerning some shady individuals, who also happen to be rare book collectors, who bribe and later coerce Larry into selling his store, which is the only remaining active unit in a potentially lucrative property re-development scheme. This thread of narrative is of little importance, it merely exists to serve Larry's rebel credentials, not selling out to "the man" by consistently refusing suitcases full of cash. Coincidentally, Aisha reminds Larry of a woman he was once deeply in love with and it is soon revealed that he is the subject of a long-harbored secret that will bring Narma to Amsterdam. When Larry and Narma come face to face, their meeting reignites a long lost love affair that began decades ago in Morocco, where Larry and Narma first met and began a whirlwind romance that seemed ill-fated, until Aisha walked into Larry's bookstore 30 years later.

Carmen Chaplin is radiant in the role of Aisha and the scenes in which she poses for her artfully erotic photography are simultaneously tasteful and scintillating. She and Reynolds work fine together as Larry and Aisha develop their friendship and uncertain romantic attraction. However, the placement of Reynolds as an aging hippie doesn't ring entirely true, nor does the idealized romance between him and Julie Christie. It is not that the actors don't share much chemistry, it comes down to the fact that they simply don't share enough screen time to depict what is discussed in reverential tones as such a great, meaningful bond. We are led to believe that there is an elemental, pan-generational, cross-continental connection between these star-crossed lovers who seem destined for one another, yet when they finally reunite there is little to suggest the depth of their history and attraction.

There are moments in *Snapshots* that suggest the picture could have been an edgy, psychosexual indie drama, had the picture more nerve to explore the complicated relationship between Larry and Aisha. The filmmakers could have exploited the red-herring suggestion that Aisha may in fact be Larry's daughter, but the picture is rarely so daring as to suggest Larry's misjudged feelings for Aisha may actually contain some unintended incestuous longing; the film is too good-natured to approach anything so salacious. Ultimately, with its genial tone, wistful nostalgic yearnings, coming-of-age enlightenment, and exotic travelogue locations, *Snapshots* evinces the kind of simple pleasures and temperate dramatics of a lightweight chick-lit romance novel.

Time of the Wolf

(2002)

"Sometimes a man takes a gun and puts it in his hands and life gets real simple. All his troubles and all his problems are right there in front of him. All he's got to do is squeeze the trigger."—Archie

After the untimely death of his parents, Aaron McGregor (Devin Douglas Drewitz) begins a new life with his aunt Rebecca (Marthe Keller) and uncle Archie (Burt Reynolds) in the Canadian countryside. The youngster finds it tough settling into his new school and into his new surrogate family. Rebecca and Archie are somewhat reluctant guardians of the young orphan; Archie was estranged from his brother, Aaron's father, while Rebecca doesn't feel she is morally or psychologically strong enough for the role of substitute mother. She is initially cold and bitter towards Aaron, chiding him for not finishing his dinner, even on the day of his parents' burial, but this form of aggression actually masks unfortunate wounds of the past: the death of her and Archie's child, whom Aaron closely resembles. While in mourning and struggling to adapt, Aaron also becomes the victim of the school bully, which gains him the sympathy of his conscientious schoolteacher Mr. Nelson (Jason Priestley). But where Aaron truly finds comfort is in the company of wolves, which he discovers after finding an injured wolf and nursing it back to health. As Aaron develops a unique bond with these animals in the wild backwoods, Archie warns Aaron not tell anyone about his new friends as they would soon be hunted down and slaughtered by local farmers. Aaron continues to roam his new homeland and discovers a love of the wilderness while coming to terms with the loss of his parents. Just as he begins to feel settled into his new way of life, Aaron learns that his well-to-do cousin is willing to adopt him into a comfortable suburban middle-class life. The child is soon torn between the stability that they offer and the call of the wild.

Time of the Wolf is based on Thomas A. MacDonald's 1994 Young Adult novel, though rather than being set in the late nineteenth century the film transposes the tale to a more modern milieu. The story's enchanting setting in the wilderness of rural Toronto and within the MacGregors' rustic farmhouse instills in the picture a timeless quality. This is a pleasant melodrama though it does falter somewhat as it invites more drama than it delivers. Dark themes are present but rarely explored with any great depth, such as the revelation that Aaron's bully is a victim of physical abuse at the hands of a fierce disciplinarian father. While that issue is confronted and sensitively handled, the script soft-pedals its depiction of emotional abuse at the hands of Aunt Rebecca. Her bullying and resentment of Aaron is tempered by Archie's warm and humane treatment of the situation. He makes some excuses for her behavior: "She's had a lot of pain in her life, she has just built this wall where she won't let anything bad come in. Unfortunately the wall keeps the bad things out, but also keeps out good things. Just give her some time, she's a good woman."

Reynolds brings warmth and tenderness to his role, affording the actor another opportunity to explore the themes of patriarchy and surrogate familial bonds that have recurred throughout his career. But Archie's benign nature makes his and Keller's relationship feel imbalanced and dulls the potentially dramatic effect of Aaron being thrown into a harsh environment. With Archie there as a constant figure of support, Rebecca's unpleasant demeanor is softened and is rarely threatening. With Archie around, the child is in no danger of being unloved. As Archie puts Aaron to work on the farm, he is always present as a source of familial comfort and moral guidance. Devin Douglas Drewitz brings a fine sense of melancholy to his role of the bereaved Aaron as he strives to survive the emotional and physical struggle of adapting to his new life.

"It's a very sweet film," Reynolds said of *Time of the Wolf*. Regarding his eminent co-star John Neville, who plays Preacher: "I was watching John the other day, and I was looking at his face, and I just wanted to take a bite out of his cheek. Every line he uttered was like he wrote it…. I hope when I'm his age [76] that I can do it with as much class and dignity as he does."[1] The respect was mutual, Neville commenting, "We're very fond of each other…. He has incredible charisma."[2]

Notes

1. Gayle MacDonald, "Still Slim. Still Gorgeous. Still Burt," *The Globe and Mail*, December 3, 2001, https://www.theglobeandmail.com/arts/still-slim-still-gorgeous-still-burt/article4157114/.
2. *Ibid.*

Miss Lettie and Me
(Made-for-Television, 2002)

"What's wrong with this place, where are the sirens and stuff?"—Travis

Mary Tyler Moore is "Miss" Lettie Anderson, a senior spinster who has shut off her heart to the world after enduring much heartbreak throughout the years. Lettie will not break her self-imposed emotional exile even for a precocious nine-year-old named Travis who arrives to her doorstep claiming to be her grandniece. Lettie is unaware of even having such a relation and refuses to embrace the new addition to her life. It turns out that Lettie is estranged from her wayward niece Alison (Jennifer Crumbley Bonder), who Lettie raised after her mother died with the expectation that Alison would eventually take over the family farm raising sheep. But the youngster decided to leave their rural Georgia idyll to pursue her dreams of stardom as a rock singer in Los Angeles. Those plans didn't pan out and Alison ended up a struggling single mother waiting tables for a living and supporting a deadbeat significant other, a similarly failed musician. Lettie's handyman Isaiah Griffin (Charlie Robinson) and his mother "Mama" Rose Griffin (Irma P. Hall) live next door and open their hearts and home to Travis; during her stay, Travis discovers that Smalltown USA is a lot different from the big city. "Dumb town doesn't even have sidewalks!" is just one of the young visitor's observations.

Travis soon embraces some of the finer things on offer in town, such as the newly opened drug store and its charming owner, Sam Madison (Reynolds). A former professional baseball player, Sam has traded sports stardom for the tranquility of his hometown. But rural serenity is not the only thing that Sam's return offers, as his presence resurrects some dormant emotions in the cold, steely heart of Miss Lettie. When Travis is chastised by Lettie for playing baseball, it later makes sense why the sport elicits such pejorative response, as Sam sacrificed a once-burgeoning relationship with Lettie to pursue his career as baseball star.

Unfortunately, Reynolds isn't given a whole lot to do here and is underused. As someone who is so important to Lettie's past, the character of Sam Madison is not given enough screen time with his old flame to support the suggestions that theirs is truly a love lost. We need Madison and his understanding of Lettie's malaise to afford the audience an empathetic reaction to her too-often brusque and bitter demeanor; even Isaiah, with his patience of a saint, calls out Lettie for what she is: "Ain't nothin' worse than an obstinate old woman!"

Predictable to the end, *Miss Lettie and Me* is unadulterated sugar for the soul. In spite of such calculated confection, the excellent performances make it quite hard to escape the film's emotional clutches. Charles Robinson and Irma P. Hall are stunning as mother and son Griffin, who offer sympathy and warmth to those around them to offset Miss Lettie's cynical cold shoulder. Their relationship is depicted with a sense of emotional depth and respect, making it all the more heartbreaking when Isaiah cares for and, ultimately, buries his beloved mama. Rose is the film's heart, its figure of tenderness and inclusion, of unquestioning charity and good will; when she dies, a part of the film dies with her. The film is worth watching for Robinson and Hall's performances alone.

Johnson County War
(Made-for-Television, 2002)

"I'm not your 'head bobby,' I'm a marshal!"—Hunt Lawton

Johnson County War was written by eminent western author Larry McMurty and Diana Ossana, based on Frederic Manfred's 1957 novel *Riders of Judgment*, the fifth book in Manfred's series *The Buckskin Man Tales*. Manfred based this particular tale on the real-life Wyoming range war waged between wealthy land owners and independent settlers between 1889 and 1893. McMurthy and Ossana's adaptation focuses on the brothers Hammett, standing together against the corrupt Hunt Lawton (Reynolds), who is made sheriff upon the arrival of a disgraced nobleman, Lord Peter (Christopher Cazenove). Peter covets the valley for his own enterprise and has hired Lawton to muscle the farmers off their land. As part of the parade of oppression, the settlers are accused of cattle rustling, which is enough of an excuse for Lawton to execute his orders with extreme prejudice. The Hammett brothers are Cain (Tom Berenger), Dale (Adam Storke) and Harry (Luke Perry), and aside from the impending war against ruthless capitalists, the three are at war with each other over various personal grievances. Particular tension mounts between Cain and Dale due to the undeniable romantic chemistry between Cain and Dale's wife, Rory (Michelle Forbes). When Dale is gunned down, Cain assumes the role of surrogate father and husband to Dale's family, despite Harry's attempts at seducing Rory. Harry, the youngest of the Hammetts and a rogue charmer, is known across the valley for his womanizing ways and showing up to help

Reynolds as Marshal Hunt Lawson in *Johnson County War* (2002).

"all the pretty widows" in their vulnerable time of need. Harry is not one for settling down; when asked by the bereaved Clara Jager (Fay Masterson) if he would get married, Harry typically deflects the query with "That's such a deep question, I'd have to answer it after breakfast." Despite the familial acrimony, the three brothers band together to protect their homesteads and their lives from the ruthless Lawton and his band of mercenary killers, including the psychopathic, aptly named Mitch Slaughter (Silas Weir Mitchell) and Jesse Jacklin (Jack Conley).

Johnson County War is directed with great skill by David S. Cass Sr., who has proven to be one of Reynolds' more underrated collaborators, considering the quality work produced by the pair. Reynolds, so rarely a villain, is marvelous as the menacing Lawton and it is to Cass' credit that he was able to take one of the most likable of Hollywood performers and make him a credibly unlikable and snarling villain. Cass was a Hollywood stuntman turned actor-producer-writer-director; he had worked in various capacities (including that of stunt coordinator and second unit director) on several films on which Reynolds appeared briefly, such as *Six Pack* (1982), *Smokey and the Bandit Part 3* (1983) and *Uphill All the Way* (1986). A bit part in the *B.L. Stryker* film *Winner Takes it All* would preface their more significant run of collaborations beginning with the first installment of the *Hard Time* trilogy. Cass wrote and produced *Hard Time* (Burt Reynolds, 1998), directed the second film, *Hard Time: The Premonition* (1999), and produced *Hard Time: Hostage Hotel* (Hal Needham, 1999). Cass and Reynolds followed that enjoyable crime trilogy with a duo of excellent westerns, including this picture and *Hard Ground*.

At three hours in length, Cass keeps things nicely unrushed as the story unfolds at a pace that privileges character development and allows for the foreboding atmosphere and simmering tension to build and ultimately explode. While there is action a-plenty for western aficionados, the more intimate personal conflicts between the gunplay are deftly served up by writers McMurthy and Ossana. The interweaving subplots often set the stage for the most dynamic dramatics and dialogue of the film, and certainly one of the greatest elements of the piece is Rachel Ward's turn as prostitute Queenie. Ward seems to relish the role of the mature temptress, who will "sleep with thieves but draws the line at killers." In the face of death threats, she can still smirk and display her heaving bosom toward her aggressors in a gesture of feminist defiance as well as self-promotion as Lord Peter's cowboys are her most loyal customers. Ward, tall and elegant, gracefully aged and naturally beautiful, is an exotic rarity in a picture of hardened faces. Cass' picture is stunningly shot by Douglas Milsome (*Full Metal Jacket*, *Hawks*, *Robin Hood: Prince of Thieves*) and his brooding, atmospheric cinematography is some of the finest you will find in a made-for-television picture. Standing in for Wyoming is the handsome Calgary, Alberta, countryside, a location which provides a suitably cold stand-in for the harsh Wyoming winter scenes and which affords Milsome the opportunity to compose some truly epic, sepia-toned vistas which give the picture an evocative vintage quality. All of this is complimented by Ken Rempel's production design.

Johnson County War premiered as a Hallmark Channel miniseries in 2002 and in its promotion as a prestige broadcast the network celebrated the picture's connection to McMurthy's award-winning 1989 CBS western miniseries *Lonesome Dove*. And while *Johnson County War* wasn't as widely acclaimed as that classic television western drama, McMurthy and Ossana justly celebrated several years later when they won a 2005 Academy Award for their screenplay adaptation of Annie Proulx's short story *Brokeback Mountain*.

Hard Ground
(Made-for-Television, 2003)

"I don't fit in this century, and it won't be long before you don't fit in either."
—John "Chill" McKay

The story of *Hard Ground* is nothing new for western aficionados. Two men of the old world, John "Chill" McKay (Reynolds) and his brother-in-law Nate Hutchinson (Bruce Dern) face a changing frontier, one of younger and meaner outlaws. McKay is a former bounty hunter serving a 99-year term in Yuma Territorial Prison when he flees after a fellow detainee, the psychotic Billy Bucklin (David Figlioli), escapes in a murderous jailbreak. Bucklin has ideas on deposing revolutionary Gen. Jesus Navarro (Sergio Calderón) and taking over control of the Mexican border. In an effort to take the unpredictable Bucklin down, McKay saddles up with Hutchinson, the man who sent him to prison in the first place. McKay's estranged son, Joshua (Seth Peterson), one of Hutchinson's deputies and a fine tracker, is one step ahead in the pursuit of Bucklin and rescues a feisty and beautiful

John "Chill" McKay (Reynolds) is about to taste freedom—or a bullet—in *Hard Ground* (2003).

captive, Liz Kennedy (Amy Jo Johnson). Liz's family was slaughtered by Bucklin and with no life to go back to, she decides that she too will join in the hunt for the sadistic fugitive.

This entire surface plot is just an excuse to present a discourse on familial relations. The antagonism between the outlaw and lawman (McKay and Hutchinson) masks what is essentially a brotherly falling out, while the end goal of the story is to have McKay and Joshua reconciling their familial discord. But McKay is a stubborn old cynic and isn't immediately receptive to mending broken bonds. "You are a cold-hearted soul, sir," Hutchinson tells McKay. "The name 'Chill' fits you like a glove."

Hard Ground was written by David S. Cass Sr. and directed by Frank Q. Dobbs with the kind of workmanlike efficiency of filmmakers like Andrew V. McLaglen, painting his narrative with skill, economy and a full embrace of the harsh exterior locations of the western milieu: a hard land for hard men. Dobbs began his Hollywood career as a writer on *Gunsmoke* before working his way up to producing and directing features including *Uphill All the Way*, which featured a cameo by Reynolds. The film is vastly superior to most non-theatrical westerns and is also better than quite a few contemporary, theatrically released ones.

Reynolds embraced the western genre in his later career as though he were making up for lost time. While the likes of Charles Bronson and Clint Eastwood cleaned up at the box office with their prolific appearances in western films since the late '60s, it would take Reynolds some catching up to do as he hadn't starred in a western since *The Man Who Loved Cat Dancing* in 1973. By the time he did rediscover his inner cowboy, the western genre had faded from box office glory and become the domain of the straight-to-video picture. It is a pleasure to see Reynolds and Dern share the screen once again, their first time since appearing in *The Premonition* (1999). The two bring a believable sense of history to their characters while Figlioli chews the scenery like some cartoon version of a Wild West villain, mugging and gunning his way through the picture. The sobriety of Reynolds and Dern balances the equation.

The Librarians
(2003)

"These punks today and their drive-by shootings … 'drive-by'! They'd shoot their own grandmother and then write a rap song about it and make a million dollars. Don't get me started!"—Irish

William Forsythe plays Simon, an enigmatic former government mercenary, solicited by a wealthy old friend to track down his granddaughter, who has gone missing in Miami. Simon assembles a team of professionals to infiltrate a white slavery ring run by feared crime boss Marcos (Andrew Divoff). Knowing Marcos' involvement in fight promotion, Simon uses his colleague Toshko's (Daniel Bernhardt) martial art skills to gain the trust of the mobster, and from there they follow a trail of underworld sleaze and moral corruption to uncover a shocking world of abuse and prostitution. Along the way Simon meets the beautiful Sandi (Erika Eleniak), who is also seeking her lost sister, another Marcos victim; along their journey into the underworld, Simon and Sandi become romantically entwined. Reynolds briefly appears to add an air of movie star class to the film with his character of Irish, a shady informant living a decadent lifestyle in the sun and with a cadre of beach babes by his side. In staying true to his character's name, Reynolds adopts a brogue which is more in line with John Ford's version of Ireland (as in *The Quiet Man*) than anything resembling a real, contemporary Irish dialect. But we are thankful for his presence in this otherwise routine and inconsequential picture.

The Librarians was directed by Mike Kirton, who also shared co-writing duties with star William Forsythe. The picture was his second and, to date, last feature film, Kirton having previously directed Forsythe in the 1999 action thriller *The Last Marshal*. Kirton's name is perhaps more familiar to film fans as a stuntman on major studio pictures, notably working on several Reynolds pictures throughout the decades, including *Smokey and the Bandit Part 3*, *Heat*, *Cop and a Half* and *The Crew*. Kirton assembled a great cast of character actors, including the formidable Forsythe and Reynolds, along with Andrew Divoff, Ed Lauter, Michael Parks, Matthias Hues and Erika Eleniak. The picture is also shot by the great cinematographer, Gary B. Kibbe, who is most lauded for his stunning work on the films of John Carpenter (*Prince of Darkness*, *They Live*, *Body Bags*, *In the Mouth of Madness*, etc.). Kibbe's framing is usually excellently composed and intricately crafted, with a distinct *mise-en-scéne* that makes interesting use of color; however, his work on *The Librarians* is flat and more suited to episodic television than anything cinematic, lacking any kind of character and nuance.

The most egregious element of the film is the editing of Rinaldo Marsili, which is fine for the dramatic scenes but purely inept when the action kicks into gear. Fight scenes and gunplay are assembled confusingly with ill-timed cuts which seem to disregard spatial and temporal awareness. But taken as a B-movie and forgiven its occasional aesthetic ineptitude, *The Librarians* is not the worst of its kind and the lineup of actors present make it worth watching. The picture suffers most whenever it needs to kick into gear as something more explosive than it can handle; as it remains, it is simply a parade of action genre clichés delivered to the screen without ever truly coming to life.

Without a Paddle
(2004)

"Come with me, or I'll shoot your testicles off and stuff 'em and mount 'em on my mantelpiece."—Del Knox

Childhood friends Jerry (Matthew Lillard), Dan (Seth Green) and Tom (Dax Shepard) decide to honor the death of a member of their childhood clique by continuing the adventurous efforts of their fallen friend by tracing the missing treasure of mythological bandit D.B. Cooper, an airplane hijacker who decades ago parachuted into the mountains with $200,000 in ransom money, along with his partner in crime Del Knox. Not adept in the ways of the wilderness, the trio soon runs afoul of both nature and some unsavory though inept drug dealers working for the corrupt local law enforcer, Sheriff Briggs (Ray Baker), by growing illegal herbs in a mountain compound.

Stripped naked of clothes and dignity, while vulnerable to the elements, the trio is saved by an old mountain man. Through mounds of scraggly hair and aging prosthetics, we just about recognize that mountain man to be Reynolds, while Jerry, Dan and Tom find out he is Del Knox. Del harbors the men at his log cabin while offering them a selection of his clothes that have been sitting in a suitcase since the 1970s and which remain cut for the style of that era. "I'd get dressed fast if I was you because I've been alone in this cabin for 30 years," Del warns lecherously. And so Jerry is bestowed with a tight red shirt and blue flare jeans in a nod to the Reynolds' wardrobe of *Smokey and the Bandit*, while Dan and Tom are resplendent in dated cowboy shirt and plaid trousers, respectively. With Del's help, the trio evades the bumbling criminals and the dastardly Briggs, escaping back to civilization a hundred thousand dollars richer courtesy of Del's treasure.

There is a neat chemistry between the three leads which is crucial to this kind of film. In a very funny scene, the three alpha male friends are encouraged by M.D. Dan to huddle together to share body heat to keep them from contracting hypothermia; the scene is scored by R Kelly's "Bump N' Grind" to hilarious effect and this is the kind of humor that this film trades in. There is nothing fresh about *Without a Paddle*; it is a screwball farce about city slickers who venture into dangerous backwoods territory in a haze of childhood nostalgia only to be met with antagonism in the form of the land and its indigene. By right, the film has all the ingredients to be a chore and a bore, but it is, surprisingly, neither of those. The film is good-natured enough to get by on its sense of absurd silliness and is directed with breezy style by Steven Brill (*Heavyweights*, 1995; *Little Nicky*, 2000; *Mr. Deeds*, 2002); it is as professional and efficient as filmmaking of this style and genre needs or demands to be.

Brill no doubt cast Reynolds in reference to the thematic reflections between *Without a Paddle* and *Deliverance*, and Reynolds hams it up a charm as Del, a man out of time and place thanks to being stranded in the wilderness for 30 years. It seems as though filmmakers of director Steven Brill's generation were keen to pay tribute to Reynolds as a star of their youth when he briefly became a familiar face in the work of a coterie of Brill's contemporaries, including Adam Sandler, Kevin James and *Jackass* alumnus Johnny Knoxville. *Without a Paddle* marks Reynolds' first appearance in a series of high-prolife studio pictures that were star vehicles for these Hollywood funnymen, which included the remake of *The Longest Yard*, *The Dukes of Hazzard* and the highly rated television shows *The King of Queens* and *Robot Chicken*. Reynolds' appearances in these commercially successful entities seemed to suggest a cultural revival, or perhaps a nostalgic appreciation, was on his horizon. With the trendiest funnymen saluting the actor, who had long been underappreciated for his comedic gifts, Reynolds would be afforded an opportunity to reveal his considerable comedic chops in some of Hollywood's most popular films and shows of the period.

Appearing in *Without a Paddle* did not bring Reynolds the critical accolades of previous weightier performances, but he did get the nod of approval from one very important viewer: "My son couldn't care less that I worked with Henry Fonda and Jimmy Stewart," Reynolds recalled. "He was terribly excited because I worked with a guy from *Scooby-Doo* [Lillard] and *Austin Powers* [Green]. He told me about them so I knew this must be good."[1]

Note

1. Burt Reynolds, "MTV's Making the Movie: Without a Paddle," DVD Supplement, *Without a Paddle*, Paramount Home Entertainment, 2005.

The Longest Yard

(2005)

"Let's try some schoolyard bullshit!"—Paul Crewe

Paul Crewe (Adam Sandler) is a former football pro for the Pittsburgh Steelers; now burned out, he spends his days drinking and arguing with his girlfriend Lena (Courteney Cox). One particularly debauched evening, he steals her prized Bentley and crashes it in a drunken stupor. Crewe is sent to prison and becomes the pawn in a power struggle between sadistic Warden Rudolph Hazen (James Cromwell) and Capt. Knauer (William Fichtner); Hazen seizes upon the opportunity of having the pro-footballer join his team as he aspires to become governor and thinks that a winning high-profile team may boost his appeal come election time. Knauer doesn't like the idea of prisoners on his team of guards, and tries to influence Crewe to resist Hazen's proposition; Knauer initially convinces Crewe with a heavy hand. When Crewe suggests a "tune-up" exhibition match to Hazen, to get the guards in shape for a real game, he is told to put together a team consisting of his fellow inmates. Crewe's reputation amongst the prison population is in a precarious position, having lost his career to an act considered most "un–American": He was the first person to be indicted on federal racketeering charges for point shaving. But Crewe's tough demeanor earns him some respect amongst the cons and secures him a friend in Caretaker (Chris Rock), who assists in assembling "The Mean Machine."

The Longest Yard is not the first remake of Tracy Keenan Wynn's original script, the first was *Mean Machine* (Barry Skolnick, 2001), a flashy and vacuous British adaptation of the script starring ex-professional soccer player Vinnie Jones in the Paul Crewe role. Director Peter Segal's 2005 version is a contemporary update of Robert Aldrich's 1974 original; save for a few changes, Segal's film takes on the familiar narrative trajectory of recruiting the various team members who come in wildly varying shapes and sizes. But for fans of the original, their saving grace comes in the form of Burt Reynolds, this time playing the role of revered former football pro Nate Scarborough, who coaches the team to success.

Reynolds' presence gives this remake a sense of legitimacy, gravity and respect for the original film. His role is substantial enough to make it more than a mere acknowledgment; it is in fact one of the more interesting roles in the picture. "I didn't want to do a cameo. I said I don't want to give you, you know, the Good Housekeeping Burt seal of approval."[1] One of the actor's other conditions for accepting the role was being allowed to take part in the on-field action for the final game. "I wouldn't have done the picture if they hadn't let me play. I said look, if you're going to have someone tackle me, have somebody with a reputation...."[2] And sure enough someone with a reputation was on-hand: former Seattle Seahawks linebacker Brian Bosworth. Reynolds' presence also served to legitimize his iconic standing within the world of actors and athletes. WWE star Steve Austin succinctly summed up Reynolds' icon status: "I've always said there's only one Elvis Presley, there's only one John Wayne, and there's only one Burt Reynolds."[3] When Reynolds later looked back on his involvement with the remake, he said:

> Anything that makes money, they figure that they'll do another picture with the same title and a number after it, and they're going to beat it to death. That second one, *The Longest Yard*, I totally just sold out. I kept saying, no, I don't want to do it, I don't want to do it, I don't want to do it, but the money got so good for the amount of time I was going to work that I said, okay, I'll do it. But it wasn't a good picture.[4]

At first glance of the promotional campaign for the 2005 *Longest Yard*, one might balk at the lineup of actors filling in for iconic stars Reynolds, Michael Conrad, James Hampton, Eddie Albert and Ed Lauter. At the time of release, Adam Sandler and Chris Rock were two of the biggest names in comedy, and with WWE athletes and pop stars like Nelly rounding out the Mean Machine, fans of the original film could be forgiven for thinking the tough, sober resolve of Robert Aldrich's version may be compromised for the sake of big names and big laughs. But Sandler & Co. acquit themselves with fine regard for the 1974 picture. Interestingly, one of the few differences between this version and the original is how it dilutes some of Crewe's more questionable traits. In the opening depiction of Crewe's relationship with women and his subsequent arrest, he is neither violent to women or police officers. What this politically correct rendering of the character does is to neuter him of his more deliberate self-destructive ways; thus Crewe's more buffoonish and less boorish misbehavior here aligns more with irresponsible frat boy shenanigans than that of the hard-living, liquor-swilling, anguished brute we meet at the start of Aldrich's film. Perhaps the family-friendly Sandler wished not to be depicted as so feral, but what the original film did so well was to make us remember that its "heroes," those who make up the Mean Machine, are still offending convicts, including Paul Crewe.

While this remake ticks all the boxes of what a contemporary version of the film should achieve, it lacks the original film's unique personality and formal originality—although it does pay homage to the split-screen action of Aldrich's picture. While the original had its share of eccentricities and humorous absurdities, this version takes it to a heightened level of farce with cameos from legends of lowbrow such as Rob Schneider and Tracy Morgan. But just as the more comedic elements of the film do threaten to undermine the tension and suspense of the drama, director Segal does a fine job with the physical aspects of the film. The New Mexico State Penitentiary is rendered an imposing structure and a menacing backdrop for the action. William Fichtner gives one of the film's best performances as the intimidating Capt. Knauer, while fans of Aldrich's film will welcome the casting of original Capt. Knauer, Ed Lauter, in a cameo role. Other familiar faces of crime cinema appear, including real-life ex-con turned actor-author-screenwriter Eddie Bunker (of *Straight Time*, *Reservoir Dogs*, *Animal Factory*). Despite a 30-year gap since Aldrich's original, audiences were all-embracing of Segal's new version, with the film earning $158 million in box office returns, doubling its $80 million budget and narrowly missing out on making the top ten earners list of 2005.

Notes

1. Burt Reynolds, "First Down & Twenty-Five to Life: The Making of The Longest Yard," DVD Supplement, *The Longest Yard*, Sony Pictures Home Entertainment, 2006.
2. *Ibid.*
3. Steve Austin, "First Down & Twenty-Five to Life: The Making of *The Longest Yard*," DVD Supplement, The Longest Yard, Sony Pictures Home Entertainment, 2006.
4. Mike Fleming Jr., "Encore: Burt Reynolds Has Tales to Tell: Passing on 'Cuckoo's Nest,' 007, 'Die Hard,' Bonding with Eastwood, McQueen, Newman & Carson but Not Brando," *Deadline Hollywood*, September 6, 2018, https://deadline.com/2018/09/burt-reynolds-book-clint-eastwood-johnny-carson-die-hard-1201670957/.

The Dukes of Hazzard
(2005)

"Actually, we prefer 'Appalachian-Americans.'"—Luke Duke

Based on the original TV series, the film version of *Dukes of Hazzard* tells the story of cousins Bo and Luke Duke (played respectively by Johnny Knoxville and Sean William Scott), who run an illegal moonshine business on behalf of their uncle Jesse Duke (Willie Nelson) from their 1969 Dodge Charger, the iconic vehicle ("the General Lee") resplendent in orange and emblazoned with a rooftop Confederate flag. The family's arch nemeses are the corrupt local official, County Commissioner Jefferson Davis Hogg, known to the world as "Boss" Hogg (Reynolds), and his enforcer Sheriff Roscoe P. Coltrane (M.C. Gainey). Hogg is engaged in some nefarious civil engineering scheme, wanting to make Hazzard County a strip coal mine, and is seeking the Duke family's farmland for his redevelopment plan. As he is unable to locate Jesse's whiskey stills or gather any tangible evidence of liquor manufacturing, Hogg plants evidence of a moonshine operation so that Sheriff Roscoe can seize the property. After hearing of Hogg's devious plan, Bo and Luke uncover containers from a local construction site that turn out to carry core samples of a mineral that will stand as evidence of the mining operation that Hogg is planning.

Throughout the first two decades of the millennium, adapting beloved, successful television shows became a *de rigueur* practice for the major Hollywood studios: other examples include *21 Jump Street*, *The A-Team*, *Baywatch*, *Charlie's Angels*, *CHiPs*, *Get Smart* and *Starsky and Hutch*. If there is one consistent element that links them, it is that they are invariably awful. *The Dukes of Hazzard*, based on the 1979–1985 CBS series, is no exception, though it has some redeeming features. For some reason, the method of the filmmakers and the studios that produce them is to amplify any murmur of idiocy, reduce them to the lowest common denominator of base humor (generally crude scatological and sexual humor will suffice) and present previously endearing characters as lobotomized halfwits. In merging the elemental parts of older works with the aesthetics of contemporary cinema, gone is any semblance of what made the original shows work. These cinematic versions are rarely flattering towards their original incarnations and are more than a little insulting to their fans.

Essentially a car chase comedy with occasional pit stops for exposition, *The Dukes of Hazzard* is not without moments of amusement. Upon arriving in Atlanta and stumbling onto the wrong street corner in the wrong neighborhood while covered in enough soot to make it seem like they are wearing blackface makeup, Bo and Luke are confronted by a gang of ghetto thugs. Taking offense, one gang member asks threateningly, "Why don't you two hillbillies join us up here for a minute?" Luke guilelessly affirms, "Actually, we prefer 'Appalachian-Americans.'" Another enjoyable moment comes as Boss Hogg is leaving the police lockup where the Duke boys are being held and his famous all-white regalia encourages a fellow detainee to emerge screen-left alerting Hogg that he is engaging in a social *faux pas*: "Don't you know you're not supposed to wear white after Labor Day?"

The picture also has some fun with the symbolism of the Confederate flag and how that image resonated on a completely different level in 2005 than it did in 1975. As the Duke boys arrive in Atlanta, they are met with equal parts hospitality and hostility. "Yeah, baby! Southern by the grace of God! Yee-haw!" hollers one trucker upon seeing the General Lee's rooftop flag. Others aren't so pleased: "Hurry up, you're late for your Klan meeting, asshole!" shouts one aggrieved lady, which results in them gaining some unsolicited support from the Jeep behind: "Aww, don't listen to her. The South will rise again! Yee-haw!" Finally, one seemingly polite woman offers them a double flip of the bird as she intones, "Nice roof, redneck!"

It's easy to see why Reynolds and other Southern folk heroes such as Willie Nelson and Joe Don Baker (he who brought the legendary Sheriff Buford Pusser so memorably to the screen in *Walking Tall*) saw something appealing about this project. On paper, it sounds like a tribute to the great tradition of Southern cinema culture, particularly as the origins of the film go back to a classic of the genre, director Gy Waldron's 1975 film *Moonrunners*. Waldron went on to co-create the successful television version of *The Dukes of Hazzard* along with former real-life moonrunner Jerry Rushing. The *Dukes of Hazzard* plot and characterizations are almost entirely based on those of *Moonrunners*, as that film's protagonist cousins Bobby and Grady Lee Hagg became Bo and Luke Duke, while Uncle Jesse Hagg was revised as Uncle Jesse Duke. The Haggs' beloved stock car "Traveller" became the iconic General Lee. The latter was named after the famed Confederate general, Robert E. Lee, and the former referred to Lee's horse Traveller.

Despite this picture's DNA link to the Southern cinema of the '70s, aesthetically it couldn't be further from Waldron's initial film version of the story. *Moonrunners* was a largely sober piece of work with little levity, while the subsequent TV show was constructed in a family-friendly variation of the premise, wherein the illicit shenanigans of the Duke clan was benign and largely inconsequential in terms of legal and moral ramifications. Such humor paved the way for this contemporary film version with its bawdy sorority house shenanigans, crass dialogue and tasteless sexual references; the *Dukes of Hazzard* of 2005 has much more in common with the slew of unfortunate *Porky's* clones (*American Pie, Sex Drive, Road Trip*) than it does with anything like *Hot Summer in Barefoot County* (Will Zens, 1974), *Moonshine County Express* (Gus Trikonis, 1977), *Bad Georgia Road* (John C. Broderick, 1977) or even *Smokey and the Bandit* (1978).

One example of the film's unfortunate adherence to adolescent humor is Sean William Scott's rendering of Bo Duke, who, while far from being of brain surgeon levels of intellect in the TV series, is here presented as a certified simpleton and delusional maniac. "I love this car…. I'm gonna make sweet love to it!" enthuses Bo in ecstasy having retrieved their Dodge Charger. "You mean you're going to make sweet love *in* it," Luke corrects his cousin. "Oh no, I want to *fuck* it!" confirms Bo. Yes, the film can be that depressingly crude and moronic.

As Bo's cohort and "BFF" (Best Friend Forever) Luke Duke, Johnny Knoxville essentially channels the persona that audiences came to know as his own from the MTV reality show and film franchise *Jackass*, and he floats through here with the attendant sense of humor and daredevil attitude that his fans would expect. Jessica Simpson, like Catherine Bach before her, is stunningly beautiful as Daisy Duke, and the film isn't shy about lingering on her toned legs and ample attributes. But the best thing about the picture is without doubt Reynolds as Boss Hogg. He relishes the performance, which is an about-face for the actor who would normally be the one behind the wheel, foot on the gas, thumbing his nose at the law while leaping through the air in a modified muscle car. And even as the villain of the piece, Reynolds' Hogg refuses to sink to the same levels of vulgarity or stupidity as the majority of the other characters do. The star emerging from the production with some semblance of dignity as few others don't.

Cloud 9
(2006)

> "These are not hookers. These are strippers. And let me tell you something … they didn't come from a lot of money, they didn't go to college, they're not the brightest bulbs in the building, or even the room, but get used to their faces, you're gonna see 'em again."—Billy Cole

Billy Cole (Reynolds) is a genial con artist–moocher who spends his days luxuriating in the Malibu homes of local movie stars when they're away; Cole can be seen lounging around Barbara Streisand's swimming pool; making cocktails in Tom Arnold's backyard; defrauding corporate investors in Anthony Hopkins' living room; interrupting Gary Busey berating his dog for producing unusually large excrement … yes, it's that kind of film. Billy's friends and associates include his adoptive son Tenspot (D.L. Hughley) and blond beach bum Jackson Fargo (Paul Wesley). With gambling addiction crippling his finances, Billy hatches a potentially lucrative plan born of his combined prurient interests in female athletes and strippers. Taking into account the physically demanding nature of exotic dancing, Billy's idea is to construct and manage a volleyball team comprised of his favorite local strippers and enter them into potentially lucrative competitions. They are a colorful bunch of beautiful rogues: the ditzy but decent blond Crystal (Marnette Patterson); sassy African-American Champagne (Kenya Moore); the formidable Latino, Corazon (Patricia De Leon); and the steely Russian, Olga (Katheryn Winnick). Cue the clichéd sporting film scenarios which ends with the underdogs overcoming insurmountable odds.

Cloud 9 is produced by distinguished filmmaker Albert S. Ruddy. To name but a few of the fine works Ruddy has contributed to the great American film library, consider *Little Fauss and Big Halsy* (1970), *The Godfather* (1972), *The Longest Yard* (1974), *Million Dollar Baby* (2004) and the two *Cannonball Run* pictures. Unfortunately, *Cloud 9* is not on the level of *The Godfather*, nor *Cannonball Run II* for that matter; it is very much a product of the teen movie machine that pumped out the second wave of raunchy adolescent rites-of-passage pictures of the late 1990s and early 2000s (*American Pie*, *Road Trip*, *Euro Trip* and their ilk). In that context, *Cloud 9* is far from being the worst of the cycle, thanks to Reynolds channeling his charming rapscallion persona to keep the film afloat. Reynolds has the ability to make the most morally questionable and scheming of characters somehow likable. Meanwhile, professional volleyball player Gabrielle Reece appears as a standout athlete on the opposing team for the final game. Reece's casting would lend the film some credibility within the sporting community, but it is hard to imagine *Cloud 9* ever strived for anything as relevant as credibility.

End Game

(2006)

"The question is who would gain the most by the death of the president.… Would you like to stay for breakfast?"—General Montgomery

Former presidential bodyguard Alex Thomas (Cuba Gooding Jr.) is suffering survivor's guilt following the assassination of his charge and is wasting his days drinking himself into oblivion. Investigative journalist Kate Crawford (Angie Harmon) is striving to discover what exactly occurred on that fateful day. Together, Thomas and Crawford uncover a trail of deceit and corruption that involves Thomas' boss Vaughan Stevens (James Woods) and reveals Stevens' association with Jack Baldwin (Peter Greene), a contract assassin for the C.I.A. Their investigation leads all the way to the corridors of power and implicates those closest to the fallen president.

Cue the procession of clichéd political intrigue and contrived conspiracy thriller tropes where closets are relieved of their skeletons, affairs are indiscreet, and everyone you suspect to be involved is indeed involved. Did the filmmakers really think they could cast James Woods (looking every bit as shifty as one would expect), or Anne Archer (alluring and furtive), and have us assume they are innocent in the espionage plot? Why else would they be in the picture if they didn't play a larger role in the big final act reveal? Reynolds appears in a glorified cameo as Gen. Montgomery, who comes out of retirement to put pressure on Stevens to solve the murder of his close friend, the president. Reynolds wanders in every so often to briefly lend some dignity and gravitas to the proceedings, though his actual character lends little to no substance to the actual narrative other than to put the fear of God into Woods' character.

End Game is an overtly stylish affair, drowned in blue tinting, restless camerawork and relentless editing, the sum of which feels like an afterthought of the subgenre of Asian-inspired Hollywood action pictures which were seemingly instigated by the importation of John Woo to U.S. cinema in the early '90s. Along with Woo (*Broken Arrow, Face/Off*) came several lauded directors from the East, including Tsui Hark (*Double Team, Knock Off*), Ringo Lam (*Maximum Risk*), Ching Siu-tung (*Belly of the Beast*) and here, Andy Cheng. Erstwhile stunt coordinator Cheng directs *End Game* with a fine kinetic energy but the picture suffers in the drama department and particularly from its casting. Cheng brought great actors on board but limits their screen time. The picture is dominated by Gooding and Harmon, whose passable screen presence pales in comparison to that of Woods and Reynolds. Even the edgy energy of Peter Greene tips the scales in his favor over the charm-less leads.

Cheng's film was produced for theatrical release though ultimately went straight-to-video amidst shifting corporate affairs with the studios involved in its distribution. Despite some occasional flair for the cinematic, *End Game* is just another routine dead president picture.

Forget About It
(2005)

"If you ever get rich, you can hire a chiro to be your caddie!"—Eddie O'Brien

Sam LaFleur (Reynolds), Eddie O'Brien (Charles Durning) and Carl Campobasso (Robert Loggia) are lifelong friends and war veterans (Vietnam, World War II, Korean War, respectively) enjoying the twilight of their lives, "a nice quiet retirement" in sunny Arizona. But it won't remain quiet for very long. Life in the trio's palatial home in Sunrise Village ("for affordable resort living") is upset when gangster who has turned state's evidence, Angelo Vittorio Nitti (Michael Paloma), arrives on the scene. Nitti wants out of the mob and deliberately sabotages a bank raid in order to get caught and to name names—including that of his uncle Don Giovanni—so he can go into the Witness Protection Program. To avoid "sleeping with the fishes in a pair of concrete boots," Nitti is transplanted from his native Hoboken to a dusty desert town out west under the pseudonym of Michael Brandon while he awaits his call for the trial. In an attempt to maintain a low-profile existence, Angelo stashes $4 million in cash. Sam, Eddie and Carl stumble across the loot and spend lavishly. Their ostentatious display of wealth without means attracts the attention of corrupt cops and Angelo's former colleagues in crime, leading to Angelo's cover being compromised. Sam, Eddie and Carl may have survived the horrors of war, but can they survive some New Jersey hoods and some New York cops on the take?

Raquel Welch plays Sunrise Village sexpot Christine DeLee, a former Las Vegas show-girl with a checkered past. DeLee is the kind of lady who cunningly utilizes her feminine assets to get what she wants from men, and Sam, Eddie and Carl are more than willing suckers (there is at least a genuine romantic attraction between her and Sam). This was the fourth time Reynolds and Welch appeared together. Indeed, the cast of the picture is its greatest asset, as any of the film's charm and entertainment value is entirely derived from the chemistry between the four ensemble players. It is a joy seeing Reynolds sharing some long-lost chemistry with Welch, three decades after their previous fireworks display in *100 Rifles* and *Fuzz*. Similarly, the three male stars have a long history as showbiz comrades; Durning and Reynolds have been co-starring with one another for decades and their natural bonhomie is something that could never be staged, while Robert Loggia's association with Durning goes back to his days on Broadway when they starred together in the 1973 production of David Rabe's *In the Boom Boom Room*. Together the great veteran actors bring a rich sense of history and friendship to their characters, the kind where they can insult each other with the worst kind of language or throw each other off their golf game yet know deep down they love and care for each other.

As a satire of gangster picture tropes, with the numerous expected *Godfather* references, the film follows a similar pattern to Reynolds' previous gangster-comedy *The Crew*. However, *Forget About It* is amateurish in comparison to that slick, well-budgeted Disney film; in fact, the scenes shot in New York are badly photographed and wildly incongruous. The footage feels as though the filmmakers didn't even have a professional lighting crew on hand. In contrast, the scenes filmed in Arizona are nicely framed, expertly lit, and aesthetically sound. If it weren't for the great casting of Reynolds, Durning, Loggia and Welch, who share good times and great chemistry when on screen together, it is unlikely *Forget About It* would be anything other than forgettable.

Broken Bridges
(2006)

"That's a special little girl you got there. I hope you'll get to know her a bit better."—Jake Delton

Bo Price (Toby Keith) and Angela Denton (Kelly Preston) were childhood sweethearts when Angela fell pregnant with their daughter. Fearing domesticity and responsibility, Bo abandoned his love and their unborn child, leaving Angela to bring up the little girl alone while educating herself in order to make a new life far away from home. Bo left small town life behind and became a successful country artist, touring with the likes of Willie Nelson while Angela became a high-flying big city career woman as a television news reporter in Miami, and that onerous work puts her under constant pressure to produce ratings-winning content for the station; their now-16-year-old daughter, Dixie Leigh Delton (Lindsey Haun), is a rebellious alternative punk who writes her own discordant music influenced by the likes of the Flaming Lips.

Bo is broken by life on the road and a dalliance with alcoholism. Onstage he is no longer flanked by skilled session musicians, but by empty whiskey glasses; his music has taken on a depressive tone that fails to impress his booking agents. Bo and Angela are burned out with their respective lives and are brought back into each other's orbit when they both lose brothers in a military aircraft accident. Returning to their hometown, Bo and Angela confront the ghosts of the past. Bo makes amends to his fallen brothers and the people of his hometown by organizing a benefit concert featuring him and some high-powered friends: singers Willie Nelson and BeBe Winans. The funds from the concert will be distributed to the families of the dead soldiers who are enduring hard times. Bo also takes this opportunity to showcase a reluctant Dixie Leigh's considerable musical abilities, as the finale of the picture is built around the polished performance of her song "Broken."

Supporting players include Reynolds as the gruff Delton patriarch, Jake, while Tess Harper is his delicate wife, Dixie Rose; it's all rounded out with a fine ensemble of clichéd but colorful locals. The theme of the difficulties of going home again, returning to the people and places of our youth as adults, is adequately handled if not especially deep. While some barbs are aimed at Bo's wealth, stature and well-maintained physique, it's not long before everybody in town is his pal once again, as the idea of family and communal resolve is the central concept of this genial film. The harmony of the idyllic small-town setting is only broken once, when Dixie Leigh almost ends up a victim of sexual assault by a local thug. Bo straightens things out with some swift action.

Reynolds had circled the periphery of the country music scene since the early 1970s. In 1973, he released an excellent country–easy listening album produced and performed by some of Memphis and Nashville's finest musicians. In 1975, county icons Furry Lewis, Jerry Reed, Mel Tillis and Don Williams co-starred alongside an awestruck Reynolds in *W.W. and the Dixie Dancekings*, while Reynolds' friends Willie Nelson and Kenny Rogers appeared onscreen and provided soundtracks to many of his projects down the years. So when Country Music Television began producing feature-length motion pictures, it was perhaps only a matter of time before they would knock on the door of the South's favorite adopted son. There is a subtle, nicely played tension between Bo and Jake, and Keith's sincere performance instills his flawed character with a decent amount of respect for his elder. Even for an absentee father, Bo is made of such good moral fiber that you can't help but root for him. Reynolds plays Jake with dignity, poise and, ultimately, warmth, the very qualities this picture trades on. So agreeable is the tone here that it can't sustain a sour note for very long, a picture where even a character as justifiably cranky as Jake eventually relents and becomes a supportive and welcoming grandfather, as we see in the scenes with Reynolds and Haun bonding over the simple pleasures of gardening while getting to know one another.

By the time *Broken Bridges* was released in 2006, Keith was a huge star with ten studio albums to his credit. Co-star Lindsey Haun was signed to Keith's independent record label, Show Dog Nashville, and the film essentially functions as a showcase for their musical talent, not a bad thing considering their formidable abilities. With its terrific soundtrack, affectionate depiction for homely small-town life, and sincere performances, *Broken Bridges* is a pleasant, heart-warming and undemanding entertainment.

In the Name of the King
(2007)

"Wisdom is our hammer. Prudence will be our nail."—King Konreid

Peace in the Kingdome of Ehb is disturbed by a band of marauding creatures called the Krug. Functioning under the orders of a disgraced evil sorcerer named Gallian (Ray Liotta), they lay waste to the town of Stonebridge. In the process the Krug kidnap Solana, the wife of a hard-working peasant simply named Farmer (Jason Statham) and kills their child. Spurred to seek vengeance, Farmer mounts a rescue mission with the help of his comrades Bastian (Will Sanderson) and Norrick (Ron Perlman). Meanwhile, King Konreid (Reynolds) rallies his troops to fight Gallian but is betrayed by his alcoholic nephew, Duke Fallow (Matthew Lilliard), who goes over to the dark side. The kingdom of Ehb needn't fear Fallow becoming its future ruler, as Farmer, who was found abandoned and brought up by the peasantry of Stonebridge decades ago, turns out to be King Konreid's rightful son and heir to the throne. And so father and son Konreid join forces to protect Ehb from Gallian's attempt to overthrow their rule and rescue Solana from the clutches of the mega-lomaniacal wizard.

Reynolds plays the king of Ehb with theatrical grandeur, the actor relishing this rare moment in patrician garb to stalk the castle halls with the power and authority of royalty. It only took over four decades in the film business before he starred in his first historical epic, as noted by producer Shawn Williamson: "The first piece of the puzzle that fell in was Burt Reynolds. And so Burt as the king was a coup from our point of view. It's a role he'd never done; he hadn't done a lot of period pieces. He's got a regal sense about him that comes across on screen that actually was fabulous."[1] Liotta and Lillard provide the film with an abundance of inspired lunacy, while Statham renders Farmer as a stoic hero. That kind of reserve usually served him well in the genre pictures *The Transporter* (Corey Yuen and Louis Letterier, 2002), *Crank* (Mark Neveldine and Brian Taylor, 2006) and *The Expendables* (Sylvester Stallone, 2010), though Statham's simple qualities are lost in the quagmire that is this film's over-plotting and stilted dialogue.

In the Name of the King is an expensive adaptation of the 2002 video game *Dungeon Siege*. However, only rare parts of the film, namely the logistically complicated exterior battle sequences, suggest that there is a budget of $60 million behind it, as the special effects look like the work of a production one-tenth of such a budget. In fairness, the film's Canadian location work is spectacular, while the invading villains, the Krug, are decent screen adversaries with their monstrous, decaying design. Unfortunately for the filmmakers,

In the Name of the King failed to catch the imagination of audiences, perhaps too soon after the hefty slog of the *Lord of the Rings* trilogy concluded in 2003 with *Return of the King*, and ended up taking a worldwide gross of $13 million, not even a quarter of its impressive budget. The comparisons with Peter Jackson's adaptation of J.R.R. Tolkien's fantasy novels aren't helped by the inclusion *Lord of the Rings* alumni, John Rhys-Davies, here playing Merick. Director Uwe Boll is known primarily for low-priced schlock horror fare such as *House of the Dead* (2003) and *Alone in the Dark* (2005), but *In the Name of the King* presented him with an opportunity to cast A-list names and funding to match. Unfortunately, Boll's sword-and-sorcery epic is as wooden as any of his low-budget pieces, an ambitious project with fantastic location shooting, grand production design, but which is let down by awkward dialogue and a plodding pace which makes this a dirge of a film at two hours in length.

Note

1. Shawn Williamson, "Making of…," DVD Supplement, *In the Name of the King*, Metronome Video, 2008.

Deal

(2008)

"I'll whip the kid into shape and then I'm out of here!"—Tommy Vinson

Tommy Vinson (Reynolds) is a retired card shark with an enduring love of the game, but his wife Helen (Maria Mason) errs on the side of caution and frugality by not allowing her husband to gamble any more. Tommy enjoyed five years at the top of his game, but after losing his confidence he spiraled into a black hole of debt and regret. Worst of all, Tommy's gambling addiction almost cost him his marriage, leading him to vow to never gamble again. Despite being 20 years free of his addiction, Tommy still possesses the desire for one final win that will set him and his wife up for the rest of their lives, but he cannot renege on his promise to Helen. However, Tommy's skill won't go to waste as he begins to mentor an ambitious law student, Alex Stillman (Bret Harrison), who has taught himself by playing virtual poker but is somewhat lacking at the tables. Tommy is watching when Alex loses during a tournament which is broadcast online and feels that the kid has potential, if only he had the right mentor, which is about the time that Tommy offers his services to assist the rookie on high-stakes games. The wary kid initially brushes the veteran off until he sees Tommy reading the body language and the hands of several players with accuracy.

Alex accepts tutoring from the old master in return for a 50–50 split of any winnings, including the big prize at the World Poker Tournament in Las Vegas. Tommy and Alex win some and lose some while along the way Alex is introduced to the beautiful Michelle (Shannon Elizabeth). Alex's concentration is thrown when he realizes that Michelle is a prostitute who was hired by Tommy to ease some of the youngster's increasing tensions. Also conflicting with Alex's poker apprenticeship is his burgeoning career at his father's law firm;

Alex's father, who paid $60,000 school tuition for his son, is not happy that Alex has been skipping out on his work as a law clerk to play poker. Matters are further complicated when Helen learns that Tommy has been using some of their savings to fund Alex's training. With Helen gone, Tommy has nothing to lose and so enters the competition himself. What Tommy doesn't realize is that he will end up facing his apprentice in the final showdown. Neither side is without encouragement, as both Alex's parents and Tommy's wife turn up at the Las Vegas tournament to lend moral support for the two competitors.

On hand to lend the film some credibility are real-life poker aces Phil Laak, Antonio Esfandiari, Chris Moneymaker, Isabelle Mercier and Mike Sexton. But unless one is intimate with the details of poker playing, it is hard to tell just how legitimate a sports picture this is within that context. All the elements of the sports film genre are present: the master-student relationship, the seemingly insurmountable odds overcome, the distraction (women, college, disapproving parents), personal hurdles and the ultimate challenge accepted. *Deal* is such a slave to the conventions of genre that the filmmakers could have substituted any sport of their choosing, and applied the same script with the same narrative beats and plot points.

But neither the structure nor the clichés are the main problem; many sports films utilize the aforementioned clichés and have succeeded on some level of interest, but poker is a particularly curious subject to craft a film around. The poker table is not a prime piece of land ripe for cinematic construction, as there are only so many shots of the stone-faced players bluffing, stacking chips and throwing down cards to keep the poker philistine attentive. Without one's active involvement in the game, poker makes for an incredibly boring spectator sport. The picture could have offered something more interesting about the mechanics and psychology of the game and those who participate, but it seems that besides the accumulation of wealth, there isn't much motivation. When Helen asks Tommy's cautious best friend Charlie (Charles Durning). "What could he possibly need with cards now?" Charlie replies solemnly, "Dignity … respect…. He just wants to hit that home run before he walks off into the sunset with you. He wants the title he never got. Something nobody can ever take away from him." Charlie's response to Helen offers a glimmer of depth to the character of Tommy, but little is explained about his moral waywardness, why gambling took him over so powerfully, and why he "lost focus."

In a story that struggles to produce much pathos, Reynolds brings considerable gravitas and cinematic class to what he has to play with; he and Harrison have some decent scenes together and they build a solid relationship from the beginning. Most intriguing is the element of father-son dependency under the surface of the pair's capitalistic concerns. Tommy doesn't have a son of his own around, and Alex doesn't have a particularly good relationship with his father, and so after having transcended the mere master-student bond to genuinely affect each other's lives, it makes the face-off in the final game a particularly tense moment. During the scene, there is a symbolically loaded image of the two of them separated by a mountain of cash; it is a witty and thematically relevant piece of composition, as Tommy is well aware that money has driven a wedge between him and his loved ones in the past and has the potential to damage his meaningful relationship with Alex. But the happy ending sees both men win on personal and professional levels; together, Tommy and Alex fill a familial void in each other's life while pursuing and claiming the almighty dollar.

A Bunch of Amateurs

(2008)

"Richard III it is! What's that about again?"—Jefferson Steele

In this 2008 British comedy, Reynolds satirizes his image and place within the acting fraternity with his rendering of Jefferson Steele, a boorish Hollywood action movie star who craves credibility as an artist from his work while also craving credibility as a father with his emotionally estranged daughter. To get a glimpse of the kind of material that has made Steele his fortune, the film opens with his new release, *Ultimate Finality 4*. Steele's star has faded and most often gets recognized not for his own striking features, but for his resemblance to Sean Connery, and usually the only time he is asked for his signature is to sign documents. Steele is represented by his well-meaning but out-of-touch agent, Charlie Rosenberg (Charles Durning), who is seeking quality material for his client and accepts an offer to perform the eponymous role in Shakepeare's *King Lear* in the Bard's hometown of Stratford-upon-Avon. What Steele doesn't realize is that Charlie misunderstood the proposed location; rather than the hallowed grounds of Shakepeare's place of birth, Steele will be performing in a quaint East Anglican farming village in Stratford St. John, Suffolk, and instead of treading the boards of the Royal Shakespeare Theatre he will be gracing the floor of a converted barn with an amateur drama group, the Stratford Players.

Samantha Bond plays Dorothy Nettle, who is responsible for soliciting Steele in the hope that his presence will revive her ailing drama society's finances. Some of the locals resent Steele's presence, namely classically trained thespian Nigel Dewberry (Sir Derek Jacobi), who covets the role of King Lear for himself and who balks at the presence of a film star playing the prestigious lead. Steele's vanity and casual approach to acting irks the devoted Dewberry. Others are more welcoming of the handsome Hollywood star, chiefly Bed and Breakfast host Mary (Imelda Staunton), who is besotted with her guest. Along the way, Steele becomes a target for the unscrupulous tabloid media, becoming unwittingly embroiled in fake sex scandals and local feuds. Of course none of that gets in the way of a triumphant performance at a genuinely historic theater, London's Old Vic, for the film's reassuring ending.

Endearing but slight, *A Bunch of Amateurs* is essentially a culture-clash comedy in which the coddled film star must reconcile with the lack of creature comforts he is used to and rein in his prima donna tendencies to ultimately embrace the rustic charms of the humble country hamlet and its people. While Reynolds would effectively say goodbye to his astonishing career and to his legions of fans with the elegiac *The Last Movie Star*, it wasn't the first time that the actor re-assessed his place within the acting community. Reynolds was considering his fame as a movie star and life as an actor as far back as his self-deprecating cameo in Mel Brooks' *Silent Movie*, and he parlayed the motif even further with the likes of *Hooper*, *The Last Producer* and *Hamlet and Hutch*. *A Bunch of Amateurs* also indulges Reynolds' taste for familial drama and another recurring theme of his work: familial disconnection and paternal longing. Steele's daughter Amanda (Camilla Arfwedson) is a struggling actress who has immersed herself into the experimental theater scene;

she has changed her surname so as not to be associated with her famous father, balking at his lavish Hollywood lifestyle and embarrassed by his crassly commercial work. Of course, Steele isn't too keen on her work either, "I think the director is a pretentious, talentless pervert," he says of the avant garde fringe production of *Pride and Prejudice* that Amanda is appearing in. In this context, *A Bunch of Amateurs* is another avenue of reconciliation for Reynolds, to make peace with and make fun of his career as an action movie performer. Perhaps more importantly, it provides an opportunity to once again confront the important themes which have interested him for much of his career, those that have often provided the subtext and central themes behind much of his work. "[King] Lear is going mad and so is my character, Mr. Steele, he is going crackers and he has lost communication with his daughter," Reynolds says. "He longs for his daughter to say something nice to him. Eventually before the play is over and the movie is over, they connect and it is quite touching."[1] Just like Jefferson Steele brought some beguiling glamour to Stratford St. John, so too did Reynolds himself make an impression upon this modest independent production.

According to Samantha Bond, working with Reynolds "is extraordinary … it takes your breath away. There is this huge star and you have to work quite hard to not let that keep you overawed, you have to deal with him as a regular actor and deal with him as a regular person, but you do have to take a very deep breath and go 'It's okay, it's only Burt Reynolds!' but it's very thrilling."[2]

Producer David Parfitt imagined Jefferson Steele as a distillation of gruff male stars such as Harrison Ford, Michael Douglas and Reynolds, but never counted on any of them agreeing to send themselves up in such a satirical, self-reflexive manner. "When you get involved in some of these scripts, you often have an actor in mind for it. I can't say that we initially said, 'Burt Reynolds,' but … you need somebody like Burt Reynolds who is really prepared to take the piss out of themselves."[3] But just as Parfitt assumed he would never get the star on board, Reynolds' agency ICM read the script and noted that it was an ideal part for their client. For director Andy Cadiff, casting Reynolds was an opportunity to work with a hero of his film going youth, having grown up in the era of *Deliverance*, *The Longest Yard*, etc. Cadiff affirmed:

> Those are the movies that made me want make movies, so Burt's image was definitely impactful to me … [H]e could laugh at himself, laugh at his own career in terms of what it was like to be #1 and then kind of discarded, and then he was elevated again during *Boogie Nights*, and then discarded and he has a sense of humor about it. If he didn't have a sense of humor about his journey through Hollywood stardom, he never could have embraced a role like this. For a director, when you get to work with an actor who you grew up with admiring their work, it's always a thrill.[4]

While critics were not bowled over by the rustic charms of *A Bunch of Amateurs*, one viewer of high power was indeed taken by it. *A Bunch of Amateurs* was chosen for the 2008 Royal Film Performance and was seen by Queen Elizabeth and Prince Philip. And just what did the queen think of the film? "Quite amusing,"[5] her majesty ruled.

Notes

1. Burt Reynolds, "Burt Reynolds: On How the Play Mirrors the Film," DVD Supplement, *A Bunch of Amateurs*, Entertainment in Video, 2009
2. Samantha Bond, "Samantha Bond: on Burt Reynolds," DVD Supplement, *A Bunch of Amateurs*, Entertainment in Video, 2009

3. David Parfitt, "David Parfitt: on Burt Reynolds," DVD Supplement, *A Bunch of Amateurs*, Entertainment in Video, 2009

4. Andy Cadiff, "Andy Cadiff: on Burt Reynolds," DVD Supplement, *A Bunch of Amateurs*, Entertainment in Video, 2009

5. "Queen spends night with Amateurs," *BBC News*, November 18, 2008, http://news.bbc.co.uk/2/hi/entertainment/7734921.stm

Reel Love

(Made-for-Television, 2011)

"If you know anything about the Bible, you would know the Lord was a fisherman, and if the Lord had a hat like this one, he would be wearing it right now."—Wade Whitman

In 2011, U.S. cable TV channel CMT (Country Music Television) launched its CMT Original Movies division, an endeavor which added original feature-length movies to the channel's production slate. The films were crafted specifically with the CMT audience and their tastes in mind and, despite being filmed in Canada, would feature rural America-themed narratives and star Nashville music artists such as Bell Bundy and LeAnn Rimes. The first two films out of the gate were *To the Mat* (starring Bundy and Ricky Schroeder) and the charming romantic comedy *Reel Love*. Essentially a star vehicle for country music sensation Rhimes, it didn't hurt that her co-star would be the South's cultural icon himself, Burt Reynolds, a boon for all concerned. Said director Brian K. Roberts:

> Getting Burt was a big deal for CMT, their target audience is really a Burt Reynolds one, but it was also a huge deal for me as I'm a big fan of Burt's. But it really all began as a LeAnn Rimes project because they wanted to work with her. It was made for television; it was one of the first movies that CMT embarked on that were spearheaded by Ira Pincus at eOne as part of their launch campaign to produce and screen their own line of movies. With regards to Burt, I had a buddy of mine, Tim O'Donnell, re-write the script which Burt then read and he liked it. I was in Vancouver shooting when I heard that Burt was going to do it. I was so thrilled.[1]

And so these two titans of Southern pop culture came together playing estranged father and daughter, Wade and Holly Whitman. Having long left behind the limited trappings of small-town life for a career with a Chicago law firm, Holly is summoned home to Lake Manion, Alabama, an idyllic Southern rural community, when she learns of Wade's heart attack. Lake Manion is the kind of town where a store called Bobby's Bait and Boat is the hub of activity, the most enterprising business, and the only place in town with an available Internet connection. It's here that Wade and seemingly the rest of the town's male population structures their lives around fishing; in particular, anticipating the town's annual fish fry. Upon revisiting the land she left behind, Holly reluctantly engages old friends and former suitors, most of whom ended up marrying each other and have now settled down; it also means returning to a family that has been fractured since her mother's death two decades ago. Wade is particularly irascible and refuses to let a little thing like a heart attack get in the way of his fishing schedule, let alone an upwardly mobile daughter who he sees as having abandoned the life he provided. The gruff patriarch has little time for rehabilitation and medication, and even less time for fruit and salad, but unfortunately for Wade he is curtly informed, "Your bacon and gravy days are over!" Another obstacle to Holly is her simpleton brother, Everett (Christian Potenza), who is devoted to his father but can't seem to keep his own life and family together.

Holly is at her wits' end and on the verge of returning North when she meets local stud mechanic Jay (Shawn Roberts). Holly has been seeing a colleague back in the city, Carl (Jeff Roop), a self-proclaimed Rhodes Scholar who wears his education and high-powered car like badges of honor. From the beginning we sense that Holly may be just another trophy to Carl and his status symbol collection, and so when she develops a burgeoning romance with Jay she may just have found a new reason to embrace her former homeland. Things get complicated when the "big-time Yankee lawyer" Carl arrives in town to take Holly home, only for him to realize that Holly is getting close to Jay and is starting to feel at home again in the town that she felt she had outgrown. True antagonism doesn't exist in the warm environs of Lake Manion and so rather than being run out of town along with his snooty attitude and boorish manner, Carl gets a taste of the local hospitality when Jay introduces him to the joys of moonshine. Despite his uncouth manner and vocal disrespect for the blue collar residents of the town, a vicious hangover is the worst smiting he receives.

Despite the warm, hazy vibe of the film and deceivingly humid Southern summer aesthetic, cast and crew worked in the harsh conditions of an Ontario cold snap: The location was in the grip of one of the worst winters of recent times. As Roberts was prepping the location for the springtime shooting schedule, the lake was still frozen over and the foliage dead from winter damage. According to Roberts,

> [*Reel Love*] was supposed to have the feel of a summer movie, but at this stage of pre-production we were still wondering if we would have any green trees or even if the ice on the lake would melt on time for shooting. Fortunately things let up a little bit and we did have some beautiful days of shooting but it was still extremely cold and it was that way throughout the entire shoot, we didn't have one warm day. There are scenes in the movie that look like it was 80 degrees out, but it was actually unbearably cold.[2]

Wade Whitman (Reynolds) refuses to let a heart attack get in the way of fishing in *Reel Love* (2011).

With the film due to air in September 2011, the production schedule was afforded three weeks of principal photography, and of the 15 days given, Reynolds would be available for five. Luckily, Roberts and crew were met with a star of great skill and economy, with Reynolds shooting as much as ten pages a day. "It was a bit of a logistical nightmare," Roberts affirms. "The good news was, 'Burt's going to do the movie!' but the bad news was 'You have him for a week'—and he's in a lot of the material—which for us meant having to visit locations twice, which is pretty challenging when you have only 15 days of shooting. But for somebody who dropped in on a 90-plus-minute movie for five days where there were many complicated set-ups, he was just a dream to work with."[3]

While Reynolds lends the film the weight of a seasoned veteran actor, the star of the picture was somewhat greener, though given her celebrity her presence led to the kind of media scrutiny that in the past would have plagued her former tabloid cover star colleague. Rhimes had gone through very public struggles with her family, management, record label and marriage, attracting the undesirable attention of the paparazzi. Roberts recalled:

> LeAnn was going through her own tough times while making the film, and the press was hounding her all the time, to the point where there was paparazzi hiding in bushes trying to get a shot of her, and later I would see these photos that were taken while we were filming and it would be published with captions that said "LeAnn Rimes having an affair with co-star" and it was absolute bullshit. One day when we were getting ready for a shot, I noticed that LeAnn has this tattoo on the inside of her forearm that says "Trust" and I asked her what that meant and she said it was to remind her that it is okay to trust people; that not everybody is out to mistreat you or take advantage of you. You know, Burt's been through all of that pretty intensely over the decades and I see the kind of humility with which he treats people and the sense of humor that he views the world through. LeAnn seems to have followed a similar experience and come through it with the same kind of outlook and good humor. Burt handles the attention he receives with total grace and dignity, but that can be hard to do. But it was a fun set. Burt is a blithe spirit and a practical jokester, he and Christian Potenza just got along like a house on fire and every morning there would be some kind of fun, whether it was Burt putting mashed potatoes in Christian's shoe or Christian taking some of Burt's clothes and recreating the *Cosmopolitan* pose, which he would print out and plaster it on Burt's trailer. There's a scene near the end of the film where they catch the fish and it's in a cooler, but there was one complicated line that Burt had some trouble with. And on the very last take when he opens the cooler, I took a big piece of paper and wrote "I love you Burt" with a big kiss on it. He laughed and it made for a great outtake, and the next take he nailed the line. I have fond memories of working on the film and a tremendous warmth and respect for Burt.[4]

As a mainstream romantic comedy, *Reel Love* is a formula film, but the ingredients make it a pleasure to watch. As always, Reynolds' ease of charm and magnetic screen presence belie any of his character's miserly transgressions. Roberts is a director more than aware of Reynolds' abilities beyond his macho action star image and is skillfully able to draw from the actor the required pathos and dramatic heft that Reynolds has displayed in some of his lesser known works. The picture's theme of familial relations is also relevant to the Reynolds canon. Here, the actor is afforded another opportunity to develop this dramatic motif that he has been working on throughout his career. The strained father-daughter relationship is driven by his emotional absence and disconnect that has brewed in his bereavement for his wife, having driven his daughter to the other side of the country while conversely making his son Everett more dependent on him. Everett might be a beer-guzzling halfwit but his heart is in the right place, and often hilariously so. When Wade is given a low-calorie fruit plate by Holly, Wade mutters his son's name under his breath and no sooner can you say the word "cholesterol" than Everett obliges with "I'm on it, Daddy, I'll fry you a steak!"

Of course, the broken bond between Wade and Holly is mended over a fishing trip, a symbolic gesture that Jay calls "the day the old man has been waiting for his entire life." It is here that we are given a glimpse into what makes him "such a miserable grouch." Wade explains to his daughter that after years of working hard to provide a solid home life, going from the Marines into the police force and then becoming a long-haul trucker, he finally found the kind of close-knit community and good quality of life that he wanted for his family. However, his emotional withdrawal in the aftermath of his wife's death meant the burden of substitute matriarch fell to his daughter, an obligation which Holly resented. Wade regretfully admits, "In my grief, I turned you into a parent." It's a strong scene, the best in the film, and is played with tenderness and the right amount of residual bitterness at the unpredictable nature of life.

The film nicely considers the culture clash and the divide of urban and rural sensibilities, but it ultimately settles on the virtues of the country life as a warmer, more meaningful way of living in contrast to the fast-paced cash-grab middle-class milieu of the city folk. Holly revels in the kind of friendships that she has missed out on since leaving Lake Manion, and in Jay she finds a sincere man who values people and community over commodities and wealth. These values are those that followers of Reynolds' career will find throughout his body of work, for despite the massively good fortune the star has enjoyed, he remained a symbol of the America Everyman. Reynolds' films often place emphasis on family values, moral decency and the resolve of good personal and work ethics over the accumulation of wealth. His good-natured screen persona is a wholesome image, sometimes tempered with raw masculinity and sex appeal, one which was never sleazy, vulgar or threatening, always presented with good humor or an underlying sense of irony. With these characteristics, Reynolds has on many occasions been able to parlay a kind of sentimentality that in the wrong hands could easily be seen as manipulative or trite, or could invite cynical eyes to comment pejoratively on such frank displays of emotion. The poignancy of many of Reynolds' creations is underscored with the kind of optimistic sentimentality portrayed by James Stewart or Gary Cooper in the old Frank Capra pictures; rather than mawkish or schmaltzy, it is rooted in a value system dictated by an inherent code of decency and sensitive compassion for people, no matter their social milieu or affiliation.

Reel Love has all the elements required for Reynolds to wield his considerable acting tools and play to his own audience's expectations. It offers him an environment in which there are fools, family, comic absurdity and human drama a-plenty, all of which allows him to assume the kind of grizzled disposition, reluctant churlishness, self-deprecating humor, keen sensitivity and romantic tenderness that has appealed to both male and female audiences for decades. The picture tapped into all of these elements of Reynolds' screen persona and despite his character's gruff façade, we know it will eventually crumble when it hits that crucial weak, nay human, spot in the narrative that will ultimately unmask the real Wade Whitman, a man not devoid of but rather devoted to his family, and allow him to reconcile with himself, his daughter and with life.

Notes

1. Brian K. Robert, *interview with author,* telephone, June 29, 2018.
2. *Ibid.*
3. *Ibid.*
4. *Ibid.*

An Interview
with Brian K. Roberts

Brian K. Roberts is a prolific, award-winning filmmaker who has worked on some of the biggest television shows of the last 30 years. His early work includes writing duties on *The Simpsons* and as an editor on *Max Headroom* and *The Tracy Ullman Show*; he later embarked on a directing career which began with *The George Carlin Show* and included episodes of *The Drew Carey Show, Lizzie Maguire, Sabrina, the Teenage Witch, The King of Queens* and *Everybody Loves Raymond*. In 2011, with the support of Ira Pincus at eOne, Roberts directed his first feature film, *Reel Love*, starring LeAnn Rimes and Burt Reynolds. A lifelong fan of Reynolds, Roberts details his professional relationship with the star and his personal admiration for the intricate methods and considerable abilities of Reynolds' acting craft.

Reel Love director Brian K. Roberts with Reynolds (photograph courtesy Brian K. Roberts Collection).

Was this a major coup for you have to Burt signed on for Reel Love?

I absolutely love Burt; he is an utmost pleasure to work with and also one of my favorite movie stars, so I was very happy to have him in the film. *Reel Love* was my first feature-length film and it's a recurring thing in my life that when I get to do something new, it always ends up being me working with someone I truly admire. My first job directing episodic television meant working with one of my childhood idols, George Carlin [on *The George Carlin Show*]. It seems I don't get to ease into anything I do in the beginning, I'm straight into working with these people who mean a lot to me and so here I was directing my first movie and it's with Burt Reynolds!

Was he aware of your admiration?

I did tell him early on how I feel about his film career, how many of these other movies—the ones he is perhaps less celebrated for—are so important to me and part of my filmmaking life. I've always been a big Burt Reynolds fan but not really for the action movies that he is perhaps most well-known for, which are fun, but for me it was movies like *Starting Over*, *Deliverance*, *The Longest Yard* and *The End* that really fascinated me. I love his comedic style but I also really appreciate his wide range and it's those movies that I just mentioned which really showcase his talent for the dramatic and the absurd, as well as the physical stuff, and it is those kinds of movies that I think of when I think of Burt Reynolds.

What is it about those films that you find so intriguing?

He took so many risks when he decided to do those films, especially *Starting Over* where he was playing completely against type. It is a comedic performance but it is also a dramatic performance, and this was a time when he could have just kept making very successful action pictures. It is such a shame that so few people think of the great movies that Burt made before and in between those major action movies. *The End* is just one of my favorite films of all time and it's one that Burt directed, and you have this great pairing of him and Dom DeLuise; it is just so dark and so bold for a major movie star to do. That was one of the things I told him that I respected so much about him, I said, "You were at the top of your career and you took the power that you had and made these really risky moves with the material that you were selecting. I know you know your body of work and these are the things that mean the most to me." And with that, Burt said, "That's so nice to hear." He appreciated it.

And so here was your own chance to contribute to that body of work. How did you find directing him?

It was a dream. Every morning, Burt and I would meet with whoever was in the scene with us that particular day, Christian or LeAnn, and we would get together in a little cabin and go over the material for the day and make sure they were all cool with the lines. Burt has a divining rod on building characterization, he would make suggestions on changing things and he would bounce ideas around; he would say, "I'll do it the way you want me to do it, but then let me try something else and see what you think." I come from the comedy world where we change stuff all the time, I'm not married to the script, I'm not one of those guys that says you have to say each word to the letter as it is in the script, I much prefer natural, organic performances. There are certain things I want to get, but we have these meetings in the morning and read the scenes, go over them and make little adjustments so by the time we hit the floor to shoot the scenes, all the kinks have been ironed out. Burt was just so smooth to work with like that, he has a great connectivity to the character, he knew the through line of his character and knew what he wanted to accomplish, and I've never seen a more giving actor.

Burt is a noted acting teacher as well. Did he spend time with the actors in developing the characters' relationships or support them on set?

Absolutely. I've worked with uncooperative actors, people who disappear and don't stick around when the camera is not on them, they'll get other people to do the off-camera lines, but Burt is not like that. He was either near or on the set all the time, unless he had to do a costume change or something, but he was always thinking of other people and that blew me away. This was only LeAnn's second or third film and Burt really worked with her as much as he could to get her to be present. I mean, she's a singer and there's a tendency for singers to want to get everything about their performance pitch perfect and so sometimes they pre-think where they are going to be, so it's important to get them into the state of being present and not to worry so much about being perfect. It's just a slightly different skill set and Burt would have certain ways of drawing her in. Burt's a mentor to a lot of people and so giving of himself and his experience. He is not just generous with other actors, but generous and cognizant of the crew.

How so?

If it meant not putting a crew member through something rigorous, he would suggest to me another way of doing it. This shows you what a class act this guy is: He drops into this movie and immediately became family and friends with everybody, a total delight to work with. He ingratiated himself with the cast and crew; he would sit on breaks and tell great stories of every famous actor of his generation, his experiences of playing football, and he would also tell brilliant Johnny Carson stories, and I was enjoying all of this so much to the point where I was like "Oh, we've got to go make a movie!" A scene would be set up and ready to go but we were enthralled with and enjoying Burt so much that you tend to forget you're there to do the work. Also, at the end of the show, when it was his final day of shooting, he went out and located a caterer and arranged for an open bar and buffet with shrimp cocktail, crab, lobster, you name it … he must have spent about six or seven grand to throw us a wrap party after his last shot, and everybody stuck around and enjoyed themselves. Burt is just a total class act all the way.

I sense that you would be happy to work with him again.

I would love to work with Burt again. After we wrapped the movie, Burt said, "I really liked working with you. Why couldn't I have been here for the whole thing?" and I said, "I don't know! It would have been great." But I'm just the director, and as such I'm not privy to the negotiations behind the scenes that dictate the schedules. So he said, "Let's do something in the future where I'm on the film from beginning to end." Of course I loved that idea, so about a year after the movie wrapped, I flew down to Jupiter, Florida, and spent a couple of days with Burt. He screened *Reel Love* at his workshop and we spent a lot of time together and I asked him if there was anything of interest to him that he would like to work on. So he turned me on to this play which would be an interesting piece of material if done right; it's a Midwestern father-son relationship drama. Burt's assistant sent me the play and I optioned it and turned it into a script. My dream for the project has been that I want to bring Burt and Sally Field back together again. I've been working on getting Burt and Sally on the project for the last three or four years, and who wouldn't want to see those two together again? The real question is, how many will want to see them in dramatic material? This would be a mature picture. They have great chemistry together and I know there's a lot of affection between them and I think a lot of people would be happy to see them share the screen again.

That would be amazing. Did Burt ever surprise you with his techniques as a performer?

Having worked with him, I would say that the word which sums up Burt Reynolds for me is "gravitas." He is a director's dream because not only is he thoroughly familiar with the material, he is proactive, he listens to actors, he maintains eye contact and is fully present when he is doing a scene. It was wonderful to watch him work with some of the actors. He is as much of a giver as he is an actor, he would never disappear; even when we were on breaks, on turnarounds, he would be working on the material or run lines, he would just be wonderfully engaging. There's the famous Spencer Tracy story that Burt has told many times and it really says a lot about his approach to acting. The story goes that when he was a young actor under contract working on the television show *Riverboat* at Universal Studios, he used to spend his off-time watching the film *Inherit the Wind* being shot there because his acting hero Spencer Tracy was starring in it. So Burt used to follow behind Tracy when he would finish and walk back to his trailer until one day Tracy realized it and said, "Come on, kid," and invited Burt to talk to him. Tracy asked Burt what he did and finding out he was an actor gave Burt advice, and it is this advice that explains a lot of the genius of Burt: "Don't let anybody catch you at it. Don't act, just behave."

Burt came out of the late '50s studio system, and like a lot of that generation of actors he started out in television shows which were being filmed on movie lots. It was there that they could go and watch these giants of film acting, such as Spencer Tracy or Cary Grant, and they could watch and learn, or have the chance to go up and talk to them. Burt's Spencer Tracy story says a lot about the curiosity that he has for the craft of acting and the drive that he has to be so good. It's a total fluke that Burt ended up an actor, and thankfully for us that he did use this absolutely natural talent, but he should have been a football player, that's what he really wanted to do early on except that he injured his knee and that effectively killed his career as an athlete, so he went into acting! I have the utmost respect for Burt as an artist and someone who just has a God-given talent and instinct.

I would say that Burt is one of the few remaining actors of that Old Hollywood caliber, with the attendant star power and screen presence.

I would agree with you, I think Burt is one of the last of his generation of actors, of the old studio system guys, alongside someone like Clint Eastwood. I used to be a director for *Entertainment Tonight* and for that I would have to go out and do four or five shoots a day and it could involve me interviewing people like Jimmy Stewart, Frank Sinatra, Dean Martin, Debbie Reynolds—real "Old Hollywood" people. And I remember Debbie saying to me, "Sorry, sir, but your key light is in the wrong place. Can you lower that?" And that's the kind of stuff that these guys were used to, having come up through the studio system where they had to go through schools for camera, lighting, makeup, voice, where it was a like a factory. These guys knew all the elements of filmmaking because they had to understand it; they had to know how to hit their marks and how to work with the camera. And Burt really is one of the last Old Hollywood stars, he knows all of that stuff. Nothing would make me happier than to see this guy get his due.

He is probably one of the few movie professionals left who can teach that style of performance from having actually experienced it himself.

He is very adroit. When I visited his master class in Jupiter, Florida, I saw him work with his students on material that they were working on. Some students were very green in some cases, and others had been there a while, and I watched the way he worked with them and I saw him able to pull real performances from some of these people who just came off the street. That's a gift! He's really dedicated to helping people, especially young actors. He really knows how to break down a scene, he knows the beats of a scene, he knows how to show people the beats of a scene, and I really learned a lot from watching him. He is doing the Actor's Studio quality instruction at his acting classes. I'm astounded he hasn't directed more than he has. I asked why and his answer was something along the lines of "I don't want to work too much, directing is a lot of work," which is true! I told him he is really good at getting to the heart of a scene, but that's completely natural to him, it's who he is and what he is capable of doing with people.

Being that you went down to Jupiter and saw Burt in his own time and away from the camera, did you get an insight into the private side of Burt Reynolds?

I don't know if the Burt Reynolds Museum is still there, but he gave me the whole tour of that and it was amazing. I remember when I was in his house, he brought me into his office which has all these great photographs of classic actors like Cary Grant, and as I'm looking around I see these five awards, each a statue of an old-school cameraman operating an old-fashioned tripod and I said, "Hey, Burt, what are these?" and he said, "Look closer and read them," and when I took a closer inspection I saw that it said "Number One Box Office Draw for the Year..." and these five awards were for five consecutive years from 1978 to 1982. While I was there, he had the original *Smokey and the Bandit* Trans Am in his driveway. Which we drove around and it was a real kick. It was just a lovely thing, we would go out to his favorite little restaurant on the water, everybody knows him, I mean, it's a small town and he's just another local guy. He's a lot of fun to hang around with. He is a very gentle guy. He has people coming up to him all the time, both young and old, but he will totally engage with them, ask them where they're from, how their family is, that kind of thing. It's a very charming thing and makes his fans feel special. He is an incredibly gifted, talented, artistic guy.

I find it a shame that despite the wealth and celebrity that he has enjoyed as a performer, a good portion of his work has been largely under-appreciated.

I don't want to say that Burt has been mistreated or anything because he has received his share of accolades and attention, but here's a guy who is probably one of the most gifted actors of his generation but to many people he's just another big star who they see as this mere commercial entity. But to his credit, he really tried to step out of it and do something different. Here's a guy who was at the Actor's Studio with Marilyn Monroe, Paul Newman, Marlon Brando and he came out of the New York Actor's Studio scene and is an extremely gifted actor but his talents and qualities as a serious performer are often overshadowed by his tremendous success with the likes of *Smokey and the Bandit* and *The Cannonball Run*. I know that he looks back on his career and sometimes thinks of the roles he turned down. "I could have been in *Terms of Endearment*, I could have been in *Star Wars*..."—he was approached to do all these films that went on to become huge events, and why wouldn't he be under consideration for *Terms of Endearment*? He was more than capable of bringing what that film required, and I get the impression that there's an element of regret in having turned some of those roles down. I think Burt underestimates himself, but I know he also looks back with a certain worldview which is very much his own. He has a wistful quality about him and that comes with this idiosyncratic sense of humor and a wry consideration of his place in the world. He was an absolute joy to work with and we will all eventually have to accept the fact that one day he may not be around. And that is sad because he truly is a valued American treasure.

Apple of My Eye

(2017)

"Well, I guess puppies aren't everybody's thing, huh?"—Charlie

For teenage competitive equestrian Bailey Andrews (Avery Arendes), horse riding is her life, but a freak accident sees the youngster launched off her steed in a moment that will change things irrevocably. Initially everything seems okay, but Bailey unknowingly suffered a head injury which devastatingly affects her eyesight and she eventually becomes legally blind. Bailey's father Jason (Liam McIntyre) is a figure of towering support while his wife Caroline (Amy Smart) carries the additional burden of breadwinner and caregiver. Enter Burt Reynolds, who plays Charlie, head trainer at Southeastern Guide Dogs. Charlie knows that Bailey is finding it difficult to establish a bond with a dog, and so given his history in horse training, he finds Bailey the perfect companion who will act as her surrogate eyes: Apple. But Apple is no guide dog; she is a horse. Of course, *Apple of My Eye* wouldn't be much of a teen film without a romantic subplot, and this is where Charlie's assistant Sebastian (Jason Griffo), who is also blind, is introduced. With the support of Charlie, Sebastian and Apple, Bailey and her family are able to come to terms with her disability.

Apple of My Eye is a warm family film that touches upon the important subject matter of a child's disability and how it affects their life and those around them. While the theme could have been mined for something deeper, the filmmakers opted to make this a frothier affair to cater to a younger audience. Some difficult scenarios are raised in the opening scenes but rarely followed through, such as the suggestion that the Andrews family is struggling economically, and the fact that Caroline has just received a promotion at work which means longer working hours away from her family; Jason is seemingly unemployed and so they must consider selling their house. However, after Bailey's accident, nothing is mentioned regarding the financial and emotional strain of supporting their disabled child. One would think that having to blind-proof their home and deal with additional medical costs would contribute further to the economic hardship, but it is rarely touched upon in the proceedings. Doting dad Andrew playfully cavorts with his daughter without a care in the world, while Caroline grimaces grimly from time to time as the burdened bread winner; surely she deserves more sympathy than is allotted to her here, given the heavy load of responsibility she carries.

Ultimately, *Apple of My Eye* tells its tale simply and efficiently. Bailey's traumatic event and subsequent major life adjustments are dealt with in too lightweight a manner to allow for much pathos to be observed, but the picture functions just fine as a frivolous young adult-teen romance soap opera. Reynolds' role is an extended cameo, and here he adds just the right amount of old world charm and grace to a well-intentioned family film.

Hamlet and Hutch

(2017)

"I wasn't in movies, I was a real actor."—Hutchinson "Papa Hutch" Byrne

Hutchinson "Papa Hutch" Byrne (Reynolds) was once a Broadway star. However, old age and its attendant afflictions have made him relocate to Georgia where he lives with his daughter Tatum (Elizabeth Leiner) and granddaughter Liv (Emma Rayne Lyle). Liv is a precocious entity whose hero is Audrey Hepburn, and the little miss tries her best to shake her grandfather out of his crotchety ways by getting him back on the stage. But Hutch is suffering from Alzheimer's and struggles to remember lines that were once his second tongue. Even more of a battle for Hutch is maintaining a cordial relationship with his daughter, whom he perceives as a failure and a deserter, having left her parents and a burgeoning career in acting behind when she met the man who would father her child. Despite Tatum being a successful businesswoman and self-sufficient single mother, Hutch remains recalcitrant. The eponymous Hamlet is a handsome retired racing greyhound who now functions as a therapy animal "looking for his forever home." After much convincing by Liv, Tatum adopts Hamlet and the dog becomes an essential companion for Hutch, whose illness and memory loss makes him feel increasingly isolated. The dog's name, which evokes the great work of the Bard, contains great meaning for Hutch, who trod the boards as a Shakespearean actor in his heyday. Hamlet's therapeutic qualities work their magic, allowing Hutch to rediscover his empathy and understanding of his family's—and his own—distinctly human flaws.

Hamlet and Hutch is a sweet-natured picture which handles its delicate themes with the right amount of sensitivity and humor, featuring a nicely depicted intergenerational relationship between Liv and Hutch. Wholly unnecessary is the subplot centered on a trailer trash kleptomaniac named Rusty (Travis Young) who compulsively steals cars and anybody's property not tied down. Later in the film, one of Rusty's illicit acquisitions is Hamlet, which leaves the Hutch family temporarily bereft of the canine emotional core that has brought them together. This strand of the narrative deviates from a story already rich enough to sustain itself without such trivial detours. The film benefits from some very nice cinematography courtesy of Carelton Holt and Chance White. It nicely captures the lush beauty of Georgia and there are moments where they frame the action exquisitely, particularly during Hutch's lonesome trek back to Central Park … from Georgia!

The Last Movie Star

(2017)

"You were the one who loved me before anybody else even knew my name." —Vic Edwards

Vic Edwards (Reynolds) was once the toast of Hollywood, a megastar movie actor who lived large on fame, fortune and fandom. That has all faded with time. He is haunted by reminders of old B-Westerns he made when he was making a name for himself in the film industry, with titles such as *Squanto* ("Fierce…Swift…Savage") and *Nine Lives to Kathmandu*. Even Vic's own doctors poke fun in prescribing medicine to him under the name "Squanto Edwards."

But not everybody has forgotten the true legacy of Vic Edwards: Die-hard fans Doug (Clark Duke) and Shane (Ellar Coltrane) have bestowed the actor with the honor of a Lifetime Achievement Award at their International Nashville Film Festival—not to be confused with the Nashville International Film Festival. Doug and Shane's humble festival takes place in a shabby pub with a makeshift screening room in which they project Vic's films on a 4×6 pull-up tripod screen. They managed to attract Vic by mentioning that Clint Eastwood, Jack Nicholson and Robert De Niro are all past recipients of the award being given to him. What these would-be festival programmers failed to mention was that those stars never acknowledged their award and of course never showed up in Nashville to receive them. On the advice of fellow actor Sonny (Chevy Chase), Vic decides to accept the award in person and arrives in Nashville to be greeted by Doug's sister Lil (Ariel Winter), a heavily pierced and multi-tattooed alternative girl with serious attitude issues. The actor means nothing to Lil. Vic is initially dismayed at the obscure environment of the film festival and makes a swift exit once the opening credits roll on *Nine Lives to Kathmandu*, escaping to his shelter of pills and booze. Doug and Shane find a drunk and angered Vic ready to leave town but the two convince him to stay and arrange for a classic Nashville breakfast of ribs the following morning. But on the way to the meal, Vic convinces Lil—his chauffeur for the weekend—to take the next exit to Knoxville, Tennessee. From here the film takes us on Vic's journey to say goodbye to his past as he embraces his legacy. Over the course of the film, the two troubled souls who were antagonistic to each other upon introduction end up becoming crucial to each other's discovery of their respective sense of value and self-worth.

When we think of graceful swan songs, we think of John Wayne in *The Shootist* (Don Siegel, 1976), Henry Fonda in *On Golden Pond* (Mark Rydell, 1981), Burt Lancaster in *Field of Dreams* (Phil Alden Robinson, 1989), and Harry Dean Stanton in *Lucky* (John Carroll

Old Burt meets Young Burt in *The Last Movie Star* (2017).

Lynch, 2017). Well, now to be ranked up there with the Duke *et al.* is Burt Reynolds with his tender and elegant farewell to film and to his fans. The film closes just as it opens: with Reynolds staring us directly through the lens of the camera. While the opening shot sees a tired, despondent Vic, the closing image poignantly frames Vic once again engaging us directly, but this time Reynolds is breaking the fourth wall to acknowledge his audience with a smile that would suggest a peaceful, satisfactory end to a truly rich and wonderful career.

Directed by lifelong Reynolds devotee Adam Rifkin, *The Last Movie Star* parallels Reynolds' own life with sometimes biographical detail. Edwards was once a celebrated athlete; he was once the biggest film star in the world; he enjoyed romances with high-profile women; he punched a director on-set; he was a Hollywood heartthrob with Southern roots and here Tennessee stands in for Reynolds' home state of Florida. Vic Edwards is essentially Burt Reynolds. Rifkin wrote the film specifically for the actor and the film is littered with references to his films and career. In a neat touch, scenes from *Smokey and the Bandit* and *Deliverance* are spliced in, serving as Vic's memory flashbacks in which we get to see present-day Reynolds (Vic) speaking with 1970s Reynolds (Vic). There are also various Easter Eggs for Reynolds fans to appreciate when spotted, such as a "Smokey" sign hanging in the bar, or an overzealous fan rhapsodizing about *Operation F.B.I.* (an obvious nod to *Operation C.I.A.*). Doug considers being on the receiving end of Vic's coruscating humor as being "like I'm on Carson!" Moments like these make *The Last Movie Star* a genuine treat for the Reynolds historian.

Adam Rifkin directs Reynolds in *The Last Movie Star* (2017) (photograph courtesy Adam Rifkin Collection).

Ariel Winter provides the right amount of bratty attitude for Lil's over-medicated, hyper-cynical millennial who is completely at odds with Vic's wise, old-world sage wisdom. In one hilarious scene, Lil lists off her entire history of mood-altering prescription drugs (far too numerous to replicate here). Vic balks at his companion's reliance upon chemicals to remain cocooned from the malaise of life, but he is as dependent on distracting substances as she, namely whiskey. While it is never explained where Lil's depression and anxiety, and penchant for morbid art, comes from, Vic's vices seem designed to cloud his perception of his place in life, having fallen hard from the heights of his illustrious career. Lil gives herself and the audience a snippet of Vic's well-lived life when she Googles his name and comes up with memorable highlights from his (Reynolds') past, including the infamous *Cosmopolitan* spread, spraying a can of cream down Johnny Carson's pants on *The Tonight Show*, and stills of his younger, handsome self in various films. The moment reminds viewers that Reynolds had a career unlike any other. He was a pop-cultural institution who crossed the mediums of television, film, and music with ease, charm and fun.

It is on Edwards' journey through his past that we are treated to the picture's best scenes, and they are numerous. Perhaps the most poignant is when Edwards visits his childhood home. When he is invited in by the star-struck current resident, he experiences a rush of emotions that recall warm memories of a happy youth; he envisions his mother working in the kitchen before that mirage fades back to the reality of the present time. It's a powerful sequence. For Reynolds and his legion of fans, moments such as these are deeply resonant. We are watching this man that we have revered and enjoyed closing the doors on his life and his career. With *The Last Movie Star*, Rifkin takes us on a deeply sentimental journey, one tempered with moments of levity, and in crafting many soul-stirring scenes for his central character, the director affords Reynolds an opportunity for some of the greatest acting of his career, none more definitive than the scene in which Reynolds delivers a profound and heart-rending monologue where Edwards grasps the finality of his journey, looking back on his life and career and accepting that he is saying goodbye to many things:

> I've watched everyone I ever cared about die. One by one they seem to just … disappear on me. It won't be long before I disappear, too. You want to know why I needed to come to Knoxville? I needed to say goodbye. Goodbye to the town that made me who I am. Goodbye to the trees I climbed as a kid. Goodbye to the school that taught me how to break the rules. And the streets I wandered late at night. The hiding places where I left all my secrets. The town where I made so many, many mistakes. And now it's time for one … last goodbye.

An Interview
with Adam Rifkin

Director Adam Rifkin began his career as an auteur of independent genre film (*Tale of Two Sisters*, 1989; *Psycho Cop 2*, 1993) before his media satire *The Chase*—an inspired pop-culture bonanza starring Charlie Sheen, punk poet Henry Rollins, and Red Hot Chili Peppers' Anthony Kiedis and Flea—received a mainstream release by 20th Century–Fox in 1994. In the succeeding years, Rifkin found success as a writer of family films for major

Reynolds and Adam Rifkin share a moment on set of *The Last Movie Star* **(photograph courtesy Adam Rifkin Collection).**

studios (*Mouse Hunt*, 1996, *Small Soldiers*, 1997, *Underdog*, 2007) while continuing to direct films which have become cult favorites, such as *Detroit Rock City* (1999). In 2017, Rifkin realized a passion project: He wrote and directed a tribute to his hero Burt Reynolds, *The Last Movie Star*, a fond farewell.

Wayne: *It is evident from* **The Last Movie Star** *that you are a great fan of Burt Reynolds. Tell me about the impact he had on you when you first discovered his work.*

Adam: When I was 11 years old, I saw *Smokey and the Bandit* and I immediately thought this guy was the coolest, funniest movie star in the world. Before I saw the film, I was aware of Burt as this famous person who was a larger-than-life figure; he was culturally ubiquitous, you couldn't help but know who Burt Reynolds was when you were growing up in the 1970s.

Was this something that would have an influence on your career as a filmmaker?

Seeing *Smokey and the Bandit* instantly made him my favorite movie star, but *Deliverance* was another film that really struck a chord with me and I discovered that later on, at an important time when I was really getting into film as an art form. So seeing *Deliverance* at the time that I did really made a huge impact on me from a filmmaking perspective.

I wrote the [*Last Movie Star*] script for Burt and for Burt only. If Burt didn't want to do this movie, then I didn't want to make it with anyone else. So I submitted the script to Burt's manager, Eric Kritzer, and he gave it to Burt. The next day I got a phone call and I knew immediately from the voice on the other end that it was Burt. I don't get star-struck, I've met enough famous people throughout my travels in Hollywood that it doesn't faze me anymore, but as soon as I realized it was Burt Reynolds, I was 11 years old again and I was completely star-struck.

How did Burt react to the script?

He said that this film was perfect for him at this specific time in his life, that only now could he accept playing such a part. There were times in his life when he wouldn't have been able to play the role. It was a hard role for him, elements of it hit very close to home and he was forced to dig deep. There were times when I thought he would probably pass on it because some of the themes might have been too sensitive.

Once you had Burt's support and commitment, what did this mean for the film in terms of going into production?

I naïvely thought that having Burt Reynolds as the star of your picture would instantly lead to funding. It didn't. It took seven years for us to get the funding to allow us to go into production. We would get word that we had financing and then it would fall through; this happened many times. I honestly thought Burt would eventually say to me, "We tried our best, let's move on," but he stuck with me for those seven years; he said, "When you get the money, you tell me where to turn up and I'll be there!"

So he obviously recognized something special in this script, an opportunity for some great acting, and to confront his own life and career.

Being that I was a huge fan of Burt's, I was aware of the basic landmarks of his life and that allowed to me include moments for his character to reflect on that would resonate with Burt. It helped that he was in the right time of his life to embrace the confrontation of those elements of his past. I wanted to write a role that he could really sink his teeth into because I believed he was a truly great actor. Unfortunately, many people didn't consider him a formidable actor, so I wanted to create something that could change people's perception of him, to let them see just how great an actor he really was.

One scene stands out in my mind, Vic's monologue where he reflects on his mortality and considers all of the things that meant something to him in his life: his youth, his friends, his family and his home town.

I wrote that scene on the set, it wasn't in the script, and it came about because Burt was talking to me about his life and his friends, about people like Dom DeLuise, Charles Durning, Dinah Shore, and we talked about how he really missed these people. And that led to me writing that scene for him where he talks about saying goodbye to the people and places of his past. The only other thing that wasn't in the script was the location; it was originally set on the East Coast, around Philadelphia, but we changed it to Nashville.

There are scenes in which you have Burt appearing onscreen with his younger self, in moments from Smokey and the Bandit *and* Deliverance. *Were these in the original script? I would imagine those would be costly clips to license.*

Those scenes are in the script. And because they are from these two huge movies which are so iconic and are widely used, it means they are indeed astronomically expensive to license. But because we had Burt involved and had his complete support, it made it easier for us to approach Warner Brothers and Universal to get permission to use them. There is such love for Burt at those studios that they jumped on board with our idea to use those scenes and they did it for us at an affordable rate.

Did Burt's co-stars and other cast members in your film share your sense of reverence?

Clark Duke, who plays Doug in the film, was a big fan of Burt's so he certainly understood the magnitude of having Burt Reynolds in our movie and was really excited to work with him. Chevy Chase, who was himself one of the biggest stars in the 1980s, is in the film as well and he really wanted to work with Burt because he is a huge fan. Some of the other actors were aware of Burt's accomplishments but were not necessarily in awe of him the way you and I would be.

I suppose for people my age, your age and people older, Burt Reynolds meant so much more than being a famous actor; he was perhaps the best example of a superstar, he transcended mere fame.

I agree. I think unless you grew up in the era where Burt was truly at his most famous, you will not realize just how big he really was. Think of the people who are huge these days: The Rock, Brad Pitt and Tom Cruise.... Burt was much bigger than all of those guys. You have to remember that this was a time before social media. Nowadays anybody with an Instagram account can become famous, but this was before all of that.

He crossed media as well, he was hugely popular with television audiences thanks to his Johnny Carson appearances and the various TV shows he had done. He released a country music album on a major label.

No other star at that time was so beloved across that spectrum of media. At a certain point in his career, Burt could do absolutely anything he wanted to, he had his pick of projects and he had the audience to support whatever he did in film, on TV, and albums ... he was huge!

Yet in his passing, most tributes mentioned two specific movies to summarize his career, and we just mentioned both of those.

And this shows just how big he was. What other star could have made a show as successful and popular as *Evening Shade*, which was a massive hit, won awards and critical plaudits, and to not even have it mentioned when people are paying tribute to his career? If that was any other star, that show would be the first thing mentioned, but Burt was so prolific and so famous for many other things that even something as beloved as *Evening Shade* ends up way down the list when people are remembering his career. Instead of being a headline, *Evening Shade* is a footnote in his career.

What made him such a likable screen presence and such a magnetic star?

Burt had the "It Factor." He had all the elements of what makes a truly great movie star and was one of the few people genuinely born with talent. You can't teach talent, you can hone it and work on it but only a few people possess that rare quality of having complete, natural talent, and Burt had it. He also had one particular element that was distinctively his and which set him apart from everyone else: He was entirely unpretentious. Burt was a serious actor, he trained with the greats, but nothing annoyed him more than people who were pretentious about acting. *Smokey and the Bandit* was the film that made him the biggest star in the world but he was always as good as his contemporaries, as brilliant as people like Al Pacino, Dustin Hoffman, etc. Even in the films that weren't so good, Burt was always brilliant in them. He gave his best performance no matter what the material was. Burt knew he was in a very lucky position in life and so he had fun with it; it's that sense of fun which translates to the screen and to the audience. Burt Reynolds let viewers in on the fun that he is having and they responded by making him the world's premier movie star.

Afterword
by C. James Lewis

Meeting Burt Reynolds changed my life. Prior to finding my place in the movie business thanks to Mr. Reynolds' friendship and teachings, I lived in another world entirely. I was a member of the U.S. Marine Corps and that led me to Vietnam as a combat Marine squad leader. After being seriously wounded in September 1968, I spent almost a year in a U.S. Navy hospital recovering. After military discharge and my parents taking care of me for another year, I was appointed to a local sheriff's office in the state of Iowa along the Mississippi River. I made the rank of sergeant and flew the department helicopters. After seven years, I resigned in good standing and simply hit the road to find my life. I drove all the way to L.A., realized it was not the place for me to be at that time and then turned around and drove to Florida. I found my home and started college. Soon after that, I met Burt Reynolds for the very first time.

This meeting took place in February of 1979, while I was enrolled at Palm Beach Junior College, located in Lakeworth, Florida. Both my drama professor and English literature professor called me into an office meeting. I was given a script to read and told to pay particular attention to a certain character. Both teachers were sending me to audition for Burt at his newly built Burt Reynolds Dinner Theater, located in Jupiter, Florida. Nineteen seventy-nine was the first season at the new theater and the inaugural play was *The Rainmaker*. Burt was directing and starring in it alongside Sally Field. I went to the audition and gave my best at capturing the character of the deputy sheriff. Burt asked me to read again and gave a suggestion. At that moment, I knew Burt was a teacher. I read again using his suggestion as best I could. He then took me aside and told me I did a good job and how proud he was of me. He told me to return to school and continue working hard. I did not get the part. I had never failed so gently, but I learned. Returning to school, I was part of two more college productions during that year.

I graduated at the end of 1979 with a two-year degree in Theater and from there I auditioned for the Burt Reynolds Institute for Theater Training (BRITT). I was accepted and became part of the Class of 1980, a yearlong apprenticeship in which we worked all aspects of production and also auditioned for incoming plays. Burt took a chance on a disabled Vietnam Veteran, emotionally bruised and very simply put, just plain lost in life, but getting through with the care, support and love of a great woman and with Burt being my beacon and voice in the dark. And believe me, it was a very deep, dark, scary and stormy time in my life.

My first play was *Mister Roberts*, and who does Burt bring in to direct our production?

283

None other than Joshua Logan, who co-wrote the play and the movie! Now Joshua Logan is directing me in a play and I am appearing alongside Martin Sheen, Simon Oakland and Mr. Logan's daughter, Harrigan. I played the part of the Shore Patrol lieutenant that Martin Milner played in the movie version. The scene was a one-on-one with Marty and what a thrill! During the production, I went to Marty about a case of the self-doubts (more like the shakes—this acting deal wasn't as easy as I thought). He took a red lipstick tube and wrote this on my dressing room mirror: "Take courage, enter. Have fun, exit." Now there's a life lesson for you.

What a start to a year in which I worked on so many wonderful productions with so many great actors, teachers and more teachers, and all chosen by Burt. Stars of the stage and the screen would walk through the doors of the theater, check their ego, and educate Burt's acting apprentices. How really extraordinary it all was. It was unlike any other acting workshop and it could be, at times, surreal. On opening night of *Mister Roberts*, Burt walked out on stage during curtain call with a desk phone and a very long cord. He handed the receiver to Marty, and said; "This call is for you." Marty said, "Hello," and the voice on the other end was Henry Fonda and said this to Marty: "Welcome to the club, kid!" The phone call was broadcast on the auditorium speaker, so the cast, crew and audience all heard it. Only Burt…

In May of 1980, halfway through my apprentice year, Burt called the theater one day and the secretary told me that Burt wanted to speak to me. So I got on the phone and Burt said, "I need you to be in Atlanta tomorrow, we're doing a film and I've got the perfect part for you." They were shooting *The Cannonball Run* and they want me to be in it! The film was directed by Hal Needham, the legendary stuntman who became very successful as a director with *Smokey and the Bandit*. I played a Missouri highway patrolman who was to arrest Dean Martin and Sammy Davis Jr. I arrived at location the next day and the call-sheet for my first day read as follows: "Directed by Hal Needham, Produced by Albert S. Ruddy, #1 Burt Reynolds, #2 Farrah Fawcett, #3 Dean Martin, #4 Sammy Davis Jr., #5 Dom DeLuise, #6 Jack Elam, #7 Jimmy Lewis." I had only ever been in college theater, was halfway through my apprenticeship year at Burt's institute, and here I was on my first day in "the business" and I'm shooting scenes with Dean Martin and Sammy Davis Jr.! When filming concluded, I asked Burt what we were going to do next, and I'm thinking Hollywood. He smiled, and then told me how good I was, how proud of me he was and that he loved me and I was going back to the apprentice program to finish my year.

I did so and at the end of 1980, three big things happened to me: I graduated from BRITT and I performed in *West Side Story*, in which I played Lt. Shrank. Our production was directed by none other than Tony Mordente, who was in the film version; Tony's daughter Lisa Mordente co-starred and her mother Chita Rivera would be there watching from the audience. With that play, I received my Theater Equity Card. Then at the graduation ceremony, Burt did a very nice thing. As he read out the graduating students' names in alphabetical order and when he came to mine, he said, "I think I'll keep that one until last," and so when it eventually came to me, Burt handed me my graduation diploma gave me a hug and said, "I'm going to Atlanta to do a movie, somebody will be calling you." I said, "Yes sir," bid him farewell and went on my way. That movie was *Sharky's Machine*. I would play Sgt. Tommy Heller, a uniformed Atlanta Metro police officer. My life changed forever. I now had an Equity Card, a Screen Actors Guild Card [for *The Cannonball Run*] and was

Left to right: Reynolds, C. James Lewis and Martin Sheen during rehearsals of the play *Mister Roberts* in 1980 (photograph courtesy C. James Lewis Collection).

about to appear in one of the biggest studio pictures of that time, all thanks to this one year acting apprenticeship program at Burt's Theater. What a year!

Sharky's Machine changed my life. I was introduced to Nick McLean, who is someone you have to mention when talking about Burt Reynolds. Nick became a legendary Hollywood cinematographer, one of the best in the business, but on this picture he was the camera operator for another famous cinematographer, William Fraker. Burt surrounded himself with only the best in cast and crew. On my first day of shooting, while standing at

the food truck pouring a coffee, the armorer fired off a series of test shots with no audible warning and my instant reaction was to dive under the truck. You could say I was a bit "gun shy." Nick looked down at me and said, "You okay, buddy?" I was shaken, embarrassed and thought about leaving for the airport. Nick took me for a walk and talked me right down. From that moment on, Nick looked after me in life and in work. Nick made sure word had passed around the set and the result was that all further weapons tests were preceded with a yell of "Fire in the hole!"

From *Sharky's Machine* onwards, I went on to have some of the most unique experiences you can imagine. Working on major studio films such as *The Man Who Loved Women City Heat* and *Stick*, I was Burt's stand-in, photo double and stunt double, as well as being a fellow actor. I also worked with Burt on his television shows, such as in 1988 when he gave me a recurring role in *B.L. Stryker*. In 1992, I became a first assistant cameraman on his hit television sitcom *Evening Shade*, where I worked alongside Nick McLean, the show's director of pho-

Reynolds directs and C. James Lewis listens, on the set of *Sharky's Machine* (1981) (photograph courtesy C. James Lewis Collection).

tography. To think I pulled focus for Nick McLean and acted with Burt Reynolds on film, stage and television are the stuff Hollywood dreams really are made of. I truly did live the dream because of Burt Reynolds. But the best of all was trading books with Burt and enjoying the conversations about those books. Whether on set, on stage or in his living room, Burt's teachings never stopped. I consider myself the luckiest guy in the world to have been privy to such a mentor. The only way to pay Burt back is to "pay it forward," to share the lessons and the generosity that Burt taught me and so many others.

In my retirement from show business, I realized a mission that I needed to fulfill. I sponsored and raised funds to build a kindergarten in Au Xing Village, Quang Tri Province, Vietnam. I was able to attend dedication ceremonies and it was my first time back since being wounded in 1968. On March 21, 2009, the school was dedicated to Jesse Griego, my fellow Marine who was killed in action in July of 1968. I was with him when he died and held him in my arms hearing his last words and seeing the light leave his eyes. I needed to do something to honor Jesse and to help the children of Vietnam who suffer greatly. I was able to do so by giving the local village children a chance to read, to write, speak properly, and grow. They now have a school and a playground free of unexploded munitions, Funds are provided for two meals a day. On September 11, 2010, I returned to Southeast Asia again and dedicated a library that I sponsored in the Ba Long District of Quang Tri, Vietnam. The children there needed a library to continue their learning skills. The library is dedicated to Pat Lucero, my Colorado high school buddy who lost his life in Vietnam in March of 1968 while serving in the U.S. Army. Now the children continue to learn and the teachers continue to educate. All of this was possible because my two principal teachers, Nick McLean and Burt Reynolds, both supported my efforts. For that I am eternally grateful and so are the parents and the children of Au Xing Village. I am blessed for not only all that Mr. Reynolds did for me but for the people he introduced me to, like Nick McLean.

No doubt, Burt was a smart man, a true athlete and an artistic visionary, but I honestly believe that first and foremost his gift and mission in life was to teach. His love, understanding and teachings are lifelong lessons not to be forgotten. He never stopped teaching for all of those 39 years that I knew him and was doing so six days before he died. However, perhaps his best lessons were his displays of always being an absolute gentleman. His father was a gentleman, and Burt Reynolds was too. I saw Burt five weeks before he passed. I took a book for him to read called *The Greatest Beer Run Ever* by Chick Donohue, and upon leaving I kissed him on the cheek and told him I loved him. He smiled and said, "Well, I love you too." There was never a goodbye between us … ever. It was only love and respect for one another.

Thank you, Burt Reynolds. I love you.

Jimmy

Appendix 1

Additional Films:
Cameos and Appearances

Six Pack (Daniel Petrie, 1982)

Smokey and the Bandit Part 3 (Dick Lowry, 1983)

Uphill All the Way (Frank Q. Dobbs, 1986)

The Player (Robert Altman, 1992)

Wind in the Wire (Jim Shea, 1993)

Auf Herz und Nieren (Thomas Jahn, Til Schweiger, 2001)

The Legend of Frosty the Snowman (Emily Kapnek, 2005)

Grilled (Jason Ensler, 2006)

Randy and the Mob (Ray McKinnon, 2007)

Delgo (Mark F. Adler, Jason Maurer, 2008)

Not Another Not Another Movie (David Murphy, 2011)

A Magic Christmas (R. Michael Givens, 2014)

Pocket Listing (Ron Glass, 2015)

Hollow Creek (Guisela Moro, 2016)

Elbow Grease (Jason Shirley, 2016)

Shangri-La Suite (Eddie O'Keefe, 2016)

Miami Love Affair (Ralph Kinnard, 2017)

Henri (Octavian O., 2017)

Shadow Fighter (Steve Daron, 2018)

Defining Moments (Stephen Wallis, 2019)

Appendix 2

Recurring Players

Rodolfo Acosta—*Impasse, Run Simon Run*

Eddie Albert—*Riverboat, The Longest Yard* (1974), *Hustle*

Loni Anderson—*Stroker Ace, Amazing Stories: Guilt Trip, All Dogs Go to Heaven, B.L. Stryker*

R.G. Armstrong—*Riverboat, Gunsmoke, White Lightning*

Elizabeth Ashley—*Paternity, B.L. Stryker, Evening Shade*

Catherine Bach—*Hustle, Cannonball Run II*

Matt Battaglia—*B.L. Stryker, Evening Shade, Raven, Universal Soldier II: Brothers in Arms, Universal Soldier III: Unfinished Business*

Ned Beatty—*Deliverance, White Lightning, W.W. and the Dixie Dancekings, Stroker Ace, Switching Channels, Physical Evidence, B.L. Stryker*

Robby Benson—*Lucky Lady, The End, Alfred Hitchcock Presents*: "Method Actor," *Rent-a-Cop, Modern Love*

Tom Berenger—*The Hollywood Sign, Johnson County War*

Candice Bergen—*Starting Over, Stick*

James Best—*Gunsmoke, Hawk, Dan August, Run Simon Run, Nickelodeon, The End, Hooper, B.L. Stryker*

Brent Briscoe—*Evening Shade, Driven, Randy and the Mob*

Keith Carradine—*The Hunter's Moon, Hostage Hotel*

Bernie Casey—*Sharky's Machine, Alfred Hitchcock Presents*: "Method Actor," *Rent-a-Cop, Evening Shade*

Maury Chaykin—*Breaking In, Mystery Alaska*

Chevy Chase—*Not Another Not Another Movie, The Last Movie Star*

Jill Clayburgh—*Semi-Tough, Starting Over*

Ossie Davis—*Sam Whiskey, B.L. Stryker, Cop and a Half, Evening Shade*

Dom DeLuise—*Silent Movie, The End, Smokey and the Bandit II, The Cannonball Run, The Best Little Whorehouse in Texas, Cannonball Run II, Amazing Stories: Guilt Trip, All Dogs Go to Heaven, B.L. Stryker*

Bruce Dern—*Hard Ground, The Premonition*

Angie Dickinson—*Sam Whiskey, The Maddening, The Last Producer*

Lesley-Anne Down—*Rough Cut, Meet Wally Sparks*

Richard Dreyfuss—*Mad Dog Time, The Crew*

Ja'Net DuBois—*Hard Time, Hostage Hotel, Waterproof*

Charles Durning—*Hawk, Starting Over, Sharky's Machine, The Best Little Whorehouse in Texas, Stick, Amazing Stories: "Guilt Trip," Evening Shade, Harlan and Merleen, Hard*

Time, The Premonition, Hostage Hotel, The Last Producer, Forget About It, Deal, A Bunch of Amateurs

Norman Fell—*Dan August, The End, Paternity, Out of This World*

Sally Field—*Smokey and the Bandit, The End, Hooper, Smokey and the Bandit II*

Anne Francis—*Dan August, Impasse*

William Forsythe—*Big City Blues, The Librarians*

George Furth—*Hooper, The Cannonball Run*

Alice Ghostley—*Gator, B.L. Stryker, Evening Shade, Hard Time*

Burton Gilliam—*At Long Last Love, Gator, Uphill All the Way, Out of This World, Evening Shade*

Gene Hackman—*Hawk, Lucky Lady*

George Hamilton—*Angel Baby, The Man Who Loved Cat Dancing, Meet Wally Sparks*

James Hampton—*Gunsmoke, Fade In, The Man Who Loved Cat Dancing, The Longest Yard, W.W. and the Dixie Dancekings, Hustle, Evening Shade*

Marilu Henner—*The Man Who Loved Women, The Cannonball Run II, Alfred Hitchcock Presents: "Method Actor," Evening Shade*

Mike Henry—*Dan August, The Longest Yard(1974), Smokey and the Bandit, Smokey and the Bandit II, Smokey and the Bandit Part 3*

John Hillerman—*At Long Last Love, Lucky Lady*

Gregory Hines—*Mad Dog Time, The Cherokee Kid*

Earl Holliman—*Armored Command, Sharky's Machine*

Bo Hopkins—*The Man Who Loved Cat Dancing, White Lightning*

Lauren Hutton—*Gator, Paternity, Malone*

Brion James—*Nickelodeon, The Hunter's Moon*

Madeleine Kahn—*At Long Last Love, City Heat*

Richard Kiel—*The Longest Yard (1974), Cannonball Run II*

Brian Keith—*Nickelodeon, Hooper, Sharky's Machine, Evening Shade*

Fernando Lamas—*Dan August, 100 Rifles*

Ed Lauter—*The Longest Yard (1974), The Librarians, The Longest Yard (2005)*

C. James Lewis—*The Cannonball Run, Sharky's Machine, Best Friends, Stroker Ace, The Man Who Loved Women, Cannonball Run II, City Heat, B.L. Stryker, The Man from Left Field*

Matthew Lillard—*Without a Paddle, In the Name of the King*

Carol Locatell—*Paternity, Sharky's Machine, Best Friends*

Rob Lowe—*Crazy Six, Pocket Listing*

Robert Loggia—*Hard Time, Forget About It*

John Marley—*Hawk, Dan August, Hooper*

Richard Masur—*Semi-Tough, Rent-a-Cop*

Mercedes McCambridge—*Riverboat, Angel Baby*

Doug, McClure—*Riverboat, Cannonball Run II, B.L. Stryker, Evening Shade, Out of This Word*

Ted McGinley—*Physical Evidence, B.L. Stryker, Evening Shade*

Peter MacNicol—*Heat, Bean*

Liza Minnelli—*Lucky Lady, Silent Movie, Rent-a-Cop*

Julianne Moore—*B.L. Stryker, Boogie Nights*

Jim Nabors—*The Best Little Whorehouse in Texas, Stoker Ace, The Cannonball Run II*

Willie Nelson—*The Dukes of Hazzard, Broken Bridges*

Bernadette Peters—*The Longest Yard* (1974), *Silent Movie*

Mary Kay Place—*Starting Over, Citizen Ruth*

Jerry Reed—*W.W. and the Dixie Dancekings, Gator, Smokey and the Bandit, Smokey and the Bandit II, Smokey and the Bandit Part 3, B.L. Stryker, Evening Shade*

Charles Nelson Reilly—*Cannonball Run II, Amazing Stories*: "Guilt Trip," *All Dogs Go to Heaven, B.L. Stryker, Evening Shade*

Gigi Rice—*B.L. Stryker, The Premonition*

Alex Rocco—*Cannonball Run II, Stick, The Last Producer*

Casey Siemaszko—*Breaking In, The Crew*

Rod Steiger—*The Last Producer, The Hollywood Sign*

Parker Stevenson—*Stroker Ace, Alfred Hitchcock Presents*: "Method Actor"

Henry Silva—*Sharky's Machine, Cannonball Run II, Mad Dog Time*

Mel Tillis—*W.W. and the Dixie Dancekings, Smokey and the Bandit II, The Cannonball Run, Cannonball Run II, Uphill All the Way*

Charles Tyner—*Hawk, Fuzz, The Longest Yard* (1974)

Abe Vigoda—*Cannonball Run II, B.L. Stryker*

Jan-Michael Vincent—*Dan August, Hooper*

Rachel Ward—*Sharky's Machine, Johnson County War*

Ann Wedgeworth—*Hawk, Evening Shade, Harlan and Merleen, The Hunter's Moon*

Raquel Welch—*100 Rifles, Fuzz, Evening Shade, Forget About It*

Jack Weston—*The Twilight Zone: The Bard, Fuzz, Gator*

Alfie Wise—*The Longest Yard* (1974), *Smokey and the Bandit, The End, Hooper, Starting Over, The Cannonball Run, Paternity, Stroker Ace, City Heat, Heat, B.L. Stryker, Evening Shade*

Bibliography

Aaker, Everett. *Television Western Players, 1960–1975: A Biographical Dictionary.* Jefferson, NC: McFarland, 2017.

Anderson, Paul Thomas. "Interview." DVD Supplement, *Boogie Nights,* Entertainment in Video, 1999.

Armstrong, Vic, with Robert Sellers. *The True Adventures of the World's Greatest Stuntman: My Life as Indiana Jones, James Bond, Superman and Other Movie Heroes.* Titan Books, 2011, London.

Arnold, Edwin T., and Eugene L. Miller. "Aldrich Interview: Pierre Sauvage 1976" in *Robert Aldrich: interviews,* Mississippi: University Press of Mississippi, 2004.

Austin, Steve. "First Down & Twenty-Five to Life: the Making of The Longest Yard." DVD Supplement, *The Longest Yard,* Sony Pictures Home Entertainment, 2006.

Baltake, Joe. "Afterword." In *The Films of Burt Reynolds.* Nancy Streebeck, New York: Citadel Press, 1982.

Bart, Peter. *Infamous Players: A Tale of Movies, The Mob (and Sex).* New York: Weinstein Books, 2011.

Benson, Robby. *I'm Not Dead...Yet.* United States of America: Valor Editions, 2012.

Biskind, Peter. *Down and Dirty Pictures.* Great Britain: Bloomsbury Publishing, 2004.

Bond, Samantha. "Samantha Bond: on Burt Reynolds." DVD Supplement, *A Bunch of Amateurs,* Entertainment in Video, 2009.

Boorman, John. "Deliverance: The Beginning." DVD Supplement, *Deliverance,* Warner Bros., 2007.

Brace, Eric. "Striptease: Burt Reynolds Outstrips Moore." *The Washington Post,* June 28, 1996. https://www.washingtonpost.com/archive/lifestyle/1996/06/28/striptease-reynolds-outstrips-moore/28794142-1672-4f3b-a119-4e8ec6efdf1e/?noredirect=on&utm_term=.198c69f18657.

Cadiff, Andy. "Andy Cadiff: on Burt Reynolds." DVD Supplement, *A Bunch of Amateurs,* Entertainment in Video, 2009.

Cameron, Julia. "Home Movie: Blake Edwards' Life is Autobiographical." *Chicago Tribune,* September 21, 1986, https://www.chicagotribune.com/news/ct-xpm-1986-09-21-8603100965-story.html.

Canby, Vincent. "Film Festival; 'Breaking In,' Crime Primer Features Burt Reynolds." *New York Times,* October 9, 1989. https://www.nytimes.com/1989/10/09/movies/film-festival-breaking-in-crime-primer-features-burt-reynolds.html.

Caulfield, Deborah. "Welch Licks Wounds of Battle," *Los Angeles Times,* June 28, 1986, http://articles.latimes.com/1986-06-28/entertainment/ca-25727_1_cannery-row.

Cawley, John. "The Animated Films of Don Bluth: At Home in Ireland." http://www.cataroo.com/DBireland.html.

Chalen, Paul. *Get Dutch!: A Biography of Elmore Leonard.* Toronto: ECW Press, 2000.

Curtin, Michael. *Playing to the World's Biggest Audience: The Globalization of Chinese Film and TV.* California: University of California Press, 2007.

Davis, Ivor. "Reynolds Seeks Rebirth in New Year, New Film." *The Sun Senitnel,* January 19, 1988. http://articles.sun-sentinel.com/1988-01-19/features/8801040739_1_burt-reynolds-rent-a-cop-liza-minnelli.

Denby, David. "Movies: Hoopla." *New York Magazine,* 28th August, 1978.

Ebert, Roger. "Cannonball Run II." *The Chicago Sun-Times,* January 1, 1984. https://www.rogerebert.com/reviews/cannonball-run-ii-1984.

Ebert, Roger. "Striptease." *Chicago Sun-Times,* June 28, 1996, https://www.rogerebert.com/reviews/striptease-1996.

Etter, Jonathan. *Quinn Martin, Producer: A Behind-the-Scene History of QM Productions and its Founder.* Jefferson, NC: McFarland, 2003.

Farber, Stephen. "Why Couldn't This 'Lady' Have an Unhappy Ending?." *New York Times,* December 4, 1975. https://www.nytimes.com/1975/12/14/archives/why-couldnt-this-lady-have-an-unhappy-ending-why-no-unhappy-ending.html.

Fleming, Mike, Jr. "Encore: Burt Reynolds Has Tales To Tell: Passing On 'Cuckoo's Nest,' 007, 'Die Hard,' Bonding With Eastwood, McQueen, Newman & Carson But Not Brando." *Deadline Hollywood,* September 6, 2018, https://deadline.com/2018/09/burt-reynolds-book-clint-eastwood-johnny-carson-die-hard-1201670957/.

Flippo, Chet. "The Unsinkable Dolly Parton." *Rolling Stone,* December 11, 1980. https://www.rollingstone.com/music/music-country/the-unsinkable-dolly-parton-197779/.

Freeman, Mike. *Jim Brown: The Fierce Life of an American Hero.* New York: Harper Entertainment, 2006.

Froug, William. *How I Escaped From Gilligan's Island: And Other Misadventures of a Hollywood Writer-*

Producer. Wisconsin: The University of Wisconsin Press, 2005

Goldman, William. *Which Lie Did I Tell?: More Adventures in the Screen Trade.* New York: Pantheon Books, 2000.

Hagan, Ray, and Laura Wagner. *Killer Tomatoes: Fifteen Tough Film Dames.* Jefferson, NC: McFarland, 2004.

Hamilton, George, and William Stadiem. *Don't Mind If I Do.* New York: Simon & Schuster, 2008.

Harris, Thomas J. "Peter Bogdanovich Interview." In *Peter Bogdanovich: Interviews,* ed. Tonguette, Peter, Mississippi: University of Mississippi Press, 2015

Hirschberg, Lynn. "Deliverance." *The New York Times,* June 16, 1996. https://www.nytimes.com/1996/06/16/magazine/deliverance.html.

Hughes, Howard. *Once Upon a Time in the Italian West: The Filmgoers' Guide to Spaghetti Westerns.* London/New York: I.B. Tauris, 2009 reprint.

Hurwood, Bernhardt J. *Burt Reynolds.* New York: Quick Fox, 1979.

Jerome, Jim. "Kissing Hollywood Life Goodbye, Robby Benson and Karla Devito Flee to South Carolina to Make Modern Love." *People,* May 28, 1990. https://people.com/archive/kissing-hollywood-life-goodbye-robby-benson-and-karla-devito-flee-to-south-carolina-to-make-modern-love-vol-33-no-21/.

Kotcheff, Ted, with Josh Young. *Director's Cut: My Life in Film.* Toronto: ECW Press, 2017.

Leonard, Elmore. *Stick.* London: Phoenix, 2007.

Lombardi, Frederic. *Allan Dwan and the Rise and Decline of the Hollywood Studios.* Jefferson, NC: McFarland, 2013.

MacDonald, Gayle. "Still Slim. Still Gorgeous. Still Burt." *The Globe and Mail,* December 3, 2001, https://www.theglobeandmail.com/arts/still-slim-still-gorgeous-still-burt/article4157114/.

Manciewicz, Tom, and Robert Crane. *My Life as a Mankiewicz: An Insider's Journey Through Hollywood.* Kentucky: University of Kentucky Press, 2012.

McBride, Joseph. *Steven Spielberg: A Biography.* Second Edition, Mississippi: University of Mississippi Jackson, United States, 2010.

Modderno, Craig. "Burt Reynolds is The Comeback Kid." *Los Angeles Times,* January 04, 1987, http://articles.latimes.com/1987-01-04/entertainment/ca-1803_1_burt-reynolds/4.

Moore, Roger, with Gareth Owen. *My Word Is My Bond: The Autobiography.* London: Michael O'Mara Books, 2008.

Munn, Michael. *David Niven: The Man Behind the Balloon.* London: JR Books, 2009.

Needham, Hal. *Stuntman!: My Car-Crashing, Plane-Jumping, Bone-Breaking, Death-Defying Hollywood Life.* New York, Boston, London: Little, Brown and Company, 2011.

Ng, David. "The Art of Blake Edwards." *Los Angeles Times,* January 17, 2009. https://latimesblogs.latimes.com/culturemonster/2009/01/blake-edwards-a.html.

Owen, Gareth. "The Cannonball Run Collector's Booklet." DVD Supplement, *The Cannonball Run,* Fortune Star Media, 2010.

Parfitt, David. "David Parfitt: on Burt Reynolds." DVD Supplement, *A Bunch of Amateurs,* Entertainment in Video, 2009.

Parton, Dolly. "The Making of the Film." DVD Supplement, *The Best Little Whorehouse in Texas,* Universal Pictures, 2001.

Powell, Larry, and Tom Garrett. *The Films of John G. Avildsen: Rocky, The Karate Kid and Other Underdogs.* Jefferson, NC: McFarland, 2014.

Reeve, Christopher. *Still Me.* London: Arrow Books, 1999.

Resnick, Sylvia Safran. *Burt Reynolds.* London: W.H. Allen, 1983.

Reynolds, Burt. "Burt Reynolds: On How the Play Mirrors the Film." DVD Supplement, *A Bunch of Amateurs,* Entertainment in Video, 2009.

Reynolds, Burt. *But Enough About Me.* London: Penguin, 2015.

Reynolds, Burt. "Doing Time on The Longest Yard." DVD Supplement, *The Longest Yard,* Paramount Home Entertainment, 2005.

Reynolds, Burt. "First Down & Twenty-Five to Life: The Making of The Longest Yard." DVD Supplement, *The Longest Yard,* Sony Pictures Home Entertainment, 2006.

Reynolds, Burt. "Foreword." *James Arness: An Autobiography,* by James Arness with James E. Wise, Jr. Jefferson, NC: McFarland, 2001.

Reynolds, Burt. "MTV's Making the Movie: Without a Paddle." DVD Supplement, *Without a Paddle,* Paramount Home Entertainment, 2005.

Reynolds, Burt. *My Life: Burt Reynolds.* Great Britain: Hodder & Stoughton, 1994.

Rinzler, J.W., *The Making of Star Wars: The Definitive Story Behind the Original Film.* Ballantine Books, New York, 2005.

Roberts, Jerry. *Encyclopaedia of Television Film Directors,* Maryland: Scarecrow Press, 1971.

Robey, Tim. "Alfred Hitchcock biopic: Dial M for Mischief." *The Telegraph,* February 6, 2013. http://www.telegraph.co.uk/culture/film/film-news/9839836/Alfred-Hitchcock-biopic-Dial-M-for-mischief.html.

Ryan, Tom. "Sam Fuller: Survivor." In *Samuel Fuller: Interviews,* ed. Gerald Perry. Mississippi: University Press of Mississippi, 2012.

Sheperd, Cybil, with Aimee Lee Ball. *Cybill Disobedience: My Autobiography.* Great Britain: Ebury Press, 2000.

Streebeck, Nancy. *The Films of Burt Reynolds.* New York: Citadel Press, 1982.

Travers, Peter. "Breaking In." *Rolling Stone,* October 19, 1989. https://www.rollingstone.com/movies/reviews/breaking-in-19891013.

Turner, Kathleen, and Gloria Feldt. *Send Yourself Roses: My Life, Loves and Leading Roles.* Great Britain: Headline Publishing Group, 2008.

Weaver, Tom. *I Was a Monster Movie Maker: Conversations with 22 SF and Horror Filmmakers.* Jefferson, NC: McFarland, 2001.

Welles, Orson. "Foreword." In *The Films of Burt Reynolds,* Nancy Streebeck. New York: Citadel Press, 1982.

Whitley, Dianna. *Burt Reynolds: Portrait of a Superstar.* New York: Grossett & Dunlap, 1979.

Williamson, Shawn. "Making of." DVD Supplement, *In the Name of the King,* Metronome Video, 2008.

Yates, Brock. *Cannonball! World's Greatest Outlaw Road Race.* Minnesota: Motorbooks International, 2003.

Interviews

Battaglia, Matt, Telephone, November 11, 2018.
Bennett, Bill, Skype, June 16, 2018.
Fleury, Clive, Telephone, March 6, 2018.
Forsyth, Bill, Email, June 11, 2018.
Goldsboro, Bobby, Email, December 12, 2018.
Lewis, C. James, Skype, August 17, 2018.
McLean, Nick, Sr., Skype, January 15, 2019.
O'Shea, Michael D., Telephone, August 30, 2018.
Rifkin, Adam, Telephone, October 10, 2018.
Roberts, Brian K., Telephone, June 29, 2018.
Ward, Rachel, Skype, February 1, 2018.

YouTube Videos

"The Bandit: Burt and crew talk about Hal Needham Recorded 2016." uploaded by Ron Swett, July 14, 2018. https://www.youtube.com/watch?v=nbhk7lL4yhU.

"Cinéma Cinémas—Burt Reynolds—1987." uploaded by Thomas Boujut, October 9, 2012. https://www.youtube.com/watch?v=6-jEoqhXKYE.

"James Arness on working with Burt Reynolds." YouTube, uploaded by FoundationINTERVIEWS, Published May 21, 2010. https://www.youtube.com/watch?v=yJqbQm0j5gY.

"Lucky Lady 1975 Alternate Ending." YouTube, uploaded by robatsea2009, April 28, 2017. https://www.youtube.com/watch?v=5_tOdtThq0c.

"Peter Bogdanovich Interview—The Seventh Art." uploaded by The Seventh Art, May 13, 2012. https://www.youtube.com/watch?v=MLOhLTB4QoU.

"Queen spends night with Amateurs." *BBC News,* November 18, 2008. http://news.bbc.co.uk/2/hi/entertainment/7734921.stm.

"Quentin Tarantino honors Hal Needham at the 2012 Governors Awards." uploaded by Oscars, December 2, 2012. https://www.youtube.com/watch?v=-JsYTFukcgw.

"Where Stallions Run—Burt Reynolds." YouTube, uploaded by Grinnygog1975, 20 August, 2008. https://www.youtube.com/watch?v=DLMVi5UwQdU.

Index